CHE
Selected Works of Ernesto Guevara

Edited and with an introduction by
ROLANDO E. BONACHEA AND NELSON P. VALDES

THE MIT PRESS
Cambridge, Massachusetts, and London, England

CHE

Selected Works of Ernesto Guevara

To *Ana Maria*
Alisa Lynn
Ricardo

Contents

лллллллллллллллллллллллллллллл

Preface
ЛПЛЛЛЛЛЛЛЛЛЛЛЛЛЛЛЛЛЛЛЛЛЛЛЛ

The editors' objective in presenting the works of Ernesto Che Guevara has been twofold: to offer in the introduction an honest discussion of Guevara's ideology, and to present a comprehensive and reliable collection of his selected writings and speeches which will enhance the scholarly investigation of revolutionary thought and the Cuban Revolution as illustrated by the ideological evolution of Guevara in its relation to the strategy of achieving power and the building of a communist society. If we have achieved this objective, we shall be well rewarded.

The volume presented here does not include the books written by Guevara (*La Guerra de Guerrillas, Pasajes de la Guerra Revolucionaria*) or the diary kept by him during his campaign in Bolivia, as these are available in the English language. Except for official texts, the English translation throughout the volume is that of the editors. For the editors' introduction what might normally be excessive documentation is provided as an antidote to speculation and an aid to serious research.

We would like to gratefully acknowledge the following friends who in one way or another contributed to the completion of the manuscript: from the University of New Mexico, Professor Edwin Lieuwen, chairman of the History Department; Professor Martin C. Needler, director of the Inter-American Affairs Division; Professor Henry J. Tobias, director of Sino-Soviet Studies Department; Professor Edwin Hoyt, chairman of the Political Science Department; Professor Paul Eduardo Ruiperez of Argentina, visiting lecturer in the Department of Sociology; our colleague, Louis Pérez; as well as Professor Maurice Zeitlin from the University of Wisconsin at Madison.

The permission given to us to reproduce copyrighted material is gratefully acknowledged in the respective footnotes.

The assistance given by the University of New Mexico Zimmerman Library and especially by Mrs. D. Wonsmos of the Inter-Library Loan Section is thankfully recorded here, as well as that of the staff of the Hispanic Foundation at the Library of Congress in Washington, D.C., where part of the research was conducted, and especially to Mrs. Georgette Dorn, who was always available to answer questions.

We also thank the Ford Foundation for its financial support of part of this project.

The following friends helped us in the preparation of the index and we gratefully acknowledge their assistance: Maureen Heaney, Larry Hickey, Ramón L. Bonachea, José Font, Diego V. Tejera, Michael Lyle, and Salvatore Ferrara. Our gratitude also to Maxine for all her work.

Finally, there is one other person who needs no mention because all who know us know of her encouragement, patience, and her role as a sounding board for ideas.

Of course, none of the aforementioned persons is responsible for the errors and opinions in this book. This burden rests solely with the editors.

N.P.V.
R.E.B.

April 1969
Washington, D.C.

Since his death, the figure of Che Guevara has loomed ever larger in the consciousness of his contemporaries. As time passes, in fact, the figure of the Cuban-Argentine revolutionary seems less and less to belong to history and more and more to the realm of legend and myth. Indeed, many of the features of the Guevara legend are shared with the legends of the heroes of antiquity.

Thus Guevara was always a stranger, always "different." He was not merely an Argentine among Cubans; even in the memoirs of those who knew him in the early years in Córdoba he was always an outsider. Like other heroes of legend, again, he traveled and had adventures, was present at critical and symbolic events and met figures of transcendent importance, in Peru, in Bolivia, in Guatemala. Yet he also moved among the poor and dispossessed and the sick, the outcasts of the earth, in his days as an indigent wanderer and in the leper colony. The mysterious stranger spoke quietly yet "as one having authority, and not as the scribes." As a guerrilla he experienced not only normal hardships but also suffered acutely because of his asthma; he suffered, and indeed finally gave his life, for the poor and downtrodden. And, like the great classical heroes, the mystery surrounding some of the events and periods of his life extends also to his death. Where is Che Guevara's body?

Thus the bare outlines of Guevara's story qualifies him to be a hero from the Arthurian saga, from the Greek myths, or from the Bible. If we were a preliterate society, there would be material enough for the oral tradition to work on.

But Guevara's appeal to the young people who are the principal votaries of his cult has somewhat different bases. Guevara's youth, his idealism, his concern for the poor and deprived, are of course important. But equally congenial to youth, if not more so, are his self-reliance and the authentically revolutionary quality of his refusal to learn from the mistakes of others; perhaps minor points of style, such as the long hair and motorbike, are not completely irrelevant.

But beside Che, the legendary hero and symbol, there also exists Ernesto Guevara, the historical figure, a figure, moreover, of key historical importance about whom many questions need to be asked and answered. The Guevara materials that are available to us, and which the present book is so welcome in making accessible, give us an idea of the general shape of Guevara's political thinking. But how did that thinking evolve? What influences were decisive in its formation? What was the state of Guevara's thinking at those points in the history of revolutionary Cuba at which his influence was critical or decisive? How "correct" was the content of his thought? Where are the logical inconsistencies, the unfounded empirical assumptions? And finally, what role did Guevara play in the evolution of Fidel Castro's political position? What precisely was his relationship, intellectual and personal, to Fidel?

The world outside revolutionary Cuba certainly owes Guevara a debt of gratitude for his help in clarifying the theoretical rationale for the policy alternatives among which the Revolution had to choose. Che always spoke frankly and honestly of the Revolution's problems, its mistakes, and its internal difficulties. The 1964 article in *International Affairs* is especially noteworthy and an example of the candid Guevara at his best.

Guevara would doubtless make an interesting study for the psychologist. His childhood was certainly not that of the typical Latin American of good family; the recurrent asthma attacks, especially, might warrant closer investigation.

It is worth noting that Guevara earned his posthumous status of existential-hero-as-man-of-action not because of the instrumental effectiveness of anything he did—he was probably as ineffective a bank president and economic manager as he was a guerrilla leader—but because of what he said and the symbolic value of some of his acts. It is clear why he was out of place in the government of revolutionary Cuba; his proper role was as moral leader, as inspirer, as precursor, not as functionary. His ideas of creating a new man, of building through moral incentives only, were of course impractical; but they place him in a distinguished Hispanic tradition, a tradition of poets and thinkers whose function is not to change the world directly but to hold up ideals that inspire men to attempt their best. But Guevara differed from the *pensadores* at least in believing that he was a man of action.

In elucidating some of the mysteries surrounding the figure of Che we clearly stand in need of all of the relevant materials we can find. In their prodigious labor of making so many of these materials available, Rolando Bonachea and Nelson Valdés have performed a most valuable service. Their own closeness to the Cuban situation and to the events of the Revolution has helped them to understand and interpret the materials with which they are dealing—indeed, to find some of those materials in the first place. At the same time, they have maintained a measure of objectivity typically denied to exiles. Because both have been students in the program which I direct at the University of New Mexico, it is with considerable pride that I commend to the reader the volume he holds in his hands.

Martin C. Needler
Director, Division of
    Inter American Affairs
University of New Mexico
Albuquerque, New Mexico
May 22, 1969

CHE
Selected Works of Ernesto Guevara

Introduction

ЛЛЛЛЛЛЛЛЛЛЛЛЛЛЛЛЛЛЛЛЛЛЛЛЛЛЛ

The history of revolutionary processes and their leaders has always elicited the most varied responses from nations and individuals. Perceptions of historical realities are determined by values and attitudes; men who lead and influence revolutions are seen as both pragmatic and idealistic, dogmatic and open-minded, machiavellian and benevolent, democratic and authoritarian. Some are revolutionary thinkers whereas others are revolutionary actors. Ernesto Che Guevara was both—a revolutionary praxis. His friends and foes alike perceived only that which was good or evil, losing sight in the process of the various dimensions of Guevara as both the man and the revolutionary.

Ernesto Guevara was born on June 14, 1928, in Rosario de Santa Fé, Argentina. He was the oldest of five children and lived with his family in middle-class comfort occasionally interrupted by economic difficulties. At the age of two he began suffering from asthma, a condition from which he was never cured, so after living for a short time in Buenos Aires the family decided to move to the summer resort of Alta Gracia in the very conservative province of Córdoba. Because he could not attend school regularly due to his illness, his mother taught him to read and write. At the age of seven, when he entered primary school, he was one of the best students in the class.[1]

In 1941, young Ernesto commenced his studies at the Colegio Nacional Dean Funes—the equivalent of high school—and his adventurous life began. With friends he went on long camping trips and showed great interest in the life of the rural folk. In 1945 when the Guevaras returned to Buenos Aires for economic reasons, he started his university studies, concentrating on medicine, and decided to become a specialist on allergies.[2] While attending the university he obtained through his father a clerical job in the city hall of Buenos Aires and because not much was done there, he spent

[1] José Aguilar, "La niñez del Che," *Granma* (Havana), October 16, 1967, p. 10.
[2] "Un largo viaje en moto de Argentina a Venezuela," *Granma* (Havana), October 16, 1967, pp. 6–7.

most of the time reading poetry—mainly the works of Mallarmé, Verlaine, and Baudelaire. Ernesto also became familiar with the works of Simón Bolívar, Enrique Rodó, Jules Verne, Emilio Salgari, and the *Martín Fierro* of José Hernández, a masterful tale of the life of the men of the pampas.[3]

Politics interested him from a very early age but he expressed no intention of becoming a revolutionary. Ernesto participated in student demonstrations against Juan Domingo Perón, who at the time was ruling Argentina,[4] but adventures attracted him more.

In 1947 the young Guevara worked for a month on a merchant ship, but the task of male nurse and stevedore did not appeal to him.[5] Two years later, with a motorbike and a knapsack, he began a journey through the northern provinces of Argentina. He left Córdoba, went to the province of Salta, and then moved into Jujuy, Tucumán, Santiago del Estero, Chaco, and Formosa. From there he went to the Andes, crossing five other provinces. On his way home he passed through the pampas: Ernesto had traveled 3,100 miles.[6] From then on he continually spoke with his friend Alberto Granados about future trips throughout the continent to get to know the beauty of nature and the miseries of the people.

On December 29, 1951, their dreams materialized; they initiated their journey of Latin America. Before reaching the capital of Chile, however, their motorcycle broke down.[7] They continued on foot and were content in their close contact with the Chileans. They intended to reach Christmas Island to work in a leprosarium,[8] but unable to get there, they went instead to Peru where Ernesto studied the Inca ruins of Macchu Picchu.[9] From January to June of 1952 they stayed in Peru and then with the aid of Dr. Hugo Pesce— who at the time headed an antileprosy campaign—worked in the

[3] Fulvio Fuentes, "Che, niñez, adolescencia, juventud," *Bohemia* (Havana), October 20, 1967, pp. 70–77.

[4] Fernando Barral, "Che, estudiante," *Granma* (Havana), October 16, 1967, p. 18. Perón rose to power from the ranks of the military in 1944 and based his eleven-year rule on an alliance of the military and the labor sector.

[5] Julia Constela, "Cuando Ernesto Guevara aún no era el Che, una entrevista con doña Celia de la Serna de Guevara," *Bohemia* (Havana), August 27, 1961, pp. 32–33.

[6] "Ernesto Guevara: El Che," *Sucesos para todos* (Mexico), August 3, 1968, pp. 12–21.

[7] "El Che Guevara, su vida," *Alarma!* (Mexico), May 30, 1968, p. 85.

[8] Granados and Guevara were considered "specialists in leprosy" by a small town newspaper in Chile. See *Diario Austral* (Temuco), February 19, 1952.

[9] Ernesto wrote an article on the ruins but the editors have been unable to find it. Archeology was also a major interest of his.

leprosarium of San Pablo, in the province of Loreto on the shores of the Amazon.[10]

The two men organized soccer games for the patients, visited the Indians of the region and tried to entertain the sick as much as possible. The lepers were extremely moved by Guevara and Granados, and after three months of work there the patients built them a raft so they could cross the Amazon. On June 21, 1952, they sailed to Leticia, Colombia, but after a few days they sailed past the port town and ran aground a small island. There they changed the raft for a boat and tried to make it back to Leticia. At last they got there but without money and not knowing anyone. Their skills in soccer allowed them to get a job as instructors so they could save enough money to buy plane tickets for Bogotá.

Because Colombia was going through a very violent period, the two foreigners were arrested for illegal entry. Some students urged them to leave the country,[11] so on July 14, 1952, they crossed the international bridge uniting Cúcuta (Colombia) with San Cristóbal (Venezuela).[12] In Caracas the men separated. Alberto Granados, through a friend, began to work in a hospital; Ernesto Guevara met a family friend and began to work in the transportation of horses by air. On July 25, 1952, he arrived in Miami, Florida, in a cargo plane carrying race horses. In this city of affluence, he lived for a few days, existing primarily on bread and coffee, spending most of the time in Bayfront Park and the public library. A month later he was back in his homeland.

On his return he was drafted but due to his asthma he was declared unfit for military duty. Ernesto reenrolled at the university, where he wrote a thesis on allergies and obtained his M.D. degree in March 1953 at the age of twenty-five. Now he could join the ranks of the bourgeoisie in Buenos Aires, but instead Ernesto bought a ticket to La Paz, Bolivia. He had been offered a job in the leper colony at Cabo Blanco in Venezuela where his old-time friend, Alberto Granados, practiced.

The acquaintances made on the second trip throughout Latin

[10] In his adolescence Guevara worked in a leper hospital in the town of San Francisco, Argentina, during his summer vacations. See Norman Gall, "The Legacy of Che Guevara," *Commentary*, December 1967, p. 36.

[11] According to John Gerassi, Guevara and Granados escaped from jail but we have not been able to find this fact in any of our sources. See John Gerassi (ed.), *Venceremos! The Speeches and Writings of Che Guevara* (New York: Macmillan, 1968), p. 8.

[12] "Un largo viaje en moto de Argentina a Venezuela" pp. 6–7.

America were ultimately to draw Ernesto into the realm of active politics. From Bolivia he went to Peru with his friend, also an Argentinian, "Calica" Ferrer. There they met the youth section of the then revolutionary party, Alianza Popular Revolucionaria Americana (Aprista). After this group supported them for a few days, they left Lima in a bus and entered Ecuador. It was the fall of 1953. In Guayaquil Ernesto Guevara reached a turning point in his life; he was convinced by the Argentine lawyer Ricardo Rojo to go to Guatemala and participate in the social revolution occurring in that country. Ricardo Rojo writes,

"How come you're going to Venezuela," I asked him, "when there's nothing to do there except earn dollars?"
Guevara insisted that he had made a pact with his friend Granados and he had to keep his word.
"Things are happening to Guatemala, *viejo*," I went on. "An important revolution is going on there; it's something you've got to see."
"All right," Guevara gave in, "but only on the condition that we walk together." [13]

While in Ecuador their economic situation was precarious. With the aid of a socialist lawyer, however, they were able to obtain free tickets for the Great White Fleet of the United Fruit Company to go to Panama. From there they went to Costa Rica where Ernesto met Rómulo Betancourt, Juan Bosch, and Raúl Leoni, leaders of the Latin American "democratic left." Their conversations, like those of any exile group, centered on the endless discussions for achieving power to effect social change.[14] By December 24, 1953, Ernesto was in Guatemala.

His greatest wish was to work as a physician in the Guatemalan jungle, but soon he found out that to do so he would need a Communist Party card. Consequently Guevara told the Minister of Public Health, "Look friend, the day I decide to affiliate myself, I'll do it from conviction, not through obligation, understand?" [15] Contrary to a common belief in the United States, Ernesto Guevara never had any post in the Guatemalan government.[16]

It was here that he met Hilda Gadea through Juan Angel Nuñez Aguilar, a Guatemalan engineer who had studied at the La Plata university in Argentina. Hilda was a Peruvian exile residing in Guatemala City to whom he had brought a letter from the Aprista

[13] Ricardo Rojo, *My Friend Che* (New York: Grove Press, 1968), p. 40.
[14] Rojo, *My Friend Che*, pp. 50–51.
[15] *Ibid*, p. 56.
[16] See the interview with Jorge Masetti in this volume; and for the mistaken position, see Gall, "Legacy of Che Guevara," p. 36.

youth section.[17] Through her he met Cuban exiles who had partici-
pated in the attack led by Fidel Castro on July 26, 1953, on the
Moncada Barracks of Oriente Province. Che, as he was called now
by the Cubans, became the doctor of this group of political activists.
He was also a good friend of Juan José Arévalo, former president of
Guatemala.[18]

Che worked as a salesman and traveled through the countryside
assessing the way of life of the Indian poor. At the same time the
United States, defending the interests of North American corporations in that Central American country, prepared and trained a
mercenary force to invade Guatemala and crush the social revolution taking place. On June 18, 1954, the invasion began, led by
Colonel Castillo Armas, a graduate of the Army Command and
General Staff School at Leavenworth, Kansas. North American
fliers were also used in the operation. Two days later Jacobo Arbenz
was out of power. The revolution considered communist by the
United States was destroyed.[19]

From his experiences in Guatemala, Che developed a number of
conclusions as to how revolutionaries can maintain power once they
have attained it.[20] When the Guatemalan counterrevolutionary invasion began, the military, which had remained quite independent
from the political structure, refused to fight. The government reacted
by seeking to create a people's militia, but the armed forces rejected
this idea and supported the opposition. Conclusion Number One:
Destroy the traditional military institution.

While in Guatemala Guevara later recalled that,

When the North American invasion took place I tried to form a group of
young men like myself, to fight the [United Fruit] adventurers. In Guatemala it was necessary to fight and yet almost no one fought. It was necessary to resist and almost no one wanted to do it.[21]

Conclusion Number Two: At the outset mobilize the people and
arm them.

The aid the counterrevolution received from the United States

[17] "Che en Guatemala y Mexico," *Granma* (Havana), October 16, 1967, p. 8.
[18] Arévalo was president from 1944 to 1950.
[19] The literature on this subject is substantial. See David Wise and Thomas
B. Ross, *The Invisible Government* (New York: Random House, 1964); Gregorio
Selser, *El guatemalazo, la primera guerra sucia* (Buenos Aires: Editorial
Iguazu, 1961); Richard J. Barnet, *Intervention and Revolution, the United
States in the Third World* (New York: World Publishing Co., 1968), pp. 229–236.
[20] Che wrote an article in September 1954 which he called "Yo ví la caida de
Jacobo Arbenz," which the editors have been unable to obtain in its entirety.
[21] See interview with Jorge Masetti in this volume and *Granma* (Havana),
October 22, 1967, p. 6.

convinced Guevara definitely that Washington, determined to protect U.S. financial interests, would oppose any social revolution. Conclusion Number Three: The United States is counterrevolutionary.

In August, when the mercenary troops entered Guatemala City, Che sought refuge in the Argentine embassy. With a Mexican safe-conduct he departed for Mexico City. Hilda Gadea accompanied him and on the train he met for the first time Julio Roberto Cáceres, also known as "El Patojo." Cáceres was a young Guatemalan revolutionary also escaping to Mexico. Che writes about this time,

> The first time I saw El Patojo was aboard a train. We were running away from Guatemala following Arbenz' overthrow. Our destination was Tapachula, then Mexico City. He was much younger than I, but we soon became close friends. Together we made the trip from Chiapas to Mexico City, facing the same problems. We were poor and beaten, and we had to make a living amidst indifferent, if not hostile surroundings.
>
> El Patojo was completely broke and I had only a few pesos. I purchased a camera and we became clandestine photographers, taking pictures of people visiting parks, etc. Our partner was a Mexican who owned the laboratory where we developed and printed our photographs. We became thoroughly familiar with Mexico City, walking from one end to the other, delivering our miserable photos and struggling with our customers in an effort to convince them that the little child in the print really looked beautiful and that the price of one Mexican peso for such a work of art was a tremendous bargain. We practised our profession for several months and managed to eat quite regularly.[22]

In 1955 Guevara worked selling books on time payments for the Fondo de Cultura Ecónomica—Mexico's most important publishing house—and also worked as a doctor in the General Hospital of Mexico City in the allergy section. It was there that he assisted those Cuban exiles requiring medical attention.

In May 1955 the men sentenced for the attack on the Moncada Barracks were freed by Fulgencio Batista and about the same time Che married Hilda Gadea. Raúl Castro was their best man. In July or August of 1955 Che met Fidel Castro.[23] This is what he said about that meeting:

> I met him [Fidel] on one of those cold Mexican nights, and I remember that our first conversation was on international politics. A few hours later, in the early morning hours, I had already become a future revolutionary.[24]

[22] Ernesto Che Guevara, *Episodes of the Revolutionary War* (New York: International Publishers, 1968), pp. 100–101.

[23] See Castro's speech on October 18, 1967, *Granma* (Havana), October 29, 1967.

[24] Ernesto Che Guevara, "Una revolución que comienza," *Revolución* (Havana), December 4, 1959, p. 2.

And elsewhere Che states,

I spoke with Fidel a whole night. At dawn I was already the physician of the future expedition. In reality, after the experience I went through, my long walks throughout all of Latin America and the Guatemalan closing, not much was needed to convince me to join any revolution against a tyrant; but Fidel impressed me as an extraordinary man. He faced and resolved the impossible. He had an unshakable faith that once he left he would arrive in Cuba, that once he arrived he would fight, that once he began fighting he would win. I shared his optimism.[25]

Although Che was only going as the invasion's doctor, he participated in the training classes conducted by Alberto Bayo, a veteran of the Spanish Civil War.[26] In theory as well as practice he was the best student among the eighty men training on a Mexican farm close to Popocatepetl. Che was the chief of personnel and his relationship with Bayo was very friendly. As a soldier, he was a model of discipline.[27]

On June 20, 1956, he was arrested by Mexican authorities with the other Cuban revolutionaries. For fifty-seven days he was incarcerated at the Miguel Shultz prison. But Che did not lose his confidence and hope. When a Guatemalan lawyer, Alfonso Bauer Paiz, former Minister of Economy under the Arbenz government, offered his services to get him out, Guevara rejected the offer on the grounds that he would face the same hardships all his comrades were facing. Weeks later they were freed.

On November 25, 1956, their yacht, the *Granma*, embarked carrying eighty-two men. They planned to arrive in Cuba on November 30 when an uprising would take place throughout Oriente Province [28] but the invading group arrived at Belic on December 2, three days after the revolt had taken place. The day before the landing, the small band was discovered by a cargo ship which reported their position to the Cuban coast guard. In the early morning hours, the group entered a swamp:

Some comrades had to be carried by the stronger men in the group. As soon as we reached solid ground we threw ourselves on the abundant grass, exhausted, hungry, and totally covered with mud.[29]

[25] See interview with Jorge Masetti in this volume.

[26] For a concise outline of Bayo's life, see General Alberto Bayo, *150 Questions for a Guerrilla* (Boulder, Colorado: Panther Publications, 1965), pp. i–xvi.

[27] Armando Bayo, "El mejor alumno," *El Mundo* (Havana), October 19, 1967, p. 4.

[28] For a detailed account of the plan, see Marta Rojas, "¡Proa a Cuba!" *Trabajo* (Havana), second half of November 1961, pp. 34–39.

[29] Faustino Pérez, "De Tuxpán a las Coloradas," in René Ray (ed.), *Libertad y Revolución, Moncada, Granma, Sierra Maestra* (Havana: n.p., 1959), p. 25.

Che writes that on December 4,

We reached solid ground, lost, stumbling, constituting an army of shadows, ghosts that walked as if following some obscure psychic impulse. We had been through seven days of hunger and constant seasickness during the sea crossing, plus three still more horrible days on land.[30]

The following day the rebels were betrayed by a peasant to the armed forces, allowing the subsequent ambush at Alegria de Pío.[31] Completely surprised by Batista's forces, only seventeen men survived. Che was wounded in the neck and soon afterward the government officially announced the total destruction of the revolutionary movement in Oriente Province.[32]

On January 18, 1957, the chief of the Army Press and Radio Office of the Batista government disclosed that a mixed patrol formed by army and navy forces exchanged fire with a group of rebels in the region of La Plata. Che notes that this was the first victory of the rebels:

We had caught by surprise an army post of twelve to fifteen men, who surrendered after fighting for an hour. In those moments, an hour of fighting was an hour of great suffering.... Five days later, with a dozen new rifles obtained from that action, we were able to defeat the advance guard of a detachment searching for us, commanded by Sánchez Mosquera, a figure of sinister reputation. This was followed by an impasse due to a traitor within our ranks; he betrayed to the enemy our position and we were almost liquidated on three different occasions.[33]

After La Plata other battles followed. On February 22, the Rebel Army for the first time vanquished an enemy column on the march. In the ensuing weeks the guerrillas fought a number of enemy patrols and reorganized themselves. Then on May 27, 1957, the battle of El Uvero took place:

El Uvero was the fiercest battle of the war; of 120 to 140 men that participated on both sides, some 40 were put out of action, that is, the dead and wounded amounted to approximately 30 percent of all the combatants.[34]

The political significance of this battle was large, for it was fought at a moment when there was no censorship. The rebel victory moved

[30] Ernesto Che Guevara, "El desembarco del Granma," in Antonio Núñez Jiménez, Geografía de Cuba (Havana: Editorial Lex, 1959), p. 572.

[31] Angel Pérez, "Yo fuí el primer guia de Fidel al llegar el Granma," Revolución (Havana), December 2, 1959, p. 8.

[32] It is interesting to note that the Havana paper La Prensa reported that Castro was hiding in Mexico because he had given up the fight. As reported in YVKR (Caracas), January 14, 1957.

[33] Guevara, "El desembarco del Granma," p. 576.

[34] Ibid, p. 577.

many young people to join the insurgents. For example, a few days later fifty revolutionaries from Santiago de Cuba went into the ranks of the guerrillas. As the Rebel Army acquired strength, a second column was created and Che Guevara was placed in command. He became a major on June 5, 1957. Throughout the winter a number of battles were waged.[35]

From the outset Guevara stood out as an imaginative leader. In the Sierra Maestra he established a bakery, a shoe shop, an arms shop, and a clandestine radio station. His bomb factory was generally called "Sputnik" or "M-26." Che was also daring and courageous, and in every attack he was to be found at the forefront. On November 29, 1957, at the battle of Mar Verde he rescued the youngest member of the Rebel Army, Joel Iglesias, while being shot at from different positions.[36]

The 26th of July Movement up to this time had proclaimed the revolutionary general strike as the culmination of the struggle; the strike was to overthrow the dictatorship.[37] The strike was a dismal failure and many thought that the end of the anti-Batista struggle was close at hand. The government had crushed the urban structure of the revolutionary movement and began to make plans to do the same with the rural revolutionaries.

The Batista offensive opened on May 24 and lasted seventy-six days. Ten thousand government troops were sent against the rebels in the Sierra Maestra mountains but the Rebel Army repelled them. It was clear that this was the longest offensive ever waged against the rural insurgents. The cream of the government armed forces was used but the traditional army was unable to deal with the counterattack led by Fidel Castro on July 29, 1958.[38]

The Rebel Army had changed its strategy from defensive to offensive. The government forces were completely demoralized, and some officers even planned a coup to save themselves from the impending catastrophe.[39] But Fidel Castro did not accept the military proposals; instead he demanded complete power without military interference. In order not to allow the reorganization of the

[35] For this period, see Ernesto Che Guevara, *Pasajes de la guerra revolucionaria* (Havana: Edicion Union, 1963).

[36] Comandante Rogelio Acevedo *et al.*, "Siempre en la primera línea de combate," *Verde Olivo* (Havana), October 31, 1965, p. 18.

[37] This aspect of the revolutionary struggle in Cuba remains to be researched thoroughly by Cuban scholars. See "El 9 de abril de 1958," *Bohemia* (Havana), April 19, 1959, pp. 58–61; *El Mundo* (Havana), April 10, 1965, p. 5, and December 2, 1964, pp. 1, 7.

[38] *Revolución* (Havana), July 26, 1959, pp. 1, 7.

[39] "Gesta inmortal," *Verde Olivo* (Havana), August 29, 1965, pp. 7–9.

enemy, Castro ordered Ernesto Che Guevara and Camilo Cienfuegos to move with two columns into Las Villas Province in order to cut the island in half.

On August 30, 1958, Che Guevara left the Sierra Maestra with one hundred and thirty-five men, most of whom had just graduated from the military training center he had established at Minas del Frío. Che's mission was to coordinate the forces of other revolutionary organizations in that province in order to create a unified command and block the communications of the government forces with Oriente Province. A veteran of the campaign affirms that,

> The weather was very bad. A hurricane was beating down on the island and heavy rains were falling in the zone we were to pass. The first day we walked seven leagues. At night we reached the highway and found some trucks, but they were not of much use, for not far from where we began they got stuck. We had to abandon them and continue on foot under the unceasing rain, walking in deep mud.[40]

The following days turned out to be rather dangerous as Che's columns had to cross overflowing rivers while trying to avoid getting the ammunition wet. They walked through difficult terrain, suffering from almost unbearable plagues of mosquitos, eating almost nothing and drinking muddy water. In a place known as La Federal they were ambushed and two rebels were killed.[41]

During the journey Che suffered frequent asthma attacks but his willpower kept him going. It is here that he developed a rather interesting military tactic: The prisoners captured by the rebels were freed in those barracks they planned to attack in the near future—their mere presence there constituted a demoralizing factor.[42]

In the second week of October 1958, the column had contact with a patrol of the Directorio Revolucionario operating in the Escambray mountains. On the fourteenth of that month Che held a meeting close to the town of Sancti Spiritus with leaders of the Partido Socialista Popular, the Directorio Revolucionario, and labor sectors seeking to create a united front in that central province.[43] Two days later they reached the Escambray mountains where Che

[40] Comandante Oscar Fernández Mell, "De las Mercedes a Gavilanes," *Verde Olivo* (Havana), August 25, 1963, p. 15.
[41] Comandante Oscar Fernández Mell, "La Sierra, la invasión, Las Villas," *Granma* (Havana), November 28, 1967, p. 5; Comandante Angel Frías, "La Federal y cuatro compañeros," *Verde Olivo* (Havana), September 1, 1963, pp. 15–16.
[42] Comandante Rogelio Acevedo et al., "Siempre en la primera línea de combate," p. 19.
[43] "Gesta inmortal," p. 9.

was to find a disintegrating situation.[44] The Directorio Revolucionario had split and two guerrilla groups calling themselves representatives of the Directorio operated in the zone. The group led by Faure Chomón favored collaboration with the 26th of July Movement, whereas the guerrillas of Eloy Gutiérrez Menoyo were convinced that they had to remain independent. On October 9, one of the chiefs of the Second Front of the Escambray—Menoyo's group—sent a message to Guevara that stated,

Having news that you are moving toward this zone without having communicated officially with our organization, I want to warn you that this zone is controlled by our guerrillas. We ask you that before you enter this zone you sincerely make clear your intentions.[45]

Guevara disregarded the message, and two weeks later, on October 21, he discussed with Faure Chomón the possibility for unity and concerted action. Five days after, the barracks at Guinia de Miranda were attacked, and then Che moved into the encampment of the Second Front of Escambray at Gavilanes.[46] The collaboration between Chomón and Guevara increased in those days,[47] and in November, in the village of Pedrero in the Escambray mountains, the bases for unity and struggle were drawn. Meanwhile the Air Force bombed the small village.[48]

The revolutionary struggle increased throughout the island. Everywhere discontent was to be found. Batista's days were numbered and a last desperate action was made: Batista sent an armored train to Oriente Province. It consisted of 18 wagons and 401 men; but it never reached its destination. On December 29, Che Guevara reached the city of Santa Clara and after a two-hour battle captured it. On December 31, Fulgencio Batista left Cuba. The Revolution had come to power.

Euphoria swept the island; enthusiastic joy and cooperation

[44] Here we find Fernández Mell's account "De las Mercedes a Gavilanes," p. 62, to be mistaken. He gives the date of arrival as September 16, 1958.

[45] "El guerrillero," *Verde Olivo* (Havana), October 29, 1960, p. 30.

[46] Comandante Humberto Castello, "Segundo Frente Nacional del Escambray, negación del Ejército Rebelde," *Verde Olivo* (Havana), February 17, 1961, pp. 28–30.

[47] See letter of November 7, 1958, in this volume.

[48] The Pedrero Pact appears in this volume. It should be noted that the date on which that pact was signed is not clear. Faure Chomón in a magazine article states it was signed on December 1, 1958, whereas in a book he helped edit the date given is sometime in November 1958. See Faure Chomón, "Cuando el Che llego al Escambray," *Verde Olivo* (Havana), December 1, 1965, pp. 12–18, and Enrique Rodríguez Loeches, *Rumbo al Escambray* (Havana: Sección de Impresión, Capitolio Nacional, 1960), p. 100.

among all opposition groups ensued. Cuba seemed to be on the threshold of a new era of happiness and freedom.

The collaboration was short. Ideological and political differences, underscored by a conflict of generations, quickly aborted the "revolutionary honeymoon." [49] Most immediately filling the political vacuum created by the flight of Batista were largely moderates, experienced politicians from the Partido Ortodoxo who had fought in the urban resistance or had passed the period of revolutionary struggle in exile; needless to say these personalities represented the most affluent and better known leaders of the old opposition. They were ideologically weak and lacked a strong leader or organization. The traditional parties failed at the beginning to take a clear stand with regard to the dictatorship, and the people in 1959 considered them morally bankrupt.

Possibly their greatest liability was their friendly position toward the United States. Historically, *anti-yanquismo* had been the ideology of the Cubans, and at a time when emotions were high and the Revolution had to be defended, these men called for moderation and understanding. The moderates were the idealists in Cuba and time passed them by. This basic division was also to be found in the 26th of July Movement in the years 1959 and 1960. Many had fought in the urban areas for a political revolution while the guerriilas had been radicalized in their contact with the peasantry and thought in terms of social revolution. The conflict that followed was delineated to some extent by the membership of the followers. If they had fought in the urban resistance, most of them in Havana, they tended to be moderates; if they had fought in the guerrilla struggle or in the urban resistance in the provinces, their outloook tended to be more radical. [50]

The *guerrilleros* were young, politically inexperienced radicals who controlled public force and military power through the Rebel Army. Notwithstanding the fact that the moderates occupied important positions in the political structure in the first weeks of 1959, they

[49] Generational interpretations are rather common in Cuba. Indeed most people refer to Cuba's history in those terms. See Maurice Zeitlin, *Revolutionary Politics and the Cuban Working Class* (Princeton, N.J.: Princeton University Press, 1967), chapter 9; Sergio A. Regol, "La generación inmolada: tránsito y destino," *Revolución* (Havana), January 14, 1959, p. 10; Silvino Sorhegui, "La tesis generacional," *Revolución* (Havana), February 11, 1959, p. 2; and Fidel Castro's interview with Francis L. McCarthy in *El Mundo* (Havana), August 7, 1956, pp. 1, A10.

[50] This aspect of the Revolution remains to be analyzed. A point of departure is José Barbeito, *Realidad y masificación, reflexiones sobre la revolución cubana* (Caracas: Ediciones Nuevo Orden, 1964), pp. 125–145.

did not possess commensurate political power because they relied on the political and military leadership of Fidel Castro.

Guevara recognized quickly that the consensus engendered by the success of the Revolution ultimately would be strained as the Revolution began to move. He felt compelled to propagate a program of complete change of the agricultural structure of the nation. The reasons were at once economic and strategic. Che adopted the idea that the vanguard of the people was the Rebel Army, which he argued was mainly composed of peasants, and not the 26th of July Movement. The Rebel Army, he believed, was the main instrument to bring about a social revolution; it could be used to politicize and mobilize the people.[51]

The moderates admitted the need for agrarian reform and, because virtually everyone believed that it would cure all social ills, on June 3, 1959, the Land Reform Law was enacted. Although theoretically a moderate measure, the agrarian reform decree was truly revolutionary for it was enforced by radicals in the Rebel Army and the National Institute of Agrarian Reform.[52] The land reform was followed by a wave of political resignations; the Revolution was going too far and too fast. The political vacuum created by the moderates' retirement enabled the radicals to capture the political structure of the nation.

Che emerged from the revolutionary struggle a calculating speaker and strategist. To most Cubans he was an enigma, a man who spoke softly but seemed to know precisely what he wanted. Lacking charisma, he was nonetheless able to communicate with and attract the people. From the outset he was conscious of differences existing within the anti-Batista movement:

... there was within the revolutionary movement a series of contradictions which we call the *sierra* and the *llano* which manifested themselves in diametrically different analyses of the elements considered fundamental to decide the armed struggle. ... These differences were deeper than tactical discrepancies: The Rebel Army was already ideologically proletarian and thought as a dispossessed class; the urban leadership remained petty bourgeois with future traitors among its leaders and greatly influenced by the milieu in which it developed.[53]

[51] See "Social Ideas of the Rebel Army" in this volume.

[52] Boris Goldenberg, *The Cuban Revolution and Latin America* (New York: Praeger, 1965), pp. 185–189, and Antonio García, *Reforma Agraria y Economía Empresarial en America Latina* (Santiago: Editorial Universitaria, 1967), pp. 276–283.

[53] The *sierra* and the *llano* refer to the mountains and the plains, where the anti-Batista struggle was waged. See "The Role of a Marxist-Leninist Party" in this volume.

An implicit assumption in this explanation is that the countryside has a *proletarianizing* effect, whereas the city develops the process of *embourgeoisiement*. This dichotomy, however, did not express in its entirety the phenomenon that Cuba went through. The rigors of clandestine life in the city might be even more demanding than those of the rural areas; in fact most revolutionaries were killed in the city. And, besides, the guerrillas always need the support of the urban areas, a fact that in time Che seemed to discard.[54]

Revolutionaries, though consumed by their very creations, are still human. Guevara, after divorcing his first wife, married for a second time on June 2, 1959, to Aleida March, a Cuban girl who had fought alongside him. Hilda Gadea reminiscing on that event said,

When a man falls in love with another woman, there is nothing a wife can do. That is how life is, and people are not to blame. I am telling you all this because we are so far removed from one another. He met Aleida in Santa Clara, when he was on his way from the Sierra Maestra with a column of guerrillas to Havana. I arrived in Cuba in January 1959, after the fall of Fulgencio Batista. We had been apart for two years; that was a long time.[55]

On June 13, 1959, the Revolution separated Che from his family; he departed for Europe, Asia, and Africa in search of diplomatic relations and long-term economic agreements. During his absence the Revolution progressively radicalized. As far-reaching changes were made in the social structure, a number of interests were injured. The United States reacted to the Land Reform Law by expressing concern over the fate of U.S. interests, adding that if land were to be taken away from North American citizens there must be a "prompt, adequate, and effective compensation." [56] Aware that Cuba did not have the capital resources for this type of compensation, the revolutionaries regarded this as the inauguration of economic aggression.

After his return on September 8, 1959, Guevara became head of the industrial section of the National Institute of Agrarian Reform. In this post he developed tentative plans for industrialization. On No-

[54] Héctor Bejar, "Una experiencia guerrillera," *Marcha* (Montevideo), April 18, 1969, p. 29, and Simón Torres and Julio Aronde, "Debray and the Cuban Experience," in Leo Huberman and Paul M. Sweezy (eds.), *Regis Debray and the Latin American Revolution* (New York: Monthly Review Press, 1968), pp. 44–62.

[55] Interview by Franco Pierini with Hilda Gadea and Aleida March, *Manchete* (Rio de Janeiro), April 20, 1968, pp. 38–42.

[56] Robert Scheer and Maurice Zeitlin, *Cuba: An American Tragedy* (Hardmondsworth, Middlesex, England: Penguin Books, 1964), pp. 97 ff. This is probably the most informative published account on U.S.–Cuban relations during this period.

vember 26, he was appointed president of the Cuban National Bank, where he established total control over the banking system and foreign trade.

Anastas Mikoyan, heading a delegation of Russian representatives, visited Cuba in early February 1960. This created new friction between Washington and Havana. A Congressional representative from New Jersey summarized the mood of many North Americans when he said,

The visit of Russian Deputy Premier Mikoyan to Cuba is an outward manifestation of what our Central Intelligence Agency and State Department have known to exist for some time. It confirms a very definite liaison between the Communists and the Castro government.... The grave danger illustrated by Mr. Mikoyan's visit is that the Castro government is riddled with Communists desirous of displaying their allegiance to Moscow....[57]

However unfounded, Cuba's economic agreement was viewed by the United States as evidence of the political control the Soviet Union had over the Revolution. Guevara once commented,

It is none of the United States's business what treaties we sign; but this treaty does not have the political implications the United States thinks it has.[58]

Cuba, nonetheless, was changing economic orbits. New trade relations raised hopes of industrializing Cuba, that panacea searched for by all underdeveloped nations.

To Guevara, Cuban underdevelopment was the result of colonial relations with the United States. Political tutelage was concomitant to the colonial function of producing raw materials for the metropolis. He argued that independence meant political sovereignty and economic independence, that both were interrelated.[59] Consequently, economic liberation necessitated breaking away from the traditional economic patterns that bound Cuba to the neighbor of the north. Conflict escalated, and Che Guevara was a major participant in it.

The precipitant of the crisis between the United States and Cuba was the oil war. U.S. refineries in Cuba were buying each barrel of oil from their subsidiaries in Venezuela at $2.80. On November 20, 1959, the Cuban government had signed an oil agreement with a U.S. investment company in New York. This company represented the economic interests of Superior Oil Company of Venezuela.

---

[57] U.S., Congress, House, *Congressional Record*, 86th Cong., 2nd sess., 1960, 106:2265–2266.
[58] *Miami Herald*, March 21, 1960.
[59] See "Political Sovereignty and Economic Independence" in this volume.

Through the agreement Cuba acquired 250,000 barrels of crude oil at 25 percent less than the price charged by the U.S. oil refineries on the island. One of the reasons for this high price was due to a very interesting mechanism developed by the oil corporations. Che had decided that foreign capital could not repatriate more than 50 percent of its profits, and the rest was to be reinvested. So the corporations opted to take out their profits by raising prices of extra-corporate sales proportionately.[60] Moreover, the refineries were demanding cash for their oil imports. Throughout the years this transaction had been done on a credit basis, but in September 1959 U.S. banks stopped giving credits to Cuba.[61]

The oil refineries which had previously waited years for payment now required payment immediately. Because Cuba could not pay cash on the spot, the refineries withheld their oil supplies. Cuba reacted by purchasing oil from Venezuela through Superior Oil Company, but could not find transportation for it.[62] Due to this, Cuba got in touch with a Soviet oil supplier. When the crude oil reached the island the refineries refused to process it. According to a statement made by the companies, they could not refine the Russian crude because of the "historical interdependence of the integrated companies."[63] On May 17, Che sent the North American refineries a letter urging them to process the oil. They refused and a month later they were nationalized. This in turn moved the president of the United States on July 6, 1960, to cut Cuba's sugar quota.[64]

The oil war inaugurated a period of measures and countermeasures climaxing in the fall of 1960 when the whole economy was socialized and the United States cut Cuba's sugar quota. Accompanying this development was the progressive radicalization of the revolutionary ideology. By July 1960, Guevara stated that the Revolution had discovered Marxism through practice.[65]

On October 21, anticipating a United States embargo on imports to

[60] The mechanism through which the refineries obtained their oil was as follows: First, the refineries were subsidiaries of the large international oil consortiums. Second, the Cuban subsidiaries would buy their oil from the Venezuelan subsidiaries at $2.80 per barrel, when the oil could be purchased in Venezuela at $2.10 per barrel. Consequently, the Cuban consumer paid the difference. See "Una zancadilla que se volvio boomerang," *Trabajo* (Havana), August 1960, pp. 86–92.

[61] *Obra Revolucionaria* (Havana), June 11, 1960, pp. 14–15.

[62] "Cuba Gets Oil; Tanker Owners Get Warning," *Oil and Gas Journal*, July 18, 1960, p. 82.

[63] "Castro's Militia Takes Texaco Refinery," *Oil and Gas Journal*, July 4, 1960, p. 76.

[64] *Department of State Bulletin*, XLIII, July 25, 1960, p. 40.

[65] "Development of a Marxist Revolution" in this volume.

Cuba, Che Guevara went to Eastern Europe, the Soviet Union, China, North Korea, and North Vietnam to seek new trade agreements and economic aid. After encountering some economic difficulties, he was assured a new market for Cuban sugar and a new supplier of goods and credits.[66]

A period of great hopes followed. Guevara prepared a plan for the industrialization of Cuba. The plan, to say the least, as he later recognized, was excessively idealistic and naïve.[67] Cuba was to become in less than five years the first country in Latin America in per capita production of steel and electric power with a net growth of 12 percent, or 9½ percent more than the goal set by the Alliance for Progress.[68]

On February 23, 1961, he became the Minister of Industries. Four days later he outlined his plan to the people:

> In the next five years we shall invest in industry about one billion pesos— 600 million of which will go to the importation of factories, machinery, and equipment, while 400 million will go for capital goods constructed in our own factories. We shall get the major part of the 600 million pesos from credits from the socialist countries.[69]

Needless to say, Che earnestly dedicated himself to work hard to achieve that goal. Since December 1959 he had been studying economics and mathematics from 2:00 A.M. to 4:00 A.M. His commitment was impressive and his ascetism vigorous. Indeed he would work from 1:00 P.M. to 6:00 A.M.[70]

Soon, however, the revolutionaries were confronted with a stark reality. Cuba did not have sufficient resources to industrialize. The great problem faced was one of obtaining supplies; from being dependent on finished goods, they became dependent on raw materials. As time passed, the economy encountered a balance of payments deficit.[71] The socialist nations considered the situation in Cuba chaotic and opted for telling the revolutionaries that from then on the credits were to be used to solve their balance of payments problem.[72] On February 6, 1963, Che remarked sardonically,

---

[66] Mario G. Cueto, "Lo que vió el Che en la URSS," *Bohemia* (Havana), December 11, 1960, pp. 44–45, 73.

[67] See "The Cuban Economy" in this volume.

[68] See "The Alliance for Progress" in this volume.

[69] *Revolución* (Havana), February 28, 1961, pp. 1, 11.

[70] J.-P. Sartre, "Vengan temprano: a media noche," *Revolución* (Havana), August 3, 1960, p. 3.

[71] Robert S. Walters, "Soviet Economic Aid to Cuba," *International Affairs* (London), January 1966, pp. 76–86.

[72] Theodore Draper, *Castroism, Theory and Practice* (New York: Praeger, 1965), pp. 135–221.

Today the newspapers tell of the long-term credits which the Soviet Union has granted us. What are the credits for? They are not for the building of industries, which is the usual reason for extending credits. They are given to us in order that we pay for the unfavorable balance which exists in our transactions with the Soviet Union.[73]

But Che kept on working hard, pursuing different interests. By 1963 Cuba again extended priority to sugar production. On July 14 in Algiers, Guevara admitted that, distressingly, after four years of revolution Cuba was still a producer of raw materials.[74] New economic plans reduced his dream of industrialization as well as his influence in the economic structure. Enrique Oltuski affirms that at the time, after a long meeting on planning, someone complained to him about the lack of food:

...and he said that this was not so, that in his house they ate reasonably well.

Half seriously, and half in jest, I told him, "Maybe you receive an additional ration."

The next day he called us to tell us,

"It was true, until yesterday we were receiving an additional ration." [75]

At about the same time that industrialization was deemphasized in economic planning, Che moved into the realm of ideology and undertook the task of considering how socialism could be built in an underdeveloped nation.[76] Faced with the fact that Cuban industrial development was not going to be financed with credits from the industrialized socialist nations, he was moved into examining a problem to some extent similar to that encountered by Leon Trotsky fifty years earlier.

The Russian Revolution had confronted a backward economy; capital to bring about socialism could be obtained through what Evgeny Preobrazhensky called "primitive socialist accumulation," that is, securing capitalization from the backs of the working masses.[77] One logical conclusion of this approach was collectivization and Stalinism. Trotsky's alternative proposal was that,

...in a country where the proletariat has power...as the result of the democratic revolution, the subsequent fate of the dictatorship and socialism is not only, and not so much, dependent in the final analysis upon the

[73] *Revolución* (Havana), February 7, 1963, p. 5.

[74] *El Mundo* (Havana), July 16, 1963, p. 7.

[75] Enrique Oltuski, "¿Que puedo decir?" *Bohemia* (Havana), February 9, 1968, p. 21.

[76] For a philosophical discussion of Che's ideology, see Adolfo Sánchez Vazquez, "El socialismo y el Che," *Casa de las Américas* (Havana), January/February 1968, pp. 149–151.

[77] Evgeny Preobrazhensky, *The New Economics* (New York: Oxford University Press, 1965).

national productive forces as it is upon the development of the international socialist revolution.[78]

Trotsky hoped that industrial Europe would undergo a social revolution so that the Soviet Union would receive economic aid from the developed nations. Che, in contrast, did not have to hope for such occurrence: the socialist nations were industrialized and in existence. These nations, Guevara concluded, lacked true socialist solidarity. In February 1965, he stated that the advanced socialist nations should invest their capital in nations remaining underdeveloped but committed to building socialism rather than investing in their own countries in order to create more industry. He went on,

In this manner an immense force—miserably exploited but never helped in its development—could be placed in motion and a new era of authentic international division of labor begun, based not on the history of what has been done up to now but rather on the history of what could be done. The states, in whose territories the new investments are to be made, will have all the inherent rights of sovereign property over them without any payment or credit due, but they will be obliged to deliver certain quantities of products to the investor countries for a certain number of years at fixed prices.... The development of the underdeveloped countries must be underwritten by the socialist countries.[79]

Che was calling for the practice of socialist solidarity, for the demonstration through deeds of a communist morality. He contended that at the root of the problem was the stark reality that the nations that had socialized their means of production had failed to create a communist morality, ultimately concluding that there was no direct relationship between the economic base of a socialist nation and a communist consciousness.[80] Ideological and moral ideas of the past, Guevara maintained, could outlive the property relations and social conditions that produced them. A socialized economy could exist in a society in which the mentality was still capitalist, but this type of society, that is, economic socialism without communist morality, did not interest him.[81]

Communism, Che assumed, was to be achieved by a parallel development of productivity and consciousness:

Communism is a goal of humanity that is reached consciously, so the eradication of old ideas from the consciousness of the people through

[78] Irving Howe (ed.), *The Basic Writings of Trotsky* (New York: Random House, 1963), p. 15.

[79] See "Revolution and Underdevelopment" in this volume.

[80] See "On the Budgetary System of Finance" in this volume.

[81] A view to some extent similar was adopted by P. J. Proudhon. Georges Gurvitch, *Los fundadores de la sociología contemporánea: Saint-Simon y Proudhon* (Buenos Aires: Editorial Galatea, 1958).

education is a factor of great importance. We cannot forget that without parallel advances in production one can never achieve a communist society.[82]

The best education one could get, according to him, was practice. In a revolutionary war every minute teaches more than a million volumes of books; this he called the "extraordinary university of experience." [83]

Just as guerrilla struggle had a proletarianizing effect, permanent struggle was to develop the new consciousness. Guevara sought to create the permanent "spirit of October." He pointed out that during the missile crisis of October 1962 people worked harder than ever, and that this attitude should be practiced every day, every month, and every year by all the workers.

The permanent ascetism of the guerrilla fighter, full of austerity and stoicism, had to be generalized. Everyone was to become a guerrilla fighter in attitude: a man in constant struggle against illiteracy, against imperialism, against underdevelopment, against reformism; for more production, for more consciousness. This is indeed what might be called *guerrilla communism.*

The experience of guerrilla warfare found expression in Guevara's effort to guerrillaize Cuba. This required the mobilization of all the people; [84] the communists, moreover, were required to work harder, sacrifice more, and to always excel. One teaches through one's own example. The mobilization of the masses, however, could not be rewarded with material incentives. Materialism, Che argued, undermined consciousness:

In order to construct communism simultaneously with the material base of our society, we must make a new man. This is why it is so important to choose correctly the instrument for the mobilization of the masses. That instrument ought to be of a fundamentally moral nature, without forgetting the correct utilization of material incentives, especially those of a social nature.[85]

This ideological posture was at the root of his economic theories. Che Guevara dealt essentially in his economic writings with the period of transition from capitalism to socialism. The model he proposed had originality and without doubt has influenced Cuba's planning of a new society. The system he wanted to construct was one that increased the material base of the nation while creating

---

[82] See "On the Budgetary System of Finance" in this volume.

[83] "Interview with Laura Bergquist (#1)" in this volume.

[84] Richard R. Fagen, "Mass Mobilization in Cuba: The Symbolism of Struggle," *Journal of International Affairs*, No. 20, 1966, pp. 254–271.

[85] "Socialism and Man in Cuba" in this volume.

a new man. Material security and a communist mentality were his concerns, and how not to subordinate either one to the other. Consciousness could not be sacrificed to achieve greater production; instead a revolution in the economic realm required its counterpart in the value system of the nation.

The Revolution must do away with personal gain, with the profit mentality, with economic materialism.[86] With that as a goal he discussed specific issues of finance, administration, planning, and the priorities of economic categories which related in one way or another to his goal.

Che maintained that economic categories and laws were not manmade but the product of social conditions under which production, distribution, and consumption take place. The "law of value" (that is, the profitability of investments and the market system) has, according to him, its operative culmination under capitalism because of the exchange value of products that is attributed to goods by society. He went on and affirmed that exchange value results from the work put into it under given conditions and, as such, value is not a relation.[87] The law of value, he said, did not and could not function in a socialist economy. If an underdeveloped country follows it while trying to construct socialism, it will soon find that those enterprises with the greater resources will dominate the market. In an underdeveloped nation, this economic category cannot be used because it will institutionalize the uneven development of the country. Consequently, investments should not be guided by the requirements of supply and demand because this will maintain the disparities of the social system. Instead one has to follow rational priorities determined by social and political needs. Investments should be channeled, Che explained, toward those sectors of society that must be stimulated, in order to overcome their backwardness, even though those investments may not be profitable economically. To Che, a socialist society had to transcend the law of value in order to escape economic and cultural underdevelopment.[88]

[86] It must be noted that in 1965, when Che left Cuba, Fidel Castro as well as other revolutionary leaders favored the material incentive approach. This position began to change by mid-1966. In 1969, the Cuban revolutionaries favor Che's position. See Sergio de Santis, "Debate sobre la gestión socialista en Cuba," in Francisco Fernández Santos (ed.), *Cuba: una revolución en marcha* (Paris: Ediciones Ruedo Ibérico, 1968), pp. 209–236; Ronald Steel, "Letter from Havana," *New York Review of Books*, April 11, 1968, pp. 8, 10; and Joseph A. Kahl, "The Moral Economy of a Revolutionary Society," *Transaction*, April 1969, pp. 30–37.

[87] Ernesto Che Guevara, "Sobre la concepción del valor; contestando algunas afirmaciones sobre el tema," *Nuestra Industria* (Havana), October 1963, pp. 3–9.

[88] Ernst Mandel, "Le grand débat économique," *Partisans* (Paris), April/June 1967.

He believed that the law of value reaches its culmination under capitalism and decreases in importance as the socialized means of production and distribution become more rationalized and perfected through planning. Once he made known his thesis that profitability should not be the main tool to achieve economic development, his position on the budgetary system of finance becomes more clear.

The budgetary system of finance and the financial self-management system represented to him two different models used by countries building socialism. The financial self-management system, Che stated, puts emphasis on material incentives to achieve development, benefiting only a specific number of producers and enterprises directly. Those benefits take the form of money paid for overfulfilled quotas; and the entire procedure, according to Che, undermines the creation of a communist mentality because it strengthens a value system developed under capitalism. Nonetheless, he recognized the usefulness of material incentives during the transitional period but maintained that this tool should be used in a limited form while laying the foundations for a new value system. He considered this period of transition one in which underdevelopment ended by creating the material bases for prosperity and new human relations.

According to Guevara the benefits to be obtained from the budgetary system of finance were more numerous than those of any other model. First, it allowed better supervision of the economy through centralization; second, it created a communist consciousness; and third, it reinforced the creation of a new man. This thesis has been challenged by those who consider that although the model might be useful in a developed nation, it is questionable whether an underdeveloped one, lacking technical and material resources, could use a model which its level of development makes inoperative.[89] On the other hand, Che believed that in spite of the weak material bases of underdeveloped nations, socialism would be built only if new social relations were established. He could not see how socialism could preserve material incentives and practices which are not congruent with communist ethics.

Interestingly, at the same time that the socialist nations of Eastern Europe moved toward a more liberalized economy, Guevara emphasized a Cuban variant of *Stakhanovism* in reverse. Whereas in the Soviet Union uninhibited competition between individual workers was emphasized in order to achieve higher levels of production and

[89] Víctor Flores Olea, "Sobre las ideas económicas del Che Guevara," *Siempre* (Mexico), June 19, 1968, pp. II–VI.

wages,[90] Guevara stressed socialist emulation and moral incentives to obtain higher output while deemphasizing higher wages. He also defended a very strict central control of the industrial sector of the economy. Under his economic model, the state was to set production targets, fix prices, wages, select the type of goods to be produced, and decrease local management autonomy.

As a representative of the revolutionary government, Guevara often traveled abroad. His travels to Europe, Asia, and Africa in 1959 and 1960 seeking new diplomatic and commercial agreements have already been mentioned. During 1961 he went to Latin America. In Uruguay, he participated in the Inter-American Economic and Social Council Conference which drew up the charter of the Alliance for Progress. There he denounced the maneuvers that took place to remove Cuba from the Inter-American System.[91] Che also met with Richard Goodwin, a representative of the Kennedy administration. In the conversation Che proposed a *modus vivendi* between Cuba and the United States by which Cuba would pay for North American expropriated companies, would not join a political and military alliance with the communist nations, and would refrain from exporting revolution. The United States in turn would refrain from subversive activities in the island and lift the trade embargo. But nothing came out of this meeting.[92] From Uruguay, he returned to his native Argentina, where he spoke with President Arturo Frondizi, a good friend of his. On August 19, Janio Quadros, president of Brazil, bestowed his country's highest award, *Ordem Nacionál do Cruzeiro do Sul*, on Ernesto Guevara. A week later Quadros had to resign.[93]

A year later Guevara arrived in the Soviet Union heading an economic delegation and presumably discussed the placing of intercontinental missiles on Cuban soil.

In July 1963, Che attended an economic planning seminar in Algeria, at which time he also discussed with members of the Afro-Asian Solidarity Organization the problems of national liberation and guerrilla struggle.

1964 was Che's traveling year as well. In March, he headed Cuba's delegation to the United Nations Conference on Trade and Develop-

[90] Maurice Dobb, *Soviet Economic Development since 1917* (London: Routledge and Kegan Paul, 1966), pp. 468–481.

[91] S. P. Alpízar, "Punta del Este, derrota del imperialismo yanqui," *INRA* (Havana), September 1961, p. 39.

[92] Richard N. Goodwin, "Annals of Politics, a Footnote," *New Yorker*, May 25, 1968, pp. 92 ff.

[93] Luis Fernández Dos Santos, "Guevara y el Brasil," *Marcha* (Montevideo), October 27, 1967.

ment held at Geneva.[94] From there he visited France and on the twenty-fifth of the same month, he traveled once again to Algeria on "an official mission" where he spoke with Ahmed Ben Bella for long hours on world revolution and the establishment of a third world movement of nonaligned nations led from Havana and Algiers.[95] In July, Guevara held a number of conversations with Sheik Abdul Rahman, communist leader and cabinet minister in Tanzania. Rahman had been a consistent sponsor of the creation of more wars of national liberation.

On November 4, 1964, he flew to Moscow for the third time seeking more credits for Cuba, which once again reinforced his beliefs regarding the lack of socialist solidarity.[96] Che returned to Havana two weeks later. He spoke at the United Nations General Assembly on December 11, and quickly afterward went once again to Algeria where he stayed until December 25, 1964. Che was seeking the creation of a third world union. In Africa he often expressed the need for the progressive countries to constitute a homogeneous bloc in order to fight against the United States in the Congo and, after the victory there, continue the struggle on the African continent.[97]

He welcomed the New Year declaring that the revolutionary struggle against North American intervention in Latin America would take on an ever-increasing continental character.[98] Then, from January 2 to mid-February, Che went to the Congo (Brazzaville), Guinea, Mali, Ghana, Dahomey, Tanzania, Egypt, and back to Algeria. It should be noted that on February 3, 1965, Guevara headed a delegation of the United Party of the Socialist Revolution of Cuba to China.[99] It is not known what was discussed there. Sixteen days later he arrived in the United Arab Republic where he spoke with Gaston Soumialot, a Congolese rebel leader who tried to convince Guevara to join him in the fight against colonialism in the Congo.[100]

[94] See "On Trade and Development" in this volume.

[95] *Revolución* (Havana), October 12, 1964, p. 1.

[96] How strained the talks were can be surmised from the fact that no communiqué was issued at their conclusion.

[97] *Revolución* (Havana), December 23 and 28, 1964; *Revolución* (Havana), January 18, 1965.

[98] "Che Guevara, 1959–1967, cronología," *Universidad de la Habana* (Havana), July/December 1967, p. 273.

[99] *Juventud Rebelde* (Havana), October 7, 1968, p. 3.

[100] Rojo, *My Friend Che*, p. 170. According to Jay Mallin, Che arranged for his incorporation in the guerrilla struggle in the Congo during this trip. This same viewpoint has been taken by Daniel James. Rojo, on the other hand, gives the impression that Che made the plans to leave Cuba *after* he had been in Africa. See Jay Mallin, " 'Che' Guevara: Some Documentary Puzzles at the End of a Long Journey," *Journal of Inter-American Studies*, January 1968, p. 77; Daniel James (ed.), *The Complete Bolivian Diaries of Che Guevara and Other Captured Documents* (New York: Stein and Day, 1968) p. 14.

On the twenty-fourth in Algiers, he delivered an attack on the Soviet Union, and from March 2 to 12, he stayed in the United Arab Republic. Two days later he arrived in Havana where he informed Fidel Castro of his long journey during a meeting that lasted almost two days. On March 21 he addressed his last public meeting with the Cubans. Then there was silence.

As soon as Ernesto Guevara's disappearance from the public eye was noticed, a barrage of rumors ensued. There was speculation everywhere. At the end of April, he was reportedly seen cutting sugar cane in Oriente Province. Some stated that he was killed in the Dominican Republic uprising. On August 21 the official radio station of the Dominican military assured the people that Che had been killed in the early days of the revolt. On August 28, the Colombian police released photographs of Che. An Italian reporter then affirmed he had interviewed Guevara for the magazine *Le Ore* in the Peruvian Andes in April 1966. He was seen in Argentina and at the same time in Vietnam.

For the moment it is impossible to say when Che Guevara left Cuba, or how he spent most of 1965 and 1966. Doubts were not dispelled when on October 3, 1965, Fidel Castro read a letter from Che in which he stated that other hills of the world demanded his aid.[101] Many doubted the authenticity of the document, arguing that Che would not have admitted ideological indebtedness to Fidel Castro.[102] To doubt the close relationship that existed between the two men would be an error. Throughout his writings Che often stated his great admiration for Fidel; this does not mean that they did not have differences, but it was a matter of timing more than anything else. Fidel Castro was a revolutionary pragmatist who believed major declarations of policy or actions ought to be made at the time most convenient to further the revolutionary cause; Che, in contrast, was a revolutionary purist guided by a sense of ethics in which principles and statements were to be made and implemented regardless of the timing.[103]

Ernesto Guevara considered the role of the individual in history very important. He believed that, although human activity is conditioned by objective conditions, men act consciously and that therefore human activity is not predetermined. Instead, men have freedom of choice. Indeed, this is the essential element in

[101] "Letter to Fidel Castro (October 1963)" in this volume.

[102] Antonio de la Carrera, "Fidel Castro's New Phase," *New Leader,* October 25, 1965.

[103] Andrés Suárez, *Cuba: Castroism and Communism, 1959–1966* (Cambridge, Mass.: M.I.T. Press, 1967), pp. 48, 198–201.

Guevarism—the great emphasis on voluntarism, on subjective conditions. Che developed a radical categorical imperative: *The duty of the revolutionary is to make the revolution.* To push history, to catalyze, is the function of the revolutionary. This is the salient feature in his reflections on guerrilla warfare.

Guevara's experience in the Sierra Maestra gave decisive form to his guerrilla theory. The theory became explicit, however, only with the passing of time.[104] His first public speech in Havana related how the revolutionary struggle had been carried out by all classes of Cuban people, and how none of those who sailed in the *Granma* was from a proletarian or peasant background.[105] After the landing of December 1956 the peasantry did not identify with the strangers but instead tolerated them. Due to the repression which the peasants suffered from the dictator's forces seeking to destroy the guerrillas, the peasants were pushed into joining the insurgents. Thus an army of civilians became an army of peasants.[106] With time and due to the failure of the revolutionary strike of April 9, 1958, he commented that the Rebel Army realized that the Revolution had to be made by all the people.

Having thus initially formulated the foundations of his vision of the Cuban Revolution, Che continued to refine his rudimentary theory in an effort to offer the Cuban experience as a revolutionary model. His book, *Guerra de guerrillas,*[107] showed two basic changes from his early position. Proceeding from the premise that armed struggle could be waged only in the countryside rather than in the cities, he argued that guerrilla warfare must ultimately lead to an agrarian revolution because land had to be promised to the peasantry. A strategic postulate leads him to a social conviction. The Cuban Revolution, Guevara notes, provides three fundamental lessons:

1. The forces of the people can defeat an army.

2. It is not necessary to wait until all the conditions for making a revolution exist; the insurrection can create those conditions.

3. In underdeveloped Latin America the countryside is the basic area for armed struggle.[108]

[104] Sergio de Santis, "Guerrilla y revolución en el pensamiento del Che Guevara," *Casa de las Américas* (Havana), November/December 1967, pp. 115–128.

[105] See "Social Ideas of the Rebel Army" in this volume.

[106] *Ibid.* It should be noted that Che uses the term *civilian* as if denoting a class.

[107] Ernesto Che Guevara, *La guerra de guerrillas* (Havana: MINFAR, 1960), p. 16.

[108] *Ibid.*

These propositions soon antagonized traditional communist parties in Latin America.[109] According to them, it was heresy to suggest that the revolutionary conditions could be created by a small, determined group of guerrilla fighters, revolutionary catalyzers who could propel historical development. Until then the communist orthodoxy provided a mechanical rationale of history that justified inertia; Havana challenged the complacency of Latin American communists. In Cuba, Che's thesis collided with the thinking of old party members who argued that the "radical petty bourgeoisie" had played the predominant role in the revolutionary struggle.[110] This assertion prompted Guevara to reaffirm his theory of the peasant revolution.[111] He then discussed the role of the national bourgeoisie when armed struggle is waged by revolutionaries to achieve power.[112] He acknowledged its potentially useful role during the revolutionary struggle, but also noted its tendency to compromise with the ruling power.[113] By 1963 Guevara was convinced that the national bourgeoisie had united with North American imperialism and consequently that this class was to play no revolutionary role whatsoever in the struggle for liberation.[114] The consistent theme that remained was —*the revolutionary can create the revolutionary conditions.* The function of the revolutionary was to expose the possibility of revolutionary change to the masses. The duty of the revolutionary became that of radicalizing the masses by confronting the established authorities. The people had to be shown that this type of activity could be carried out. This view soon clashed with the foreign policy of the Soviet Union.

From the outset he considered the guerrilla fighter a man who had to possess certain qualities. He wrote,

[109] Alain Joxe, *El conflicto chino-soviético en América Latina* (Montevideo: Ediciones Arca, 1967).

[110] Draper, *Castroism*, p. 84.

[111] See "Cuba: Exceptional Case or Vanguard in the Struggle against Colonialism?" in this volume.

[112] Guevara believed in the existence of a national bourgeoisie prior to 1959 in Cuba; the evidence, however, seems to indicate the opposite. See Robin Blackburn, "Prologue to the Cuban Revolution," *New Left Review* (London), October 1963, pp. 59–64; Lisandro Otero, "Cuba: literatura y revolución," *Siempre* (Mexico), June 15, 1966; and Roberto Rozsa and José A. Fidalgo, "Colonia y lucha de clases hasta 1868," *Casa de las Américas* (Havana), September/October 1968, p. 52.

[113] A number of scholarly studies have pointed out this tendency. Jorge Graciarena, *Poder y clases sociales en el desarrollo de América Latina* (Buenos Aires: Paidós, 1967); Claudio Véliz (ed.), *The Politics of Conformity in Latin America* (London: Oxford, 1967); and James Petras and Maurice Zeitlin (ed.), *Latin America, Reform or Revolution* (New York: Fawcett Premier, 1968).

[114] See "Guerrilla Warfare: A Method" in this volume.

The guerrilla fighter ... must have a moral conduct that shows him to be a true priest of the reform to which he aspires. To the stoicism imposed by the difficult conditions of warfare should be added an austerity born of rigid self-control that will prevent a single excess, a single slip, whatever the circumstances. The guerrilla soldier should be an ascetic. ... The peasant must always be helped technically, economically, morally, and culturally. The guerrilla fighter will be a sort of guiding angel who has fallen into the zone, helping the poor always and bothering the rich as little as possible in the first phases of the war.[115]

Che consistently emphasized that leadership posed the biggest problem in Latin America. Revolutionary conditions existed; leaders conscious of the necessity of change and confident of the possibility of revolutionary change were absent. His theory of guerrilla warfare was considered a formula for Latin American national liberation, but this theory was a posteriori reflection on the Cuban experience; it was a formulization of the Cuban success even though the guerrilla fighters during the struggle did not subscribe to a preconceived theory. The *foco guerrillero* (guerrilla focus) was a product of national characteristics and improvisation.[116] By 1963, the model of armed struggle developed by Che incorporated a new element: Liberation would only be achieved by a continental struggle. Latin American liberation became an all-or-nothing affair. The premise was now one of an historicocultural homogeneity. Latin America was perceived as a unit. By 1965, the concept of a continental revolution was enlarged by Che to encompass the whole underdeveloped world. Now to achieve national liberation a world revolution had to be fought.[117]

The Cuban Revolution during its insurrectional stage did not become a bone of contention between the Soviet Union and the United States. Guevara thought that this would not occur again in Latin America. He was convinced that the Vietnam war and the establishment of a socialist state in the hemisphere would prompt the U.S. to give political and military support to all governments of Latin America. Therefore, the revolutionaries would have to present a united front, waging guerrilla warfare on a continental and later a world scale.[118] In his letter to the Tricontinental organization with headquarters in Havana he stated,

[115] Norman Gall, "Legacy of Che Guevara," p. 37.

[116] For a good critique of the Guevara/Debray thesis, see the articles by Gerardo Unzueta in *El Siglo* (Santiago, Chile), January 21, 28, 1968, and Joe Slovo, "Latin America and the Ideas of Regis Debray," *African Communist* (London), second quarter, 1968, pp. 37–54.

[117] See "Message to the Tricontinental" in this volume.

[118] Bruce Jackson, "Whose Men in Havana?" *Problems of Communism*, May/June 1966; Albert P. Lentin, *La lutte tricontinentale: impérialisme et révolution après la conférence de la Havane* (Paris: Maspero, 1966).

What role shall we, the exploited people of the world, play? The people of the three continents focus their attention on Vietnam and learn their lesson. If imperialists blackmail humanity by threatening it with war, the wise reaction is not to fear war. The general tactics of the people should be to launch a constant and firm attack on all fronts where the confrontation is taking place....

And he adds,

On this continent for all practical purposes only one tongue is spoken (with the exception of Brazil, with whose people those who speak Spanish can easily make themselves understood, owing to the great similarities of our languages). There is also such a great similarity among the classes of the different countries that an identification exists among them, of an "international American" type, much more complete than that of other continents. Language, customs, religion, a common foreign master unite them.... Owing to the similarities of our national characteristics, the struggle of our America will achieve continental proportions.... America, a forgotten continent in the world's more recent liberation struggles, which is now beginning to make itself heard through the Tricontinental in the voice of the vanguard of its peoples, the Cuban Revolution, has before it a task of much greater relevance: to create a second or a third Vietnam.... What a luminous, near future would be visible to us if two, three, or many Vietnams appeared throughout the world with their share of death and immense tragedies, their everyday heroism and repeated blows against imperialism, obliging it to disperse its forces under the attack and the increasing hatred of all the peoples of the earth! [119]

Because he considered the objective conditions for armed struggle present in Latin America, what was absent was revolutionary consciousness. Just as he believed that consciousness was necessary for the building of socialism, he also regarded it as a creator, if the conditions did not exist, of armed struggle. Only a cadre of professional revolutionaries was needed; everything else would follow as a by-product of the dynamics of the struggle.[120]

The theory, however, is not perfect. The guerrilla cadres do not revolutionize the peasantry, but rather it is the government repression against the peasantry that impels the people to join the guerrilla. The weakness of the Guevara theory of armed struggle lies in the problem of how it deals with the dilemma of radicalizing the peasants through its own armed struggle and at the same time carrying on an armed struggle independent of the peasantry. It is in this first period that the guerrilla is at its weakest and open to destruction. To suggest that the army will take vengeance on the peasantry because the *guerrilleros* are elusive underestimates the

[119] "Message to the Tricontinental" in this volume.
[120] This voluntarism was criticized by Marx himself. See Karl Marx and Frederick Engels, *Werke* (Berlin: Dietz Verlag, 1962), II, 614.

intelligence of the military of Latin America. Similarly to think that the rootless sugar cane worker or the minifundia peasant of Cuba who joined the guerrilla movement in Cuba had its counterpart in the Indian population of the Andes overlooks cultural and historical differences.[121]

Guevara chose Bolivia as his main center of operations because, as two British writers with close relation to Havana state,

Bolivia ... presents a uniquely favorable arena for the new Cuban strategy of all-out armed struggle against what Fidel Castro calls the "puppet governments of imperialism." It combines three conditions not found anywhere else in South America:
  1. a militant, revolutionary working class armed with its own weapons —the miners;
  2. a disgruntled, conspiratorial middle class which controlled power for a decade, lost it to its own military and is determined to have its revenge—the M.N.R.; and
  3. a wretchedly equipped and trained soldadeska with no "background" or "tradition," weak in numbers and jittery in morale.[122]

It should be indicated that among the "conditions," the role that the Indian peasants are to have is not considered. The Bolivian guerrillas under Guevara were structured following the insurrectional thesis developed by Guevara through a number of years and coherently expounded by Debray. Its guiding principles were

1. A revolution requires a political vanguard, but the vanguard of the revolutionary movement does not necessarily have to be the communist party.

2. The guerrilla struggle will create the revolutionary party and not the reverse. The guerrilla movement will create the people's army and from it will arise the vanguard party.

3. The political and military leadership of the revolutionary movement will have to be controlled by the guerrilla movement.

4. The guerrilla movement is the vanguard of the revolutionary movement and, as such, it controls the revolutionary activity in the cities.[123]

On November 7, 1966, Ernesto Guevara began the guerrilla struggle in Bolivia. From the very start, Che tried to unite all the revolu-

---

[121] Carlos R. Rodríguez, "The Cuban Revolution and the Peasantry," *World Marxist Review*, October 1965, pp. 62–71; G. C. Alroy, "The Peasantry in the Cuban Revolution," *Review of Politics*, January 1967, pp. 87–99; Juan Carlos Santos, "La marcha al Segundo Frente Frank País," *El Mundo* (Havana), September 17, 1966, pp. 1, 7.

[122] Perry Anderson and Robin Blackburn, "The Debray Dossier," *Bertrand Russell Peace Foundation London Bulletin*, September 1967, p. 27.

[123] Regis Debray, ¿*Revolución en la Revolución?* (Havana: Casa de las Américas, 1966).

tionary forces of the country, but his efforts found little support. The Communist Party of Bolivia and the two Trotskyist factions, as well as the pro-Chinese Communist Party, expressed their solidarity with the guerrilla movement in April 1967, but they gave it no material support.[124]

The CPB proposed three conditions for aiding the guerrillas.[125] According to Che's diary, the first secretary of the party, Mario Monje, met with him at the end of December 1966, and stated that he would resign from his post but would obey the norms of the CPB. Second, Monje would become the political and military leader of the revolutionary struggle as long as it took place in Bolivia. And third, Monje would seek aid from all Latin American communist parties.[126] Guevara rejected the proposal that would remove him from the leadership of the struggle, arguing that he was leading a continental army that required a leadership with continental prestige. To accept the proposal would have meant to set the precedent of allowing others to claim leadership of the revolutionary force once it had begun to function within the boundaries of a particular nation.[127]

After the split with the CPB, the guerrillas had no contacts with any other political party; consequently they decided to form their own political organization, the Ejército de Liberación Nacional.[128]

By mid-March, an oil engineer reported suspicious movements in the region of Ñancahuazú to the army. A military patrol was dispatched to investigate; it was ambushed by a guerrilla column on March 23, 1967. Guerrilla warfare began in Bolivia only two days after Che had written in his diary, "Everything gives the impression

---

[124] *La Mañana* (La Paz), May 19, 1967; *Le Monde* (Paris), November 16, 1967.

[125] Mario Monje maintains that his proposals were different. According to his version his conditions were (1) a meeting of the communist parties of Latin America to coordinate actions; (2) the formation of a wide political front, from which should come a revolutionary command; (3) political and military leadership in the hands of someone chosen by the revolutionary command. Monje has also stated that Che offered him the political leadership of the guerrilla movement. On the other hand, a veteran of the guerrilla movement who was able to escape to Chile from Bolivia in 1968 affirmed that Monje insisted that the pro-Chinese Bolivian communists not be allowed to participate in the movement, that the CPB be allowed to control the political and military command of the movement, and that aid be sought from all Latin American communist parties. See *El Diario* (La Paz), February 5, 1968, p. 3; *Latin America* (London), March 1, 1968, pp. 67–68; Daniel James (ed.), *Complete Bolivian Diaries*, pp. 95, 227–228.

[126] "The Diary of Che Guevara," *Ramparts*, July 27, 1968, p. 18.

[127] Mario Monje, "Las divergencias del PC Boliviano con el Che Guevara," *Punto Final* (Santiago), February 27, 1968.

[128] *La Siniestra* (Rome), November/December 1967.

of complete chaos; they [the guerrillas] don't know what to do." The ambush represented an act of disobedience on the part of one of the Cubans who was ordered not to engage the enemy under any circumstances. As a result, the man lost his command and the guerrillas their secrecy.

From March through October, twenty-six battles were fought.[129] On April 12, 1967, U.S. "advisers" arrived from Panama. Five days later the guerrilla group was divided in two. One group was led by Che and the other by "Joaquín," a Cuban. By late July, the Bolivian army launched a major offensive seeking to locate and annihilate the *guerrilleros*. In September after a major clash, the army captured documents and information which allowed the Bolivian government to destroy the logistical rear guard of the guerrillas in the urban areas. On August 31, the forces of Joaquín were ambushed at the Masicuri River, when all the guerrillas tried to cross the river at the same time! [130] From September 22 through 25, Che and his men stayed in Alto Seco, a village high in the Andean mountains. On the twenty-third, six hundred Bolivian rangers, who had completed an intensive course in counterinsurgency under officers of the United States Special Forces Mobile Units, were deployed to the area.

On September 27, the Manchego regiment was able to ambush the guerrillas, killing four of their members a few miles from the village of La Higuera on the Piarinambi River. Among the casualties were Roberto Peredo, Guevara's hight-hand man and supposed leader of the Bolivian guerrillas, and the Cuban Major Orlando Pantoja Tamayo, who had fought alongside Che in Cuba. Taking advantage of the confusion that followed, one of the *guerrilleros* deserted the group and hid in the wilderness where he shaved and cut his hair. He then proceeded to the town of Mizque Loma where he asked for employment. He was told to solicit employment at Pucara; there he was later arrested by Lieutenant Colonel Luis Penaililo, one of the ranger's chiefs operating from Valle Grande. The deserter provided precise information to the armed forces.

With the death of "Coco" Peredo, Che and his group found themselves dispirited and began moving back and forth from canyon to canyon. In the meantime, the insurgents had been encircled by approximately 1,500 troops. The guerrillas were trapped.

On Sunday morning, October 8, 184 Bolivian rangers pursued the

---

[129] Major ones were Iripiti, El Mesón, Taperilla, Ñancahuazú, Samaipata, La Tranca, Yajo Pampa, and Quebrada del Yuro.
[130] *Presencia* (La Paz), October 4, 1967.

guerrillas into a canyon four miles from the village of Higueras. At 1:15 P.M. the battle began. The first shot hit Che's mule; hours later he was captured. The next day Ernesto Guevara was murdered by his captors.[131]

Che's action always reflected his profound belief that the best way of teaching was by example. To assume leadership of continental armed struggle in Latin America was the logical conclusion of the apostle of continental revolution, particularly when he was convinced such a leader was lacking. Perhaps there is another reason why Che began a guerrilla movement again: The Cuban revolutionaries have implicitly admitted in almost all of their declarations that the fighting days in the mountains were a kind of past golden age, an age of revolutionary innocence to which they aspired to return.[132]

Guerrilla struggle meant a kind of communism in microcosm—an environment that suppressed differences and acted as a midwife for the surfacing of the best of man, a community of fellowship in which all performed according to their abilities and shared alike.

Bolivia was to be a training ground, a revolutionary center from which guerrillas were to spread to other nations of Latin America. Che's main objectives were Peru and Argentina. He had worked closely with his very good friend, journalist Jorge Masetti of Argentina, who had tried to create an insurrectional center in the province of Salta. At the end of 1964, Masetti was discovered and killed by the military. He had trained in Bolivia since June 1963 and moved into Argentina three months later.[133] Che had argued that the training of Argentine guerrillas had to take place outside its boundaries; the Bolivian guerrilla force was to become a highly mobile unit, which after setting up a guerrilla group in Bolivia was to move to the other two countries.[134]

The guerrilla force committed multiple blunders.[135] In April 1967

[131] "Como murió el Che," *Sucesos para todos* (Mexico), February 17, 1968; Carlos Núñez, "Responso y Zafarrancho," *Marcha* (Montevideo), October 27, 1967; Michele Ray, "How the C.I.A. Executed Che," *Ramparts*, March 1968; *El Mundo* (Havana), October 17, 1967; *Guardian* (London), October 11, 1967; Richard Gott, "La experiencia guerrillera en Bolivia," *Estudios Internacionales* (Santiago), April/June 1968, pp. 85–114.

[132] Carlos Franqui (ed.), *The Twelve* (New York: Lyle and Stuart, 1968), and Edmundo Desnoes, *Gente del llano* (Havana: Casa de las Américas, 1965).

[133] Rojo, *My Friend Che*, p. 154. A similar procedure was used by Che's former brother-in-law Ricardo Gadea, when he trained in Bolivia and infiltrated into Peru in 1964.

[134] Philippe Labreveux, *Bolivia bajo el Ché* (Buenos Aires: Colección Replanteo, 1968); Hugo Gambini, *El Ché Guevara* (Buenos Aires: Editorial Paidos, 1968).

[135] See "A Guerrilla's Diary [factors in the failure of Che Guevara's Bolivian insurgency]," *Far Eastern Economic Review*, August 15, 1968, pp. 313-316.

the army appropriated a diary from one of the guerrillas in which it was stated that Guevara was leading the struggle. There were also two photographs of Che in a guerrilla camp. All began to disintegrate when the guerrilla force revealed itself to the armed forces.

Indeed, the guerrillas were not supposed to start their activities until 1968. They began in defeat because since the time the revolutionary war began they had failed to establish a supported recruitment network in the cities due to disagreements with the Bolivian Communist Party. Guevara's theory of the city becoming subordinated to guerrilla leadership had as a consequence a lack of urban support. From the outset, the guerrilla movement was isolated and left to its fate. Soon a problem of leadership and discipline developed within the guerrilla force itself. The Bolivians were the only deserters because, among other things, they disliked playing a secondary role to the Cubans, who tended to control all positions of command.

After losing the logistical rear guard, the guerrillas ran out of supplies and often fell ill. It must have been an anxiety-provoking sight to watch Guevara suffer from recurrent asthmatic and rheumatic attacks which often forced him to ride a mule. His very performance now was contrary to the prerequisite he had set as guerrilla theoretician on the matter of leadership. The heavy losses they suffered by August had a demoralizing effect. It was also at this time that supplies became scarce, the desertions increased, and the graduates of counterinsurgency warfare became available to the Bolivian military.

At the root of all the erroneous calculations was his theory of guerrilla warfare, which incredibly was not founded on a realistic analysis of the Cuban revolutionary process. Guevara had too much iron will and too little political sophistication.

Che failed to see that the Cuban Revolution had been exceptional. First of all, the dynamics of struggle between Batista's forces and the guerrillas were more complex than he admitted. Undoubtedly the Rebel Army inflicted heavy casualties on the regular armed forces, but this was a product of the very tactics used by Batista. Conventional warfare was used to fight a guerrilla war. Consequently, all the offensives made by the dictatorship ended in dismal failure. The ranks of the regular forces began to lose morale as they found themselves unable to deal with an enemy that did not follow the "rules of warfare." Once morale disintegrated and battles continued, the flexibility, mobility, and better military ability of the rebels overwhelmed Batista's forces. It would be erroneous, however, to definitely state that the Rebel Army defeated the regular troops in battle. Che himself stated once that the army did not fight but retreated, leaving behind weapons and equipment.[136]

Cuba in 1958 was completely different from the Bolivia of 1967. The Cuban peasantry had nothing in common with the peasant masses of the Andes; their historical and cultural development had been distinct. For example, in Bolivia if the peasants aided the guerrillas, they would lose their land.[137] Forced to fight, Guevara had no other choice but to follow his premise that armed struggle had to be carried on in the countryside; but in Bolivia the paradox is that although the countryside is suitable for guerrilla warfare, the peasantry is conservative.[138] In contrast, the miners are a revolutionary force which exists in an environment not suitable for this type of activity—the *altiplano*.

Guevara was caught in the vicious circle of his own theory of the *foco insurreccional*, not to mention the maneuvers to undermine the revolutionary struggle by other left-wing groups. To survive the guerrilla needs the support of the peasants but to achieve that support the guerrilla has to demonstrate that it can survive.

The revolutionary is dead. The myth now begins. Through his life, Ernesto Guevara expressed a desire to better the human condition. He had a certain intellectual blindness but he was a man of action. No other Cuban revolutionary has produced such a detailed account of the revolutionary war as he did. His narratives, while not exhaustive, rigorous, or objective, present a starting point for any student of the Cuban Revolution. He wrote about history while making it. His flaws as analyst or historian are obvious, but he never pretended to be either. As theoretician he was imaginative; his convictions were basically rooted in ethical ideas. To relieve the suffering of the people, no matter how much sacrifice had to be undergone, was his driving principle. He had the courage to fight and die for his convictions. A committed man, he sought a simple formula of revolutionary struggle and, as a consequence, his end was dramatic. It is his commitment, his idealism, and his absolute belief that the individual could change history which has made him a romantic and, at the same time, a legendary figure of great attraction. In an

[136] See his interview in the Escambray mountains in this volume.

[137] In fact, Guevara was reported to the army by a peasant. Thomas Molina, "La última trinchera del Che," *Punto Final* (Santiago), October 22, 1968, pp. 20–22.

[138] Johan Vellard, *Civilisations des Andes* (Paris: Gallimard, 1963), pp. 201–261.

age of routine and mechanical behavior, Guevara rises as an ascetic symbol, a man ready to sacrifice. It would be erroneous, nevertheless, to view this man as a materialization of humanism; in doing so, one would lose sight of his many dimensions. He believed in a set of ideas and he killed to defend them.

His death represents a great paradox: The failure of his political strategy is also the victory of his example. His military defeat gave him an existential victory.

WRITINGS

Pedrero Pact

ЛЛЛЛЛЛЛЛЛЛЛЛЛЛЛЛЛЛЛЛЛЛЛЛЛ

The disintegration of Fulgencio Batista's dictatorial government has entered its definitive stage. All the efforts of the dictatorship were directed to maintaining itself until the electoral farce of November 3; [1] that date is now past and it constituted a sonorous slap from the people to the candidates of the dictatorship, whether officials or not.

A new date is now set before the eyes of the tyranny's weary soldiers: February 24, [2] a theoretical moment in which the presidential mandate should be transferred. But each time Batista's soldiers believe less in deceitful dates and each time they feel more the effectiveness of the people's arms in their own flesh.

In this manner has become evident the full identification which exists in the struggle against the tyranny between the 26th of July Movement and the Directorio Revolucionario. Both organizations have called on the people of Las Villas from the Sierra de Escambray, where their forces struggle for Cuba's freedom.

The goal of the 26th of July Movement and the Directorio Revolucionario is to maintain a perfect coordination in their military actions, culminating in the synchronization of operations so that members of both the 26th of July and the Directorio Revolucionario will participate in combat simultaneously, and to utilize jointly, for the benefit of the Revolution, the channels of communication and supply which are under the control of one or the other organization.

In administrative policy, the liberated territory has been divided into zones which are under the jurisdiction of the Directorio Revolucionario and the 26th of July and in which each organization will collect war tributes.

"Pacto de Pedrero, Noviembre 1958," 13 *Documentos de la Insurrección* (Havana: Organización Nacional de Bibliotecas Ambulantes y Populares, December 1959), pp. 63–64. The Directorio Revolucionario began to operate in the Sierra de Escambray in February 1958. Shortly afterward Guevara arrived in Las Villas; the leaders of both organizations met in the hamlet of Pedrero and discussed a common strategy. Eds.

[1] On November 3, 1958, elections were held in Cuba and, as expected, Batista's candidate won the presidential election. Eds.

[2] On February 24, 1959, Fulgencio Batista was supposed to hand over power to his presidential appointee, Andrés Rivero Agüero. Eds.

Concerning agrarian policy and the administration of justice, the 26th of July and Directorio Revolucionario are assessing plans for agrarian reform and a penal code.

This declaration is an example of the revolutionary movement's cohesion in the Las Villas front where the 26th of July and the Directorio Revolucionario represent the purest ideals of youth struggling as brothers, bearing to a large degree the weight of Cuba's insurrection and shedding their blood. Without this there would be guerrilla war in neither the Sierra Maestra nor the Sierra Escambray. Nor would we have dates such as the twenty-sixth of July at the Moncada or the thirteenth of March at the presidential palace.

We are conscious of our duty to the fatherland and in the names of the revolutionary postulates of Frank País and José Antonio Echevarría we call on all revolutionary factions to unite, and invite the organizations in the territory which possess insurrectional forces to adhere publicly to this appeal, thus coordinating their action for the benefit of the Cuban nation.

TO UNITE IS THE WORD OF ORDER: Together we are ready to win or die.

Ernesto (Che) Guevara
Commander in Chief of
Las Villas Regiment
Movimiento 26 de Julio

Rolando Cubelas [3]
Commander in Chief of
Las Villas Regiment
Directorio Revolucionario

[3] Rolando Cubelas was a major and a leader of the Directorio Revolucionario's guerrillas in the Escambray mountains. During the first months of the Revolution he was a military attaché to the Cuban embassy in Spain; by mid-1959, he was subsecretary in the Ministry of Government. In October 1959 he became the president of the University Federation of Students. On March 10, 1966, he was sentenced to twenty-five years in prison for allegedly plotting the assassination of Fidel Castro. Eds.

Latin America as Seen from the Afro-Asian Continent

ЛЛЛЛЛЛЛЛЛЛЛЛЛЛЛЛЛЛЛЛЛЛЛЛ

For Asians to speak of America (our America, the unredeemed one) is to speak of an unknown continent; Latin America is as unknown to them as Asia, that immense part of the world whose libertarian aspirations found appropriate expression in the Bandung Pact,[1] is unknown to us.

Nothing is known of Latin America except that it was a gigantic section of the world where dark-skinned natives lived with loin-cloths and spears, a place where once Christopher Columbus arrived, more or less about the same time that Vasco da Gama rounded the Cape of Good Hope. Nothing is known about our centuries of cultural, economic, and political history. Nothing concrete is added to this knowledge, except a semiabstract event called the Cuban Revolution.

In reality, Cuba is an abstraction for those faraway lands that have just begun to awaken. A mythological being arises named Fidel Castro—beard, long hair, olive green uniform, and an unclear position in a country whose very name is unknown to them. Many do not know that Cuba is an island or that Fidel Castro is the Cuban Revolution. Those bearded men are Castro's, those men, originating on an island difficult to find on a map, moved by the magic spring of a mythological man, are Latin America, the new America that stretches its limbs after many years of kneeling down.

The other Latin America is disappearing. The one with unknown men who work miserably in tin mines and in whose name Indonesian tin workers are exploited into martyrdom; the America with amazonic rubber plantations worked by men with malaria and in whose name infinitesimal salaries are paid in Indonesia and Ceylon; the America with fabulous oil resources due to which small salaries are paid to workers in Iraq, Saudi Arabia, and Iran; the one with cheap sugar that forces the Indian worker to labor under savage conditions and receive low wages, is disappearing.

Africa and Asia, surprised by the bold desires to be free, begin

Humanismo (Mexico), September/October 1959, pp. 46–48.
[1] Afro-Asian Conference held at Bandung, Indonesia, in April 1955, which emphasized self-determination and opposition to colonialism. Eds.

to look beyond their seas. Could it be that those large grain and raw material suppliers have had their culture arrested by colonialism and millions of Asians and Africans have the same hopes we have? Could it be that our brotherhood transcends distances, different languages, and the absence of close cultural links, and unites us in the struggle? Should a Japanese worker be closer to an Argentine laborer, a Bolivian miner, the man working for United Fruit Company or the Cuban sugar cutter than to a Japanese samurai? Could it be that Fidel Castro is, more than an isolated case, the vanguard of the American people in their ever-increasing struggle for freedom? Perhaps he is a man of flesh and blood like Sukarno, Nehru, or Nasser.

The liberated people are becoming conscious of the great deceit they have been subjected to, the so-called racial inferiority, and they now know that they could have been mistaken about how they judged other people in the world.

To this conference of Afro-Asian peoples Cuba has been invited—one country of our American continent before this august meeting of our Afro-Asian brothers. Cuba has not come by chance but rather as the result of the historic convergence of all oppressed peoples in this hour of liberation. It has come to tell that a true Cuba exists and that Fidel Castro is a man, a popular hero, and not an abstract myth. It will also explain that Cuba is not an isolated event but rather the first signal of America's awakening.

When you tell them about the hardly noticed popular heroes of Latin America, all the men without names who died in battle for a whole continent, or about the Colombian "bandits" who fight against the alliance of the cross and the sword; when you talk to them about the Paraguayan *mensú* [2] and the Bolivian miners killing each other while representing, without knowing it, the oil interests of England and the United States, then you will see surprise in their eyes. It is not the amazement of hearing something unprecedented in history, but the amazement of listening to a new version, identical in development and consequences to the old colonial version that they suffered for shameful centuries.

Latin America is taking shape and concretizing. Latin America, which is to say Cuba; Cuba, which means Fidel Castro (a man representing a continent with the mere presence of his guerrilla beard), is acquiring life. The Latin American continent is becoming alive in the Afro-Asia imagination with real men who suffer and fight for similar ideals.

[2] Peon on a maté plantation. Eds.

From my new perspective I learned to judge all the events in which I participated from the sublime moment of "twelve," [3] and now I see all small contradictions disappear and Cuba attains a real transcendence in the continent. With this perspective I can value the childish gesture, due to its simplicity and spontaneity, of the man from another land who touches my beard and in a strange tongue asks, "Fidel Castro?" adding, "Are you a member of the guerrilla army that leads the struggle for freedom in Latin America? Are you our allies from the other side of the sea?" And I have to answer him, and millions of Afro-Asians like him who live in new and insecure atomic times, in the affirmative. Furthermore I tell him that I am his brother, one among many from this side of the world who await with infinite anxiety the moment when our continents will unite and destroy, once and for all, the anachronistic presence of colonialism.

[3] Refers to when the guerrillas numbered only twelve men in 1956. Eds.

The Most Dangerous Enemy
and Other Stupidities

Sometimes we even thought it was rather pompous to refer to Cuba as if it were in the center of the universe (she is so small, poor thing): Nonetheless it is true, or almost true. If someone doubts the Revolution's importance, he should read the headlines, "The United States Threatens Poland because of Pact with Cuba." Man, we're strong and dangerous. We have poisoned the American environment and threatened the sweet democracy of Trujillo and Somoza,[1] so now the champions of freedom threaten Poland because it signed an agreement with Cuba.

We can imagine the uneasy surprise of the Polish minister presently visiting the United States. In the middle of his breakfast he hears the terrible news; poor man, he probably sadly lamented the irresponsibility of his counterpart who signed that agreement with that terrible "communist country" called Cuba.

It does not matter if Poland is a country that calls itself communist, or that it forms part of the Warsaw Pact and proclaims everywhere its alliance with the Soviet Union. The quarrel is not with us, but with those who signed an agreement with us. The quarrel is all about certain helicopters the United States does not want us to have.

Cuba should not be allowed to buy helicopters because she is communist and now communist Poland is threatened by the United States with not selling her helicopters which are then sold to Cuba (don't ask me to explain this any better; I don't understand it either).

By the way, the Polish minister should tell the North Americans to jump in the lake because Cuba does not have to account to anyone for what it does with its sovereignty.

Oh, it's so great and comfortable to belong to such a strong world power as dangerous Cuba!

To fight against such a powerful communist nation as Cuba, with

Verde Olivo (Havana), April 17, 1960, p. 7. This article was written by Guevara under the pseudonym Francotirador.
[1] Rafael Trujillo of the Dominican Republic and Luis Somoza of Nicaragua. Eds.

very dangerous missile bases in Camagüey, one cannot declare war; instead, it has to be attacked with a curtain of terrible truths broadcast everywhere. This is not a new method. The Voice of America is broadcast throughout the so-called Iron Curtain to Eastern Europe in every language. For those Cubans who do not know their country, it is very convenient every so often to listen to the Voice of America broadcast. Many truths invented at UPI or AP will be learned; the ignorant Cubans will find out, for example, that our public landmarks are called Fidel Castro Avenue, Che Boulevard, Almeida Fountain, and so on. Also, you will learn that that sinister Raúl Castro heads a network of sneaky international spies who are training to invade the United States. You will inform yourselves about all the threats faced by the Free World, and this is why it is indispensable to crush this Caribbean "center of disturbance."

Many interesting things are narrated by the "voice of freedom" to innocent Cubans; the only thing we do not understand is why the United States has to make all these broadcasts if its internal satellites, such as *Diario de la Marina* and *Prensa Libre*,[2] repeat obediently all that they say. Could it be that Conte Agüero [3]—"hero of freedom of the press"—realized sadly the danger in which he found himself here and decided to go abroad and use the magnificent vehicle of "the voice of war criminals"?

A little bit scared because we do not know the true intentions of these people, we ask ourselves: Why so much stupidity?

[2] Havana dailies, conservative and liberal respectively. Eds.

[3] Luis Conte Agüero was a radio commentator who fought the Batista dictatorship; he was a good friend of Fidel Castro until 1960. Eds.

Notes for the Study of the Ideology
of the Cuban Revolution

꒥꒥꒥꒥꒥꒥꒥꒥꒥꒥꒥꒥꒥꒥꒥꒥꒥꒥꒥꒥꒥꒥꒥

This is a unique Revolution which some people assert contradicts one of the most orthodox premises of the revolutionary movement expressed by Lenin: "Without a revolutionary theory, there is no revolutionary movement." It would be suitable to state that a revolutionary theory, as the expression of a social truth, is beyond any enunciation of it, that is to say, the revolution can be made if the historical realities are interpreted correctly and if the forces involved are utilized correctly, even if the theory is not known. It is clear that an adequate understanding of the theory simplifies the task and prevents us from falling into dangerous errors as long as the theory corresponds to the reality. Besides, speaking concretely of this Revolution, it should be emphasized that the principal actors were not exactly what one might call theoreticians, but neither were they completely ignorant of the great social phenomena and the laws which control them. With some theoretical knowledge as a base and a profound understanding of reality, it was possible to create a revolutionary theory with the passing of time.

The aforesaid should be considered an introduction to the explanation of this curious phenomenon which has the whole world intrigued: the Cuban Revolution. It is an event worthy of study in contemporary world history: How and why a group of men shattered by an army greatly superior in technique and equipment was able at first to survive, later to become strong and even stronger than the enemy in the battle zones, and still later to migrate into new zones of combat, finally defeating that enemy on the battlefield though still with fewer troops.

Naturally, we who do not often show the required preoccupation with theory have not come today to expound on the truth of the Cuban Revolution as if we were its masters. Rather we will simply try to give the bases which will enable us to interpret this truth. In fact, the Cuban Revolution must be separated into two absolutely different stages: that of armed action until January 1, 1959, and the political, economic, and social transformation since then.

Verde Olivo (Havana), October 8, 1960, pp. 10–14.

Even these two stages deserve to be broken down into further subdivisions, but we shall not approach them from a point of historical exposition but rather from a viewpoint of the evolution of the revolutionary thought of the leaders through their contact with the people. Incidentally, at this point one must introduce a general attitude toward one of the modern world's most controversial terms: Marxism. Our position, when asked whether we are Marxists or not, is the same as that of a physicist when asked if he is a "Newtonian" or a biologist if asked whether he is a "Pasteurian."

There are truths so evident, so embedded in the people's knowledge, that they are now useless to discuss. One should be a "Marxist" as naturally as one is a "Newtonian" in physics, or a "Pasteurian" in biology, considering that if new facts determine new concepts these new concepts will never take away that part of truth which the older concept had. Such is the case of Einsteinian relativity or of Planck's quantum theory with respect to Newton's discovery. It subtracts nothing from the greatness of the wise Englishman. Thanks to Newton, physics was able to advance until new concepts of space were reached. The wise Englishman was the necessary stepping stone for it.

In Marx as a thinker, as an investigator of social doctrines and of the capitalist system in which he lived, one could evidently object to certain inaccuracies. We as Latin Americans, for example, could not agree with Marx's interpretation of Bolívar [1] or with Marx's and Engels' analysis of the Mexicans to whom they gave some race and nationality theories as fact which are inadmissible today.[2] But great men, discoverers of illuminating truths, live on in spite of their minor faults, and they only serve to demonstrate that they are human—that is to say, human beings who can incur errors in spite of the clear awareness reached by these giants of thought. This is why we acknowledge the essential truths of Marxism as part of the cultural and scientific heritage of the people and take it with the naturalness of something which needs no further discussion.

The advances in the social and political sciences, as in other fields, belong to a long historical process, the links of which connect with one another—adding up, gathering, and achieving perfection con-

---

[1] Simón Bolívar (1783–1830), leader of Latin America's independence movement. Eds.

[2] Marx approved of the annexation of Texas and California because the Mexicans were "lazy." See Max Nomad, *Apostles of Revolution* (New York: Collier Books, 1961), p. 103. Eds.

stantly. In the origins of peoples, there existed Chinese, Arabian, or Hindu mathematics; yet today mathematics has no frontiers. Thus throughout history there was a Greek Pythagoras, an Italian Galileo, an English Newton, a German Gauss, a Russian Lovachevsky, an Einstein, and so on. Thus in the field of social and political sciences, from Democritus to Marx, a long series of thinkers added their original investigations and accumulated a body of experience and doctrine.

Marx's merit is that in the history of social thought he suddenly produces a qualitative change. He interprets history, understands its dynamics, foresees the future; but in addition to foreseeing it, which would end his scientific obligation, he expresses a revolutionary concept: Not only must one interpret nature, it must be transformed. Man ceases to be a slave and becomes the architect of his own destiny. At this point, Marx begins to place himself in such a situation that he becomes the necessary target of all those who have a special interest in maintaining the old, similar to what happened to Democritus, whose work was burned by Plato and his disciples, the ideologues of Athenian slave aristocracy.

Starting with the revolutionary Marx, a political group with concrete ideas established itself, taking as a basis giants such as Marx and Engels and developing through successive stages with personalities such as Lenin, Mao Tse-tung, and the new Soviet and Chinese rulers, establishing a body of doctrine and, let us say, examples to follow.

The Cuban Revolution takes up Marx where he left science to take up his revolutionary rifle. And the Revolution takes him up at that moment not in the revisionist spirit of going against that which follows Marx, of reviving "pure" Marx, but simply because up to that point Marx, the scientist, placed himself outside of the history he studied and predicted. Afterward, Marx the revolutionary would fight within history. We, practical revolutionaries, when initiating our struggle, simply fulfilled laws foreseen by Marx the scientist. Through that path of rebellion, struggling against the old power structure, basing ourselves on the people to destroy that structure, and having as the basis of our struggle the happiness of the people, we are simply adjusting ourselves to the predictions of Marx the scientist. That is to say, and it is well to emphasize it once again, the laws of Marxism are present in the events of the Cuban Revolution, independently of what the leaders profess or know fully of those laws from a theoretical viewpoint.

For a better understanding of the Cuban revolutionary movement up to January 1 [1959], it must be divided into the following stages: before *Granma*'s landing; from there to the victories of La Plata and Arroyo del Infierno; from there to the battle of Uvero and the formation of the second guerrilla column; from then on to the creation of the third and fourth columns, the invasion of the Sierra de Cristal, the establishment of the Second Front; the April strike and its failure; the repulsing of the great offensive; and the invasion of Las Villas.

Each of those brief historical moments in the guerrilla war enclosed distinct social concepts as well as different appreciations of the Cuban reality which shaped the thought of the military leaders of the Revolution, those who with the passing of time would also reaffirm their qualities as political leaders.

Before the landing of the *Granma* a mentality predominated which to some degree might be called "subjectivist": blind confidence in a rapid popular explosion, enthusiasm and faith in the power to liquidate Batista's might by a swift armed uprising combined with spontaneous revolutionary strikes and the subsequent fall of the dictator. The movement was the direct heir of the Ortodoxo party, and its main slogan was "Shame against Money," that is to say, administrative honesty as the principal idea of the new Cuban government.

However, Fidel Castro pointed out in "History Will Absolve Me" the bases which have been almost completely fulfilled by the Revolution, but which have also been surpassed by it, moving toward a deeper reassessment in the field of economics. This has brought a similar deepening in politics at the national and international levels.

After the landing came the defeat, the almost total destruction of the forces, and their regrouping and integration as a guerrilla force. Characteristic of the small group of survivors, embued with a spirit of struggle, was the understanding that to imagine spontaneous outbursts throughout the island was an illusion. Also, they understood that the struggle was to be a long one and that it should count on a large peasant participation. It is at this point that the first peasants entered the guerrilla war. Shortly after, two battles were fought—not important in the number of combatants involved but of a great psychological importance because the antagonism of the city people, which comprised the central group of this guerrilla, against the peasants was erased. The peasants in turn had distrusted the group and above all were afraid of the government's barbarous reprisals. Two facts were revealed at this stage, both very important for their interrelated factors: to the peasants, that the bestialities of the army and all the persecution would not be sufficient to put an end to the guerrilla even though the army would be capable of destroying their homes, crops, and families. Thus to take refuge amidst the guerrilla, where their lives would be protected, was a good solution. At the same time the guerrilla fighters learned the ever-increasing necessity of winning the peasant masses, which required, obviously, that they be offered something they desired with all their soul. There is nothing that a peasant wants more than land.

Then followed a nomadic stage in which the Rebel Army progressively conquered zones of influence. It could not remain for any length of time, but neither could the enemy army and it could not even enter those zones. Through several battles a sort of front between the two sides was established.

May 28, 1957, marks a milestone, when at Uvero an attack was launched against a well-armed and rather well-situated garrison, with ready access to reinforcements, close to the sea and with an airport. The victory of the rebel forces in this battle, one of the bloodiest fought for 30 percent of the forces that participated in the battle were killed or wounded, changed the panorama completely. It showed that the Rebel Army could function in a territory from which intelligence never leaked out to the enemy and from which we could dart to the plains and attack enemy positions.

Shortly thereafter, the first segregation took place and two fighting columns were created. The second column, for military reasons, and a little bit childishly, called itself the fourth column. Immediately the two columns demonstrated their activism. On July 26 they attacked Estrada Palma, and five days later, Bueycito, which is 30 kilometers away. From then on the battles were more important, and we stood firm against the oppressors. Every time they tried to climb the mountains we resisted them, and fighting fronts with vast zones of no man's land were established, vulnerable only to punitive incursions from both sides, but approximately the same battle lines were maintained.

However, the guerrillas gained strength with the substantial contribution of the peasants from the zone and from members of the Movement in the cities. The guerrillas became more combative and increased their fighting spirit. In February 1958, after repelling some offensives, Column 3, led by Almeida [3] left to occupy a place close to Santiago, while Raúl Castro's Column 6, named in honor of

[3] Juan Almeida, a veteran of the Moncada attack. Eds.

our hero Frank País, who died a few months earlier, managed the feat of crossing the central highway in the first days of March of that year, establishing itself in the hills of Mayarí, and creating the Second Oriental Front "Frank País."

The growing successes of our rebel forces became known as they filtered through the censorship, and the people were rapidly reaching the climax of revolutionary activity. At this moment, Havana offered the idea of a nationwide struggle through a general revolutionary strike to destroy the might of the enemy by attacking it simultaneously at all points.

The function of the Rebel Army would then be that of a catalyst, of an "irritating thorn," to unleash the movement. In those days, our guerrillas increased their activity, and the heroic legend of Camilo Cienfuegos began, as he fought for the first time in the lowlands of Oriente, following strict orders from the central command.

The revolutionary strike, however, was not adequately planned, for it did not consider the importance of the workers' unity and it was not emphasized that the workers, in the exercise of their own revolutionary activity, should choose the appropriate time. They sought to give a clandestine blow, announcing the strike from a radio station, ignoring that the secret of the day and the hour had filtered down to Batista's henchmen but not to the people. The movement that advocated the strike failed, and a great and select number of revolutionary patriots were assassinated mercilessly.

There is an interesting fact which should be noted in the history of the Revolution: Jules Dubois,[4] the *correveidile*[5] of North American monopolies, knew beforehand the date on which the strike was to occur.

At this point, one of the most important qualitative changes in the development of the war occurred for we acquired the certainty that victory would be achieved only by increasing the guerrilla forces until the enemy was defeated in frontal battle.

By then a firm relation had been established with the peasantry; the Rebel Army had drawn up civil and penal codes, administered justice, distributed food, and collected taxes in the administered zones. The adjacent zones also felt the influence of the Rebel Army. Major offensives were prepared, which in two months of fighting resulted in 1,000 casualties for the enemy (who was completely demoralized) while increasing by 600 weapons our fighting capacity.

[4] Former reporter for the Chicago *Tribune.* Eds.
[5] *Correveidile:* an informer. Eds.

By then it was demonstrated that the army could not defeat us; there was no force in Cuba capable of bending the peaks of the Sierra Maestra and the hills of the Second Oriental Front "Frank País"; every road became untraversable in Oriente province for the troops of the tyranny. Once the offensive was defeated, Camilo Cienfuegos, with Column 2, and the author of this article with Column 8, named "Ciro Redondo," were ordered to cross the province of Camagüey in order to establish ourselves in Las Villas, cutting the enemy's communications. Camilo was to later continue advancing to repeat the feat of the hero after which his column was named, Antonio Maceo:[6] the total invasion from east to west.

The war at this point showed a new characteristic; the correlation of forces changed favorably to the side of the Revolution. Our two small columns, which included 80 and 140 men, crossed during a month and a half the plains of Camagüey, constantly surrounded and harassed by an army that mobilized thousands of soldiers. We reached Las Villas province and went on to cut the island in half.

At times it may seem strange, incomprehensible, and even incredible that two columns of such small size, without communications, mobility, or the most elemental weapons of modern warfare could fight against an army well-trained and overarmed. What was fundamental was the characteristic of each group: The more uncomfortable the guerrilla fighter is, and the more he experiences the rigors of nature, the more the guerrilla fighter feels himself at home, his morale is higher, his sense of security greater. At the same time, under any circumstances he has come to risk his life, to trust it to luck like a tossed coin and, in general, for the final outcome of the battle it matters little whether the individual guerrilla survives or not.

The enemy soldier in the present example is the junior partner of the dictator, the man who receives the last crumbs left by the last of the profiteers, a long line that begins in Wall Street and ends up with him. He is willing to defend them, to the degree that they are important. Their salaries and sinecures are worth some suffering and some dangers, but they are never worth his life. If the price of maintaining them will cost his life, he opts for abandoning them, that is to say, he will retreat from the face of the guerrilla danger. From these two concepts and morales springs the difference which would cause the crisis of December 31, 1958.[7]

[6] Black military leader of the Cuban war of independence in the period from 1868 to 1898. Eds.
[7] Batista fled to the Dominican Republic on this date. Eds.

The superiority of the Rebel Army was established more clearly and, also, with the arrival of our columns to Las Villas the greater popularity of the 26th of July Movement among all others was demonstrated, the Directorio Revolucionario, the Second Front of Las Villas, the Partido Socialista Popular, and some small guerrilla bands of the Organización Auténtica.[8] This was due in large degree to the magnetic personality of its leader, Fidel Castro, but the justice of its revolutionary line was an influence.

Here ends the insurrection, but the men who arrived in Havana after two years of arduous struggle in the mountains and plains of Oriente, on the plains of Camagüey, and the mountains, plains, and cities of Las Villas, were not ideologically the same men who landed on the beaches of Las Coloradas,[9] or who were incorporated in the first phase of the struggle. Their distrust of the peasant had been converted into affection and respect for his virtues; their total lack of knowledge of life in the country had become a deep knowledge of the needs of our peasants. Their flirtations with statistics and with theory have been nullified by practice.

With agrarian reform as the banner, the execution of which began in the Sierra Maestra, these men confronted imperialism. They know that agrarian reform is the basis on which the new Cuba must be built. They also know that the agrarian reform will give land to all dispossessed but that it will dispossess the unjust possessors. And they know that the greatest of the unjust posessors are also influential men in the State Department or in the government of the United States of America. But they learned to overcome difficulties with courage, audacity, and above all with the support of the people, and they have seen already the future of liberation which awaited us on the other side of our sufferings.

To arrive at this final idea of our goals, we traveled far and changed much. Parallel to the successive qualitative changes which took place on the battlefields, there occurred changes in the social composition of our guerrilla and ideological transformations in their leaders. Each of these processes or changes constitutes a qualitative change in the composition, strength, and revolutionary maturity of our army. The peasant progressively gave it vigor, capacity to suffer,

[8] Directorio Revolucionario was a student-based organization; most of its members were to be found at the University of Havana. The Second Front of Las Villas was a guerrilla front under the leadership of the Directorio and members of the Partido Auténtico. The Partido Socialista Popular was the Cuban communist party. The Organización Auténtica was formed by men of action of the Partido Auténtico.

[9] This is where the *Granma* landed. Eds.

knowledge of the terrain, love of the land, and hunger for agrarian reform. The intellectual of whatever type made his small contribution by beginning a sketch of a theory. The worker contributed his sense of organization, his inherent tendency toward unification. Above all these, there is the example of the rebel forces which had proved to be much more than an "irritating thorn" and whose example gave faith and uplifted the masses until they lost all fear of their executioners. Never before was the concept of interaction so clear to us. We could feel how this interaction progressively matured in us, we taught the value of armed insurrection, the strength that a man has when, with a weapon at hand and the will to fight, he faces other men; and the peasants taught us the tricks of the mountains, the strength necessary to live and triumph there, and the efforts and sacrifices that must be made to move forward the destiny of the people.

Thus, when bathed in peasant sweat, with a horizon of mountains and clouds, beneath the radiant sun of the island, the rebel chief and his cortege entered Havana, on a new "staircase of the winter garden climbed history with the feet of the people."

Cuba: Exceptional Case or Vanguard in the Struggle against Colonialism?

Jᒐᒐᒐᒐᒐᒐᒐᒐᒐᒐᒐᒐᒐᒐᒐᒐᒐᒐᒐᒐᒐᒐᒐᒐᒐᒐᒐᒐ

The working class is the productive and creative class; the working class produces what material wealth exists in the country. As long as power is not in their hands, as long as the working class allows power to be in the hands of the managers, in the hands of the speculators, in the hands of the landowners, in the hands of monopolies, in the hands of foreign or national vested interests while armaments are in the hands of those in the service of the vested interests and not in their own hands, the working class will be forced to lead a miserable existence no matter how many crumbs those interest groups let fall from their banquet table.

—FIDEL CASTRO

Never in America has there been an event of such extraordinary character, such deep roots, and such far-reaching consequences for the destiny of the progressive movements of this continent as our revolutionary war. It has been called by some the cardinal event in the history of America and next in importance to the trilogy composed of the Russian Revolution, the social transformations which followed the triumph over Hitler's armies, and the victory of the Chinese Revolution.

This movement, although heterogeneous in its forms and manifestations, has followed—and it could not be otherwise—the general lines of all the great historical events of this century which are characterized by anticolonial struggle and the transition to socialism.

Certain groups, however, either in good faith or from self-interest, have claimed to see a number of exceptional causes and characteristics in the Cuban Revolution which are magnified in importance to the extent of making them the determining factors in interpreting these profound social and historical events. The "exceptionalism" of the Cuban Revolution is cited when compared with the lines of other progressive parties in America; thus, it is affirmed that the forms and paths of the Cuban Revolution are a unique product and that the historical transition of the peoples in other countries of America will be different.

We recognize that there were exceptional factors which gave dis-

Verde Olivo (Havana), April 9, 1961, pp. 22–29.

tinctive characteristics to the Cuban Revolution. It is a clearly established fact that every revolution contains individual factors; but it
also is an established fact that revolutions obey certain laws which
societies cannot escape. Let us analyze, then, the factors in this
supposed exceptionalism.

The first, the most original, and perhaps the most important is
this charismatic force named Fidel Castro Ruz, who in a few years
has reached historic dimensions. The future will assign an exact
place to our prime minister, yet we hope and believe that he is to
be ranked with those of the greatest figures in the history of Latin
America. What are the exceptional circumstances surrounding the
personality of Fidel Castro?

There are several characteristics in his life that make him stand
clearly above his companions and followers. Fidel is a man of such
tremendous personality that he would lead any movement in which
he participated. This he has done throughout his career, from the
days in which he was a student to the premiership of our country.
He possesses the qualities of a great leader. These qualities, joined
with his personal traits of audacity, force, and courage, and with his
extraordinary avidness always to listen for the will of the people,
have carried him to the place of honor and sacrifice which he occupies today. He also has other important qualities: his ability, for
example, to assimilate knowledge and experience in order to understand a given situation as a whole without losing sight of the small
details, his immense faith in the future, his broad vision in foreseeing events and acting ahead of them, always seeing further than
his companions. With these cardinal qualities, combined with his
capacity to hold and unite and to oppose the divisions that weaken,
with his capacity to direct the action of the people, with the infinite
love the people have for him and his faith in the future and his ability to foresee it, Fidel Castro has done more than anyone else in Cuba
to build the formidable apparatus of the Cuban Revolution of today
from nothing.

However, no one could state that in Cuba the political and social
conditions were totally different from those of other countries of
America or that Fidel Castro was able to carry out the Revolution
precisely because of such differences. Fidel, a great and able leader,
directed the Revolution in Cuba at the moment he did and in the
way he did by interpreting the profound political disturbances that
prepared the people for the great leap along revolutionary paths.
Also, certain conditions existed which, though not peculiar to Cuba,

will be difficult to exploit again by other peoples because imperialism, unlike some progressive groups, learns from its mistakes.

The condition we could call exceptional is that North American imperialism was disoriented and unable to measure the true depth of the Cuban Revolution. This in a way explains many of the apparent contradictions in the so-called North American fourth power. The monopolies, as is habitual in these cases, began to think about a successor to Batista precisely because they knew that the discontented people were also looking for one—but one with a revolutionary approach. What stroke could have been more intelligent and clever than to remove the unserviceable little dictator and put in his place the new "youngsters," who would in their day be able to serve the interests of imperialism? The imperialists played for awhile with this card from their continental deck and lost miserably. They were suspicious of us before our triumph, but did not fear us; or rather, they played two cards, using their experience at this double game which habitually they could not lose. Emissaries from the State Department arrived several times disguised as journalists to determine the nature of the unknown revolution but were never able to discover any symptom of impending danger. When imperialism tried to react, when it realized that the group of inexperienced young men had a clear understanding of their political duty and was determined to live up to it, it was already too late. Thus, in January 1959, the first social revolution in the Caribbean and the most fundamental of all American revolutions was born.

We do not believe that there was anything exceptional in the fact that the bourgeoisie, or at least a part of it, showed itself in favor of the revolutionary war against the tyranny but at the same time supported and promoted movements tending toward a search for negotiated solutions which would allow a replacement of Batista by elements disposed to slowing down the Revolution.

In view of the conditions in which the revolutionary war was fought and the complexity of the political forces which opposed the tyranny, it is not exceptional that some landlord elements adopted a position of neutrality or at least of nonbelligerency toward the insurrectionary forces.

It is understandable that the national bourgeoisie, ruined by imperialism and by the tyrant whose troops plundered small property and made a daily livelihood from bribery, saw with a certain amount of sympathy that these youngsters from the mountains punished a mercenary army which was serving as the armed instrument of imperialism. Thus, nonrevolutionary forces helped the Revolution to win power.

Granting the utmost of the argument, we can add a new factor of exceptionalism, namely, that in most parts of Cuba the rural populace had been proletarianized by the operation of large capitalist semimechanized forms of cultivation, and had entered a stage of organization which gave them a stronger class consciousness. We can admit this. But we should point out in respect for the truth that the first territory occupied by the Rebel Army and made up of the defeated column that had arrived aboard the *Granma* was inhabited by a class of peasants completely different in its cultural and social roots from those country dwellers who predominate in the regions of extensive, semimechanized Cuban agriculture. In fact, the Sierra Maestra, locale of the first revolutionary column, is a section that served as a refuge to all those peasants who struggled daily against the landlords. Thus, the peasants went there as squatters on land which belonged to the state or some rapacious landowner, searching for a small piece of land that would yield them some small wealth. They struggled continuously against the extortions of the soldiers who were always allied with the landowning power; and their horizon ended with the document of title to their land. The soldiers who formed our first guerrilla army of rural people came from that part of this social class which was most aggressive in demonstrating love for the possession of its own land and which expresses most perfectly the spirit catalogued as petty bourgeois. These peasants fought because they wanted land for themselves and their children and because they wanted to manage it, sell it, and enrich themselves through their work.

Despite his petty bourgeois spirit, the peasant learns quickly that he cannot satisfy his desire for land without breaking the latifundia system. Thus, a radical agrarian reform, which alone can give land to the peasants, clashes directly with the interests of the imperialists, the big landowners, and the magnates of sugar and cattle. The bourgeois fears those interests, but the proletariat has no such fear. In this way the very march of the Revolution unites workers and peasants. The workers support the struggle against the latifundia. The poor peasant, benefited by the ownership of land, loyally supports the revolutionary power and defends it from its imperialist and counterrevolutionary enemies.

We believe that no other factors of exceptionalism exist and we have been generous in granting this many.

We shall look now at the permanent roots of all social phenomena in America and at the contradictions that mature in the bosom of modern societies bringing about changes that can acquire the magnitude of a revolution like the one in Cuba.

First in chronological order, not according to importance, stands the system of latifundia which was the basis of economic power of the dominant class throughout the period after the liberating, anticolonial revolutions of the past century. This landowning social class, which exists in all countries, generally is at the rear of the social events that move the world. In some cases, however, the more alert and farsighted of this class recognize the danger and begin to change the form of their capital investments, advancing at times into mechanized agricultural production, transferring some of their wealth into industry, or becoming commercial agents of monopoly interests. At any rate the first liberating revolution did not destroy the latifundia and did not touch a reactionary element that stands for servitude on the land. This is the phenomenon which appears without exception in all the countries of Latin America and serves as the substratum of all the injustices committed since the time when the king of Spain granted land to the most noble conquerors, leaving for the natives, creoles, and mestizos, in the case of Cuba, only *realengos*—parcels of land left between three large circular tracts that touch one another.

The landowner joined in alliance with the monopolies when he realized that he could not survive by himself. North American capital arrived to impregnate the virgin lands and later to carry away all the foreign exchange that had been "generously" donated earlier, plus further amounts that were several times greater than the sum originally invested in the "beneficiary" country.

America was one large field of imperialist struggle. The "wars" between Costa Rica and Nicaragua, Panama's separation from Colombia, the infamy committed against Ecuador in its dispute with Peru, the struggle between Paraguay and Bolivia are only expressions of this gigantic battle among the great monopolistic powers of the world. By the end of World War II this struggle had been decided almost completely in favor of North American monopolies. Since then, the imperialists have dedicated themselves to strengthening their colonial possessions and to perfecting their system against intrusion by old and new imperialist competitors. All this resulted in a monstrously distorted economy which has been described by economists of the imperialist regimes with a phrase demonstrative of the profound charity that they feel for us, the inferior human beings. They refer to our Indians, who are miserably exploited and reduced to ignominy, as *"inditos."* [1] And they refer to Negroes and mulattoes, who are discriminated against both as a people and as a class, as "colored." They do so in order to divide the working masses in their struggle for better economic conditions. They give to all the peoples of America another decorous and smooth name—the "underdeveloped."

What is underdevelopment?

A dwarf with an enormous head and a swollen chest is "underdeveloped" in the sense that his weak legs and short arms do not match the rest of his torso; he is the product of a malformation which has distorted his development. This is what we are in reality, countries that are colonial, semicolonial, or dependent. Ours are countries with distorted economies because of imperialist policy which has abnormally developed the industrial or agricultural branches to complement the imperialists' own complex economies. "Underdevelopment" or distorted development brings along a dangerous specialization in raw materials that holds over our peoples the threat of hunger. We, the underdeveloped, are also countries of monoculture, of a single product, of a single market. A single product, the uncertain sale of which depends on a single market that imposes and fixes conditions, holds the great formula of imperialist economic domination as expressed in the old and eternal Roman precept, "divide and rule."

The large landholding system through its connections with imperialism completely determines so-called "underdevelopment," which results in low wages and unemployment. The phenomenon of low salaries and unemployment, sharpened by the great contradictions of the system and constantly at the mercy of the cyclical variations of the economy, is the common denominator of all the Latin American countries from the Rio Bravo to the South Pole. This common denominator, which serves as the basis of analysis and which goes in capital letters, is called HUNGER OF THE PEOPLE: weariness from being oppressed, abused, and exploited to the maximum; weariness from selling one's labor day after day for fear of becoming a part of the great mass of unemployed—all so that the maximum of profit is squeezed from each human body only to be squandered in the orgies of the owners of capital. These are important and inescapable common denominators in Latin America. We cannot say that we were exempt from any of these related evils

[1] "Little Indians." Eds.

that result in the most terrible and permanent of all evils—hunger of the people.

Large landholdings, either as a form of primitive exploitation or as the expression of capitalist monopoly of the land, conforms to new conditions and is allied to economic imperialism, which results in low salaries, underemployment, unemployment, and hunger—all of this is euphemistically called "underdevelopment." All this existed in Cuba. Here we had hunger as well as one of the highest percentages of unemployment in Latin America; imperialism was more aggressive here than in many Latin American countries. And here large landholdings existed as much as in any sister country.

What did we do to free ourselves from this powerful imperialist phenomenon with its puppet governments in every country and its mercenary armies willing to defend those puppets and its complex social system of exploitation of man by man? We applied certain formulas that on other occasions we have called discoveries of our empirical medicine, which has rapidly become a part of the explanation of scientific truth.

The objective conditions for the struggle are given in the hunger of the people, in the reaction against this hunger, in the fear unleashed to check the popular reaction, and in the wave of hate that repression creates. Subjective conditions were missing in America— the most important being the consciousness of the possibility of victory through violent struggle against the imperialist powers and their internal allies. These conditions are created through armed struggle, which serves to make more clear the necessity of change (and permits it to be foreseen) and of the defeat and total liquidation of the army (an indispensable condition to every true revolution) by popular forces.

In addition to pointing out that these conditions are created by means of armed struggle, we must explain once more that the terrain of that struggle should be the countryside. The peasantry, with an army made up of their own class, fighting for their own great objectives—the first which must be a just distribution of land—will come from the country to take over the cities. On the ideological base of the working class, whose great thinkers discovered the social laws that rule us, the peasant class in America will provide the great liberation army of the future, as it has already done in Cuba. This army, created in the countryside where subjective conditions ripen for the seizure of power, proceeds to conquer the cities from the outside, uniting with the working class and giving greater meaning to the content of its own ideology by these contacts. It can and should demolish the oppressor army, at first in skirmishes, combats, surprises, and finally in great battles, when it will have grown into a large popular army of liberation. The stage in the consolidation of revolutionary power will be the liquidation of the old army, as we stated earlier.

If all of these conditions present in Cuba were found in the rest of the Latin American countries, what would happen in other struggles to conquer power for the dispossessed classes? Would it be feasible or not? If it is feasible, would it be easier or more difficult than in Cuba?

We must explain the difficulties that in our view will make the new revolutionary struggles in America more difficult. There are general difficulties confronting all countries and particular difficulties for some in which their stage of development or national peculiarities distinguish them from the others. We have already pointed out at the beginning that certain factors could be considered exceptional, such as the attitude of imperialism at the time of the Cuban Revolution (one of disorientation) and, to a certain extent, the attitude of national bourgeoisie itself, also disoriented and at times looking sympathetically at the rebels' actions due to the pressure of imperialism on their interests (a situation which is common to all our countries). Cuba has drawn the line in the sand and once again we see Pizzaro's dilemma: on one side there are those who love the people, and on the other those who hate the people. The line between them increasingly divides these two great social forces—the bourgeoisie and the working class—who are defining their respective positions with greater clarity as the process of the Cuban Revolution advances.

This means that imperialism has learned, fully, the lesson of Cuba and that it will not again be taken by surprise in any of our twenty republics or in any of the existing colonies. This means that great popular battles against powerful invading armies await those who now attempt to violate the peace of the sepulchers, the Pax Romana. This is important because if the Cuban war of liberation with its two years of continual combat, anxieties, and instability was difficult, the new battles that await the people in other parts of Latin America are going to be infinitely more difficult.

The United States hastens the delivery of arms to the puppet governments they see as being increasingly threatened; it makes them sign pacts of dependence to legally facilitate the shipment of instruments of repression and death and of troops to use them. Moreover, it increases the military preparation of the repressive armies with the intention of making them efficient weapons against the people.

And what about the bourgeoisie? The national bourgeoisie generally is not capable of maintaining a consistent struggle against imperialism. It shows that it fears popular revolution even more than the oppression and despotic dominion of imperialism which crushes nationality, tarnishes patriotic sentiments, and colonizes the economy.

A large part of the bourgeoisie opposes revolution openly, and since the beginning has not hesitated to ally itself with imperialism and the landowners to fight against the people and close the road to revolution.

A desperate and hysterical imperialism, ready to undertake any maneuver and to give arms and even troops to its puppets in order to annihilate any country which rises up; ruthless landowners, unscrupulous and experienced in the most brutal forms of repression; and, finally, a bourgeoisie willing to close, through any means, the roads leading to popular revolution: These are the great allied forces which directly oppose the new popular revolutions of Latin America.

Such are the difficulties that must be added to the ones arising from struggles of this kind under the new conditions found in Latin America since the consolidation of that irreversible phenomenon which the Cuban Revolution represents.

There are still other, more specific problems. It is more difficult to prepare guerrilla bands in those countries that have a concentration of population in large centers and have a greater amount of light and medium industry, even though it may not be anything like effective industrialization. The ideological influence of the cities inhibits the guerrilla struggle by increasing the hopes for peacefully organized mass struggle. This gives rise to a certain "institutionalization," which in more or less "normal" periods makes conditions less harsh than those usually inflicted on the people. The idea is even conceived of possible quantitative raises in the congressional ranks of the revolutionary elements until a point is reached someday which allows a qualitative change.

It is not probable that this hope will be realized given present conditions in any country of America, although a possibility that the change can begin through the electoral process is not to be excluded. However, current conditions in all countries of America make this possibility very remote.

Revolutionaries cannot foresee all the tactical variables which can arise in the course of the struggle for their liberating program. The real capacity of a revolutionary is measured by his ability to find adequate revolutionary tactics in every different situation and by keeping all tactics in mind so that he might exploit them to the maximum. It would be an unpardonable error to underestimate the gain that a revolutionary program can make through a given electoral process, just as it would be unpardonable to look only to elections and not to realize other forms of struggle, including armed struggle, to achieve power, which is the indispensable instrument for applying and developing the revolutionary program. If power is not achieved, all other conquests, however advanced they appear, are unstable, insufficient, and incapable of producing necessary solutions.

When we speak of winning power via the electoral process, our question is always the same: If a popular movement takes over the government of a country by winning a wide popular vote and resolves as a consequence to initiate the great social transformations which make up the triumphant program, would it not come into conflict right away with the reactionary classes of that country? Has the army not always been the repressive instrument of that class? If this is so, it is logical to suppose that this army will side with its class and enter the conflict against the new constituted government. By means of a coup d'état, more or less bloodless, this government can be overthrown and the old game renewed again, which will seem never to end. It can also happen that the oppressor army could be defeated by an armed popular reaction in defense and support of its government. What appears difficult to believe is that the armed forces would accept profound social reforms with good grace and peacefully resign themselves to their liquidation as a caste.

Where there are large urban concentrations, even when economically backward in our humble opinion, it may be advisable to engage in struggle outside the limits of the city in a way that can continue for a long time. The existence of a guerrilla center in a mountain of a country with populous cities maintains a perpetual focus of rebellion because it is very improbable that the repressive powers will be able, either rapidly or over a long period of time, to liquidate guerrilla bands established with social bases in territory favorable to guerrilla warfare if the strategy and tactics of this type of warfare are consistently employed.

What would happen in the cities is quite different. Armed struggle against the repressive army can develop to an unsuspected degree, but this struggle will become a frontal one only when there is a powerful army which fights against another army. A frontal fight against a powerful and well-equipped army cannot be undertaken by a small group.

For the frontal fight, many arms will be needed, and the question arises: Where are these arms to be found? They do not appear spontaneously; they must be seized from the enemy. But in order to seize them from the enemy, it is necessary to fight; and it is not possible to fight openly. Thus, the struggle in the big cities must begin as a clandestine operation, capturing military groups or weapons one by one in successive assaults.

If this happens, a great advance can be made. But we would not dare say that victory will be denied to a popular rebellion with a guerrilla base inside the city. No one can object on theoretical grounds to this strategy; at least we have no intention of doing so. But we should point out how easy it would be as the result of a betrayal or simply by means of continuous raids to eliminate the leaders of the revolution. In contrast, if while employing all conceivable maneuvers in the city (such as organized sabotage and above all that effective form of action which is suburban guerrilla warfare) and if, besides, a base is kept in the countryside, the revolutionary political power because it is relatively safe from the contingencies of the war will remain untouched even if the oppressor government defeats and annihilates all the popular forces in the city. *It should be relatively safe, but not outside the war, not giving directions from some other country or from distant places. It should be within its own country fighting.* These are the considerations that lead us to believe that even in countries where the predominance of the cities is great, the central political focus of the struggle can develop in the countryside.

Returning to the case of counting on help from the military class in dealing the coup and supplying the weapons, there are two problems to be analyzed: first, if the military really joins with the popular forces to strike the blow, supposing them to be an organized nucleus and capable of independent decision, in such a case there would be a coup by one part of the army against another part, probably leaving the structure of the military caste intact. The other case, in which armies unite rapidly and spontaneously with popular forces, can only occur after the armies have been beaten violently by a powerful and persistent enemy, that is, in conditions of catastrophe for the constituted power. In this case, with the army defeated and its morale broken, this phenomenon can occur; but in order to occur, struggle is necessary and we always return to the question of how to carry on that struggle. The answer leads us toward the development of guerrilla struggle in the countryside on favorable ground and supported by struggle in the cities, counting always on the widest possible participation of the working masses and guided by the ideology of that class.

We have sufficiently analyzed the obstacles which revolutionary movements in Latin America will encounter. The question can now be asked whether or not there are favorable conditions for the preliminary stage, mainly that of Fidel Castro in the Sierra Maestra. We believe that here, too, there are general conditions which facilitate these centers of rebellion and specific conditions in certain countries which are even more favorable. We should point out two subjective factors which are the most important consequences of the Cuban Revolution: the first is the possibility of victory, knowing that the capability exists to crown with success an enterprise like the one undertaken by the group of deluded expeditionaries on the *Granma* who struggled for two years in the Sierra Maestra. This indicates immediately that there can be a revolutionary movement that operates from the countryside, that mixes with the peasant masses, that will grow from weakness to strength, that will destroy the army in a frontal fight, that will capture cities from the countryside, that will strengthen through its struggle the subjective conditions necessary for seizing power. The importance of this fact is seen by the great quantity of "exceptionalists" who have appeared at the present time. The "exceptionalists" are those special beings who say they find in the Cuban Revolution a unique event which cannot be followed—led by a man who has few or no faults, who led the Revolution through a unique path. This is completely false, we affirm.

The possibility of victory by the popular forces in Latin America is clearly seen in the form of guerrilla warfare undertaken by an army of peasants in alliance with the workers which defeats the oppressor army in a frontal assault, takes cities by attack from the countryside, and dissolves the oppressor army as the first stage in completely destroying the superstructure of the colonial world.

We should point out a second subjective factor: The masses not only know the possibility of triumph, they know their destiny. They know with increasing certainty that whatever the tribulations of history during short periods, the future belongs to the people because the future will bring about social justice. This will help to raise revolutionary ferment to even greater heights than those which prevail in Latin America.

We can mention some less general factors which do not appear in the same intensity from country to country. One of these very important factors is that there is greater exploitation of the peasants in Latin America than there was in Cuba. Let us remind those who pretend to see in our insurrectional stage the proletarianization of the peasantry that in our concept it was precisely this which accelerated the cooperative stage as well as the achievement of power and the agrarian reform (in spite of the fact that the peasant of the first battles, the core of the Rebel Army, is the same one to be found today in the Sierra Maestra, proud owner of his parcel of land and intransigently individualistic).

There are, of course, particularities in America: an Argentine peasant does not have the same outlook as a communal peasant in Peru, Bolivia, or Ecuador. But the hunger for land is permanently present in the peasants, and it is generally they who hold the keynote to America. Because in some countries they are even more exploited than in the case of Cuba, the possibilities increase that this class will rise up in arms.[2]

There is also another fact. The army of Batista, with all its enormous defects, was an army structured in such a way that all, from the lowest soldier to the highest general, were accomplices in the exploitation of the people. They were complete mercenaries, and this gave some cohesiveness to the repressive apparatus. The armies of America as a whole include a professional officers' corps and recruits called up periodically. Each year the young recruits leave their homes where they have known of the daily sufferings of their parents, have seen them with their own eyes, and have felt the misery and social injustice. If one day they are sent as cannon fodder to fight against the defenders of a doctrine that they feel in their own flesh to be just, their capacity to perform aggressively will be seriously affected. Thus, with adequate systems of propaganda the recruits will see the justice of the struggle and the reasons for the struggle, and magnificent results will be achieved.

We can say, after this brief study of the revolutionary struggle, that the Cuban Revolution had exceptional factors which give it its own peculiarities and factors which are common to all the countries

[2] It is to be noted that in theories of revolutionary struggle it is those who are not more exploited but less exploited who tend to revolt. This has been pointed out by Brinton, Davies, Tocqueville, and others. Eds.

of America which express the internal need for revolution. There are new conditions that will make the flow of these revolutionary movements easier as they give the masses consciousness of their destiny and the certainty that it is possible. There are, on the other hand, obstacles that will make it harder for the armed masses to achieve power rapidly such as imperialism's close alliance with the bourgeoisie in order to fight to the utmost against the popular forces. Gloomy days await Latin America. . . .[3] Thus, once the anti-imperialist struggle begins, we must constantly strike hard where it hurts the most, never retreating, always marching forward, counterstriking against each aggression. This is the way to victory. . . .[4]

[3] Guevara indicates that gloomy days await the world also judging by the "latest statements of U.S. leaders." He points out Lumumba's assassination in the Congo, perhaps as an index of future conflicts. Eds.

[4] Guevara concludes by promising another article dealing with the Revolution after January 1959 in order to analyze the same question which the title of this essay indicates. Eds.

On Ideological Investigations

CONSIDERING: that the Declaration of Havana, endorsed by the people of Cuba, proclaims the complete dignity of man and the civil, social, and political equality of all citizens;

CONSIDERING: that within the laws that direct the socialist development of society is found the free unfolding of each man and the achievement of his most adequate utilization for the benefit of the collectivity;

CONSIDERING: that the right of work is a consecrated principle of our Fundamental Law; [1]

CONSIDERING: that there is news that in some labor centers the management has practiced ideological investigations of the workers, a limitation of the complete liberty of man resulting from this practice;

CONSIDERING: that the Ministry has full power to set the most convenient norms to achieve its goals, it is resolved by this Ministry:

First: to prohibit the managers of the labor centers operated by this Ministry to create or administer ideological interrogations of workers;

Second: to establish that ideological investigations can only be carried out when the workers under this Ministry solicit entrance in revolutionary organizations; in this case the investigations are to be carried out by the persons appointed by the revolutionary organizations.

Resolution 61–127 of the Ministry of Industries, May 19, 1961, *Marcha* (Montevideo), October 20, 1967, pp. 19–20.

This resolution was released by Guevara as Minister of Industries at a time when old members of the Cuban Communist Party influential in Cuba's economic structure were conducting ideological investigations of workers. Eds.

[1] The 1940 Constitution. Eds.

The Cadre, Backbone
of the Revolution

It is not necessary to insist on the characteristics of our Revolution. Its original form has its own spontaneity which marked the transition from a revolution of national liberation to a socialist revolution. The transition was rapid, led by the same people who participated in the initial assault on the Moncada Barracks. The revolutionary leaders are the men who sailed on the *Granma* and finally declared the socialist character of the Cuban Revolution. New sympathizers, cadres, and organizations joined the weak structure in its initial stages until they gave our Revolution its present mass character.

When it became clear that a new social class had definitely taken power in Cuba, we realized too the great limitations the exercise of state power would encounter. There was a lack of cadres to cope with enormous revolutionary tasks.

Soon after taking power, the bureaucratic administration was appointed by "rule of thumb." At first there were no major problems because the old structure had not been destroyed yet. The administrative apparatus functioned in its old, slow, and lifeless way. But it had organization and sufficient coordination to maintain itself through inertia, disdaining the political changes which came about as a prelude to the changes in the economic structure.

The 26th of July Movement, deeply injured by the internal struggles of its right and left wings, was unable to dedicate itself to constructive tasks. The Partido Socialista Popular had not been able to develop intermediate cadres to cope with the newly arising responsibilities because it had suffered fierce attacks and had been illegal for many years.

When the first state interventions in the economy took place, the task of finding cadres was not very complicated. It was possible to choose cadres from among many people who had at least the minimum requirements for assuming leadership positions. But with the radicalization of the revolutionary process after the nationalization of North American and large Cuban enterprises, a demand for ad-

Cuba Socialista (Havana), September 1962, pp. 17–22.

ministrative personnel began. At the same time, we felt an urgent need for production technicians due to the exodus of many of them who were attracted by better offers from imperialist companies in other parts of America or in the United States. And the political apparatus had to make great efforts, in the midst of its task of structuring, to give ideological attention to the masses who had joined the Revolution and were eager to learn.

We all performed our roles as well as we could, but it was not without pain and anxiety. Many mistakes were made by political administrators. Enormous mistakes were made by the new administration of enterprises, who had overwhelming responsibilities on their hands.

In the political apparatus we committed great and costly errors. Thus the political apparatus little by little began to fall into the hands of a contented and inactive bureaucracy which was completely isolated from the masses. The apparatus became a springboard for promotions and for bureaucratic posts of major or minor importance.

Our main mistake was our lack of feeling for reality at a given moment. But the tool which we lacked, which blurred our capacity to perceive, and which was converting the party into a bureaucratic entity, endangering production and administration, was the lack of developed cadres at the intermediate level. Our policy of finding cadres is now synonymous with going back to the masses, establishing contact anew with the masses—a contact which had been closely maintained by the Revolution in its first stages. But it had to be established through an apparatus that would afford the most beneficial results. The apparatus should allow for feeling the pulse of the masses and transmitting political orientation which in many cases had been given mainly through the personal appearances of Prime Minister Fidel Castro or other revolutionary leaders.

We can now ask ourselves, "What is a cadre?" A cadre is an individual who has attained sufficient political development to be able to interpret orders emanating from the central power, making these orders his own and conveying them to the masses. At the same time, the cadre should become aware of the masses' needs and desires and their most intimate motivations.

A cadre is an individual who possesses ideological and administrative discipline, who knows and practices democratic centralism. He knows how to evaluate existing contradictions. The cadre knows how to practice the principle of collective discussion and decision making. His loyalty has been tested. His physical and moral courage have matured with his ideological development. He is always willing to engage in discussion on any matter and to respond to the extent of giving his life for the Revolution.

Also, he is an individual capable of analyzing by himself, which enables him to make decisions and to exercise creative initiative without conflicting with discipline.

The cadre is a creative leader, a technician with a good political understanding who can reason dialectically, carrying forward his sector of production or developing the masses politically from his post of leadership.

This exemplary human being, surrounded by virtues which are difficult to achieve, is present among the people of Cuba. We find him daily. It is essential to use all the opportunities available to develop him to the fullest—educating him and obtaining from him the greatest benefit for the nation.

The development of a cadre is achieved through daily tasks; but the tasks must be undertaken in a systematic manner in special schools where competent teachers, who are examples at the same time to the students, will encourage rapid ideological advancement.

In a regime which is beginning the construction of socialism, one cannot imagine a cadre who is not highly developed politically. However, by political development, we mean not only the learning of Marxist theory but also individual responsibility for his actions. Political development is a discipline which will do away with any transitory weakness without clashing with a big dose of initiative and constant preoccupation with the Revolution's problems.

Therefore, to develop him we must establish principles of selection among the masses. It is here we must find the incipient personalities who have been tested by sacrifice or who have begun to demonstrate their social preoccupation. We must place them in special schools. If special schools are not available, we must give them positions of greater responsibility so that they can be tested in practical work.

We have found many new cadres who have developed during these years, yet their development has been uneven. This is because the young *compañeros* have had to face the reality of revolutionary creation without adequate orientation by the party. Some have succeeded whereas others were left midway or were simply lost in the bureaucratic labyrinth or in the temptations which come with power.

To assure the victory and the total consolidation of the Revolution, we must develop different types of cadres. The political cadre will be the base of our mass organizations and will orient them through the action of the United Party of the Socialist Revolution (PURS). We have begun to establish these foundations with the national and provincial schools of revolutionary instruction and with study groups at all levels.

Also, we need military cadres. For these cadres, we can utilize the selection which war itself made among our young fighters, for there are many alive who were tested under fire but who lacked theoretical knowledge. They were tested under difficult conditions and have proved their loyalty to the revolutionary regime with which they have been intimately connected since its birth and development.

We shall have to encourage economic cadres dedicated specifically to the difficult tasks of planning and organizing the socialist state. It is necessary to work with the professionals and to encourage youth to study important technical careers. We should give science some ideological impetus so that our accelerated development will be guaranteed. It is imperative to create an administrative team that will take advantage of the specific technical knowledge of others and at the same time knows how to coordinate and lead production. It will have to move at the pace of the Revolution.

The common denominator for all cadres is political awareness. This does not consist of unconditional support of the Revolution's postulates, but rather a great capacity for sacrifice and a capacity for dialectical analysis which encourages the making of continuous contributions on all levels to the rich theory and practice of the Revolution. These *compañeros* should be selected from the masses by merely applying the principle that the best will come to the forefront and that the best should receive the greatest opportunities for development.

In all of these situations, the function of the cadre, in spite of occupying different posts, is the same. The cadre is the key to the ideological vanguard of the United Party of the Revolution. It is what we could call the dynamic element of this mechanism. The cadre should not simply become a transmitter of slogans or demands but a creator who will help in the masses' development and in the formation of the leaders. The cadres serve as points of contact between the leaders and the masses. The cadre has the important mission of watching over things so that the great spirit of the Revolution will not become dormant. He cannot allow the revolutionary pace to decrease. The cadre is sensitive as he transmits what comes from the masses to the leaders and infuses in the masses the orientation of the party.

The development of the cadres is a task that cannot be delayed. The development of the cadres has been undertaken by the revolutionary government with great eagerness by making scholarships available based on selective principles, and also with its programs of study for workers which offer various opportunities for technological development.

Finally, we have developed slogans—study, work, and revolutionary vigilance for the whole country—based fundamentally on young communist unions from which the future cadres and the Revolution's future leaders should emerge.

Intimately tied to the cadre concept is the capacity for sacrifice, for showing the Revolution's truths and watchwords through personal example. The cadre as political leader must gain the workers' respect through his actions. It is absolutely necessary that he earn the respect and affection of the *compañeros* whom he must guide. Above all, there is no better cadre than the man elected by the masses in their assemblies—cadres chosen from among our vanguard workers.

These exemplary workers will become part of PURS along with the old members of the Integrated Revolutionary Organization (ORI). They will have to pass the selective tests which are required. At first our party will be a small party, but its influence among the workers will be enormous; the party will grow as socialist consciousness develops. Work will be considered a moral necessity and there will be total devotion to the people's cause.

With leaders of this caliber, the difficult tasks which lie ahead will be completed with few setbacks. After a period of confusion and faulty methods, we have achieved a just policy which will never be abandoned. With the ever-renewed impulse of the working class, an inexhaustible fountain filling the ranks of the future PURS, and with the leadership of our party, we undertake in earnest the task of forming the cadres which will guarantee the forceful development of our Revolution. We must triumph in this undertaking.

Tactics and Strategy
of the Latin American Revolution

⊓⊔⊓⊔⊓⊔⊓⊔⊓⊔⊓⊔⊓⊔⊓⊔⊓⊔⊓⊔⊓⊔⊓⊔⊓⊔⊓⊔⊓⊔⊓⊔⊓⊔⊓⊔

Tactics show us how to use armed forces in combat and strategy teaches us how to use combat encounters in order to obtain the war's objective.
—KARL VON CLAUSEWITZ

I began this work with a quotation from Clausewitz, the military author who fought against Napoleon and who theorized so brilliantly about war; Lenin loved to quote him because of the clarity of his thinking, in spite of the fact that he was, of course, a bourgeois analyst.

Tactics and strategy are the two main elements of the art of war, but war and politics are intimately related by a common denominator: the effort to reach a specific goal, whether it be annihilation of the adversary in armed conflict or the taking of political power.

But analysis of the essential tactics and strategies that rule political or military struggles cannot be reduced to a schematic formula.

The richness of each one of these concepts can be measured only by combining practice with the analysis of the complex activities that they imply.

There are no unalterable tactical and strategic objectives. Sometimes tactical objectives attain strategic importance, and other times strategic objectives become merely tactical elements. The thorough study of the relative importance of each element permits the full utilization, by the revolutionary forces, of all of the facts and circumstances leading up to the great and final strategic objective: *the taking of power.*

Power is the sine qua non strategic objective of the revolutionary forces, and everything must be subordinated to this basic endeavor.

But the taking of power, in this world polarized by two forces of extreme disparity and absolutely incompatible in interests, cannot be limited to the boundaries of a single geographic or social unit. The seizure of power is a worldwide objective of the revolutionary forces. To conquer the future is the strategic element of revolution;

According to the Cuban government this article was written during the missile crisis of October 1962, yet was not published until Guevara's death. *Juventud Rebelde* (Havana), October 2, 1968.

freezing the present is the counterstrategy motivating the forces of world reaction today, for they are on the defensive.

In this worldwide struggle, position is very important. At times it is decisive. Cuba, for example, is a vanguard outpost, an outpost which overlooks the extremely broad stretches of the economically distorted world of Latin America. Cuba's example is a beacon, a guiding light for all the peoples of America. The Cuban outpost is of great strategic value to the major contenders who at this moment dispute their hegemony of the world: imperialism and socialism.

Its value would be different if it had been located in another geographic or social setting. Its value was different when prior to the Revolution it merely constituted a tactical element of the imperialist world. Its value has increased, not only because it is an open door to America but because, added to the strength of its strategic, military and tactical position, is the power of its moral influence. "Moral missiles" are such a devastatingly effective weapon that they have become the most important element in determining Cuba's value. That is why, to analyze each element in the political struggle, one cannot extract it from its particular set of circumstances. All the antecedents serve to reaffirm a line or position consistent with its great strategic objectives.

Relating this discussion to America, one must ask the necessary question: What are the tactical elements that must be used to achieve the major objective of taking power in this part of the world? Is it possible or not, given the present conditions in our continent, to achieve it (socialist power, that is) by peaceful means? We emphatically answer that, in the great majority of cases, this is not possible. The most that could be achieved would be the formal takeover of the bourgeois superstructure of power and the transition to socialism of that government which, under the established bourgeois legal system, having achieved formal power will still have to wage a very violent struggle against all who attempt, in one way or another, to check its progress toward new social structures.

This is one of the most debated and most important topics, and possibly, it is a topic on which our Revolution disagrees the most with other revolutionary movements of America. We must clearly state our position and try to analyze its rationale.

Today America is a volcano. Although not in a state of eruption it is shocked by subterranean vibrations which announce its coming. There are visible and audible signs everywhere. The Second Declaration of Havana is the concrete expression of those subterranean movements. It strives to achieve an awareness of its objective, that is, an awareness of the necessity and, even more so, the certainty of the possibility of revolutionary change. Evidently, this American volcano is not divorced from the revolutionary movements that have appeared in the contemporary world in this moment of crucial confrontation of forces between two opposing conceptualizations of history.

We could refer to our fatherland with the following words from the Declaration of Havana: "What is the history of Cuba if it is not the history of Latin America? And what is the history of Latin America if it is not the history of Asia, Africa, and Oceania? And what is the history of all of these peoples if it is not the history of the most merciless and cruel imperialistic exploitation in the modern world?"

America like Africa, Asia, and Oceania, is part of a whole where economic forces have been distorted by imperialism. But not all the continents present similar characteristics; the forms of economic exploitation—imperialist, colonialist, or neocolonialist—employed by the European bourgeois forces have had to cope not only with the liberation struggle of the oppressed peoples of Asia, Africa, and Oceania, but also with the penetration of U.S. imperialist capital. This has created different correlations of forces in different areas, and has permitted peaceful transition toward national independent or neocolonialist bourgeois systems.

But in America such systems have not developed. Latin America is the parade ground of U.S. imperialism, and there are no economic forces in the world capable of supporting the struggle that the national bourgeoisies have waged against imperialism elsewhere; that is why these forces, relatively much weaker than in other regions, back down and compromise with imperialism.

The frightened bourgeoisie is faced with a terrible choice: submission to foreign capital or destruction by domestic popular forces. This dilemma has been accentuated by the Cuban Revolution; through the polarization created by its example, the only alternative left is to sell out. When this takes place, when the pact is sanctified, the domestic reactionary forces ally themselves with the most powerful international reactionary forces, and the peaceful development of social revolutions is prevented.

Pointing out the present situation, the Second Declaration of Havana states,

In many Latin American countries revolution is inevitable. This fact is not determined by the will of anyone. It is determined by the horrible conditions of exploitation under which the American people live, the development of a revolutionary consciousness in the masses, the world-wide crisis of imperialism, and the universal liberation movements of the subjugated nations.

Today's restlessness is an unmistakable symptom of rebellion. The entrails of the continent are stirring after having witnessed four centuries of slave, semislave, and feudal exploitation of man by man, from the aborigenes and slaves brought from Africa to the national groups that arose later—whites, blacks, mulattoes, mestizos, and Indians—who today share pain, humiliation, and the Yankee yoke, and share hope for a better tomorrow.

We can conclude, then, that when faced with the decision to bring about more socially just systems in America, we must think fundamentally in terms of armed struggle. There exists, nevertheless, some possibility of peaceful transition; this is pointed out in the studies of classical Marxist authors and it is sanctioned in the declaration of the parties. However, under the current conditions in America, every minute that goes by makes a peaceful commitment more difficult. The latest events in Cuba are an example of the cohesion that exists between the bourgeois governments and the imperialist aggressor on the fundamental aspects involved in the conflict.

Remember this point we have continually emphasized: Peaceful transition is not the achievement of formal power by elections or through public opinion movements without direct combat, but rather it is the establishment of socialist power, with all of its attributes, without the use of armed struggle. It is reasonable, then, that all the progressive forces do not have to initiate the road of armed revolution but must use—until the very last moment—every possibility of legal struggle within the bourgeois conditions.[1]

With regard to the form the revolutionary movements must adopt after seizing power, a number of very interesting questions of interpretations that characterize the times arise. The Declaration of the 81 Communist Parties states,

Our epoch, whose fundamental content consists of the transition from capitalism to socialism, as initiated by the great October Socialist Revolution, is the epoch of the struggle between two diametrically opposed social systems; it is the epoch of socialist revolutions and of national liberation revolutions; it is the epoch of the collapse of imperialism and of the liquidation of the colonial system; it is the epoch of the constant advance of more and more peoples on the socialist road; it is the epoch of the triumph of socialism and of universal communism.

The main feature of our epoch is the fact that the international so-

[1] Guevara made a note calling for the insertion of a quotation from the Declaration of the 81 Communist Parties, an insertion he did not make. Eds.

cialist system is becoming the decisive factor in the development of human society.

It is stated, then, that though the people's struggle for liberation is very important, what characterizes the present time is the transition from capitalism to socialism.

On all of the exploited continents there are countries whose social systems have reached different levels of development, but almost all of them have strong social divisions with feudal characteristics and heavy dependence on foreign capital. It would be logical to think that in the struggle for liberation, following the natural process of development, one would reach national democratic governments in which the bourgeoisie more or less predominates. This has occurred in many cases. Nevertheless, those peoples who have had to use force to achieve independence have made greater advances in the path of social reforms and many of them are building socialism. Cuba and Algeria are the most recent examples of the effects of armed struggle on the development of social transformation. If we conclude, then, that the peaceful road is almost nonexistent in America as a possibility, we can point that it is very probable that the outcome of the victorious revolutions in this area of the world will produce regimes of a socialist structure.

Rivers of blood will flow before this is achieved. Algeria's wounds have not yet healed; Vietnam continues to bleed; Angola struggles bravely and alone for its independence; Venezuela, whose patriots identify with the Cuban cause, has recently demonstrated its high and expressive solidarity with our Revolution; Guatemala is waging a difficult, almost underground struggle. All of these are good examples.

The blood of the people is our most sacred treasure, but it must be used in order to save more blood in the future.

Other continents have achieved liberation from colonialism and have established more or less strong bourgeois regimes. This was accomplished without, or almost without, violence but we must realize that following the logic of events up to this moment, that this national bourgeoisie in constant development at a given moment will find itself in contradiction with other strata of the population. When the yoke of the oppressor country is removed, this national bourgeoisie is no longer a revolutionary force and transforms itself into an exploiting class, renewing the cycle of social struggle. It could advance or not on this peaceful road, but irrevocably two great forces will confront each other: the exploiters and the exploited.

The dilemma of our time, regarding how power should be seized, has not escaped the penetration of Yankee imperialists. They also want a "peaceful transition." They favor the liquidation of the old feudal structures that still exist in America and want to ally with the most advanced sectors of the national bourgeoisies, carrying out some monetary reforms, some kind of reform in the land structure, and a moderate industrialization, preferably in consumer goods, with technology and raw materials imported from the United States.

The perfected formula consists in allying the national bourgeoisie with foreign interests; together they create new industries in the country, setting up for these industries tariff advantages of such magnitude that it permits the total exclusion of competition from other imperialist countries. Profits obtained in this manner can be taken out of the country with protection afforded by the many loopholes in exchange regulations.

Through this new and more intelligent system of exploitation, the "nationalist" country assumes the role of protecting U.S. interests by setting up tariffs that allow an extra profit (which the North Americans re-export to their country). Naturally, the sale prices of articles, without competition, is fixed by the monopolies.

All of this is reflected in the projects of the Alliance for Progress which is nothing more than an imperialist attempt to block the development of the revolutionary conditions of the people by sharing a small quantity of the profits with the native exploiting classes, thus making them into firm allies against the highly exploited classes. In other words, this suppresses the internal contradictions of the capitalist system as much as possible.

As we mentioned previously, there are no forces in America capable of intervening in this economic struggle and therefore the game of imperialism is very simple. The only possibility left is the impetuous development of the European Common Market, under German leadership, which could reach the economic strength sufficient to compete with the Yankee capitalists in this region. But the development of contradictions and their violent resolution is so rapid and so eruptive today that it appears that America will become much earlier the battlefield of exploiters and exploited than the scene of an economic struggle between the two imperialisms. It should be said that the intentions of the Alliance for Progress will not materialize because the consciousness of the masses and objective conditions have matured too much for them to fall into such naïve trap.

The decisive factor today is that the imperialist-bourgeois front be consistent. During the recent O.A.S. voting there were no discordant voices on fundamental problems and only a few governments tried to cover up their shame with legalistic formulas, without denouncing the aggressive tendency of these resolutions, which are contrary to law.

The fact that Cuba had atomic missiles served as a pretext for all to side with the United States: Playa Girón did not produce the opposite effect.[2] They know very well that these are defensive weapons, they also know who is the aggressor. Even though they do not say so, the fact is that they all recognize the true danger posed by the Cuban Revolution. The most submissive countries and consequently, the most cynical, talk about the threat of Cuban subversion, and they are right. The greatest threat of the Cuban Revolution is its own example, its revolutionary ideas, in the fact that the government has been able to raise the combat ability of the people, led by a leader of world stature, to heights seldom equaled in history.

Here is the electrifying example of a people prepared to suffer atomic immolation so that its ashes may serve as the foundation for new societies. And when an agreement was reached by which the atomic missiles were removed, without asking our people, we were not relieved or thankful for the truce; instead we denounced the move with our own voice. We have demonstrated our firm stand, our own position, our decision to fight, even if alone, against all dangers and against the very atomic menace of Yankee imperialism.

This causes other peoples to quake. They hear the call of the new voice that emanates from Cuba, stronger than all fears, lies or prejudices, stronger than hunger and all the hooks used in trying to destroy our people. It is stronger than the fear of any reprisal, the most barbarous punishment, the cruelest death, or the most bestial oppression of the exploiters. A new voice, clear and precise, has sounded in every corner of our America.

That has been our mission and we have fulfilled it, and we shall continue to fulfill it with all the decision of our revolutionary convictions.

We could ask the question: Is this the only road? Why not use the imperialist contradictions? Why not seek the backing of the bourgeois sectors that have been struck and humiliated by imperialism? Could we not find a less severe, less self-destructive formula than this Cuban position? Is it not possible to attain the survival of

[2] Refers to the exile-supported invasion of April 1961. Eds.

Cuba through the combination of force and diplomatic maneuvers? We answer: When faced with brute force, use force and determination; when faced by those who want to destroy you, you can only reply with the will to fight to the very last man in order to defend yourselves.

And this formula is valid for all of America in the face of those who at any cost want to remain in power against the will of the people. Fire and blood must be used until the last exploiter has been annihilated.

How can the revolution be carried out in Latin America? Let us listen to the Second Declaration of Havana:

In our countries two circumstances are joined: underdeveloped industry and an agrarian system of feudal character. That is why no matter how hard the living conditions of the urban workers are, the rural population lives under even more horrible conditions of oppression and exploitation. But, with few exceptions, it also constitutes the absolute majority, sometimes more than 70 percent of the Latin American population.

Not counting the landlords who often live in the cities, this great mass earns its livelihood by working as peons on plantations earning miserable wages. Or they till the soil under conditions of exploitation no different than those of the Middle Ages. These circumstances determine in Latin America that the poor rural population constitutes a tremendous potential revolutionary force.

The armies are set up and equipped for conventional warfare. They are the force whereby the power of the exploiting classes is maintained. When they are confronted with the irregular warfare of peasants based on their home ground, they become absolutely powerless; they lose ten men for every revolutionary fighter who falls. Demoralization among them mounts rapidly when they are beset by an invisible and invincible army which provides them no chance to display their military academy tactics and their military fanfare, of which they boast so much, to repress the city workers and students.

The initial struggle of small fighting units is constantly nurtured by new forces; the mass movement begins to grow bold, the old order bit by bit breaks into a thousand pieces, and that is when the working class and the urban masses decide the battle.

What is it that from the very beginning of the fight makes those units invincible, regardless of the number, strength, and resources of their enemies? It is the people's support, and they can count on an ever-increasing mass support.

But the peasantry is a class which, because of the ignorance in which it has been kept and the isolation in which it lives, requires the revolutionary and political leadership of the working class and the revolutionary intellectuals. Without that, it cannot alone launch the struggle and achieve victory.

In the present historical conditions of Latin America, the national bourgeoisie cannot lead the antifeudal and anti-imperialist struggle. Experience demonstrates that in our nations this class—even when its interests clash with those of Yankee imperialism—has been incapable of confronting imperialism, paralyzed by fear of social revolution and frightened by the clamor of the exploited masses.

That is what the Second Declaration of Havana says and it can be seen as an outline of revolution in Latin America. We cannot think of alliances that are not absolutely led by the working class, we cannot think of collaboration with a frightened and treacherous bourgeoisie that destroys the forces on which it based itself to attain power. The weapons must be in the hands of the people and all of Latin America must become a battlefield. The peasants have to fight for their land, the oppressor must be killed mercilessly in ambushes, and the revolutionary must fight and die with honor. This is what counts.

This is the panorama of America, a continent which is preparing to fight, and the sooner the people take up arms and bring their machetes down on the landowners, the industrialists, the bankers, and all the exploiters, as well as their main instrument, the oppressor army, the better.

Whether guerrilla action should always be the tactic or whether it is feasible to institute other actions as the central axis of the struggle can be argued at length. Our opposition to using any other tactic in Latin America is based on two arguments:

First: Accepting as truth the statement that the enemy will fight to stay in power, one must think in terms of the destruction of the oppressor army. In order to destroy it, a people's army must be raised to oppose it directly. This army will not spring up spontaneously; it will have to arm itself with the weapons taken from the enemy's arsenal and this implies a very long and hard struggle in which the popular forces and their leaders will always be exposed to attack from superior forces without adequate conditions for defense and maneuverability. On the other hand, a guerrilla nucleus established in favorable terrain guarantees the security and permanence of the revolutionary command ·and the urban contingents can be directed from this central command of the people's army. They can carry out actions of incalculable importance.

The eventual destruction of urban groups will not destroy the soul of the revolution; its leadership, from its rural bastion, will continue catalyzing the revolutionary spirit of the masses and organizing new forces for other battles.

Second: The continental character of the struggle. Can we conceive of this new epoch in the emancipation of Latin America as the contest between two local forces struggling for power over a given territory? Obviously not. It will be a fight to the death between all the popular forces and all the repressive forces.

The Yankees will intervene because of the solidarity of interests and because the struggle in Latin America is decisive. They will intervene with all of their resources and also will turn all their available destructive weapons upon the popular forces. They will not allow revolutionary power to consolidate itself, and if it succeeds in doing so, they will attack it again and again. They will not recognize defeat and will try to divide the revolutionary forces, introducing saboteurs of every kind. They will try to destroy the new state economically; in a word, they will try to annihilate it.

Given this over-all panorama of Latin America, we find it difficult to believe that victory can be achieved in one isolated country. The union of repressive forces must be countered with the unity of the popular forces. In every country where oppression reaches the limits of tolerance, the banner of rebellion must be raised, and this banner will, of historical necessity, be continental in character. The Andean Cordilleras are destined to be the Sierra Maestra of America, as Fidel has said, and all the immense territories of this continent are destined to be the scene of a struggle to death against imperialist power.

We cannot say when the struggle will take on these continental characteristics or how long it will last, but we can predict its coming, for it is the product of historical, political, and economic circumstances. Its advance cannot be stopped.

Faced with this continental tactic and strategy, some people offer limited formulas: minor election campaigns, an election victory here or there, two deputies, a senator, four mayors, a large popular demonstration broken up by gunfire; an election lost by fewer votes than the preceding one; one labor strike won, ten strikes lost; one step forward, ten steps back; one sectoral victory here, ten defeats there. And then, at that precise moment, the rules of the game are changed and one has to start all over again.

Why these formulas? Why the weakening of the people's energies? There is only one reason: Among the progressive forces of some Latin American nations there exists a terrible confusion between tactical and strategic objectives. Small tactical positions have been interpreted as great strategic objectives. One must credit the reactionary forces with the success of having forced their class enemy to make these minimal offensive positions their fundamental objective.

Where these grave errors occur, the people organize their legions year after year to achieve gains which cost them immense sacrifices and do not have the least value.

There is the hill of parliament, legality hill, the hill of legal economic strikes, the salary increase hill, the bourgeois constitution hill, the liberation of a popular figure hill . . . and the worst of it all is that in order to gain these positions one must enter into the political game of the bourgeois state. And in order to get permission to play this dangerous game one must show that one is a good boy, that one is not dangerous, that one would never think of assaulting army garrisons or trains, or destroying bridges, or bringing revolutionary justice to hired thugs of the reaction or to torturers, or going to the mountains. One cannot state resolutely the only and violent affirmation of Latin America: the final struggle for her redemption.

Latin America offers a contradictory picture. There are progressive forces which are not up to the level of those whom they lead; people who rise to unknown heights, people who boil with a desire to act and leaders who frustrate those desires. The hecatomb is almost here and the people have no fear; they try to move toward the moment of sacrifice, which will mean the definitive achievement of redemption. The educated and prudent ones, on the other hand, put all available brakes on the movement of the masses, attempting to divert the irrepressible yearnings of the masses for the great strategic objectives: the taking of political power, the annihilation of the army and the destruction of the system of exploitation of man by man. The picture is contradictory but full of hope because the masses know that "the role of Job is not for the revolutionary," so they prepare for battle.

Will imperialism continue to lose one position after another or will it, in its bestiality, as it threatened not long ago, launch a nuclear attack and burn the entire world in an atomic holocaust? We cannot say. We do assert however, that we must follow the road of liberation even though it may cost millions of atomic victims. In the struggle to death between the two systems we cannot think of anything but the final victory of socialism or its relapse as a consequence of the nuclear victory of imperialist aggression.

Cuba is at the brink of an invasion, threatened by the most powerful imperialistic forces of the world, and as such, threatened with atomic death. From its trench, refusing to retreat, Cuba issues a call to arms to all of Latin America. This is a struggle that will not be decided in a few minutes or an hour of terrible battle. The end of the struggle will take years of bitter encounters causing atrocious suffering. The attack of the allied imperialist and bourgeois forces will time and again force the popular movements to the brink of destruction, but they will always come back strengthened by the support of the people until total liberation is achieved.

From here, from its lonely vanguard trench, our people make their voice heard. This is not the song of a revolution headed for defeat; it is a revolutionary anthem destined to be sung eternally from the lips of Latin American fighters. It will be echoed by history.

Guerrilla Warfare:
A Method

ЛЛЛЛЛЛЛЛЛЛЛЛЛЛЛЛЛЛЛЛЛЛЛЛЛЛЛЛ

Guerrilla warfare has been employed on innumerable occasions throughout history in different circumstances to obtain different objectives. Lately it has been employed in various popular wars of liberation when the vanguard of the people chose the road of irregular armed struggle against enemies of superior military power. Asia, Africa, and Latin America have been the scene of such actions in attempts to obtain power in the struggle against feudal, neo-colonial, or colonial exploitation. In Europe, guerrilla units were used as a supplement to native or allied regular armies.

In America, guerrilla warfare has been employed on several occasions. As a case in point, we have the experience of César Augusto Sandino fighting against the Yankee expeditionary force on the Segovia of Nicaragua.[1] Recently we had Cuba's revolutionary war. Since then in America the problem of guerrilla war has been raised in discussions of theory by the progressive parties of the continent with the question of whether its utilization is possible or convenient. This has become the topic of very controversial polemics.

This article will express our views on guerrilla warfare and its correct utilization. Above all, we must emphasize at the outset that this form of struggle is a means to an end. That end, essential and inevitable for any revolutionary, is the conquest of political power. Therefore, in the analysis of specific situations in different countries of America, we must use the concept of guerrilla warfare in the limited sense of a method of struggle in order to gain that end.

Almost immediately the question arises: Is guerrilla warfare the only formula for seizing power in all of Latin America? Or, at any rate, will it be the predominant form? Or simply, will it be one formula among many used during the struggle? And ultimately we may ask: Will Cuba's example be applicable to the present situation on the continent? In the course of polemics, those who want to undertake guerrilla warfare are criticized for forgetting mass struggle, implying that guerrilla warfare and mass struggle are opposed to each other. We reject this implication, for guerrilla warfare is a

Cuba Socialista (Havana), September 1963, pp. 1–17.
[1] In 1928. Eds.

people's war; to attempt to carry out this type of war without the population's support is the prelude to inevitable disaster. The guerrilla is the combat vanguard of the people, situated in a specified place in a certain region, armed and willing to carry out a series of warlike actions for the one possible strategic end—the seizure of power. The guerrilla is supported by the peasant and worker masses of the region and of the whole territory in which it acts. Without these prerequisites, guerrilla warfare is not possible.

We consider that the Cuban Revolution made three fundamental contributions to the laws of the revolutionary movement in the current situation in America. First, people's forces can win a war against the army. Second, one need not always wait for all conditions favorable to revolution to be present; the insurrection itself can create them. Third, in the underdeveloped parts of America, the battleground for armed struggle should in the main be the countryside. (*Guerrilla Warfare*) [2]

Such are the contributions to the development of the revolutionary struggle in America, and they can be applied to any of the countries on our continent where guerrilla warfare may develop.

The Second Declaration of Havana points out,

In our countries two circumstances are joined: underdeveloped industry and an agrarian system of feudal character. That is why no matter how hard the living conditions of the urban workers are, the rural population lives under even more horrible conditions of oppression and exploitation. But, with few exceptions, it also constitutes the absolute majority, sometimes more than 70 percent of the Latin American population.

Not counting the landlords who often live in the cities, this great mass earns its livelihood by working as peons on plantations earning miserable wages. Or they till the soil under conditions of exploitation no different than those of the Middle Ages. These circumstances determine in Latin America that the poor rural population constitutes a tremendous potential revolutionary force.

The armies are set up and equipped for conventional warfare. They are the force whereby the power of the exploiting classes is maintained. When they are confronted with the irregular warfare of peasants based on their home ground, they become absolutely powerless; they lose ten men for every revolutionary fighter who falls. Demoralization among them mounts rapidly when they are beset by an invisible and invincible army which provides them no chance to display their military academy tactics and their military fanfare, of which they boast so much, to repress the city workers and students.

The initial struggle of small fighting units is constantly nurtured by new forces; the mass movement begins to grow bold, the old order bit by bit breaks into a thousand pieces, and that is when the working class and the urban masses decide the battle.

[2] Ernesto Guevara, *La Guerra de Guerrillas*. Eds.

What is it that from the very beginning of the fight makes those units invincible, regardless of the number, strength, and resources of their enemies? It is the people's support, and they can count on an ever-increasing mass support.

But the peasantry is a class which, because of the ignorance in which it has been kept and the isolation in which it lives, requires the revolutionary and political leadership of the working class and the revolutionary intellectuals. Without that, it cannot alone launch the struggle and achieve victory.

In the present historical conditions of Latin America, the national bourgeoisie cannot lead the antifeudal and anti-imperialist struggle. Experience demonstrates that in our nations this class—even when its interests clash with those of Yankee imperialism—has been incapable of confronting imperialism, paralyzed by fear of social revolution and frightened by the clamor of the exploited masses.

Completing the foresight of the preceding statements, which constitute the essence of the revolutionary declaration of Latin America, the Second Declaration of Havana in the following paragraphs states:

The subjective conditions in each country, the factors of revolutionary consciousness, of organization, of leadership, can accelerate or delay revolution, depending on the state of their development. Sooner or later, in each historic epoch, as objective conditions ripen, consciousness is acquired, organization is achieved, leadership arises, and revolution is produced.

Whether this takes place peacefully or comes into the world after painful labor does not depend on the revolutionaries; it depends on the reactionary forces of the old society. Revolution, in history, is like the doctor who assists at the birth of a new life: he does not use forceps unless necessary, but he will unhesitatingly use them every time labor requires them. It is a labor which brings the hope of a better life to the enslaved and exploited masses.

In many Latin American countries revolution is inevitable. This fact is not determined by the will of anyone. It is determined by the horrible conditions of exploitation under which the American people live, the development of a revolutionary consciousness in the masses, the worldwide crisis of imperialism, and the universal liberation movements of the subjugated nations.

We shall begin from this basis to analyze the whole matter of guerrilla warfare in Latin America.

We have already established that it is a means of struggle to attain an end. First, our concern is to analyze the end in order to determine whether the winning of power in Latin America can be achieved in other ways than armed struggle. Peaceful struggle can be carried out through mass movements compelling—in special crisis situations—the governments to yield; thus, eventually the popular forces would take over and establish a dictatorship of the proletariat. Theoretically this is correct. When analyzing this in the Latin American context, we must reach the following conclusions: Generally on this continent there exist objective conditions which propel the masses to violent actions against their bourgeois and landlord governments. In many countries there exist crises of power and also some subjective conditions for revolution. It is clear, of course, that in those countries where all of these conditions are found, it would be criminal not to act to seize power. In other countries where these conditions do not occur, it is right that different alternatives will appear and out of theoretical discussions the tactic proper to each country should emerge. The only thing which history does not admit is that the analysts and executors of proletarian policy be mistaken.

No one can solicit the role of vanguard of the party as if it were a diploma given by a university. To be the vanguard of the party means to be at the forefront of the working class through the struggle for achieving power. It means to know how to guide this fight through shortcuts to victory. This is the mission of our revolutionary parties and thus the analysis must be profound and exhaustive so that there will be no mistakes.

At the present time we can observe in America an unstable balance between oligarchical dictatorship and popular pressure. We mean by "oligarchical" the reactionary alliance between the bourgeoisie and the landowning class of each country which has a greater or lesser preponderance of feudalism.

These dictatorships carry on within a certain "legal" framework which they adjudicated themselves to facilitate their work throughout the unrestricted period of their class domination. Yet we are passing through a stage in which the masses' pressure is very strong and is straining bourgeois legality so that its own authors must violate it in order to halt the impetus of the masses.

Barefaced violation of all legislation or of laws specifically instituted to sanction ruling class deeds only increases the tension of the people's forces. Thus the oligarchical dictatorship attempts to use the old legal order to change constitutionality and further oppress the proletariat without a frontal clash. Nevertheless, at this point, a contradiction arises. The people no longer support the old much less the new coercive measures established by the dictatorship and try to smash them. We should never forget the class character, authoritarian and restrictive, which typifies the bourgeois state. Lenin refers to it in the following manner: "The state is the product and the manifestation of the irreconcilability of class antagonisms. The state arises when, where, and to the extent that class antagonisms objectively cannot be reconciled. And, conversely, the existence of the state proves that class antagonisms are irreconcilable." (*State and Revolution*)

In other words, we should not allow the word "democracy" to be utilized apologetically to represent the dictatorship of the exploiting classes and to lose its deeper meaning and acquire the meaning of granting the people certain liberties, more or less good. To struggle only to restore a certain degree of bourgeois legality without considering the question of revolutionary power is to struggle for the return of a dictatorial order established by the dominant social classes. In other words, it is to struggle for a lighter iron ball to be fixed to the prisoner's chain.

In these conditions of conflict, the oligarchy breaks its own contracts, its own mask of "democracy," and attacks the people, though it will always try to use the superstructure it has formed for oppression. Thus, we are faced once again with a dilemma: What must be done? Our reply is: Violence is not the monopoly of the exploiters and as such the exploited can use it too and, what is more, ought to use it when the moment arrives. Martí said, "He who wages war in a country, when he can avoid it, is a criminal, just as he who fails to promote war which cannot be avoided is a criminal."

Lenin said, "Social democracy has never taken a sentimental view of war. It unreservedly condemns war as a bestial means of settling conflicts in human society. But social democracy knows that as long as society is divided into classes, as long as there is exploitation of man by man, wars are inevitable. In order to end this exploitation we cannot walk away from war, which is always and everywhere begun by the exploiters, by the ruling and oppressing classes." He said this in 1905. Later in the "Military Program of the Proletarian Revolution," a far-reaching analysis of the nature of class struggle, he affirmed: "Whoever recognizes the class struggle cannot fail to recognize civil wars, which in every class society are the natural, and under certain conditions, inevitable continuation, development, and intensification of the class struggle. All· the great revolutions prove this. To repudiate civil war, or to forget about it, would mean sinking into extreme opportunism and renouncing the socialist revolution." That is to say, we should not fear violence, the midwife of new societies; but violence should be unleashed at that precise moment in which the leaders have found the most favorable circumstances.

What will these be? Subjectively, they depend on two factors which complement each other and which deepen during the struggle: consciousness of the necessity of change and confidence in the possibility of this revolutionary change. Both of these factors, with the objective conditions (which are favorable in all Latin America for the development of the struggle), with the firm will to achieve it as well as the new correlation of forces in the world, will determine the mode of action.

Regardless of how far away the socialist countries may be, their favorable influence will be felt by the people who struggle, just as their example will give the people further strength. Fidel Castro said on July 26 [1963]: "And the duty of the revolutionaries, especially at this moment, is to know how to recognize and how to take advantage of the changes in the correlation of forces which have taken place in the world and to understand that these changes facilitate the people's struggle. The duty of revolutionaries, of Latin American revolutionaries, is not to wait for the change in the correlation of forces to produce a miracle of social revolutions in Latin America but to take full advantage of everything in it that is favorable to the revolutionary movement—and to make revolution!"

There are some who say, "Let us admit that in certain specific cases revolutionary war is the best means to achieve political power; but where do we find the great leaders, the Fidel Castros, who will lead us to victory?" Fidel Castro, as any human being, is the product of history. The political and military chieftains who will lead the insurrectional uprisings in America, merged if possible in one man, will learn the art of war during the course of war itself. There is neither trade nor profession that can be learned from books alone. In this case, the struggle itself is the great teacher.

Of course, the task will not be easy nor is it exempt from grave dangers throughout. During the development of armed struggle, there are two moments of extreme danger for the future of the revolution. The first of these arises in the preparatory stage and the way with which it is dealt will give the measure of determination to struggle as well as clarity of purpose of the people's forces. When the bourgeois state advances against the people's positions, obviously there must arise a process of defense against the enemy who at this point, being superior, attacks. If the basic subjective and objective conditions are ripe, the defense must be armed so that the popular forces will not merely become recipients of the enemy's blows. Nor should the armed defense camp be allowed to be transformed into the refuge of the pursued.

Guerrilla warfare may adopt a defensive movement at a certain point, yet it carries within itself the capacity to attack the enemy and must develop it constantly. This capacity is what determines, with the passing of time, the catalytic character of the people's forces. That is, guerrilla warfare is not passive self-defense; it is defense with attack. And from the moment we recognize it as such, it has as its final goal the conquest of political power.

This moment is important. In social processes the difference between violence and nonviolence cannot be measured by the number of shots exchanged; rather, it lies in concrete and fluctuating situations. And we must be able to see the right moment in which the people's forces, conscious of their relative weakness and their strategic strength, must take the initiative against the enemy so the situation will not deteriorate. The equilibrium between oligarchic dictatorship and the popular pressure must be changed. The dictatorship tries to function without resorting to force. Thus, we must try to oblige the dictatorship to resort to violence, thereby unmasking its true nature as the dictatorship of the reactionary social classes. This event will deepen the struggle to such an extent that there will be no retreat from it. The performance of the people's forces depends on the task of forcing the dictatorship to a decision—to retreat or unleash the struggle—thus beginning the stage of long-range armed action.

The skillful avoidance of the next dangerous moment depends on the growing power of the people's forces. Marx always recommended that once the revolutionary process has begun the proletariat strike blows again and again without rest. A revolution which does not constantly expand is a revolution which regresses. The fighters, if weary, begin to lose faith; and at this point some of the bourgeois maneuvers may bear fruit—for example, the holding of elections to turn the government to another gentleman with a sweeter voice and more angelic face than the outgoing tyrant or the staging of a coup by reactionaries generally led by the army with the direct or indirect support of the progressive forces. There are others, but it is not our intention to analyze such tactical stratagems.

Let us emphasize the military coup mentioned previously. What can the military contribute to democracy? What kind of loyalty can be asked of them if they are merely an instrument for the domination of the reactionary classes and imperialist monopolies and if, as a caste whose worth rests on the weapon in their hands, they aspire only to maintain their prerogatives?

When, in difficult situations for the oppressors, the military establishment conspires to overthrow a dictator who in fact has been defeated, it can be said that they do so because the dictator is unable to preserve their class prerogatives without extreme violence, a method which generally does not suit the interests of the oligarchies at that point.

This statement does not mean to reject the service of military men as individual fighters who, once separated from the society they served, have in fact now rebelled against it. They should be used in accordance with the revolutionary line they adopt as fighters and not as representatives of a caste.

A long time ago Engels, in the preface to the third edition of *Civil War in France*, wrote,

The workers were armed after every revolution; for this reason the disarming of the workers was the first commandment for the bourgeois at the helm of the state. Hence, after every revolution won by the workers, a new struggle ending with the defeat of the workers. (Quoted by Lenin in *State and Revolution*)

This play of continuous struggle, in which some change is obtained and then strategically withdrawn, has been repeated for many dozens of years in the capitalist world. Moreover, the permanent deception of the proletariat along these lines has been practiced for over a century.

There is danger also that progressive party leaders, wishing to maintain conditions more favorable for revolutionary action through the use of certain aspects of bourgeois legality, will lose sight of their goal (which is common during the action), thus forgetting the primary strategic objective: the seizure of power.

These two difficult moments in the revolution, which we have analyzed briefly, become obvious when the leaders of Marxist-Leninist parties are capable of perceiving the implications of the moment clearly and of mobilizing the masses to the fullest, leading them on the correct path of resolving fundamental contradictions.

In developing the thesis, we have assumed that eventually the idea of armed struggle as well as the formula of guerrilla warfare as a method of struggle will be accepted. Why do we think that in the present situation of America guerrilla warfare is the best method? There are fundamental arguments which in our opinion determine the necessity of guerrilla action as the central axis of struggle in Latin America.

First, accepting as true that the enemy will fight to maintain itself in power, one must think about destroying the oppressor army. To do this, a people's army is necessary. This army is not born spontaneously; rather it must be armed from the enemy's arsenal and this requires a long and difficult struggle in which the people's forces and their leaders will always be exposed to attack from superior forces and be without adequate conditions of defense and maneuverability.

On the other hand, the guerrilla nucleus, established in terrain favorable for the struggle, ensures the security and continuity of the revolutionary command. The urban forces, led by the general staff of the people's army, can perform actions of the greatest importance. However, the eventual destruction of these groups would not kill the soul of the revolution; its leadership would continue from its rural bastion to spark the revolutionary spirit of the masses and would continue to organize new forces for other battles.

Moreover, in this region begins the construction of the future state apparatus entrusted to lead the class dictatorship efficiently during the transition period. The longer the struggle becomes, the larger and more complex the administrative problems; and in solving them, cadres will be trained for the difficult task of consolidating power and, at a later stage, economic development.

Second, there is the general situation of the Latin American peasantry and the ever more explosive character of the struggle against feudal structures within the framework of an alliance between local and foreign exploiters.

Returning to the Second Declaration of Havana,

At the outset of the past century, the peoples of America freed themselves from Spanish colonialism, but they did not free themselves from exploitation. The feudal landlords assumed the authority of the governing Spaniards, the Indians continued in their painful serfdom, the Latin American man remained a slave one way or another, and the minimum hopes of the peoples died under the power of the oligarchies and the tyranny of foreign capital. This is the truth of America, to one or another degree of variation. Latin America today is under a more ferocious imperialism, more powerful and ruthless, than the Spanish colonial empire.

What is Yankee imperialism's attitude confronting the objective and historically inexorable reality of the Latin American revolution? To prepare to fight a colonial war against the peoples of Latin America; to create an apparatus of force to establish the political pretexts and the pseudo-legal instruments underwritten by the representatives of the reactionary oligarchies in order to curb, by blood and by iron, the struggle of the Latin American peoples.

This objective situation shows the dormant force of our peasants and the need to utilize it for Latin America's liberation.

Third, there is the continental nature of the struggle. Could we imagine this stage of Latin American emancipation as the confrontation of two local forces struggling for power in a specific territory? Hardly. The struggle between the people's forces and the forces of repression will be to the death. This too is predicted by the paragraphs cited previously.

The Yankees will intervene due to solidarity of interest and because the struggle in Latin America is decisive. As a matter of fact, they are intervening already as they prepare the forces of repression and the organization of a continental apparatus of struggle. But, from now on, they will do so with all their energies; they will punish the popular forces with all the destructive weapons at their disposal. They will not allow a revolutionary power to consolidate; and, if it ever happens, they will attack again, will not recognize it, and will try to divide the revolutionary forces. Moreover, they will infiltrate saboteurs, create border problems, will force other reactionary states to oppose it, and will impose economic sanctions attempting, in one word, to annihilate the new state.

This being the panorama in Latin America, it is difficult to achieve and consolidate victory in a country which is isolated. The unity of the repressive forces must be confronted with the unity of the popular forces. In all countries where oppression reaches intolerable proportions, the banner of rebellion must be raised; and this banner of historical necessity will have a continental character.

As Fidel stated, the cordilleras of the Andes will be the Sierra Maestra of Latin America; and the immense territories which this continent encompasses will become the scene of a life or death struggle against imperialism.

We cannot predict when this struggle will reach a continental dimension nor how long it will last. But we can predict its advent and triumph because it is the inevitable result of historical, economic, and political conditions; and its direction cannot change.

The task of the revolutionary forces in each country is to initiate the struggle when the conditions are present there, regardless of the conditions in other countries. The development of the struggle will bring about the general strategy. The prediction of the continental character of the struggle is the outcome of the analysis of the strength of each contender, but this does not exclude independent outbreaks. As the beginning of the struggle in one area of a country is bound to cause its development throughout the region, the beginning of a revolutionary war contributes to the development of new conditions in the neighboring countries.

The development of revolution has normally produced high and low tides in inverse proportion. To the revolution's high tide corresponds the counterrevolutionary low tide and vice versa, as there is a counterrevolutionary ascendancy at moments of revolutionary decline. In those moments, the situation of the people's forces becomes difficult; and they should resort to the best means of defense in order to suffer the least damage. The enemy is extremely powerful, it is of continental scope. For this reason, the relative weakness of the local bourgeoisie cannot be analyzed with a view toward making decisions within restricted boundaries. Still less can one think of an eventual alliance by these oligarchies with a people in arms.

The Cuban Revolution sounded the bell which gave the alarm. The polarization of forces will become complete: exploiters on one side and exploited on the other. And the mass of the petty bourgeoisie will lean to one side or the other according to their interests and the political skill with which they are handled. Thus, neutrality will be an exception. This is how revolutionary war will be.

Let us think how a guerrilla focus can start. Nuclei with relatively few persons choose places favorable for guerrilla warfare, with the intention of unleashing a counterattack or to weather the storm, and there they start taking action. However, what follows must be very clear: At the beginning the relative weakness of the guerrilla is such that they should work only toward becoming acquainted with the terrain and its surroundings while establishing connections with the population and fortifying the places which eventually will be converted into bases.

A guerrilla force which has just begun its development must follow three conditions in order to survive: constant mobility, constant vigilance, constant distrust. Without the adequate use of these three conditions of military tactics, the guerrilla will find it hard to survive. We must remember that the heroism of the guerrilla fighter, at this moment, consists of the scope of the planned goal and the enormous number of sacrifices that he must make in order to achieve it. These sacrifices are not made in daily combat or face-to-face battle with the enemy; rather, they will adopt more subtle and difficult forms for the guerrilla fighter to resist physically and mentally.

Perhaps the guerrillas will be punished heavily by the enemy, divided at times into groups with those who are captured to be tortured. They will be pursued as hunted animals in areas where they have chosen to operate; the constant anxiety of having the enemy on their track will be with them. They must distrust everyone, for the terrorized peasants in some cases will give them away to the repressive troops in order to save themselves. Their only alternatives are life or death, at times when death is a concept a thousand times present and victory only a myth for a revolutionary to dream of.

This is the guerrilla's heroism. This is why it is said that walking is a form of fighting and to avoid combat at a given moment is also another form. Facing the general superiority of the enemy at a given place, one must find a form of tactics with which to gain a relative superiority at that moment either by being capable of concentrating more troops than the enemy or by using fully and well the terrain in order to secure advantages that unbalance the correlation of forces. In these conditions, tactical victory is assured; if relative superiority is not clear, it is better not to act. As long as the guerrilla is in the position of deciding the "how" and the "when," no combat should be fought that will not end in victory.

Within the framework of the great politicomilitary action, of which they are a part, the guerrilla will grow and reach consolidation. Thus, bases will continue to be formed, for they are essential to the success of the guerrilla army. These bases are points which the enemy can enter only at the cost of heavy losses; they are the revolution's bastions, both refuge and starting point for the guerrilla's more daring and distant raids.

One comes to this point if difficulties of a tactical and political nature have been overcome. The guerrillas cannot forget their function as vanguard of the people—their mandate—and as such they must create the necessary political conditions for the establishment of a revolutionary power based on the masses' support. The peasants' aspirations or demands must be satisfied to the degree and form which circumstances permit so as to bring about the decisive support and solidarity of the whole population.

If the military situation will be difficult from the very first moment, the political situation will be just as delicate; if a single military error can liquidate the guerrilla, a political error can hold back its development for long periods. The struggle is politico-military and as such it must be developed and understood.

In the process of the guerrilla growth, the fighting reaches a point where its capacity for action covers a given region for which there are too many men in too great a concentration in the area. There begins the beehive action in which one of the commanders, a distinguished guerrilla, hops to another region and repeats the chain of development of guerrilla warfare. He is, nevertheless, subject to a central command.

It is imperative to point out that one cannot hope for victory without the formation of a popular army. The guerrilla forces can be expanded to a certain magnitude; the people's forces, in the cities and in other areas, can inflict losses; but the military potential of the reactionaries will still remain intact. One must always keep in mind the fact that the final objective is the enemy's annihilation. Therefore, all these new zones which are being created, as well as the zones infiltrated behind enemy lines and the forces operating in the principal cities, should be under one unified command.

Guerrilla war or war of liberation will generally have three stages: First, the strategic defensive when the small force nibbles at the enemy and runs; it is not sheltered to make a passive defense within a small circumference but rather its defense consists of the limited attacks which it can strike successfully. After this comes a state of equilibrium in which the possibilities of action on both sides—the enemy and the guerrillas—are established. Finally, the last stage consists of overrunning the repressive army leading to the capture of the big cities, large-scale decisive encounters, and at last the complete annihilation of the enemy.

After reaching a state of equilibrium when both sides respect each other and as the war's development continues, the guerrilla war acquires new characteristics. The concept of maneuver is introduced: large columns which attack strong points; mobile warfare with the shifting of forces and means of attack of relative potential. But due to the capacity for resistance and counterattack that the enemy still has, this war of maneuver does not replace guerrilla fighting; rather, it is only one form of action taken by the guerrillas until that time when they crystallize into a people's army with an army corps. Even at this moment the guerrilla, marching ahead of the action of the main forces, will play the role of its first stage, destroying communications and sabotaging the whole defensive apparatus of the enemy.

We have predicted that the war will be continental. This means that it will be a protracted war; it will have many fronts; and it will cost much blood and countless lives for a long period of time. But another phenomenon occurring in Latin America is the polarization of forces, that is, the clear division between exploiters and exploited. Thus when the armed vanguard of the people achieves power, both the imperialists and the national exploiting class will be liquidated at one stroke. The first stage of the socialist revolution will have crystallized, and the people will be ready to heal their wounds and initiate the construction of socialism.

Are there possibilities less bloody? Awhile ago the last dividing up of the world took place in which the United States took the lion's share of our continent. Today the imperialists of the Old World are developing again—and the strength of the European Common Market frightens the United States itself. All this might lead to the belief that there exists the possibility for us merely to observe as spectators the struggle among the imperialists trying to make further advances, perhaps in alliance with the stronger national bourgeoisie. Yet a passive policy never brings good results in class struggle and alliances with the bourgeoisie, though they might appear to be revolutionary, have only a transitory character. The time factor will induce us to choose another ally. The sharpening of the most important contradiction in Latin America appears to be so rapid that it disturbs the "normal" development of the imperialist camp's contradiction in its struggle for markets.

The majority of national bourgeoisie have united with North American imperialism; thus their fate shall be the same as that of the latter. Even in the cases where pacts or common contradictions are shared between the national bourgeoisie and other imperialists, this occurs within the framework of a fundamental struggle which will embrace sooner or later *all the exploited and all the exploiters.* The polarization of antagonistic forces among class adversaries is up till now more rapid than the development of the contradiction among exploiters over the splitting of the spoils. There are two camps: the alternative becomes clearer for each individual and for each specific stratum of the population.

The Alliance for Progress attempts to slow that which cannot be stopped. But if the advance of the European Common Market or any other imperialist group on the American market were more rapid than the development of the fundamental contradiction, the forces of the people would only have to penetrate into the open breach, carrying on the struggle and using the new intruders with a clear awareness of what their true intentions are.

Not a single position, weapon, or secret should be given to the class enemy, under penalty of losing all. In fact, the eruption of the Latin American struggle has begun. Will its storm center be in Venezuela, Guatemala, Colombia, Peru, Ecuador? Are today's skirmishes only manifestations of a restlessness that has not come to fruition? The outcome of today's struggles does not matter. It does not matter in the final count that one or two movements were temporarily defeated because what is definite is the decision to struggle which matures every day, the consciousness of the need for revolutionary change, and the certainty that it is possible.

This is a prediction. We make it with the conviction that history will prove us right. The analysis of the objective and subjective conditions of Latin America and the imperialist world indicates to us the certainty of these assertions based on the Second Declaration of Havana.

The Role of a
Marxist-Leninist Party

ⲛⲖⲛⲖⲛⲖⲛⲖⲛⲖⲛⲖⲛⲖⲛⲖⲛⲖⲛⲖⲛⲖⲛⲖⲛⲖⲛⲖⲛⲖⲛ

This small book is designed to introduce our party militants to the wide and rich field of Marxist-Leninist ideas.... [1] It shows us with clarity what a Marxist-Leninist party is: "Persons fused by a community of ideas who organize themselves to give life to Marxist conceptualizations, that is, to carry out the historical mission of the working class." The book also explains how the members of the party cannot be isolated from the masses, how they have to be in constant touch with the people, how they should exercise criticism and self-criticism and be severe with their own mistakes. It also points out how the party should be positive in all its ventures; it should fight for something and not against something. The Marxist parties cannot cross their arms and wait for the objective and subjective conditions to appear—formed through the mechanical process of class struggle. This book shows the leading and catalyzing role of the party—vanguard of the working class—that guides the workers to the path to victory and accelerates the momentum toward new social situations. It insists that even in moments of social flux one has to know how to retreat and maintain firmly the cadre structure so as to be able to move more effectively on another opportunity and advance toward the fundamental goal of a Marxist-Leninist party: the acquisition of power.

It is logical that this is a class party. A Marxist-Leninist party could not call itself so if it were not a class party, for its mission is to find the shortest route to achieve the dictatorship of the proletariat. Its most valuable cadres, its leaders, and its tactics arise from the working class.

It is inconceivable that the building of socialism can begin with a bourgeois party, a party that would have for a great many of its members exploiters who are in charge of shaping the political line of the party. Evidently, a group of this sort can only lead the struggle in the stage of national liberation to a certain point and in given circumstances. Afterward, the revolutionary class would transform

Prologue to the book, *El partido marxista-leninista* (Havana: Dirección Nacional del Partido Unido de la Revolución Socialista de Cuba), 1963.

[1] Guevara mentions the contents of the book, essays on Marxism-Leninism by Fidel Castro and O. V. Kuusinen, a Soviet theoretician. Eds.

itself into a reactionary one and new conditions would appear to force the creation of a Marxist-Leninist party which would lead the revolutionary struggle. Already, at least in Latin America, it is practically impossible to talk of liberation movements led by the bourgeoisie. The Cuban Revolution has polarized all forces; faced with the dilemma of choosing between the people and imperialism, the weak national bourgeoisies have chosen imperialism and have definitely betrayed their countries. This removes almost totally the possibility of a peaceful transition to socialism in this part of the world.

If the Marxist-Leninist party is able to foresee the historical stages that it will face and is capable of becoming the vanguard of the people even before the stage of national liberation has ended, then that party will have fulfilled two historical missions and will be able to face the tasks of socialist construction with greater strength and more prestige among the masses.

The Cuban Revolution has been a rich experience because of the new contributions it has made to revolutionary developments in Latin America. This experience, with its many errors, has taught many lessons because the errors were analyzed and corrected publicly. Particularly important are the speeches of *compañero* Fidel (which appear in this book) on the United Party of the Socialist Revolution and the working methods of the Integrated Revolutionary Organizations. These two speeches mark two fundamental stages of our development. In the first stage a truly revolutionary leader frankly confesses, after reaching the pinnacle of his thought, his Marxist-Leninist convictions. But this is done, not as a simple verbal affirmation, but outlining the most important facets in the evolution of the leader, the evolution of the movement and the party, which finally integrate themselves in the United Party of the Socialist Revolution.

In his self-analysis, *compañero* Fidel recognizes all the regressive ideas inculcated in him by the environment, and tells us how instinctively he fought against those ideas and how he resolved his many doubts.

At this stage, the 26th of July Movement constituted something new and very difficult to define. Fidel Castro, hero of the Moncada Barracks, prisoner on the Isle of Pines, trained a group of expeditionaries who had as their mission reaching the coast of Oriente and initiating the revolutionary struggle in that province, trying to separate it from the rest of the island or advancing, according to objective conditions, to Havana in a succession of more or less bloody victories.

Reality hit us: all the subjective conditions necessary for the materialization of our plan did not exist; we did not follow all the rules of revolutionary war which we later learned with our own flesh in two years of hard struggle. We were defeated and there began the most important history of our movement. We became aware that tactical mistakes were committed and that some important subjective factors were lacking. The people were conscious of the need for change but lacked the certainty of the possibility of change. To create the certainty of that possibility was our task and in the Sierra Maestra began the long process that served as catalyst to the movement in the island which provoked uninterrupted revolutionary outbursts in the entire territory.

It was demonstrated with deeds that the Rebel Army with the faith and enthusiasm of the people, in favorable terrain, could increase its force through the adequate use of weapons and destroy the enemy's army. That is a great lesson in our history. Before victory, the correlation of forces began to change, becoming immensely favorable to the revolutionary movement; the necessary subjective conditions were created. A new revolutionary experience occurred in Latin America: It was demonstrated how the great truths of Marxism-Leninism always happen—in this case, that the mission of the leaders of revolutionary movements is to create the necessary conditions for the takeover of power and not to await a revolutionary wave that will appear from the masses.

At the same time, the Cuban experience shows the necessity for the armed groups that defend the people's sovereignty to be safe from surprise attacks, and indicates the importance of armed struggle as well as the favorable terrain in which the guerrilla forces should function. This is another contribution of our Revolution to the Latin American struggle for emancipation: from the countryside one goes to the city, from the small to the large—one creates the revolutionary movement that culminates in the city of Havana.

Elsewhere Fidel clearly expresses that the essential condition of a revolutionary is to know how to interpret reality. Referring to the April 1958 strike, he explains how we failed to interpret that moment and as a consequence we suffered a catastrophe. Why was the April strike called? Because there was within the revolutionary movement a series of contradictions which we call the *sierra* and the *llano* [2] manifesting themselves in diametrically different analyses of the elements considered fundamental to decide the armed struggle.

[2] *Sierra* should be understood as a mountainous region or the countryside. This is the region where the 26th of July Movement carried out most of its struggle. *Llano* should be understood as the plains or the urban centers. Eds.

The *sierra* was ready to engage the army as often as necessary, to win battle after battle, capturing its weapons, and to arrive one day at the total seizure of power with the Rebel Army as a foundation. The *llano* favored generalized armed struggle throughout the country, culminating in a revolutionary general strike that would expel the Batista dictatorship and establish a government of "civilians," converting the new army into an apolitical institution.

The clash between these theses was continuous and did not facilitate the unity of command necessary at such moments. The April strike was prepared and ordered by the *llano* with the consent of the *sierra* leadership—which did not consider itself able to prevent it, even though it had serious doubts on its outcome—and with the stated reservations of the Partido Socialista Popular,[3] which warned of the danger at the time. The revolutionary commanders went to the *llano* to help out, and it was thus that our unforgettable army commander, Camilo Cienfuegos, made his first incursions into the Bayamo area.

These differences were deeper than tactical discrepancies: The Rebel Army was already ideologically proletarian and thought as a dispossessed class; the urban leadership remained petty bourgeois, with future traitors among its leaders and greatly influenced by the milieu in which it developed.

It was a minor struggle for internal control in the framework of the great struggle for power. The revolutionary wing did not allow itself to be displaced from power and struggled to conquer all power. The Rebel Army is the genuine representative of the triumphant Revolution.

The clashes occurred periodically and unity of command (not yet respected by all) was achieved when Fidel became prime minister a few months after the triumph of the Revolution. Until that moment, what had we done? We had acquired, as Fidel stated, the right to begin. We had only reached the culmination of one stage, which was based on the fight to the death against a system established in Cuba represented by dictator Batista, but our revolutionary tendency to go beyond this and to improve our society and liberate our nation from all economic shackles took us, by necessity, into a frontal fight with imperialism.

Imperialism has been a very important factor in the development of our ideology; every imperialist blow called forth a rebuttal; every time the Yankees reacted with their habitual arrogance by taking a

[3] Communist Party of Cuba during the struggle against Batista's dictatorship. Eds.

measure against Cuba, we had to take the necessary countermeasures and this deepened the Revolution.

The Partido Socialista Popular joined this front and the old revolutionary militants and the guerrilla fighters began to fuse. Already at this stage Fidel warned against some dangers of sectarianism and criticized them.

At the time of the armed struggle there was a group of *compañeros* that tried to defend the movement against the apparent caudillism [4] of Fidel, committing the error—which was to be repeated later at the time of the sectarianism—of confusing the great merits of the leader of the Revolution and his undeniable gift of command with the individual whose sole preoccupation is to secure the unconditional support of his followers so as to establish a system of bossism. It was a fight without reason carried out by a small group, a fight that did not end the first of January or when Fidel became prime minister, but much later when the right wing of the 26th of July was destroyed. In this manner fell—for opposing the popular will—Urrutia, Miró Cardona, Ray, Hubert Matos, David Salvador, and many other traitors.[5] With the defeat of the right wing arose the need to structure a party, the United Party of the Socialist Revolution, expounder of Marxism-Leninism according to Cuban conditions. This party was supposed to have its cadres selected from the masses; the party was to be centralized and elastic at the same time. For all these we blindly trusted the authority that the Partido Socialista Popular won through many years of struggle, leaving aside almost all of our organizational criteria. In this manner a condition was created that allowed sectarianism to appear.

Compañero Aníbal Escalante was in charge of the organization process and a black period began. This period was—happily enough —short in our revolutionary development. Mistakes were made in the methods of direction; the party lost its essential qualities of close contact with the masses and democratic centralism. The spirit of sacrifice disappeared. Often people without experience and without merit were put in charge of important posts just because they accommodated themselves to the existing situation. The Integrated Revolutionary Organizations lost their function of ideological leadership and control of the productive apparatus and became an administrative institution. Under these conditions, the warning signals which should have come from the provinces, explaining the series

4 Caudillism: the dominance of a man who leans on his personal magnetism, on his charisma. It has the connotation of strong rule over the people. Eds.

5 Leaders of the anti-Batista struggle who became disaffected with the Revolution. Most of them had a social democratic outlook with variants in their attitude toward the United States. Eds.

of problems which existed there, would get lost because the ones who had to analyze the administrative functionaries' work were precisely the leaders of the nucleus fulfilling a double function of party and public administration.

The stage of mistaken ideas, of great errors and mechanical transplants, has ended fortunately. The old foundations on which this sectarian monster was built have been torn apart.

Faced with the problem, the national directorate of the party presided over by Fidel opted for returning to the masses, and this is why the system of consultation with all the work centers for the election of the exemplary workers from the masses was established. Those selected have the possibility of becoming a member of the party—a party intimately united with the masses.

As part of the changes in the party system, an educational program within the party was begun. The best workers, the men that demonstrate a revolutionary attitude with their daily labor, are rewarded. The rewards do not go, as in the past, to friends, to those with "clear thinking," or to the "bachelors of Marxism." [6]

A new epoch of party vigor has begun. A wide and bright path to constructing socialism unfolds before us. The party has the task of leading that construction.

The party of the future will be closely united with the masses and will get its ideas from the masses. The leadership will concretize those ideas. It will be a party that rigidly applies its discipline following the principles of democratic centralism. To improve its work the party will always discuss, criticize, and self-criticize. Its members will be the best people, and these cadres will have to fulfill its dynamic task of being in contact with the people and transmitting their experiences to their superiors. The cadres will have to be the first in their studies, in their work, in their revolutionary enthusiasm, in their sacrifice; at every moment they have to be the best, the purest, the most humane.

It should be remembered always that a Marxist is not a robot or a fanatic machine directed like a torpedo by a mechanism toward a determined object. Fidel discussed this problem in one of his speeches when he said,

Who has said that Marxism is the renunciation of human sentiments, or renunciation of fellowship, or renunciation of the love one has for a comrade, or the respect one has for another person? Who has said that

---

[6] "Bachelors of Marxism": this term arose from within the ranks of the guerrillas who fought against the Batista dictatorship. It refers to the old members of the Cuban Communist Party who did not participate in armed action, preaching revolution while not practicing it. Eds.

Marxism has no soul, no feelings? It was precisely love for man which conceived Marxism, it was love for man, for humanity, the desire to combat misery, injustice, and all the exploitation suffered by the proletariat which made Marxism rise from the mind of Karl Marx when precisely Marxism could arise, when precisely a real possibility and more than a real possibility could arise—that historical necessity of a social revolution of which Karl Marx was the interpreter. But what could this interpreter have been but for the wealth of human sentiment of men like him, like Engels, like Lenin?

This appraisal by Fidel is essential for the new party militant. It should always be remembered. Record it in your memory as the most efficient weapon against all deviations. The Marxist must be the best, the most complete of human beings but, always, above everything else, a human being: a party militant who lives and vibrates when in contact with the masses; a tireless worker who gives all to his people; a hard worker who gives his hours of rest, his personal tranquillity, his family, or his life to the Revolution; a man who is never alien to the warmth of human contact.

On the international scene our party has very important duties. We are the first socialist country in America, an example to be followed by other countries, a living experience to be perceived by all the other brother parties, an experience that shows all of its achievements and mistakes. In this form, it is more instructive and does not hold the aspiration to be raised only before those who have professed their faith in Marxism-Leninism, but before the popular masses of America.

The Second Declaration of Havana is the guide of the proletariat, the peasantry, and the revolutionary intellectuals of Latin America. Our own attitude will be a permanent guide. We should be worthy of the place we have, we should work every day thinking of our America. We should strengthen daily the foundations of our state, its economic organization, and its political development so as to improve our internal structure and convince the peoples of America of the practical possibility of initiating socialist development in the present state of the international correlation of forces.

All this without forgetting that our emotional capacity facing the aggressors' excesses and the suffering of the people cannot be confined to America, not even to America and the socialist countries. We must practice true proletarian internationalism, feel any aggression as one committed on us, any affront, any act that goes against the dignity of man, against his happiness anywhere in the world.

We, the militants of a new party, in a newly liberated region of the world, should always hold high the flag of human dignity which our Martí held—leader of many generations, present today in our reality, who once said, "Every true man ought to feel on his own cheek the blow given to the cheek of any man."

On the Budgetary System
of Finance

ЛЛЛЛЛЛЛЛЛЛЛЛЛЛЛЛЛЛЛЛЛЛЛЛЛЛЛЛ

Many statements have been made on the budgetary system of finance, but they are not sufficient. It is imperative to begin a thorough analysis of this subject so as to get a clear idea of its methodology and implications.

The budgetary system has been officially sanctioned in the *Law regulating the financing of state enterprises*, and it has been used in the internal workings of the Ministry of Industries. The history of this finance system is rather short in Cuba; it began to acquire some consistent use in 1960. But our purpose is not to analyze its development but the system as it exists today, with the understanding that its development has not ended.

Our interest is to make a comparison between the budgetary system of finance and the cost accounting system; within the latter we emphasize the aspect of financial autonomy, for this is the fundamental difference between the two systems. We shall also discuss their relation to material incentives, for they are the basis on which the system of cost accounting is established.

The explanation of differences is difficult because they are often obscure and subtle. Also, the budgetary system has not been developed thoroughly enough to enable us to explain it as clearly as cost accounting.

We shall begin with some quotations. The first comes from Marx's writings on economics, dating from the time of his intellectual production named that of *the young Marx*. At this time his language shows the influence of philosophic ideas that contributed to his development, whereas his economic ideas were less precise. Nevertheless, Marx was in the prime of his life. He had already embraced the cause of the poor and explained it philosophically, although without the rigorous scientific method of *Das Kapital*. At the time he thought in philosophic terms; therefore, he referred more concretely to man as a human individual and to the problems of his liberation as a social being without considering the inevitable crumbling of the social structures of his time opening the door to a transition, the dictatorship of the proletariat. In *Das Kapital*, Marx

Nuestra Industria: Revista Económica (Havana), February 1964, pp. 3–23.

arises as a scientific economist analyzing in detail the transitory character of social epochs and their connection with production relations; in this work he does not allow philosophical disquisitions to enter his analysis.

The influence of this monument of human intelligence is such that it has made us frequently forget the humanist character (in the best sense of the word) of his concerns. The mechanism of production relationships and their consequence, the class struggle, hides, to some extent, the objective fact that men are the actors in history. Now we are interested in man and that is the reason for this quotation. The fact that the quotation comes from the youthful period does not lessen its value as an expression of the philosopher's thought.

Communism is the positive abolition of private property, of human self-alienation, and thus the real appropriation of human nature through and for man. It is, therefore, the return of man himself as a social, that is, really human being, a complete and conscious return which assimilates all the wealth of previous development. Communism as a fully developed naturalism is humanism and as a fully developed humanism is naturalism. It is the definitive resolution of the antagonism between man and nature, and between man and man. It is the true solution of the conflict between existence and essence, between objectification and self-affirmation, between freedom and necessity, between individual and species. It is the solution of the riddle of history and is *conscious* of this solution.[1]

The word *consciousness* is emphasized because it is basic in the presentation of the problem. Marx thought about man's liberation and considered communism the solution to the contradictions that produced man's alienation, but he considered that solution a conscious act. It should be stated that communism cannot be seen merely as the product of class contradictions in a highly developed society, contradictions that will be resolved in a transitional period leading to the final goal. Man is the conscious actor of history. Without the *consciousness*, which encompasses his awareness as a social being, there can be no communism.

During the writing of *Das Kapital*, Marx did not abandon his militant attitude. In 1875, when the Gotha Congress was held to unite all labor organizations in Germany (Social Democratic Workers' Party and General Association of German Workers) and the program named after the Congress was drawn up, Marx answered with his *Critique of the Gotha Program*. This document, written in the midst

[1] C. Marx, *Manuscritos Económico-Filosóficos de 1844* (Mexico: Editorial Grijalbo), 1962, pp. 82–83.

of his main work and with a clear polemical orientation, is important because in it Marx deals in passing with the subject of the transitional period. In his analysis of point three of the Gotha Program, he discusses at length some of the most important matters of this period—a period he considered a result of the cracking of the developed capitalist system.

In this stage the use of money is not foreseen, but there is individual distribution of labor because,

What we have to deal with here is a communist society, not as it has developed on its own foundations but, on the contrary, as it emerges from capitalist society; which is thus in every respect, economically, morally, and intellectually, still stamped with the birthmarks of the old society from whose womb it emerges. Accordingly the individual producer receives back from society—after deductions have been made—exactly what he gives to it.[2]

Marx could only sense the development of a worldwide imperialist system; Lenin examined it and gave his diagnosis:

Uneven economic and political development is an absolute law of capitalism. Hence, the victory of socialism is possible first in several or even in one capitalist country taken singly. The victorious proletariat of that country, having expropriated the capitalists and organized its own socialist production, would stand up against the rest of the world, the capitalist world, attracting to its cause the oppressed classes of other countries, raising revolts in those countries against the capitalists, and if necessary coming out even with armed force against the exploiting classes and their states. The political form of society in which the proletariat is victorious by overthrowing the bourgeoisie will be a democratic republic, which will more and more centralize the forces of the proletariat of the given nation, or nations, in the struggle against the states that have not yet gone over to socialism. The abolition of classes is impossible without the dictatorship of the oppressed class, the proletariat. The free union of nations in socialism is impossible without a more or less prolonged and stubborn struggle of the socialist republics against the backward states.[3]

A few years later Stalin systematized the idea to the point of considering socialist revolution in the colonies possible:

The third contradiction is the contradiction between the handful of ruling "civilized" nations and the hundreds of millions of colonial and dependent peoples of the world. Imperialism is the most barefaced exploitation and the most inhuman oppression of hundreds of millions of people inhabiting vast colonies and dependent countries. The purpose of this exploitation and oppression is to squeeze out super-profits. But in exploiting these countries, imperialism is compelled to build railroads,

[2] C. Marx, *Crítica del Programa de Gotha.*
[3] Lenin, *Sobre la consigna de los Estados Unidos de Europa.*

factories, and mills there, to create industrial and commercial centers. The appearance of a class of proletarians, the emergence of a native intelligentsia, the awakening of national consciousness, the growth of the movement for emancipation—such are the inevitable results of this "policy." The growth of the revolutionary movement in all colonies and dependent countries without exception clearly testifies to this fact. This circumstance is of importance for the proletariat in that it radically undermines the position of capitalism by converting the colonies and dependent countries from reserves of imperialism into reserves of the proletarian revolution.[4]

The theses of Lenin were proved in practice by his achievement of power in Russia and the establishment of the U.S.S.R. We are faced with a new phenomenon: the advent of a socialist revolution in one country, economically backward, with 22 million square kilometers, a low population density, a greater degree of poverty as a result of war and, as though this were not enough, attacked by imperialist powers.

After a period of wartime communism, Lenin established the basis for the NEP and with it the foundations for the development of Soviet society up to our own day. Here it is necessary to point out the moment through which the Soviet Union was going, and for that purpose there is no one better than Lenin:

Thus, in 1918, I was of the opinion that in relation to the economic condition of the Soviet Republic at that time, state capitalism would be an advance. This sounds very queer and perhaps even absurd, for already at that time our republic was a socialist republic; at that time, every day, we hurriedly—perhaps too hurriedly—adopted various new economic measures. Nevertheless, I then held the view that compared with the economic position of the Soviet Republic as it was at that time, state capitalism was an advance, and I explained my idea simply by enumerating the main elements of the economic system of Russia. In my opinion these elements were the following: (1) patriarchial, that is, the most primitive form of agriculture; (2) small commodity production (this includes the majority of the peasants who trade in grain); (3) private capitalism; (4) state capitalism; and (5) socialism. All these economic elements were represented in Russia at that time. I set myself the task of explaining the relation in which these elements stood to one another and whether one of these nonsocialist elements, namely state capitalism, should not be appraised higher than socialism. I repeat: It seems very strange to everyone that a nonsocialist element should be appraised higher than, should be regarded as superior to, socialism in a republic which declares that it is a socialist republic. But it will become intelligible if you remember that we did not regard the economic system of Russia as something homogeneous and highly developed; we fully appreciated the fact that we had in Russia patriarchal agriculture, the

[4] J. Stalin, *Sobre los fundamentos del leninismo.*

most primitive form of agriculture, side by side with the socialist form. What role could state capitalism play under such circumstances?

Having emphasized the fact that already in 1918 we regarded state capitalism as a possible line of retreat, I shall now deal with the results of our New Economic Policy. I repeat: At that time it was still a very vague idea but, in 1921, after we had passed through the most important stage of the civil war, and passed through it victoriously, we encountered a great—I think it was the greatest—internal political crisis of Soviet Russia, which caused discontent among a considerable section, not only of the peasantry, but also of the workers. This was the first and I hope the last time in the history of Soviet Russia that large masses of peasants were hostile toward us, not consciously, but instinctively. What gave rise to this peculiar and for us, of course, very unpleasant situation? The fact that we had advanced too far in our economic offensive, the fact that we had not created an adequate base, that the masses sensed what we ourselves were not yet able consciously to formulate, that the direct transition to purely socialist forms, to purely socialist distribution, was beyond our strength, and that if we were not able to retreat, to confine ourselves to easier tasks, we were doomed.[5]

As can be seen, the economic and political situation of the Soviet Union made necessary the retreat that Lenin mentioned. This whole policy can be characterized as a tactic closely tied to the historical situation of the country and as a result one should not give it universal validity. We believe that two factors of considerable importance should be taken into account if one is to follow this policy in other countries:

(1) The characteristics of czarist Russia at the time of the revolution, including the development of technology at all levels, the special character of the people, the general conditions of the country, to which must be added the destruction created by a world war, the devastation made by the White hordes and the imperialist invaders.

(2) The general characteristics of the times with respect to the techniques for the direction and control of the economy.

Oskar Lange, in his article, "Present Economic Problems in Poland," states the following:

Bourgeois economic science has still another function. The bourgeoisie and the monopolies do not apportion large sums for the establishment of institutions of higher learning and institutes of scientific analysis in the field of economic sciences merely as an aid to apologize for the capitalist system. They expect something more from economists, that is, help in solving the numerous problems connected with economic policy. In the period of free enterprise capitalism, the tasks in this field were somewhat limited; they related solely to financial management, monetary policy, credit policy, tariff policy, transportation, and so forth.

[5] Lenin, *Problemas de la edificación del socialismo y del comunismo en la URSS.*

But under the conditions of monopolistic capitalism and especially under the conditions of increasing penetration of state capitalism into economic life, problems of this type grow. We can enumerate some: market analysis to facilitate the price policy of the large monopolies; methods used by a complex of centrally controlled industrial enterprises; reciprocal accounting regulations among these enterprises; the programmed interlocking of their activities, development, location, and subsequent policies of amortization and investment. From all these arise the issues related to the activity of the capitalist state today, such as the criteria of nationalized industries, their investment and location policies (in the energy field, for example), and to politico-economic intervention in the entire national economy. To all these problems a series of technical and economic procedures have been added, which can be partially used by us in the building of socialism in certain fields, such as market analysis, programming of enterprises forming a group, internal accounting procedures within each factory or group, amortization criteria, and others. Undoubtedly the workers of the future will use them during the transition of today's capitalist countries to socialism.

It must be noted that Cuba had not made its transition nor even begun its Revolution when this was written. Many of the technical advances described by Lange existed in Cuba; that is, the conditions of Cuban society at the time permitted centralized control over some enterprises whose headquarters were in Havana or New York. The Consolidated Petroleum Enterprise, created when the three imperialist refineries (Esso, Texaco, and Shell) were unified, maintained and, in some cases, perfected its system of controls. Today this enterprise is considered a model by the Ministry of Industries. In those enterprises in which neither the centralized tradition nor the practical conditions existed, the conditions were created on the basis of national experience. Such was the case with the Consolidated Flour Enterprise, which achieved first place among the enterprises under the jurisdiction of the Vice-Ministry of Light Industry.

Although practice during our first days of industrial management fully convinced us of the impossibility of following any other path, it would be idle to discuss now whether the organizational measures taken then would have produced similar or better results than the system of self-financing at the unit level. The important thing is that it was accomplished under very difficult conditions and that centralization permitted the liquidation—in the case of the shoe industry, for example—of a great number of inefficient *chinchales* [6] and allowed the transfer of 6,000 workers to more productive endeavors.

With this series of quotations, we have attempted to define elements basic to an understanding of the system:

[6] Small artisanlike workshops. Eds.

First: Communism is a goal of humanity that is reached consciously, so the eradication of old ideas from the people's consciousness through education is a factor of great importance. We cannot forget, of course, that without parallel advances in production one can never reach a communist society.

Second: The most advanced forms of technology must be borrowed, regardless of where they come from, as long as they can be adapted to the new society. The technology of petrochemicals of the imperialists can be used by the socialist camp without fear of becoming *contaminated* by bourgeois ideology. With reference to techniques of management and control of production, the same can be said. Without seeming too pretentious, we could paraphrase Marx's reference to Hegel's dialectics and say that these capitalist techniques can be turned right side up.

An analysis of accounting techniques habitually used in the socialist countries shows us that their techniques and ours are separated by a distance equivalent to the difference existing in the capitalist camp between competitive and monopolistic capitalism. After all, earlier techniques served as the foundation for the development of both systems, *turned right side up*, but from then on their paths separated because socialism has its own production relationships and requirements.

We can say that, technically, the predecessor of the budgetary system of finance was the imperialist monopoly located in Cuba, which had undergone the variations inherent in the process of developing the techniques of management and control—a process that extends from the dawn of the monopolistic system to our times, in which it reaches its highest levels. When the monopolists withdrew, they took with them their top- and intermediate-level men. At the same time our immature concept of revolution led us to tear down a number of established procedures merely because they were capitalist. This is why our system has not attained the high degree of effectiveness that the Cuban subsidiaries of monopolies had in the management and control of production. We are moving in that direction, leaving behind dead leaves from the past.

General Differences Between Cost Accounting and the Budgetary System of Finance

There are differences of varying degrees between the two systems. We shall attempt to divide them into two large groups and explain each concisely. There is a methodological difference—practical, we should say—and differences of a more profound character, whose nature might cause analysis to seem futile if one does not proceed with great caution.

It should be understood that what we seek with both systems is a more efficient way of reaching communism; there is no dispute about principle. Cost accounting has demonstrated its practical efficiency. We believe that our system's plan of action, if properly developed, could increase the effectiveness of the economy of the socialist state while deepening the consciousness of the people and uniting the world socialist system on the basis of concerted action.

The most immediate difference arises when we speak about the enterprise. To us an enterprise is a conglomerate of factories or units that have a similar technological basis, a common destination for their production, or in some cases the same limited geographic location. Cost accounting defines an enterprise as a production unit with its own juridical personality. A sugar mill is an enterprise according to that method, whereas for us all the sugar mills and other units related to sugar production constitute the Consolidated Sugar Enterprise. Recently in the U.S.S.R. there have been some attempts at this type of system adapted to the particular conditions of that brother country. (See "Los Combinados de Empresas Soviéticas, La nueva forma de administración de las industrias," I. Ivonin, *Nuestra Industria: Revista Económica*, no. 4.)

Another difference is the way in which money is used. In our system it operates only as arithmetic money, as a price reflection of the enterprise's activity. The central organizations analyze the price index in order to control the enterprise's operation. In cost accounting it is not only this, but also a means of payment that acts as an indirect instrument of control, for these funds allow the unit to operate and its relations to the banking system are similar to those of a private producer in contact with capitalist banks to which it must explain its plan exhaustively and demonstrate its solvency. Naturally, in this case what operates is not an arbitrary decision but compliance with a plan and maintenance of relations among state organizations.

In accordance with our method of using money, our enterprises have no funds of their own. Separate bank accounts exist for the purpose of withdrawals and deposits; the enterprise can withdraw funds, according to the plan, from the general expense account and from a special account to pay salaries but when the enterprise deposits money it automatically becomes state property.

The enterprises of the majority of our brother countries have their own funds in the banks which they strengthen with credits on which they pay interest. It must never be forgotten that these funds of *their own*, as well as the credits, belong to society and their movement expresses the enterprise's financial position.

As for work methods, cost accounting enterprises use overtime work as well as piecework or work paid by the hour (or by the job). We are trying to make all our factories institute overtime work, with limited rewards for overfulfillment of quotas. This will be discussed later.

In the fully developed cost accounting system there is a rigorous method of hiring. There are monetary penalties for nonfulfillment of quotas based on a legal structure established after years of experience. In our country such a structure does not exist, even for self-managed organizations like INRA; [7] and it becomes particularly difficult to establish the system because of the coexistence of two systems that are so dissimilar. Now we have the Arbitration Commission, which lacks executive powers, but its importance is growing gradually and it could become the basis of a new juridical structure in the future. Internally, among organizations subject to the budgetary system of financing, decision making is easy because administrative measures are taken if the control accounts are well operated and up to date (this already occurs in most enterprises under this Ministry).

Starting from the basis that in both systems the state's general plan is the highest authority, adherence to which is compulsory, one can synthesize operating analogies and differences by stating that self-management is based on a complete centralized control and a more marked decentralization. Indirect control is exercised through "the ruble," by the bank, and the monetary result of the operation serves as a measure of rewards. Material interest is the great lever that moves the workers individually and collectively.

The budgetary system of financing is based on the centralized control of the enterprise's activity; its plan and economic operation are controlled by central organizations directly. It has no funds of its own and receives no bank credits. It uses on an individual basis material incentives, that is, monetary rewards and punishments, and at the opportune time it will use collective ones; but direct material incentives are limited by the method of payment of the salaries.

More Subtle Contradictions:
Material Incentives versus Consciousness

Now we enter the realm of more subtle contradictions, which should be better explained. The matter of material incentives versus

[7] National Institute of Agrarian Reform. Eds.

moral incentives has given origin to many discussions among those interested in the subject. It is necessary to make one thing clear: *We do not negate the objective need for material incentives*, but we are reluctant to use them as a fundamental element. We believe that in economics such a lever becomes an end in itself and then begins to impose its own force on the relationships among men. We should not forget that material incentives come from capitalism and are destined to die under socialism.

How are we going to make them die?

Little by little, through gradual increase in consumer goods for the people, which will make this type of incentive unnecessary—we are told. We see in this answer a very rigid mechanism. Consumer goods, that is the watchword and the great molder, in the end, of consciousness, according to the defenders of the other system. We believe that direct material incentives and consciousness are contradictory terms.

This is one of the points at which our disagreement reaches concrete dimensions. It is no longer a matter of variations. To the defenders of financial self-management direct material incentives—projected into the future and accompanying the society in the diverse stages of building communism—do not contradict the "development" of consciousness. For us, they do. That is why we fight against their predominance; they mean a delay in the development of socialist morality.

Yes, material incentives are opposed to the development of consciousness, but they are efficient for obtaining production achievements. Should we say that if one pays greater attention to the development of consciousness this will retard production? In comparative terms, it is possible in a given situation, even though no one has made the pertinent calculations. We affirm that in a relatively short time the development of consciousness does more for production development than material incentives and we base this on the general projection of development necessary to society before entering communism—which presupposes that labor ceases to be a painful necessity and becomes a pleasant imperative. This statement, loaded with subjectivism, requires the sanction of experience and this we are trying to do. If in the course of that experience it is demonstrated that consciousness is a dangerous brake to the development of productive forces, we shall have to stop and return to well-traveled roads. Up to now this has not occurred and the method with the improvement practice provides is acquiring even more consistency and demonstrating its inner coherence.

What, then, is the correct handling of material incentives? We believe that their existence cannot be forgotten, whether as a collective expression of the masses' strivings or as an individual presence; they are a reflection of the workers' mental habits from the old society.

We do not have a clearly defined idea as to how to use material incentives collectively due to insufficiencies in the planning apparatus which prevent us from having absolute faith in the system and from having organized a structure until now that would permit us to steer clear of difficulties. We see the greatest danger in the antagonism created between the state administration and production organizations. This antagonism has been analyzed by the Soviet economist Liberman, who concludes that the methods of collective incentives should be changed, abandoning the old formula of rewards based on the fulfillment of quotas and moving to more advanced ones.

Even if we disagree with Lieberman on the matter of how much emphasis should be given to material incentives (as a lever), we believe that his concern with the aberrations that the concept "fulfillment of the quota" has suffered is quite correct. The relations between enterprises and central organizations acquire contradictory forms and the methods used by the enterprises to obtain benefits sometimes have taken on characteristics that have nothing to do with socialist morality.

We believe that in a certain way the possibilities of development offered by the new production relationship for promoting the evolution of man in the direction of "the kingdom of freedom" are being wasted. We gave a detailed account of precisely this in our definition of the essential agreements of the system of interrelationships that exist between education and the development of production. One can embark on creating the new consciousness because there are new production relationships and, although in a general historical sense consciousness is a product of production relationships, the characteristics of the present period must be considered because there is a fundamental contradiction (on a worldwide level) between imperialism and socialism. Socialist ideas have influenced the consciousness of the whole world; that is why consciousness can develop and advance further than the particular stage of productive forces in a given country.

In the U.S.S.R. of the early days, the regime was characterized as a socialist state in spite of the existence of productive relationships of a much more backward type. Under capitalism there are remainders of feudalism, but capitalism is the system that characterizes the country after it has dominated the main aspects of the economy. In Cuba, the development of contradictions between the two world systems permitted the establishment of a socialist revolution. A socialist character was acquired through a conscious act, thanks to the knowledge acquired by the leaders, the deepening of the masses' consciousness, and the correlation of forces in the world.

If all this is possible, why not think of the role of education as a pertinent aid to the socialist state in its task of eliminating the defects of a society that has died and carries its old production relationships to the grave? Lenin states,

Infinitely stereotyped, for instance, is the argument they learned by rote during the development of Western European social democracy, namely, that we are not yet ripe for socialism, that as certain "learned" gentlemen among them put it, the objective economic conditions for socialism do not exist in our country. It does not occur to any of them to ask: But what about a nation that found itself in a revolutionary situation such as that created during the first imperialist war? Might it not, influenced by the hopelessness of its situation, fling itself into a struggle that would offer it at least some chance of securing conditions for the further development of civilization that were somewhat unusual? "The development of the productive forces of Russia has not attained the level that makes socialism possible." All the heroes of the Second International, including, of course, Sukhanov, beat the drums about this proposition. They keep harping on this incontrovertible proposition in a thousand different keys, and think that it is the decisive criterion of our revolution.

But what if the situation, which drew Russia into the imperialist world war which involved every more or less influential Western European country and made her a witness to the eve of the revolutions maturing or already begun in the East, gave rise to circumstances that put Russia and her development in a position which enabled us to achieve precisely that combination of a "peasant war" which the working class movement suggested in 1856 by no less a Marxist than Marx himself as a possible prospect for Prussia?

What if the complete hopelessness of the situation, by stimulating the efforts of the workers and peasants tenfold, offered us the opportunity to create the main requisites of civilization in a different way from that of the Western European countries? Has that altered the basic relations between the basic classes of all the countries that are being or have been drawn into the general course of world history? If a definite level of culture is required for the building of socialism (although no one can say just what that definite "level of culture" is, for it differs in every Western European country), why can we not begin by first achieving the prerequisites for that definite level of culture in a revolutionary way, and then with the aid of the workers' and peasants' government and the soviet system proceed to overtake the other nations? [8]

[8] Lenin, *Problemas de la edificación del socialismo y del comunismo en la URSS.*

With regard to material incentives on an individual basis, we recognize it (even though we fight against it and try to accelerate its elimination through education) and we apply it to overtime work norms and to the subsequent punishment in wages when there is no compliance with them.

The subtle difference between the two systems rests on the arguments for paying salaries according to work quotas. The production quota is the average amount of labor required to make a product in a certain amount of time and in specific conditions of equipment utilization. It is the delivery of a work quota made to society by one of its members; it is the fulfillment of a social duty. If the quotas are overfulfilled there is a greater benefit to society, and it can be assumed that the worker who fulfills his duty better deserves more material rewards. We accept this conception as a necessary evil in a transitional period. But we do not accept that the principle of *from each according to his capacity, to each according to his work* be interpreted as the complete payment, bonus pay, for the overfulfillment of a given quota (these are cases in which the pay exceeds the percentage of fulfillment in order to provide extraordinary incentives for industrial productivity). Marx explains very clearly in his *Critique of the Gotha Program* that a considerable part of the worker's pay goes to items that are far removed from his immediate needs:

Let us take first of all the words "proceeds of labor" in the sense of the product of labor; then, the cooperative proceeds of labor are to social product. From this is to be deducted: First, cover for replacement of the means of production used up. Second, additional portion for expansion of production. Third, reserve or insurance fund to provide against misadventures, disturbances through natural events, and so forth. These deductions from the "undiminished proceeds of labor" are an economic necessity and their magnitude is to be determined by available means and forces, and partly by calculation of probabilities, but they are in no way calculable by equity. There remains the other part of the total product, destined to serve as means of consumption. Before this is divided among the individuals, there has to be deducted from it: First, the general costs of administration not belonging to production. This part will, from the outset, be very considerably restricted in comparison with present-day society and it diminishes in proportion as the new society develops. Second, that which is destined for the communal satisfaction of needs, such as schools, health services, and so forth. From the outset this part is considerably increased in comparison with present-day society and it increases in proportion as the new society develops. Third, funds for those unable to work, in short, what is included under so-called official poor relief today. Only now we come to the "distribution" which the program, under Lassallean influence, alone has in view in its narrow fashion, namely that part of the means of consumption which is divided among the individual producers of the cooperative society. The "undiminished proceeds of labor" have already quietly become converted into the "diminished" proceeds, although what the producer is deprived of in his capacity as a private individual benefits him directly or indirectly in his capacity as a member of society. Just as the phrase "undiminished proceeds of labor" has disappeared, so now does the phrase "proceeds of labor" disappear.

All this shows us that the amount of funds in reserve depends on a series of politico-economic or politico-administrative decisions. Because all existing wealth in reserve is the proceeds of unpaid labor, we have to infer that decisions on the volume of the funds analyzed by Marx imply changes in payments. This is a variation in the volume of directly unpaid labor. To all this has to be added the fact that there does not exist—if it exists, it is not known—a mathematical method for determining what is *just* in the rewards for overfulfillment (or for the basic salary), and as a result what is just has to be based essentially on the new social relations and on the legal structure that sanctions the form of distribution of part of the individual worker's labor by the collectivity.

Our quota system has the merit of establishing compulsory professional improvement in order to be promoted from one position to another. In time this will produce a considerable increase in our technological level.

Nonfulfillment of a quota means nonfulfillment of a social duty: society punishes the transgressor with a reduction of his wage. The work quota is not a mere guidepost which establishes a possible measurement of convention for calculating amounts of work; it expresses a moral obligation on the part of the worker, *it is his social duty*. Here is where administrative and ideological control have to be combined. The great role of the party in every production unit is to be its driving force; it must utilize every type of example set by its militants so that productive work, training, and participation in the economic affairs of each production unit will become an integral part of the workers' lives and an irreplaceable habit.

On the Law of Value

A profound difference (at least in the strict meaning of the terms) exists between the conception of the proponents of cost accounting of the law of value and the possibility of its conscious use and our conception. The *Manual of Political Economy* [9] states,

[9] This is a handbook of political economy published by the educational section of Cuba's communist party and like most handbooks of this type has no author. Eds.

Under capitalism, the law of value functions as a blind and spontaneous force which rules over men; in the socialist economy there is an awareness of the law of value—the state keeps it in mind and *uses* it in the practical control of the planned economy. A knowledge of how the law of value operates and its *intelligent utilization* inevitably aid the planners of the economy to channel production along rational lines, systematically improve work methods, and make use of all resources in order to produce more and better.

The italicized words indicate the spirit of the quoted paragraphs. The law of value would function as a blind but known force, and as such usable by man.

But this law has some characteristics. First, it is conditioned by the existence of a mercantile society. Second, its results are not susceptible to a priori measurement and must be reflected in the market where there is an interchange between producers and consumers. Third, it is coherent as a whole with respect to world markets, and changes and distortions in some branches of production are reflected in the total result. Fourth, given its character as an economic law, it essentially functions as a tendency and, in periods of transition, its tendency logically should be to disappear.

A few paragraphs later, the *Manual* states,

The socialist state uses the law of value through the financial and credit system to control production and distribution of the social product. The control of the law of value and its use in accordance with a plan represents an enormous advantage of socialism over capitalism. Thanks to control over the law of value, its operation in the socialist economy does not involve the waste of social labor that is inseparable from the anarchy of production in capitalism. The law of value and the categories related to it—money, prices, trade, credits, finances—are successfully utilized by the U.S.S.R. and countries with popular democracies in the interest of building socialism and communism, in the process of planned direction of the national economy.

This can only be considered exact with regard to the total magnitude of value produced for the population's direct use and the respective funds available for their acquisition—something any capitalist finance minister could do with relatively stable finances. Within this framework there is room for every partial distortion of the law. Further on it is pointed out that,

Mercantile production, the law of value, and money will disappear only when the higher stage of communism is reached. But to create the conditions that would make possible the elimination of production for profit and the circulation of money in the higher stage of communism, it is necessary to *develop* and use the law of value and monetary-commercial relations during the construction period of a communist society.

Why *develop?* We understand that for a certain time the capitalist elements will be retained and that this period cannot be ascertained beforehand, but the characteristics of the transitional period are those of a society that liquidates its old ties in order to rapidly enter a new phase. The *tendency* should be, in our opinion, to liquidate as vigorously as possible the old categories—including the market, money, and material incentives—or rather, the conditions that provoke the existence of the categories. Otherwise, we would be led to the assumption that the task of building socialism in a backward society is something like an historical accident and that its leaders in order to correct the *error* should dedicate themselves to the consolidation of all categories inherent in the intermediate society. Income distribution in accordance with work and the tendency to eliminate man's exploitation of man as fundamentals of the new society would remain. This seems insufficient in itself as a factor in the gigantic development of change of consciousness necessary in order to be able to face transition. The change in consciousness must occur by the multifaceted action of all the new relationships, education and socialist morality, replacing the individualistic concepts of direct material incentives that hinder man's development as a social being.

To summarize our differences: We believe that the law of value partially exists due to the remains of the mercantile society, which is also reflected in the type of exchange that takes place between the government supplier and the consumer. We believe that particularly in a society with highly developed foreign trade, like ours, the law of value on an international scale must be recognized as a fact that directs commercial transactions even within the socialist bloc. We have recognized the need for this trade to assume a higher form in the countries of the new society, avoiding the widening of the gap that exists between the developed and the less developed countries. It should be stated that it is necessary to find trade mechanisms that permit the financing of industrial investments in the developing countries, even if it disrupts the existing price systems in the capitalist world market. This will permit the more even advancement of the entire socialist camp, with the natural consequence of smoothing rough spots and creating cohesion in the spirit of proletarian internationalism (the recent agreement between Cuba and the U.S.S.R. is a step in this direction). We deny the possibility of using consciously the law of value, and base this opinion on the nonexistence of a free market which automatically expresses the contradiction between producers and consumers. We deny the existence of the category *merchandise* in the relations among state enterprises and we consider all such establishments to be part of the single great enterprise that is the state (although, in practice, this is not the case in our country). The law of value and planning are two terms related by a contradiction and its resolution. We can say, then, that centralized planning is the way of life in a socialist society—planning defines it and is the point at which man's consciousness achieves at last a synthesis and directs the economy toward its goal: the complete liberation of man within the framework of a communist society.

On the Fixing of Prices

On the theory of the fixing of prices there are also great differences. In self-management, prices are established "in accordance with the law of value," but there is no explanation (so far as we know) as to which expression of the law of value is considered. One recognizes socially necessary work in the production of a specific item but no attention has been paid to the fact that socially necessary work is an economic-historic concept and that, as such, it is changeable on the local (or national) level as well as internationally. The continuous advances in technology, the consequence of competition in the capitalist world, decreases the cost of necessary work and, therefore, the value of the product. A closed society can ignore the changes for a given time, but it will always have to return to these international relationships in order to establish their value. If a given society ignores these changes for a long time without developing new and exact formulas to replace the old ones, it will create interconnections that shape its own value scheme, congruent within itself but contradictory to the tendencies of highly developed technology (the case of steel and plastics, for example). This can cause relative backwardness of some importance and, at any rate, distortions of the law of value on an international level, which will not allow the comparison of economies.

The "circulation tax" is an accounting fiction through which certain income levels of enterprises are maintained by making products more expensive for the consumer in such a manner that supply is leveled with the amount of solvent demand. We believe that it is an imposition of the system but not an absolute necessity, and we work on formulas that will take these aspects into consideration.

A global stabilization of the mercantile fund and solvent demand is necessary. The Ministry of Internal Commerce would be in charge of leveling the people's purchasing power and the prices of the goods offered, always considering that a whole series of items that are basic necessities for a man's life should be offered at low prices, even though in the case of other less important ones high prices are charged with a manifest ignorance of the law of value in each concrete case.

Now a serious problem arises. What criteria would be employed by the economy to set real prices in its analysis of production relationships? It could be the analysis of necessary work in Cuban terms. This would create immediate distortions and the loss of vision of world problems because of the necessary automatic interrelationships that would be created. The world price, however, could be used; this would cause a loss of vision with respect to national problems, for our national production level is not satisfactory by world standards.

We propose, as a first approach to the problem, the creation of low price indices based on the following:

All imported raw materials will have a fixed, stable price based on an average international market price plus a few points for transportation costs and the facilities of the Ministry of Foreign Trade. All Cuban raw materials would have the price of their real production cost in monetary terms. To each we would add the estimated labor costs plus depreciation of the basic means for producing them and that would be the price of the products supplied to enterprises and to the Ministry of Internal Trade. But prices would constantly be affected by the indices that reflect the price of that merchandise on the world market plus the costs of transportation and of the Ministry of Foreign Trade. The enterprises functioning under the system of budgetary financing would do so on the basis of estimated costs and would not make profits. All profits would be made by the Ministry of Internal Trade. (Naturally, this refers to that part of the social product that is created as goods, and it is essential as a consumption base.) The indices will continuously tell us (the central organization and the enterprise) what our real assets are and would prevent our making mistaken decisions. The population would not suffer as a result of all these changes, for the prices of the merchandise they purchase are fixed independently, bearing in mind demand and the vital need for each product.

For example, in order to calculate the amount of an investment we would calculate raw materials and equipment directly imported, building and equipment installation expenses, and the cost of the planned wages, keeping an eye on real contingencies and a certain margin for the cost of the construction equipment. This could give us, after investments were made, three figures: first, the real cost of the operation in money; second, what the work should cost according to our plans; third, what it should cost in terms of world production. The difference between the first and the second would be charged to the inefficiency of the construction equipment. The difference between the second and the third would be the index of our lag in a given sector.

This permits us to make important decisions on the alternate use of materials such as cement, iron, plastics; roofs made of cement, aluminum, or zinc; iron, lead, or copper piping; wood, iron or aluminum windows, and so forth.

All decisions can disregard the mathematical optimum when there are political reasons, reasons of foreign trade, and so forth, but we would always have before us a reflection of the real world reacting to our work. Prices will never be separated from the world image, which fluctuates in certain years in accordance with technological advances and in which the socialist market and the international division of labor will have ever greater preeminence once a world socialist price system has been achieved that is more logical than the one used now.

We could go on discussing this very interesting subject, but it is preferable to outline a few primary ideas and explain that all this needs more elaboration.

Collective Rewards

On collective rewards for the administration of the enterprise, we want to refer first of all to the experiments recorded by Fikriat Tabeiev:

What shall be the fundamental and decisive index to ascertain the work of the enterprises? Economic investigations have led to several proposals.

Some economists propose as the main index the standard of accumulation; others, the cost of labor, and so forth. The Soviet press has carried the broad discussions provoked by an article by Professor Lieberman, in which he proposes as the fundamental exponent of the work of the enterprise the degree of profitability, income level, and standard of accumulation. We believe that in judging the functioning of an enterprise it is convenient to bear in mind the contribution made by the enterprise's personnel to the particular product. This, which in the final analysis does not contradict the struggle for sufficiently high income, permits better concentration of the efforts made by the enterprise's personnel in improving the productive process. The social organizations of Tartary have proposed the utilization of a standard value for the manufacturing process of each part of a product. To demonstrate the possibility of putting this proposal into practice, an economic experiment has been made.

In 1962, the standards of value of the manufacturing process for production at all branches of Tartary's industry were designed and approved. That year constituted a transition period during which the index was used parallel to the planning of over-all production. The index based on the standard of value of the manufacturing process expresses technically justified expenses in which are included the salaries and bonuses received by the workers, plus factory expenses and those of the entire fabrication of each item.

It is necessary to point out that the application of this index has nothing to do with the "infernal" accounting systems used in capitalist countries. We consistently follow a rational organization of the work processes and do not intensify work on a disproportionate scale. All work aimed at establishing work standards is done with direct participation of the enterprise's personnel and social organizations, particularly labor unions.

The standard of value of the manufacturing process, unlike the index of over-all production, does not include most material expenses—past labor of other enterprises—nor does it include profit, that is, those components of the value of over-all mercantile production which diminish the quality of the true volume of the enterprise's production. As a closer reflection of the work invested in the production of each item, the index that expresses the standard of value of the manufacturing process permits better determination of the operations relating to increased yield, lowered costs, and profit from the particular product. This index is also the most convenient from the standpoint of planning within the factory and for the organization of cost accounting within the enterprise. Moreover, it permits comparison of the productivity of labor in related enterprises.[10]

We believe that this Soviet investigation is worth studying and coincides, in some respects, with our thesis.

Summary of Ideas on the Budgetary System of Finance

To summarize our ideas on the budgetary system of finance, we should begin by explaining that it is a total concept, that is, its objective operation would be exercised when it entered into all aspects of the economy in a single whole that, starting with political decisions and going through the central planning board (JUCEPLAN), would reach the enterprises and units through ministerial channels. There it would merge with the population. Later it would return to the policy-making organization, creating a gigantic

[10] "Investigación económica y dirección de la economía," *Revista Internacional*, no. 11, 1963.

even circle within which certain rates could change more or less automatically because production controls would permit it. The ministries would have the specific responsibility of designing and controlling the plans. This would also be done by enterprises and units in accordance with decision scales that could be more or less flexible depending on the organizational thoroughness achieved, the type of production, or the particular time.

JUCEPLAN would be responsible for the over-all central controls of the economy and would be assisted in its operation by the Ministry of Finance, in all financial controls, and by the Ministry of Labor, in the planning of the labor force.

As all these do not now occur in this fashion, we shall describe our present situation, with all its limitations, small triumphs, its defects and defeats, some of them justified or justifiable, some the product of our inexperience or the result of our gross failings.

JUCEPLAN gives only the general outlines of the plan and the control figures of basic products over which it keeps a more or less strict control. The central organizations, including the Ministry of Industries, control the so-called centralized products as well as others by means of an agreement among enterprises. Once the plan is established and made compatible, agreements are signed—sometimes this is done beforehand—and work begins.

The central office of the Ministry is in charge of assuring the fulfillment of agreements at the enterprise level. The enterprise is responsible for doing the same at the unit level. It is essential that the accounting system be consolidated at the enterprise and the ministry levels. The basic means and the inventories should be centrally controlled so that unused resources can be moved easily from one unit to another. The Ministry also has the authority to move the basic means from one enterprise to another. The funds do not have a mercantile character; they are only entered on the books as debits or credits. Part of production is directly delivered to the population through the Ministry of Internal Trade and part to the units producing other items for which ours are intermediate products.

Our main idea is that in this entire process the product acquires value because of the labor that goes into it. However, there is no need for mercantile relations among the enterprises. The delivery or purchasing agreements, or the document which must be requested at a particular moment, simply mean that one has fulfilled the duty to produce and deliver a given product. Acceptance of a product by an enterprise would mean (in somewhat idealistic terms for the present, one must recognize) acceptance of the quality of the product. The product becomes merchandise when there is a legal change in ownership, when it is consumed by an individual.

The means of production for other enterprises do not constitute merchandise, but they must be valued in accordance with the indices suggested earlier. A comparison must be made with the amount of work necessary to fulfill a consumption quota in order to assign a price to the basic means of raw material involved.

Quality, quantity, and variety should be achieved following quarterly plans. The unit, in accordance with its work quotas, would pay the workers their wages directly. One aspect remains to be discussed: the method of rewarding the workers of a productive unit for their particularly brilliant performance, or a performance above the average of the economy as a whole—and whether factories which have failed to fullfill their duties should be punished or not.

The Budgetary System of Finance Today

What is happening today? One of the things happening is that the factory never has the supplies in the manner or at the time required, so it does not fulfill its production plans. But worse yet, at times it receives raw materials for some other technological process. This produces changes in the factory and its technology. Consequently, production costs, the amount of manpower, and investments are also subject to change. Sometimes they undo the entire plan, forcing frequent changes.

Today, at the ministerial level, we have had to be merely passive witnesses or mere recorders of all these anomalies. Now we are entering a phase in which we shall be able to act on certain aspects of the plan, to demand at least that any distortion of the plan be foreseen in a mathematic or accounting manner and thus be controlled. We lack the necessary automatic mechanisms to ensure that all controls be made rapidly and indices be analyzed. We have neither the sufficient analytical capacity nor the sufficient capacity to deliver indices or correct figures for interpretation.

The enterprises are connected to their factories directly, sometimes by telephone or telegraph or through a provincial delegate. In other cases they are connected through the Ministry's delegations, who exercise control. In the municipalities or economico-political places of this sort, the so-called CILOS—which are nothing but a meeting of unit administrators—function close to each other. They are responsible for analyzing unit problems and deciding about minor mutual assistance involving considerable bureaucratic red tape if done through other channels. In some cases they can lend basic means of production, but consultation with the particular enterprise is always necessary before transfers can be made.

At the beginning of each month, production statistics arrive at the Ministry, where they are analyzed at even the highest levels, and fundamental measures are taken to correct defects. In the following days, other more elaborate statistics are received which permit the taking of concrete measures to solve any problem.

What are the basic weaknesses of the system? In the first place, immaturity must be mentioned. Second, there is a scarcity of cadres who are really qualified at all levels. Third, there is the lack of complete dissemination of the whole system and its mechanisms so that the people can understand it better. We can also cite the lack of a central planning agency that functions uniformly and with an absolute hierarchy—this could facilitate work. The shortcomings in supply and transportation, which at one time force us to accumulate products and at another impede production, should be cited. We have shortcomings in our quality control and our relations with distribution organizations, particularly with the Ministry of Internal Trade. (These relationships should be close, harmonious, and well defined.) There are also shortcomings in our relationships with supply organizations, mainly the Ministry of Foreign Trade and INRA. It is still difficult to distinguish which shortcomings are the product of weaknesses inherent in the system and which are due substantially to our present degree of organization.

Neither the factory nor the enterprise at this time has any material incentives of a collective nature. This is not due to a central idea in the entire scheme but to our not having attained sufficient organizational capacity at this moment to permit us to do so on some basis other than the simple fulfillment or overfulfillment of the enterprise's main plans, for reasons already mentioned.

A bureaucratic tendency is attributed to the system, and one of the points on which one must insist constantly has to do with rationalization of the entire administrative machinery in order to reduce bureaucracy to a minimum. Well then, from the standpoint of objective analysis, it is evident that the less bureaucracy exists, the more centralized the process of recording information and the control of the enterprise and unit becomes. So if each enterprise could centralize all its administrative functions, its bureaucracy could be reduced in each unit to a small managerial nucleus and a collector of information to be sent to the central organization.

At this time that is impossible, but we have to create units of optimum size. This is something that the system facilitates if work quotas are established calling for a single type of salary, so as to destroy the narrow ideas about the enterprise as a center of individual action and move more in the direction of society as a whole.

General Advantages of the Budgetary System of Finance

We believe that this system has the following advantages:

First, in tending toward centralization it tends toward a more rational utilization of national funds.

Second, it tends toward a greater rationalization of the entire administrative machinery of the state.

Third, this same tendency toward centralization necessitates the creation of larger units within adequate limits, saving manpower and increasing the productivity of workers.

Fourth, integrated into one quota system it makes one great state enterprise of the Ministry, to mention one example, and of all ministries, if possible. It will become one great state enterprise within which one can move from one part to another and advance within the different branches or go elsewhere without salary problems. There will simply be one national wage scale.

Fifth, counting on budgeted building organizations, there can be much simplification of investment control. The contracting investor will look after investments, and the Ministry of Finance will do the financial supervision.

It is important to point out that the general idea of cooperation is instilled in the worker, the idea of belonging to a large whole which is the people of the country. In this manner one promotes the development of the worker's awareness of his social duty.

The following quotation from Marx is interesting because, stripped of the words that presuppose the capitalist system, it exposes the process of the formation of work traditions, and on that account can serve us as antecedent for the construction of socialism:

It is not enough that the conditions of labor are concentrated in a mass, in the shape of capital, at the one pole of society, whereas at the other are grouped masses of men who have nothing to sell but their labor-power. Neither is it enough that they are compelled to sell it voluntarily. The advance of capitalist production develops a working class, which by education, tradition, habit, looks on the conditions of that mode of production as self-evident laws of nature. The organization of the capitalist process of production, once fully developed, breaks down all resistance. The constant generation of a relative surplus population keeps the law of supply and demand of labor, and therefore keeps wages, in a rut that corresponds to the wants of capital. The dull compulsion of economic relations completes the subjection of the laborer to the capitalist. Direct force, outside economic conditions, is of course still used, but only exceptionally. In the ordinary run of things, the laborer can be left to the "natural laws of production," to his dependence on capital, a dependence springing from, and guaranteed in perpetuity by, the conditions of production themselves.[11]

The productive forces are developing; the relations of production are changing; everything awaits the direct action of the worker's state over the people's consciousness.

With reference to material incentive, what we want to achieve with the budgetary system of finance is to avoid making the lever into something that forces the individual, as an individual, or the collectivity to fight desperately with one another in order to ensure certain conditions of production or distribution which will place a portion of the population in a privileged position. We must make social duty the fundamental point on which the whole work effort is based, but we must watch the worker's labor with an awareness of his weaknesses. We must reward or punish by applying material incentives or restraints of an individual or collective type according to whether the worker or the production unit is able to do its social duty. Moreover, compulsory training for promotion, when we can practice it on a national scale, creates a general tendency to study on the part of the entire working mass of the nation. This training is not limited by any particular local situation, for the work area is the entire country, and consequently this provokes a tendency toward a very considerable technical perfection.

We must also consider that through a policy of subsidies student workers trained for other posts can easily withdraw from work. In this manner rough jobs will be eliminated in certain sectors and more productive factories will be created. That is more in accord with the central idea of entering communism—a society with large-scale production and the satisfaction of man's basic needs.

The educational role the party must play to transform the work center into the collective exponent of the workers' aspirations and concerns should be stressed. The work center must become the place where their desire to serve society is molded.

The work center, one could think, will be the basis of the political nucleus of the future society, whose suggestions, when transferred to more complex political organizations, will allow the party and the government to make the essential decisions for the economy and the cultural life of the individual.

[11] C. Marx, *El Capital*, vol. 1.

The Cuban Economy:
Its Past and Its Present Importance

(To write for a journal of this type is a most difficult task for a revolutionary politician who wishes to defend the views that have guided his actions and to make a cool analysis of the causes of the present state of the world which have a bearing on the situation in his own country. It is difficult to do this without making statements that may shock, given the extreme differences of opinion which separate us. However, I shall try. I apologize in advance if I do not make myself clear, but I do not apologize for what I intend to say.)

The Paris Peace Treaty of 1898 and the Platt Amendment of 1901 were the signs under which our new republic was born. In the first, the settlement of accounts after the war between two powers led to the withdrawal of Spain and the intervention of the United States. On the island, which had suffered years of cruel struggle, the Cubans were only observers; they had no part in the negotiations. The second, the Platt Amendment, established the right of the United States to intervene in Cuba whenever her interests demanded it.

In May 1902, the political-military oppression of the United States was formally ended, but her monopolistic power remained. Cuba became an economic colony of the United States and this remained its main characteristic for half a century.

In a country generally laid to waste, the imperialists found an interesting phenomenon: a sugar industry in full capitalistic expansion.

Sugar cane has been part of the Cuban picture since the sixteenth century. It was brought to the island only a few years after the discovery of America; however, the slave system of exploitation kept cultivation on a subsistence level. Only with the technological innovations which converted the sugar mill into a factory, with the introduction of the railway and the abolition of slavery, did the production of sugar begin to show a considerable growth, and one which assumed extraordinary proportions under Yankee auspices.

The natural advantages of the cultivation of sugar in Cuba are obvious, but the predominant fact is that Cuba was developed as a sugar factory of the United States.

International Affairs (London), vol. 40, no. 4 (October 1964), pp. 589–599.

North American banks and capitalists soon controlled the commercial exploitation of sugar and, furthermore, a good share of the industrial output of the land. In this way, a monopolistic control was established by U.S. interests in all aspects of a sugar production, which soon became the predominant factor in our foreign trade due to the rapidly developing monoproductive characteristics of the country.

Cuba became the sugar-producing and -exporting country *par excellence;* and if she did not develop even further in this respect, the reason is to be found in the capitalist contradictions which put a limit to a continuous expansion of the Cuban sugar industry, which depended almost entirely on North American capital.

The North American government used the quota system on imports of Cuban sugar not only to protect her own sugar industry, as demanded by her own producers, but also to make possible the unrestricted introduction into our country of North American manufactured goods. The preferential treaties of the beginning of the century gave North American products imported into Cuba a tariff advantage of 20 percent over the most favored of the nations with whom Cuba might sign trade agreements. Under these conditions of competition, and in view of the proximity of the United States, it became almost impossible for any foreign country to compete with North American manufactured goods.

The U.S. quota system meant stagnation for our sugar production. During the last years the Cuban productive capacity was rarely utilized to the full, but the preferential treatment given to Cuban sugar by the quota also meant that no other export crops could compete with it on an economic basis.

Consequently, the only two activities of our agriculture were cultivation of sugar cane and the breeding of low-quality cattle on pastures which at the same time served as reserve areas for the sugar plantation owners.

Unemployment became a constant feature of life in rural areas, resulting in the migration of agricultural workers to the cities. But industry did not develop either, only some public service undertakings under Yankee auspices (transportation, communications, electrical energy).

The lack of industry and the great part played by sugar in the economy resulted in the development of a very considerable foreign trade which bore all the characteristic marks of colonialism: primary products to the metropolis, manufactured goods to the colony. The Spanish empire had followed the same pattern, but with less ability.

Other exports were also primary products, but their proportion only reached 20 percent of Cuba's total exports. They were tobacco, principally in leaves; coffee—only occasionally, due to the small production; raw copper and manganese; and, during later years, semiprocessed nickel.

Such was the picture of the Cuban economy; in effect, a mono-productive country (sugar) with one particular export and import market (the United States), and vitally dependent on its foreign trade.

Under these conditions a bourgeoisie dependent on imports came into being and grew to be one of the greatest obstacles to the industrialization of the country. Only in later years did the bourgeoisie ally itself with North American manufacturing interests, creating industries which used North American equipment, raw materials, technology, and a cheap native labor force. The profits of those industries went to the country of the monopolies, either to the parent companies or to the North American banks which the native capitalists considered the safest place for deposits.

This twisted development brought with it great unemployment, great poverty, great parasitic strata, and the division of the working class through the appearance of a labor aristocracy made up of the workers of the imperialist enterprises, whose wages were much higher than those of the workers who sold their labor to the small native capitalists, and, naturally, infinitely higher than those of the part-time employed and totally unemployed.

The "American way of life" came to our defenseless society through the penetration of the monopolies; and the importation of luxury articles accounted for a great percentage of our trade while the sugar market stagnated and with it the possibility of acquiring precious foreign exchange. The deficit in our balance of payments became yearly greater, consuming the reserves accumulated during the Second World War.

With the exception of the two years 1950 and 1957, during which sugar prices jumped temporarily due to the war in Korea and the tense military situation in the Near East, our terms of trade showed a constant decrease during the decade following 1948. (A sad fate; only war could give the people of Cuba relative well-being.)

In that decade the flow of our exports had become stagnant and the terms of trade downward; the Cuban standard of living was bound to decline if remedial measures were not taken. And they were "taken," chiefly in the shape of budgetary increases for public works and the creation of state credit organizations to encourage private investment in industry.

Never have the state stabilization measures recommended by the

Keynesian economists been so openly employed to conceal embezzle-
ment of public funds and the illegal enrichment of politicians and
their allies. The national debt rose considerably. Expensive roads and
highways were built, as well as tunnels and enormous hotels in
Havana and the great towns; but none of these works was of any
real economic utility nor did any of them constitute the most appropriate action to be taken in an underdeveloped country.

A number of industries were created which by their characteristics
could be divided into two groups: the first consisted of factories of
relatively high technical standard, the property of North American
enterprises which used the few credit resources of a poor and
economically very underdeveloped country to increase their foreign
assets; the other, of a number of factories with obsolete equipment
and uneconomic methods, which from the very beginning required
state protection and subsidies. It was this group that served as a
means of enrichment for politicians and their capitalistic associates;
they made enormous commissions on the purchases of equipment.

In 1958, Cuba had a population of 6.5 million with a per capita
income of about $350 (calculating the national income according to
capitalist methods); the labor force comprised one third of the
total population, and one fourth of it was virtually unemployed.

Although great areas of fertile land were lying waste, and rural
labor was far from being fully utilized, imported foodstuffs and
textile fibers of agricultural origin amounted to 28 percent of the
country's total imports. Cuba had a coefficient of 0.75 head of cattle
per inhabitant, a figure exceeded only by the great cattle-breeding
countries. Nevertheless, the exploitation of this great number of
cattle was so inefficient that it was necessary to import cattle products.

In 1948, imports amounted to 32 percent of the national income;
ten years later the figure had risen to 35 percent. Exports provided 90
percent of the total income of foreign currencies. On the other hand,
profits on foreign capital transferred abroad absorbed up to 9 percent
of the foreign currency income on the trade balance.

Due to the constant deterioration of the terms of trade and the
transfer of profits abroad, the Cuban trade balance showed a total
deficit of $600 million for the period 1950–1958, the effect of which
was to reduce the available foreign currency reserves to $70 million.
This reserve represented 10 percent of the average annual imports
during the last three years.

The two main economic problems of the Cuban Revolution during its first months were unemployment and a shortage of foreign currencies. The first was an acute political problem, but the second was more dangerous, given the enormous dependence of Cuba on foreign trade.

The revolutionary government's economic policy was directed primarily toward solving these two problems. It is therefore appropriate to make a short analysis of the actions taken and the errors made during the first months.

The agrarian reform implied such a profound institutional change that it became immediately possible to make an effort toward the elimination of the obstacles that had prevented the utilization of human and natural resources in the past.

Because of the predominant part which had been played by the latifundia in agricultural production, and the enormous size of the sugar cane plantations organized along capitalistic lines, it was relatively easy to convert this type of rural property into state farms and cooperatives of considerable size. Cuba thus avoided the slow-moving development characteristic of other agrarian revolutions: the division of land into a fantastic number of small farms, followed by the grouping of such small units to enable more modern techniques, feasible only on certain levels of production, to be applied.

What was the economic policy followed in agriculture after the transfer of the large estates? As a natural part of this process, rural unemployment disappeared and the main efforts were directed toward self-sufficiency as regards the greater part of foodstuffs and raw materials of vegetable or animal origin. The trend in the development of agriculture can be defined in one word: diversification. In its agricultural policy the Revolution represented the antithesis of what had existed during the years of dependence on imperialism and of exploitation by the landowning class. Diversification versus monoculture; full employment versus idle hands: these were the major transformations in the rural areas during those years.

It is well known that, nevertheless, serious agricultural problems immediately arose, and these have only begun to be solved during recent months. How can be explain the relative scarcity of some agricultural products, and particularly the decline in sugar production, when the Revolution began by incorporating all the idle rural productive factors in the agricultural process, thus greatly increasing its potentialities? We believe we committed two principal errors.

Our first error was the way in which we carried out diversification. Instead of embarking on diversification by degrees we attempted too much at once. The sugar cane areas were reduced and the land thus made available was used for cultivation of new crops. But this meant a general decline in agricultural production. The entire economic history of Cuba had demonstrated that no other agricultural activity would give such returns as those yielded by the cultivation of the sugar cane. At the outset of the Revolution many of us were not aware of this basic economic fact because a fetishistic idea connected sugar with our dependence on imperialism and with the misery in the rural areas, without analyzing the real causes: the relation to the uneven trade balance.

Unfortunately, whatever measures are taken in agriculture, the results do not become apparent until months, sometimes years, afterward. This is particularly true as regards sugar cane production. That is why the reduction of the sugar cane areas made between the middle of 1960 and the end of 1961—and, let us not forget the two years of drought—has resulted in lower sugar cane harvests during 1962 and 1963.

Diversification on a smaller scale could have been achieved by utilizing the reserves of productivity existing in the resources assigned to the various traditional types of cultivation. This would have permitted the partial use of idle resources for a small number of new products. At the same time, we could have taken measures to introduce more modern and complex techniques requiring a longer period of assimilation. After these new technical methods had begun to bear fruit in the traditional fields, particularly in those related to exports, it would have been practicable to transfer resources from these fields to the areas of diversification without prejudice to the former.

The second mistake made was, in our opinion, that of dispersing our resources over a great number of agricultural products, all in the name of diversification. This dispersal was made not only on a national scale but also within reach of the agricultural productive units.

The change made from monoculture to the development of a great number of agricultural products implied a drastic transformation within relatively few months. Only a very solid productive organization could have resisted such rapid change. In an underdeveloped country, in particular, the structure of agriculture remains very inflexible and its organization rests on extremely weak and subjective foundations. Consequently, the change in the agricultural structure and diversification, coming simultaneously, produced a greater weakness in the agricultural productive organization.

Now that the years have passed, conditions have changed and the pressure of the class struggle has lessened, and so it is fairly easy to make a critical assessment of the analysis made during those months and years. It is for history to judge how much was our fault and how much was caused by circumstances.

At any rate, hard facts have shown us both the errors and the road toward their correction, which is the road the Cuban Revolution is at present following in the agricultural sector. Sugar now has first priority in the distribution of resources and in the assessment of those factors which contribute to the most efficient use of those resources. The other sectors of agricultural production and their development have not been abandoned, but adequate methods have been sought to prevent a dispersal of resources of which the effect would be to hinder the obtaining of maximum yields.

In the industrial sector our policy is directed toward the same two objectives: the solution of the two problems of unemployment and scarcity of foreign exchange. The agrarian reform, the revolutionary measures as regards redistribution of income, and the increase in employment observed in other sectors of the economy and in industry itself, extended the national market considerably. This market was further strengthened by the establishment of a government monopoly of foreign trade, and by the introduction of a protectionist policy as regards the importation of goods which, without any disadvantage to the national consumer, can be manufactured in Cuba.

What industry there was in Cuba only worked to a fraction of its capacity, due to the competition of North American goods, many of which entered the country practically duty-free, and also to the fact that national demand was limited by the concentration among the parasitic classes of a large part of the national income.

Immediately after the Revolution the explosive increase of demand permitted a higher degree of utilization of our industrial capacity, and nationally produced articles accounted for a greater share of total consumption. This industrial growth, however, aggravated the problem of the balance of payments, for an extraordinarily high percentage of the costs of our industry—which was nationally integrated only to a small degree—was represented by the importation of fuel, raw materials, spare parts, and the equipment for replacement.

The problem of the balance of payments, and that of urban unemployment, made us follow a policy aimed at an industrial development which would eliminate these defects. Here, too, we both achieved successes and committed errors. Already during the first years of the Revolution we ensured the country's supply of electric power, acquiring from the socialist countries new plant capacities which will meet our needs until 1970. New industries have been created, and many small- and medium-sized production units in the mechanical field have been re-equipped. One result of these measures was that our industry could be kept running when the North American embargo on spare parts hit us hardest. Some textile factories, some extractive and chemical installations, and a new and vigorous search for fresh mineral resources have all contributed to successes in the more efficient use of native natural resources and raw materials.

I have spoken of certain achievements in the industrial field during the first years, but it is only just that I should also mention the errors made. Fundamentally, these were caused by a lack of precise understanding of the technological and economic elements necessary in the new industries installed during those years. Influenced by existing unemployment and by the pressure exerted by the problems in our foreign trade, we acquired a great number of factories with the dual purpose of substituting imports and providing employment for an appreciable number of urban workers. Later we found that in many of these plants the technical efficiency was insufficient when measured by international standards, and that the net result of the substitution of imports was very limited, because the necessary raw materials were not nationally produced.

We have rectified this type of error in the industrial sector. In planning new industries we are evaluating the maximum advantages which they may bring to our foreign trade through use of the most modern technical equipment at present obtainable, taking into consideration the particular conditions of our country.

So far the industrial development achieved can be described as satisfactory, if we take into account the problems caused by the North American blockade and the radical changes which have occurred in only three years as regards our foreign sources of supply. Last year our sugar production fell from 4.8 million metric tons to 3.8 million, but this was offset by an increase, in general terms, of 6 percent in the rest of industry. This year, 1964, given the greater strength of our internal productive organization and our greater experience in commercial relations with our new sources of supply, the industrial advance should be still greater.

The transformations so far made in the Cuban economy have produced great changes in the structure of our foreign trade. As regards exports the changes have been limited chiefly to the opening up of new markets, with sugar continuing to be the main export article. On the other hand, the composition of our imports has changed completely during these five years. Imports of consumer goods, particularly durables, have decreased substantially in favor of capital equipment, while a small decrease can be noted in the imports of intermediate goods. The policy of substitution of imports is showing slow but tangible results.

The economic policy of the Revolution having attained a certain integral strength, it is clear that imports of durable consumer goods will once more increase, to satisfy the growing needs of modern life. The plans being made for the future provide for both an absolute and a relative increase in the importation of these articles, taking into account the social changes which have occurred. It will be unnecessary, for example, to import Cadillacs and other luxury cars, which in former years were paid for to a great extent with the profits derived from the labor of the Cuban sugar worker.

This is only one aspect of the problems connected with the future development of Cuba which are at present being studied. The policy we shall follow in years to come will largely depend on the flexibility of our foreign trade, and on the extent to which it will permit us to take full advantage of opportunities which may present themselves. We expect the Cuban economy to develop along three principal lines between now and 1970.

Sugar will continue to be our main earner of foreign exchange. Future development implies an increase of 50 percent in present productive capacity. Simultaneously a qualitative advance will take place in the sugar sector, consisting of a substantial increase in the yield per unit of land under cultivation, and an improvement in technology and equipment. That improvement will tend to make up for the ground lost through inefficiency during the last ten to fifteen years. During that period the complete lack of expansion of our market led to technological stagnation. With the new possibilities which have opened up in the socialist countries, the panorama is changing rapidly.

One of the main bases for the development of our sugar industry, as well as for the development of the country as a whole, is the agreement recently signed between the U.S.S.R. and Cuba. This guarantees to us future sales of enormous quantities of sugar at prices much above the average of those paid in the North American and world markets during the last twenty years. Apart from this and other favorable economic implications, the agreement signed with the U.S.S.R. is of political importance inasmuch as it provides

an example of the relationship that can exist between an underdeveloped and a developed country when both belong to the socialist
camp, in contrast to the commercial relations between the underdeveloped countries exporting raw materials and the industrialized
capitalist countries—in which the permanent tendency is to make
the balance of trade unfavorable to the poor nations.

The second line of industrial development will be nickel. The
deposits in northeastern Cuba offer great possibilities for making
this part of the island the future center of the metallurgical industry. The capacity of the nickel-smelting works will be increased,
making Cuba the second or third largest producer in the world of
this strategic metal.

The third line of this future development will be the cattle industry. The large number of cattle, great indeed in proportion to
the size of the population, offers rich possibilities for the future.
We estimate that within about ten years our cattle industry will
be equalled in importance only by the sugar industry.

As I have indicated, the role played by foreign trade in the Cuban
economy will continue to be of basic importance, but there will be
a qualitative change in its future development. None of the three
principal lines of development will imply an effort to substitute
imports, with the exception of the cattle industry, during the first
years. After these first years the character of our new economic
development will be fully reflected in our exports, and although
the policy of substitution of imports will not be abandoned, it will
be balanced by exports. For the decade following 1970 we are planning a more accelerated process of substitution of imports. This
can only be achieved on the basis of an industrialization program
of great scope. We shall create the necessary conditions for such
a program, making full use of the opportunities offered to an underdeveloped economy by our external trade.

Has the indisputable political importance in the world achieved by
Cuba any economic counterpart? If so, should that importance lead
to the contemplation of more serious economic relations with other
countries, materializing in trade? In such an event, how would we
build up this trade which has been greatly reduced due the North
American blockade?

In considering these questions I leave aside reasons of a utilitarian
nature which might lead me to make an apology for international
trade, for it is evident that Cuba is interested in an active, regular,
and sustained interchange of trade with all countries of the world.
What I am trying to do is to present an exact picture of the present

situation. The North American government is obsessed by Cuba, and not only because of its abnormal colonialist mentality. There is something more. Cuba represents, in the first place, a clear example of the failure of the North American policy of aggression on the very doorstep of the continent. Further, Cuba provides an example for the future socialist countries of Latin America and so an unmistakable warning of the inevitable reduction of the field of action of U.S. finance capital.

North American imperialism is weaker than it seems; it is a giant with feet of clay. Although its present potentialities are not seriously affected by violent internal class struggles leading to the destruction of the capitalist system, as foreseen by Marx, those potentialities are fundamentally based on a monopolistic extraterritorial power exercised by means of an unequal interchange of goods and by the political subjection of extensive territories. On these fall the full weight of the contradictions.

As the dependent countries of America and other regions of the world cast off the monopolistic chains, and establish more equitable systems and more just relations with all the countries of the world, the heavy contributions made by them to the living standard of the imperialist powers will cease, and of all the capitalist countries the United States will then be the most seriously affected. This will not be the only outcome of an historical process; displaced finance capital will be forced to seek new horizons to make good its losses and, in this struggle, the most wounded, the most powerful, and the most aggressive of all the capitalist powers, the United States, will employ her full strength in a ruthless competition with the others, adopting, perhaps, unexpected methods of violence in her dealings with her "allies" of today.

Thus the existence of Cuba represents not only the hope of a better future for the peoples of America but also the prospect of a dangerous future for the seemingly unshakable monopolistic structure of the United States. The North American attempt to strangle Cuba implies a desire to stop history; but if, in spite of all kinds of aggression, the Cuban state remains safe, its economy becoming increasingly strong and its foreign trade more important, then the failure of this policy will be complete and the move toward peaceful coexistence will become more rapid.

New relations based on mutual interests will be established. These will benefit the socialist bloc and the countries now liberating themselves. Yet the great capitalist countries, including England, facing serious economic problems and limitations of markets, could have the opportunity to lead this new interchange, as France has already tried to do to a certain extent.

To such countries the Cuban market, although not unimportant, may not be worth a break with the United States, but Latin America as a whole is a gigantic potential market of 200 million people. It is useless to close one's eyes to the reality that this continent will continue its struggle for liberation, and that it will ultimately, if gradually, establish either groups or a bloc of countries free of imperialism and with internal systems related to socialism. Therefore, the capitalist countries should decide whether it is worthwhile to use Cuba as a means of testing a situation which may prove to be of great advantage even if it represents a danger to the future of the capitalistic system.

The alternatives are clear, and in our opinion they imply the need for serious decisions: One can be an ally of the United States until the collapse of a policy of oppression and aggression and then fall victim to the same internal and external problems as will afflict the United States when that moment arrives; or one can break that alliance, which in any case is already beginning to crack in relation to Cuba, in order to help—by means of trade—the rapid development of the countries which are liberating themselves, thus not only giving greater hope to those peoples still fighting for liberation, but simultaneously creating conditions which will bring closer the disappearance of capitalism.

We think this is the great dilemma now facing countries like England. Cuba is part of that dilemma in her role as a catalyzing agent of the revolutionary ideas of a continent, and as the pioneer of these ideas.

It is not for us to say what final decision should be taken. We simply state the alternatives.

ЛГЛГЛГЛГЛГЛГЛГЛГЛГЛГЛГЛГЛГЛГЛГЛГЛГЛ

We consider it a great honor to write the prologue to this book based on the writings of General Vo Nguyen Giap, presently assistant prime minister, minister of defense, and commander in chief of the Popular Army of the Democratic Republic of Vietnam. General Giap speaks with the authority that his long personal experience and that of the communist party in the liberation struggle confer on him. This work, which is by itself of permanent value, has more interest—if that is possible—due to the tumultuous series of events that have occurred lately in this region of Asia, and because of the controversies that have arisen over the use of armed struggle as the way of solving the insurmountable contradictions that exist between exploiters and exploited in given historical situations.

The successful battles that were carried out during long years by the heroic armies and the entire people of Vietnam are repeated today. South Vietnam is in a state of war; that part of the country snatched from its legitimate owner, the Vietnamese people, is getting closer to victory. Even when the imperialist enemy threatens to send thousands of men, when the warmongers speak of using the atomic bomb and General Taylor is named ambassador to the so-called "Republic of South Vietnam," tacitly becoming commander in chief of the armies that are trying to liquidate the people's war there—nothing will stop their defeat.

Nearby in Laos, civil war has begun, provoked by North American maneuvers and supported in one way or another by U.S. traditional allies. The neutral kingdom of Cambodia (part, like its brothers Laos and Vietnam, of former French Indochina) is today subject to violation of its borders and suffers permanent attacks because of its firm defense of neutralism and national sovereignty. For all these reasons, this book goes beyond the limits set by a given historical episode and acquires the characteristics of a law for the entire region.

The problems discussed have particular importance for most of the peoples of Latin America as well because they are subject to

Prologue to Vo Nguyen Giap's book, *La guerra del pueblo, ejército del pueblo* (Havana: Editora Política, 1964).

North American imperialist domination. And it is evident that to know the Vietnamese experience would be of extraordinary interest for all the people of Africa who each day sustain ever more difficult, but repeatedly victorious, struggles against all types of colonialists.

Vietnam has special characteristics. It is a very old civilization with a long tradition of independence and an indigenous culture. Within its millenarian history, the episode of French colonialism is scarcely a minute event. Nonetheless, its fundamental qualities and those of the aggressor in general terms resemble the insurmountable contradictions existing in all the dependent nations as well as the form in which those contradictions can be resolved. Cuba, without knowing of these writings or others on the subject which narrated the experiences of the Chinese Revolution, began the road of liberation with similar methods, achieving success that today is the vision of everyone.

This work discusses questions of general interest to those who are fighting for their liberation. The book can be summarized as follows: It is possible to engage in armed struggle in specific conditions when nonviolent methods of achieving liberation have failed; armed struggle requires a favorable terrain for guerrilla operations and a significant peasant population.

Despite the fact that the book is based on a compilation of articles, they are well connected and certain repetitions add vigor to the whole. It treats the liberation war of the Vietnamese people, the definition of this fight as a people's war, and the people's army as the executive arm of the people. It shows the great experiences of the party in leading the armed struggle and organizing the revolutionary armed forces. The last chapter covers the last episode of the war, Dien Bien Phu, in which the liberation forces began a war of positions, defeating in this field the imperialist enemy.

The book begins narrating how, after World War II ended with the victory of the Soviet Union and the allied powers from the West, France disregarded all agreements and created extreme tension in the whole country. Peaceful and rational methods of solving controversies were demonstrated to be useless, so the people opted for armed struggle. Due to the characteristics of the country, the struggle had to be waged by the peasantry. It was a peasant war because of the places where action occurred and the composition of the army; but it was led by a proletarian ideology. Once again the worker-peasant alliance was proved an essential factor for victory. At first, because of the anticolonialist and anti-imperialist characteristics of the struggle, it was the war of an entire people. Many whose background did not correspond exactly to the classical definition of poor peasant or worker joined the liberation struggle; slowly sides were defined and the antifeudal struggle began achieving its true anti-imperialist, anticolonialist, and antifeudal character. From the struggle a socialist revolution was established.

Mass struggle was utilized throughout the war by the Vietnamese communist party. It was used, first of all, because guerrilla warfare is one expression of the mass struggle. One cannot conceive of guerrilla war when it is isolated from the people. The guerrilla group is the numerically inferior vanguard of the great majority of the people, who have no weapons but express themselves through the vanguard. Also, mass struggle was used in the cities as an indispensable weapon for the development of the struggle. It is important to point out that never during the period of the struggle for liberation did the masses give away any of their rights in order to get some concession from the regime. The people did not talk about reciprocal concessions but demanded liberties and guarantees, which brought inevitably in many sectors a crueler war than the French would have waged otherwise. This mass struggle without compromises—which gives it its dynamic character—gives us fundamental elements with which to understand the problem of the liberation struggle in Latin America.

Marxism was applied according to the concrete historical situation of Vietnam and because of the guiding role of the vanguard party, faithful to its people and consequently to its doctrine, a resounding victory was achieved over the imperialists. The characteristics of the struggle, in which territory had to be given to the enemy and many years had to pass in order to achieve final victory, with fluctuations, ebb and flow, was that of a protracted war. During the entire struggle one could say that the front lines were where the enemy was. At a given moment, the enemy occupied almost the entire territory and the front was spread to wherever the enemy was. Later the lines of combat were delimited and a main front was established. But the enemy's rear guard constituted another front; it was a total war and the colonialists were never able to mobilize their forces with ease against the liberated zones. The slogan "dynamism, initiative, mobility, and quick decision in new situations" is in synthesis the guerrilla tactic. These few words expressed the tremendously difficult art of popular war.

At certain times, the new guerrillas, fighting under the leadership of the party, were in regions in which the French penetration was strong and where the population had been terrorized by the French. In those cases, the guerrillas practiced what the Vietnamese called "armed propaganda." Armed propaganda is simply the presence of liberation forces in certain places where they demonstrate their power and combat ability, moving among the people as easily as fish in water. Armed propaganda, with time, catalyzed the masses of a region and revolutionized them, adding new territories to those already conquered by the people's army. In this way bases and guerrilla zones increased throughout Vietnam. This tactic has been summarized as follows: If the enemy concentrates, he loses ground; if the enemy disperses, he loses force. When the enemy concentrates to make a strong attack, one should counterattack in all the places where the enemy is dispersed. If the enemy returns to occupy specific places with small groups, the counterattack will be made according to the correlation of forces existing in each region, but the shock force of the enemy will have been diluted once again. This is another of the fundamental teachings of the liberation struggle in Vietnam.

The liberation struggle has passed through three stages that characterize, in general, the development of the people's war. It begins with small-sized guerrilla units that have extraordinary mobility and are able to mix with the physical and human geography of the region. As time goes by a quantitative process is produced which, at a given time, gives way to the great qualitative leap of the war of movements. Here we have more compact groups dominating entire zones. They have better means and their fighting capacity is much greater, but mobility is their fundamental characteristic. After another period of time the final stage of the struggle is reached. The people's army consolidates and moves into a war of positions—as happened in Dien Bien Phu—and finishes off the colonial dictatorship.

During the struggle, which dialectically culminated in the attack on Dien Bien Phu, in a war of positions, liberated or semiliberated zones were created which constituted territories of self-defense. Self-defense is also conceived by the Vietnamese in an active sense as one part of a single battle against the enemy. A self-defense zone can be defended from limited attacks, provide the people's army with men and provisions, and maintain the internal security of the region. Self-defense is no more than a minimal part of a whole, with special characteristics. One can never conceive of a self-defense zone as a whole in itself, that is, a region in which the popular forces try to defend themselves from the enemy's attack while the rest of the nation remains without disturbance. If that happened, the *foco* [1] would be localized, and destroyed, unless it moved immediately to the first phase of the people's war: guerrilla war.

The entire process of the Vietnamese struggle, as already mentioned, was based fundamentally in the peasantry. At first, without a clear definition of its outline, the struggle was solely to obtain national liberation, but as the forces defined themselves the struggle became a typical peasant war. Agrarian reform was established in the course of the struggle as the contradictions increased and the people's army became stronger. This is the manifestation of the class struggle within the society at war. The class struggle was led by the party, having as its goal the elimination of the enemy and the maximum use of the contradictions of colonialism. Correctly exploiting the contradictions, the party was able to achieve victory in the shortest time possible.

Compañero Vo Nguyen Giap also tells us of the close ties that exist between the party and the army, and how in this struggle the army is a part of the party and as such leads the struggle. We are also told of the close relationship that exists between the army and the people, how the army and the people are one, which once again, corroborates the magnificent synthesis expressed by Camilo: [2] "The army is the people in uniform." The armed forces, during the struggle and afterward, had acquired a new technique, one that allowed it to overcome the new weapons of the enemy and repel any type of offensive.

The revolutionary soldier has a conscious discipline. During the struggle his fundamental characteristic is self-discipline. The people's army, respecting all the rules of military codes, has great internal democracy and a great degree of equality with respect to the acquisition of essential items for its fighting men.

In all these manifestations General Nguyen Giap teaches us what we have learned through our own experience, an experience that occurred some years after the popular forces of Vietnam achieved victory, but an experience that reinforces the idea of the need for a profound analysis of historical processes at this time. This analysis should be done using Marxism, using all of its creative capacity and adapting it to the changing circumstances of different countries, countries different in many respects but similar in their colonized

---

[1] *Foco:* refers to guerrilla activity, not to a guerrilla base. Eds.

[2] Major Camilo Cienfuegos fought against the Batista dictatorship and disappeared mysteriously in October 1959, when the ranks of the Rebel Army were passing through a period of great disagreement. Eds.

structure, the existence of an imperialist oppressor, and of a class associated very closely with it. After an accurate analysis, General Giap reaches this conclusion:

In the present world situation, a nation, even a small and weak one, that rises under the leadership of the working class to fight resolutely for its independence and for democracy has the moral and material possibility of defeating the aggressors regardless of whom they are. In given historical conditions, this fight for national liberation can become an armed struggle of long duration—prolonged resistance—to achieve victory.

These words synthesize the general characteristics that the war of liberation in the dependent territories will have to assume.

We believe that the best declaration with which to conclude the prologue is the same one used by the editors of this book and with which we are identified: "We wish that all our friends, who like us still suffer the attacks and threats of imperialism, can find in *People's War, People's Army* what we have found: new motives of faith and hope."

Socialism and Man in Cuba

Dear *Compañero:*

I am finishing these notes during my trip through Africa, stimulated by the desire to fulfill, though tardily, my promise to you. I shall deal with the theme of the title as I believe it will be interesting to your Uruguayan readers.

It is common to hear from capitalistic spokesmen, as an argument in the ideological struggle against socialism, the statement that this social system or the period of socialist construction which Cuba has entered is characterized by the abolition of the individual for the sake of the state. I shall not try to refute this assertion on a merely theoretical basis, but shall attempt to establish the facts as they are experienced in Cuba and to add some general comments of my own. First, I shall outline a brief history of our revolutionary struggle before and after taking power.

As is known, July 26, 1953, is the precise date when the revolutionary actions were initiated which would eventually lead to triumph in January 1959. A group of men led by Fidel Castro in the dawn hours of that day attacked the Moncada Barracks in Oriente Province. The attack was a failure, and the failure became a disaster. The survivors wound up in prison and after a subsequent amnesty again undertook the revolutionary struggle.

During this process when there existed only the seeds of socialism, man was the fundamental factor. On him we relied, individualized, specific, with first and last name, and on his capacity for action depended the success or failure of a given mission.

Then the phase of guerrilla struggle began. It developed in two distinct environments: the people, a dormant mass yet in need of mobilization, and the vanguard, the guerrilla, the generator of revolutionary consciousness and enthusiasm. This vanguard was the catalyst which created the subjective conditions for victory. Throughout the proletarianization of our thought and the revolution that was taking place in our habits and our minds, the individual was the fundamental factor. Every fighter of the Sierra Maestra who achieved

Letter addressed to Carlos Quijano, editor of *Marcha* (Montevideo), March 1965. *Verde Olivo* (Havana), April 11, 1965, pp. 14–18, 66.

a high rank in the revolutionary forces had a history of notable achievements to his credit. Based on these, he attained his rank.

This was the first heroic stage in which men vied to achieve a place of greater responsibility, of greater danger, and without any other satisfaction than that of fulfilling their duty. In our work in revolutionary education we return often to this instructive theme. In the attitude of our fighters, we could glimpse the man of the future.

Total commitment to the revolutionary cause has been repeated at other times during our history. Throughout the October Crisis and the days of hurricane Flora, we saw acts of exceptional sacrifice and courage performed by all of our people. From an ideological viewpoint, our fundamental task is to find the formula which will perpetuate in daily life these heroic attitudes.

In January 1959, the revolutionary government was established with the participation of the various members of the submissive bourgeoisie. The presence of the Rebel Army as the fundamental factor of force constituted the guarantee of power. Serious contradictions arose which were resolved in the first instance in February 1959, when Fidel Castro assumed the leadership of the government in the post of prime minister. This process culminated in July of the same year with the resignation of President Urrutia due to pressure from the masses.

Into the history of the Cuban came a personage with clearly defined features which would systematically reassert itself: the masses. This multidimensional entity is not, as is sometimes pretended, the sum of the elements of one category (reduced to the same uniformity by the system imposed) acting as a docile herd. It is true that it follows its leaders, primarily Fidel Castro, without vacillating. But the degree to which he has earned this trust corresponds precisely with his ability to interpret the desires and aspirations of the people and with his sincere endeavor to fulfill the promises made.

The masses participated in the agrarian reform and in the difficult task of managing state enterprises, they went through the heroic experience of Playa Girón, forged themselves in combat against the different groups of CIA armed bandits, lived through one of the most important self-definitions in modern times during the October Crisis, and today work on toward the construction of socialism.

Looking at things from a superficial viewpoint, it would seem that those who speak about the subordination of the individual to the state are correct; the masses perform with unequaled enthusiasm and discipline the tasks assigned by the government be they of an economic, cultural, defensive, or athletic nature. Generally the initiative comes from Fidel or those in the revolutionary high command and is explained to the people, who make it their own. At other times local experience which is thought to be valuable is picked up by the party and the government and generalized following the same procedure.

However, the state makes mistakes at times. When this occurs, the collective enthusiasm diminishes due to a quantitative diminishing that takes place in each of the elements that make up the collective and work becomes paralyzed until it is reduced to an insignificant magnitude. This is the time to rectify the error.

That is what happened in March 1962, due to the sectarian line imposed on the party by Aníbal Escalante.

It is evident that the mechanism is not sufficient to assure a sequence of sensible measures. What is missing is a more structured relationship with the masses. We must improve this in years to come but for now, in the case of the initiatives arising on the top levels of government, we are using an almost intuitive method of listening to the general reactions in the face of the problems posed.

Fidel is a master at this, and his particular mode of integration with the people can only be appreciated by seeing him in action. At the great mass meetings, one can observe something like the dialogue of two tuning forks whose vibrations summon forth new vibrations each in the other. Fidel and the masses begin to vibrate in a dialogue of increasing intensity until it reaches an abrupt climax crowned by cries of struggle and of victory.

For one who has not lived the revolutionary experience, it is difficult to understand the close dialectical unity that exists between the individual and the mass, in which both are interrelated, and the mass, as a whole composed of individuals, is in turn interrelated with the leader.

Under capitalism, phenomena of this sort are observed when politicians appear who are capable of popular mobilization; but if it is not an authentic social movement, in which case it is not completely accurate to speak of capitalism, the movement will have the same lifespan as its promoter or until the popular illusions imposed by the rigors of capitalism are ended. In this type of society, man is directed by a cold mechanism which habitually escapes his comprehension. The alienated man has an invisible umbilical cord which ties him to the whole society: the law of value. It acts on all facets of his life, shaping his road and destiny.

The laws of capitalism, invisible and blind for most people, act on the individual even though he is not aware of them. He sees only a horizon that appears infinite. This is how capitalistic propaganda presents it, pretending to extract from the "Rockefeller" story —whether it is true or not—a lesson of the possibility of success. Yet the misery which necessarily accumulates in order that an example of this sort arise and the sum total of vileness resulting from a fortune of this magnitude do not appear in the picture. It is not always possible to clarify these concepts for the popular forces. (It would be fitting at this point to study how the workers of the imperialist countries gradually lose their international class spirit under the influence of a certain complicity in the exploitation of the dependent countries and how this fact at the same time wears away the masses' spirit of struggle within their own country, but this is a topic which is not within the intention of these notes.)

In any case the path is very difficult and apparently an individual with the proper qualities can overcome it to achieve the final goal. The prize is glimpsed in the distance; the road is solitary. Moreover, this is a race of wolves: One can only arrive by means of the failure of others.

I shall now attempt to define the individual, this actor in the strange and passionate drama that is the building of socialism, in his twofold existence as a unique being and as a member of the community.

I believe that the simplest way to begin is to recognize his unmade quality: man as an unfinished product. The prejudices of the past are carried into the present in the individual's consciousness and a continual effort has to be made in order to eradicate them. It is a twofold process. On the one hand, society acts with its direct and indirect education; and on the other, the individual submits himself to a conscious process of self-education.

The newly forming society has a hard competition with the past. This is so not only on the level of individual consciousness, with the residue of a systematic education oriented toward the isolation of the individual, but also on the economic level where, because of the very nature of the transitional period, mercantile relationships persist. *Mercancia* [1] is the economic cell of capitalistic society; as long as it exists, its effects will be felt in the organization of production and, hence, in the individual's consciousness.

In Marx's scheme, the period of transition was conceived as the

[1] *Mercancía:* there is no precise translation of this term into English. It has the connotation of goods for sale, commodities, merchandise, but it could also mean market relationships. Eds.

result of the explosive transformation of the capitalist system destroyed by its own contradictions; subsequent reality has shown how some countries which constitute the weak branches detach themselves from the capitalist tree, a phenomenon foreseen by Lenin. In those countries, capitalism has developed sufficiently for its effects to be felt in one way or another on the people, but it is not its own inner contradictions that explode the system after having exhausted all of its possibilities. The struggle for liberation against a foreign oppressor, misery provoked by strange accidents such as war, whose consequences make the privileged classes fall upon the exploited, and liberation movements to overthrow neocolonial regimes are the habitual unchaining factors. Conscious action does the rest.

In these countries there has not been a complete education, for social work and wealth through the simple process of appropriation is far away from the reach of the masses. Underdevelopment on the one hand and the usual flight of capital to the "civilized" countries on the other make a rapid change impossible without sacrifice. There is still a long stretch to be covered in the construction of an economic base, and the temptation to take the beaten path of material interest as the lever of accelerated development is very great.

There is the danger of not seeing the forest because of the trees. Pursuing the wild idea of trying to realize socialism with the aid of the worn-out weapons left by capitalism (the market place as the basic economic cell, profit making, individual material incentives, and so forth), one can arrive at a dead end. And one arrives there after having traveled a long distance with many forked roads where it is difficult to perceive the moment when the wrong path was taken. Meanwhile, the adapted economic base has undermined the development of consciousness. To construct communism simultaneously with the material base of our society, we must create a new man.

This is why it is so important to choose correctly the instrument for the mobilization of the masses. That instrument must be of a fundamentally moral nature, without forgetting the correct utilization of material incentives, especially those of a social nature.

As I have stated before, it is easy to activate moral incentives in times of extreme danger. To maintain their permanence, it is necessary to develop a consciousness in which values acquire new categories. Society as a whole must become a gigantic school.

In general the phenomenon is similar to the process of the formation of a capitalist consciousness in the system's first stage. Capitalism resorts to force but also educates the people in the system. Direct propaganda is carried out by those who explain to the people the inevitability of the class system, whether it be of divine origin or due to the imposition of nature as a mechanical entity. This appeases the masses, who find themselves oppressed by an evil impossible to fight.

This is followed by hope, which differentiates capitalism from the previous caste regimes that offered no way out.

For some, the caste system continues in force: the obedient will be rewarded in the afterlife by the arrival in other wonderful worlds where the good are requited, and thus the old tradition is continued. For others, innovation: the division of classes is a matter of fate, but individuals can leave the class to which they belong through work, initiative, and so on. This process, and that of self-education for success, must be deeply hypocritical; it is the interested demonstration that a lie is true.

In our case, direct education acquires much greater importance. Explanations are convincing because they are true; there is no need for subterfuge. It is carried out through the state's educational apparatus in the form of general, technical, and ideological culture, by means of bodies such as the Ministry of Education and the party's information apparatus. Education takes among the masses, and the new attitude that is patronized tends to become a habit; the masses incorporate the attitude as their own and exert pressure on those who still have not become educated. This is the indirect way of educating the masses, as powerful as the other one.

But the process is a conscious one; the individual receives a continuous impact from the new social power and perceives that he is not completely adequate to it. Under the influence of the pressure implied in indirect education, the individual tries to accommodate to a situation which he feels is just while recognizing that his lack of development has impeded him in doing so until now. He educates himself.

In this period of the construction of socialism, we can see the new man being born. His image is as yet unfinished; in fact, it will never be finished, for the process advances parallel to the development of new economic forms. Discounting those whose lack of education makes them tend toward the solitary road, toward the satisfaction of their ambitions, there are others who, even within this new panorama of over-all advances, tend to march in isolation from the accompanying mass. What is important is that men acquire more awareness every day of the need to incorporate themselves into society, and, at the same time, of their importance as motors of that society.

They no longer march in complete solitude along lost paths toward distant longings. They follow their vanguard constituted of the party, of the most advanced workers, of the advanced men who move along bound in close communion to the masses. The vanguard has their sight on the future and its rewards, but these are not envisioned as something individual; the reward is the new society where men will have different characteristics—the society of communist man.

The road is long and full of difficulties. Sometimes it is necessary to retreat, having lost the way; at times, because of a rapid pace, we separate ourselves from the masses; and on occasion, because of our slow pace, we feel the close breath of those who follow on our heels. In our ambition as revolutionaries, we try to move as quickly as possible, clearing the path, understanding that we receive our nourishment from the masses and that they will advance more rapidly if we encourage them by our example.

In spite of the importance given to moral incentives, the fact that there exist two principal groups (excluding, of course, the minority fraction of those who do not participate for one reason or another in the construction of socialism) indicates the relative lack of development of social consciousness. The vanguard groups are ideologically more advanced than the mass. The latter is acquainted with the new values, but insufficiently. Whereas in the former a qualitative change occurs which permits them to make sacrifices as a function of their vanguard character, the latter see only by halves and must be subjected to incentives and pressures of some intensity; it is the dictatorship of the proletariat operating not only over the defeated class but also individually over the victorious class.

All of this entails, for its total success, a series of revolutionary institutions. The image of the multitudes marching toward the future fits the concept of institutionalization as a harmonic unit of canals, steps, dams, well-oiled apparatus which make the march possible, which will permit the natural selection of those who are destined to march in the vanguard and who will dispense rewards and punishments to those who fulfill their duty or act against the society under construction.

The institutionalization of the Revolution has still not been achieved. We are searching for something new which will allow perfect identification between the government and the community as a whole, adjusted to the peculiar conditions of the building of socialism and avoiding to the utmost the commonplaces of bourgeois democracy transplanted to the society in formation (such as legislative houses, for example). Some experiments have been carried out with the aim of gradually creating the institutionalization of the Revolution, but without too much hurry. Our greatest restraint has been the fear that any formal aspect might separate us from the masses and the individual, making us lose sight of the ultimate and most important revolutionary ambition: to see man liberated from his alienation.

Notwithstanding the lack of institutions (which must be overcome gradually), the masses now make history as a conscious aggregate of individuals who struggle for the same cause. The individual's possibilities for expressing himself and making himself heard in the social apparatus are infinitely greater, in spite of the lack of a perfect mechanism to do so.

It is still necessary to accentuate his conscious, individual, and collective participation in all the mechanisms of direction and production and tie them in with the idea of the need for technical and ideological education, so that the individual will grasp how these processes are closely interdependent and their advances parallel. He will thus achieve total awareness of his social being, which is equivalent to his full realization as a human creature, having broken the chains of alienation.

This will be translated concretely into the reappropriation of his nature through freed work and the expression of his own human condition through culture and art.

In order for it to attain the characteristic of being freed, work must acquire a new condition; man as a commodity ceases to exist and a system is established which grants a quota for the fulfillment of social duty. The means of production belong to society and the machine is only the front line where duty is performed. Man begins to liberate his thought from the bothersome fact that presupposes the need to satisfy his animal needs through work. He begins to see himself portrayed in his work and to understand its human magnitude through the created object, through the work carried out. This no longer entails leaving a part of his being in the form of labor, power, soul, which no longer belong to him, but rather it signifies an emanation from himself, a contribution to the life of society in which he is reflected, the fulfillment of his social duty.

We are doing everything possible to give work this new category of social duty and to unite it to the development of technology, on the one hand, which will provide the conditions for greater freedom, and to voluntary labor on the other, based on the Marxist concept that man truly achieves his full human condition when he produces without being compelled by the physical necessity of selling himself as a commodity.

It is clear that work still has coercive aspects, even when it is voluntary; man as yet has not transformed all the coercion surrounding him into conditioned reflexes of a social nature, and in many cases he still produces under the pressure of the environment (Fidel calls this moral compulsion). He still has to achieve complete spiritual re-creation in the presence of his own work, without the direct pressure of the social environment but bound to it by new habits. That will be communism.

The change in consciousness is not produced automatically, just as it is not produced in the economy. The variations are slow and not rhythmic; there are periods of acceleration, others are measured, and some even involve a retreat.

We must also consider, as we have already pointed out, that we are not before a pure transition period such as that envisioned by Marx in the *Critique of the Gotha Program*, but rather a new phase not foreseen by him—the first period in the transition to communism or in the construction of socialism.

This process takes place in the midst of a violent class struggle; and elements of capitalism are present within it, which obscure the complete understanding of the essence of the process.

If to this be added the scholasticism that has delayed the development of Marxist philosophy and impeded the systematic treatment of the period in which the political economy has as yet not been developed, we must agree that we are still in diapers and it is urgent to investigate all the primordial characteristics of the period before elaborating a far-reaching economic and political theory.

The resulting theory will necessarily give preeminence to the two pillars of socialist construction: the formation of the new man and the development of technology. In both aspects we have a great deal to accomplish still, but the delay is less justifiable regarding the conception of technology as the basis: here it is not a matter of advancing blindly, but rather of following for a considerable stretch the road opened up by the most advanced countries of the world. This is why Fidel harps with so much insistency on the necessity of the technological and scientific formation of all of our people and especially of the vanguard.

In the field of ideas that lead to nonproductive activities, it is easier to see the division between material and spiritual needs. For a long time man has been trying to free himself from alienation through culture and art. He dies daily in the eight and more hours during which he performs as a commodity in order to be resuscitated in his spiritual creation. But this remedy bears the germs of the same disease: He is a solitary being who seeks communion with nature. He defends his oppressed individuality from the environment and reacts to esthetic ideas as a unique being whose aspiration is to remain immaculate.

It is only an attempt at flight. The law of value is no longer a mere reflection of production relations; the monopoly capitalists have surrounded it with a complicated scaffolding which makes of it a docile servant, even when the methods employed are purely empirical. The superstructure imposes a type of art in which the artist must be educated. The rebels are dominated by the apparatus, and only exceptional talents are able to create their own work. The remaining ones become shamefaced wage-workers, or they are crushed.

Artistic experimentation is invented and is taken as the definition of freedom. But this "experimentation" has limits which are imperceptible until they are clashed with, that is to say, when the real problems of man and his alienation are dealt with. Senseless anguish or vulgar pastimes are comfortable safety valves for human uneasiness; the idea of making art a weapon of denunciation and accusation is combatted.

If the rules of the game are respected, all honors are obtained— the honors that might be granted to a pirouette-creating monkey. The condition is to not attempt to escape from the invisible cage.

When the Revolution took power, the exodus of the totally domesticated took place; the others, revolutionaries or not, saw a new road. Artistic experimentation gained new impulse. However, the roots were more or less traced, and the concept of flight was the hidden meaning behind the word freedom. This attitude, which was a reflection in consciousness of bourgeois idealism, was frequently maintained in the revolutionaries themselves.

In countries which have gone through a similar process, there was an attempt made to combat these tendencies with an exaggerated dogmatism. General culture became something like a taboo, and a formally exact representation of nature was proclaimed as the height of cultural aspiration. This later became a mechanical representation of social reality created by wishful thinking, the ideal society, almost without conflict or contradiction, that man was seeking to create.

Socialism is young and makes mistakes. We revolutionaries many times lack the knowledge and the necessary intellectual audacity to face the task of the development of the new human being by methods distinct from the conventional ones, and the conventional methods suffer from the influence of the society that created them. (Once again the topic of the relation between form and content appears.) Disorientation is great, and the problems of material construction absorb us. There are no artists of great authority who also have great revolutionary authority.

The men of the party must take this task on themselves and seek the achievements of the critical objective: to educate the people.

What is then sought is simplification, what everyone understands, what the functionaries understand. True artistic experimentation is annulled and the problem of general culture is reduced to the assimilation of the socialist present and the dead (and therefore not dangerous) past. As such, socialist realism is born on the foundation of the art of the last century.

But the realistic art of the nineteenth century is also class art, perhaps more purely capitalist than the decadent art of the twentieth century, where the anguish of alienated man shows through. In culture, capitalism has given all that it has to give and all that remains of it is the announcement of a bad-smelling corpse—in art, its present decadence. But why endeavor to seek in the frozen forms of socialist realism the only valid recipe? "Freedom" cannot be set against socialist realism because the former does not yet exist and it will not come into existence until the complete development of the new society. But at all costs let us not attempt to condemn all post-mid-nineteenth-century art forms from the pontifical throne of realism. That would mean committing the Proudhonian error of the return to the past, and strait-jacketing the artistic expression of the man who is being born and constructed today.

An ideological and cultural mechanism which will permit experimentation and clear out the weeds that shoot up so easily in the fertilized soil of state subsidization is lacking.

In our country, the error of mechanical realism has not appeared, but rather the contrary. This has been because of the lack of understanding of the need to create the new man who will represent neither nineteenth-century ideas nor those of our decadent and morbid century. It is the twenty-first-century man whom we must create, although this is still a subjective and unsystematic aspiration. This is precisely one of the fundamental points of our studies and our work; to the extent that we make concrete achievements on a theoretical base or vice versa, that we come to theoretical conclusions of a broad character on the basis of our concrete studies, we will have made a valuable contribution to Marxism-Leninism, to the cause of mankind.

The reaction against nineteenth-century man has brought a recurrence of twentieth-century decadence. It is not a very grave error, but we must overcome it so as not to leave the doors wide open to revisionism.

The large multitudes of people are developing themselves, the new ideas are acquiring an adequate impetus within society, the material possibilities of the integral development of each and every one of its members make the task ever more fruitful. The present is one of struggle; the future is ours.

To summarize, the culpability of many of our intellectuals and artists lies in their original sin; they are not authentic revolutionaries. We can attempt to graft elm trees so they bear pears, but simultaneously we must plant pear trees. The new generations will arrive free of original sin. The possibility that exceptional artists will arise will be that much greater because of the enlargement of the cultural field and the possibilities for expression. Our task is to keep the present generation, maladjusted by its conflicts, from becoming perverted and perverting the new generations. We do not want to create salaried workers docile to official thinking or "scholars" who live under the wing of the budget, exercising a freedom in quotation marks. Revolutionaries will come to sing the song of the new man with the authentic voice of the people. It is a process that requires time.

In our society the youth and the party play a large role. The former is particularly important because it is malleable clay with which the new man, without any of the previous defects, can be constructed.

They receive treatment which is in consonance with our ambitions. Education is increasingly more complete, and we do not forget the incorporation of the students into work from the very first. Our scholarship students do physical work during vacation or simultaneously with their studies. In some cases work is a prize, in others it is an educational tool; it is never a punishment. A new generation is being born.

The party is a vanguard organization. The best workers are proposed by their comrades for membership. The party is a minority, but the quality of its cadres gives it great authority. Our aspiration is that the party become a mass one, but only when the masses have attained the level of development of the vanguard, that is, when they are educated for communism. Our work is aimed at providing that education. The party is the living example; its cadres must be lecturers of assiduity and sacrifice; with their acts they must lead the masses to end the revolutionary task, which entails years of struggle against the difficulties of construction, class enemies, the defects of the past, imperialism.

I would like to explain now the role played by the personality, man as the individual who leads the masses that make history. This is our experience, and not a recipe.

Fidel gave impulse to the Revolution in its first years, he has given leadership to it always and has set the tone; but there is a good group of revolutionaries developing in the same direction as the maximum leader and a great mass that follows its leaders because it has faith in them. It has faith in them because these leaders have known how to interpret the longings of the masses.

It is not a question of how many kilograms of meat are eaten or how many times a year someone may go on holiday to the seashore or how many pretty imported things can be bought with present wages. It is rather that the individual feels greater fulfillment, that he has greater inner wealth and many more responsibilities. In our country the individual knows that the glorious period in which it has fallen to him to live is one of sacrifice; he is familiar with sacrifice.

The first ones came to know it in the Sierra Maestra and wherever there was fighting; later we have known it in all Cuba. Cuba is the vanguard of America and must make sacrifices because it occupies the advance position, because it points out to the masses of Latin America the road to full freedom.

Within the country the leaders must fulfill their vanguard role; and it must be said with all sincerity that in a true revolution, to which one gives oneself completely, from which one expects no material compensation, the task of the vanguard revolutionary is both magnificent and anguishing.

Let me say, with the risk of appearing ridiculous, that the true revolutionary is guided by strong feelings of love. It is impossible to think of an authentic revolutionary without this quality. This is perhaps one of the greatest dramas of a leader; he must combine an impassioned spirit with a cold mind and make painful decisions without flinching one muscle. Our vanguard revolutionaries must idealize their love for the people, for the most sacred causes, and make it one and indivisible. They cannot descend, with small doses of daily affection, to the places where ordinary men put their love into practice.

The leaders of the Revolution have children who do not learn to call their father with their first faltering words; they have wives who must be part of the general sacrifice of their lives to carry the Revolution to its destiny; their friends are strictly limited to their comrades in revolution. There is no life outside it.

In these conditions, one must have a large dose of humanity, a large dose of a sense of justice and truth, to avoid falling in dogmatic extremes, into cold scholasticism, into isolation from the masses. Every day we must struggle so that this love of living humanity is transformed into concrete facts, into acts that will serve as an example, as a mobilizing factor.

The revolutionary, ideological motor of the Revolution within his party, is consumed by this uninterrupted activity that has no other end but death, unless construction be achieved on a worldwide scale. If his revolutionary eagerness becomes dulled when the most urgent tasks are realized on a local scale, and if he forgets about proletarian internationalism, the revolution that he leads ceases to be a driving force and it becomes a comfortable drowsiness which is taken advantage of by our irreconcilable enemy, by imperialism, which gains ground. Proletarian internationalism is a duty, but it is also a revolutionary need. This is how we educate our people.

It is clear that there are dangers in the present circumstances. Not only that of dogmatism, not only that of the freezing up of relations with the masses in the midst of the great task, but there also exists the danger of weaknesses in which it is possible to fall. If a man thinks that in order to dedicate his entire life to the Revolution, he cannot be distracted by the worry that one of his children lacks a certain product, that the children's shoes are in poor condition, that his family lacks some very necessary item, beneath this reasoning the germs of future corruption are allowed to filter through.

In our case we have maintained that our children must have, or lack, what the children of the ordinary citizen have or lack; our family must understand this and struggle for it. The Revolution is made through man, but man must forge day by day his revolutionary spirit.

Thus we go forward. At the head of the immense column—we are neither ashamed nor afraid to say so—is Fidel, followed by the best party cadres and, immediately after, so close that their great strength is felt, come the people as a whole, a solid conglomeration of individualities moving toward a common objective: individuals who have achieved the awareness of what must be done, men who struggle to leave the domain of necessity and enter that of freedom.

That immense multitude is ordering itself; its order responds to an awareness of the need for order; it is no more a dispersed force, divisible in thousands of fractions shot into space like the fragments of a grenade, trying through any means, in a fierce struggle with their equals, to attain a position that would give them support in the face of an uncertain future.

We know that we have sacrifices ahead of us and that we must pay a price for the heroic act of constituting a vanguard as a nation. We, the leaders, know that we must pay a price for having the right to say that we are at the head of the people who are at the head of America.

Each and every one of us punctually pays his quota of sacrifice, aware of receiving our reward in the satisfaction of fulfilling our duty, conscious of advancing with everyone toward the new man who is glimpsed on the horizon.

Allow me to attempt to come to some conclusions:

We socialists are more free because we are more fulfilled; we are more fulfilled because we are more free.

The skeleton of our freedom is formed, but it lacks the protein substance and the draperies; we shall create them.

Our freedom and its daily sustenance are the color of blood and are swollen with sacrifice.

Our sacrifice is a conscious one; it is the payment for the freedom we are constructing.

The road is long and unknown in part; we are aware of our limitations. We shall make the twenty-first-century man, we ourselves.

We shall be forged in daily action, creating a new man with a new technology.

The personality plays the role of mobilization and leadership insofar as it incarnates the highest virtues and aspirations of the people and is not detoured.

The road is opened up by the vanguard group, the best among the good, the party.

The fundamental clay of our work is the youth; in it we have deposited our hopes and we are preparing it to take the banner from our hands.

If this faltering letter has made some things clear, it will have fulfilled my purpose in sending it.

Accept our ritual greetings, as a handshake or an "Ave María Purísima."

Patria o muerte

ЛЛЛЛЛЛЛЛЛЛЛЛЛЛЛЛЛЛЛЛЛЛЛЛЛЛЛЛ

Now is the time of the furnaces, and only light should be seen.

—JOSE MARTI

Twenty-one years have already elapsed since the end of the last world conflagration; numerous publications in every possible language celebrate this event symbolized by the defeat of Japan. There is a climate of apparent optimism in many areas of the different camps into which the world is divided.

Twenty-one years without a world war in these times of maximum confrontation, of violent clashes and sudden changes, appears to be a very high figure. However, without analyzing the practical results of this peace (poverty, degradation, increasing exploitation of enormous sectors of humanity) for which all of us have stated that we are willing to fight, we would do well to inquire if this peace is real.

It is not the purpose of these notes to detail the different conflicts of a local character that have been occurring since the surrender of Japan; nor do we intend to recount the numerous and increasing instances of civilian strife which have taken place during these years of apparent peace. It will be enough just to name, as an example against undue optimism, the wars of Korea and Vietnam.

In the first of these, after years of savage warfare, the northern part of the country was submerged in the most terrible devastation known in the annals of modern warfare: riddled with bombs; without factories, schools, or hospitals; with absolutely no shelter for housing 10 million inhabitants.

Under the discredited flag of the United Nations, dozens of countries under the military leadership of the United States participated in this war with the massive intervention of United States soldiers and the use, as cannon fodder, of the drafted South Korean population. On the other side, the army and the people of Korea and the volunteers from the People's Republic of China were furnished with supplies and technical aid by the Soviet military apparatus. The United States tested all sorts of weapons of destruction, excluding

April 1967, from Bolivia. *Granma Weekly* (Havana), April 23, 1967, pp. 1, 10–11. Official Cuban government translation.

the thermonuclear type, but including, on a limited scale, bacteriological and chemical warfare.

In Vietnam the patriotic forces of that country have carried on an almost uninterrupted war against three imperialist powers: Japan, whose might suffered an almost vertical collapse after the bombing of Hiroshima and Nagasaki; France, who recovered from that defeated country its Indochina colonies and ignored the promises it had made in harder times; and the United States, in the last phase of the struggle.

There have been limited confrontations in every continent, although in our America there were only incipient liberation struggles and military coups d'état until the Cuban Revolution sounded the alert signaling the importance of this region. This action attracted the wrath of the imperialists and Cuba was finally obliged to defend its coasts first in Playa Girón and again during the October Crisis.

This last incident could have unleased a war of incalculable proportions if a United States–Soviet clash had occurred over the Cuban question.

But evidently the focal point of all contradictions is at present the territory of the peninsula of Indochina and the adjacent areas. Laos and Vietnam are torn by civil wars which have ceased being such by the entry into the conflict of United States imperialism with all its might, thus transforming the whole zone into a dangerous powder keg ready at any moment to explode. In Vietnam the confrontation has assumed extremely acute characteristics. It is not our intention, either, to chronicle this war. We shall simply remember and point out some milestones.

In 1954, after the annihilating defeat of Dien Bien Phu, an agreement was signed at Geneva dividing the country into two separate zones; elections were to be held within a term of eighteen months to determine who should govern Vietnam and how the country should be reunified. The U.S. did not sign this document and started maneuvering to substitute the emperor, Bao Dai, who was a French puppet, for a man more amenable to its purposes. This happened to be Ngo Din Diem, whose tragic end—that of an orange squeezed dry by imperialism—is well known by all.

During the months following the agreement, optimism reigned supreme in the camp of the popular forces. The last redoubts of the anti-French resistance were dismantled in the south of the country—and they awaited the fulfillment of the Geneva Agreements. But the patriots soon realized there would be no elections—unless the United States felt itself capable of imposing its will in the polls, which was practically impossible even resorting to all its fraudulent methods. Once again fighting broke out in the South and gradually acquired full intensity. At present the U.S. invading army has increased to nearly half a million troops, while the puppet forces decrease in number and, above all, have totally lost their combativeness.

Almost two years ago the U.S. started systematically bombing the Democratic Republic of Vietnam, in yet another attempt to overcome the resistance of the South and impose, from a position of strength, a meeting at the conference table. At first, the bombardments were more or less isolated occurrences and were represented as reprisals for alleged provocations from the North. Later on, as they increased in intensity and regularity, they became one gigantic attack carried out by the air force of the United States day after day for the purpose of destroying all vestiges of civilization in the northern zone of the country. This is an episode of the infamously notorious "escalation."

The material aspirations of the Yankee world have been fulfilled to a great extent despite the unflinching defense of the Vietnamese anti-aircraft artillery, the numerous planes shot down (over 1,700), and the socialist countries' aid in war supplies.

This is the sad reality: Vietnam—a nation representing the aspirations, the hopes of a whole world of forgotten peoples—is tragically alone. This nation must endure the furious attacks of U.S. technology with practically no possibility of reprisals in the South and only some of defense in the North—but always alone.

The solidarity of all progressive forces of the world with the people of Vietnam is today similar to the bitter agony of the plebeians urging on the gladiators in the Roman arena. It is not a matter of wishing success to the victim of aggression, but of sharing his fate; one must accompany him to his death or to victory.

When we analyze the lonely situation of the Vietnamese people, we are overcome by anguish at this illogical fix in which humanity finds itself.

U.S. imperialism is guilty of aggression—its crimes are enormous and cover the whole world. We already know all that, gentlemen! But this guilt also applies to those who, when the time came for a definition, hesitated to make Vietnam an inviolable part of the socialist camp, running, of course, the risks of war on a global scale —but also forcing a decision on imperialism. The guilt also applies to those who maintain a war of abuse and maneuvering—started quite some time ago by the representatives of the two greatest powers of the socialist camp.

We must ask ourselves, seeking an honest answer, Is Vietnam isolated or is it not? Is it not maintaining a dangerous equilibrium between the two quarreling powers?

And what great people these are! What stoicism and courage! And what a lesson for the world is contained in this struggle! Not for a long time shall we be able to know if President Johnson ever seriously thought of bringing about some of the reforms needed by his people—to iron out the barbed class contradictions that grow each day with explosive power. The truth is that the improvements announced under the pompous title of the "Great Society" have been poured down the drain of Vietnam.

The largest of all imperialist powers feels in its own guts the bleeding inflicted by a poor and underdeveloped country; its fabulous economy feels the strain of the war effort. Murder is ceasing to be the most convenient business for its monopolies. Defensive weapons, and never in adequate numbers, are all these extraordinary Vietnamese soldiers have—besides love for their homeland, their society, and unsurpassed courage. But imperialism is bogging down in Vietnam, is unable to find a way out, and desperately seeks one that will overcome with dignity this dangerous situation in which it now finds itself. Furthermore, the Four Points put forth by the North and the Five Points of the South now corner imperialism, making the confrontation even more decisive.

Everything indicates that peace, this unstable peace which bears the name for the sole reason that no worldwide conflagration has taken place, is again in danger of being destroyed by some irrevocable and unacceptable step taken by the United States.

What role shall we, the exploited people of the world, play? The peoples of the three continents focus their attention on Vietnam and learn their lesson. Because imperialists blackmail humanity by threatening it with war, the wise reaction is not to fear war. The general tactics of the people should be to launch a constant and firm attack on all fronts where the confrontation is taking place.

In those places where the meager peace we have has been violated, what is our duty? To liberate ourselves at any price.

The world panorama is of great complexity. The struggle for liberation has not yet been undertaken by some countries of ancient Europe, sufficiently developed to realize the contradictions of capitalism but weak to such a degree that they are unable either to follow imperialism or to start on their own road. Their contradictions will reach an explosive stage during the forthcoming years—but their problems and, consequently, their solutions are different from those of our dependent and economically underdeveloped countries.

The fundamental field of imperialist exploitation comprises the three underdeveloped continents: America, Asia, and Africa. Every country has also its own characteristics, but each continent as a whole also represents a certain unity. Our America is integrated by a group of more or less homogeneous countries and in most parts of its territory U.S. monopoly capital maintains an absolute supremacy. Puppet governments, or, in the best of cases, weak and fearful local rulers, are incapable of contradicting orders from their Yankee master. The United States has nearly reached the climax of its political and economic domination; it could hardly advance much more; and change in the situation could bring a setback. Its policy is to maintain that which has already been conquered. The line of action, at the present time, is limited to the brutal use of force with the purpose of thwarting the liberation movements, no matter of what type they might happen to be.

Under the slogan "We shall not allow another Cuba" hides the possibility of perpetrating aggression without fear of reprisal (such as the one carried out against the Dominican Republic or before that the massacre in Panama) and the clear warning stating that the Yankee troops are ready to intervene anywhere in America where the established order may be altered, thus endangering their interests. This policy enjoys almost absolute impunity: the Organization of American States is a suitable mask, in spite of its unpopularity; the inefficiency of the United Nations is ridiculous as well as tragic; the armies of all American countries are ready to intervene in order to smash their peoples. The International of Crime and Treason has in fact been organized. On the other hand, the national bourgeoisies have lost all their capacity to oppose imperialism—if they ever had it —and they have become the last card in the pack. There are no other alternatives; either a socialist revolution or a make-believe revolution.

Asia is a continent with different characteristics. The struggle for liberation waged against a series of European colonial powers resulted in the establishment of more or less progressive governments whose ulterior evolution has brought, in some cases, the reaffirming of the primary objectives of national liberation and, in others, a setback toward the adoption of pro-imperialist positions.

From the economic point of view, the United States had very little to lose and much to gain in Asia. The changes benefited its interests; the struggle for the overthrow of other neocolonial powers and the penetration of new spheres of action in the economic field is carried out sometimes directly, occasionally through Japan.

But there are special conditions in Asia, particularly in Indochina, which create certain characteristics of capital importance and play a decisive role in the entire U.S. military strategy. The imperialists encircle China through South Korea, Taiwan, South Vietnam and Thailand, at least.

This dual situation, a strategic interest as important as the military encirclement of the People's Republic of China and the penetration of these great markets—which they do not dominate yet— turns Asia into one of the most explosive points of the world today in spite of its apparent stability outside the Vietnamese war zone.

The Middle East, though geographically a part of this continent, has its own contradictions and is actively in ferment; it is impossible to foretell how far the cold war between Israel, backed by the imperialists, and the progressive countries of that zone will go. This is just another of the volcanoes threatening eruption in the world today.

Africa offers an almost virgin territory to neocolonial invasion. There have been changes which, to some extent, forced neocolonial powers to give up their former absolute prerogatives. But when these changes are carried out without interruption, colonialism continues in the form of neocolonialism with similar effects on the economic situation.

The United States had no colonies in this region but is now struggling to penetrate its partners' fiefs. It can be said that following the strategic plans of United States imperialism, Africa constitutes its long-range reservoir; its present investments, though, are only important in the Union of South Africa and its penetration is beginning to be felt in the Congo, Nigeria, and other countries where a sharp rivalry with other imperialist powers is beginning to take place (nonviolent up to the present time).

So far it does not have great interests to defend there except its assumed right to intervene in every spot of the world where its monopolies detect the possibility of huge profits or the existence of large reserves of raw materials.

All this past history justifies our concern over the possibilities of liberating the peoples within a moderate or short period of time.

If we stop to analyze Africa, we observe that in the Portuguese colonies of Guinea, Mozambique, and Angola the struggle is waged with relative intensity, with particular success in the first and variable success in the other two. We still witness in the Congo the dispute between Lumumba's successors and the old accomplices of Tshombe, a dispute which at the present time seems to favor the latter, those who have "pacified" a large area of the country for their own benefit—though the war still is latent.

In Rhodesia we have a different problem: British imperialism used every means within its reach to place power in the hands of the white minority now in control. The conflict, from the British point of view, is absolutely unofficial; this Western power with its habitual diplomatic cleverness—also called hypocrisy in plain language—presents a façade of displeasure before the measures adopted by the government of Ian Smith. Its crafty attitude is supported and followed by some Commonwealth countries, but is attacked by a large group of countries belonging to black Africa, even by some that are still docile economic vassals of British imperialism.

Should the efforts of Rhodesia's black patriots to organize armed rebellion crystallize and should this movement be effectively supported by neighboring African nations, the situation in that country could become extremely explosive. But for the moment all of these problems are being discussed in such innocuous organizations as the United Nations, the Commonwealth, and the Organization of African Unity.

Nevertheless, the social and political evolution of Africa does not lead us to expect a continental revolution. The liberation struggle against the Portuguese should end victoriously, but Portugal means nothing in the imperialist field. The confrontations of revolutionary importance are those which place at bay all the imperialist apparatus, though this does not mean that we should stop fighting for the liberation of the three Portuguese colonies and for the deepening of their revolutions.

When the black masses of South Africa or Rhodesia start their authentic revolutionary struggle, or when the impoverished masses of a nation rise up to rescue their right to a decent life from the hands of the ruling oligarchies, a new era will dawn in Africa.

Up to now army putsches have followed one another; a group of officers succeeds another or replaces rulers who no longer serve their caste interests and those of the powers who covertly manage them—but there are no great popular upheavals. In the Congo these characteristics appeared briefly, generated by the memory of Lumumba, but they have been losing strength in the last few months.

In Asia, as we have seen, the situation is explosive. The points of friction are not only Vietnam and Laos, where actual fighting is going on, but also Cambodia (where direct United States aggression may start at any time), Thailand, Malaya, and of course, Indonesia, where we cannot assume that the last word has been said despite the annihilation of the communist party of that country carried out by the reactionaries when they took power. And also naturally, there is the Middle East.

In Latin America armed struggle is underway in Guatemala, Colombia, Venezuela, and Bolivia, and the first uprisings are appearing in Brazil. Other foci [*focos*] of resistance appear and are then extinguished. But almost every country of this continent is ripe for a type of struggle that, in order to achieve victory, cannot be content with anything less than establishing a government of a socialist nature.

On this continent for all practical purposes only one tongue is spoken (with the exception of Brazil, with whose people those who speak Spanish can easily make themselves understood, owing to the great similarities of our languages). There is also such a great similarity among the classes of the different countries that an identification exists among them of an "international American" type, much more complete than that of other continents. Language, customs, religion, a common foreign master unite them. The degree and forms of exploitation are similar for both the exploiters and the exploited in many of the countries of our America. And rebellion is ripening swiftly.

We may ask ourselves: How will this rebellion come to fruition? What type will it be? We have maintained for quite some time now that, owing to the similarity of national characteristics, the struggle of our America will achieve continental proportions. It will be the scene of many great battles fought for the liberation of humanity.

Within the over-all struggle on a continental scale, the battles which are now taking place are only episodes—but they have already furnished their martyrs, who will figure in the history of our America as having given their necessary quota of blood in this last stage of the fight for the total freedom of man. These names will include Major Turcios Lima, the priest Camilo Torres, Major Fabricio Ojeda, Majors Lobatón and Luis de la Puente Uceda, all outstanding figures in the revolutionary movements of Peru, Guatemala, Colombia, and Venezuela.

But the active mobilization of the people creates new leaders: César Montes and Yon Sosa raise the flag of battle in Guatemala; Fabio Vásquez and Marulanda, in Colombia; Douglas Bravo in the western half of the country and Américo Martín in El Bachiller direct their respective fronts in Venezuela.

New uprisings will take place in these and other countries of our

America, as has already happened in Bolivia; they will continue to grow in the midst of all the hardships inherent to this dangerous profession of the modern revolutionary. Many will perish, victims of their errors; others will fall in the hard battle ahead; new fighters and new leaders will appear in the heat of the revolutionary struggle. The people will produce their fighters and leaders in the selective process of the war itself—and Yankee agents of repression will increase. Today there are military "advisers" in all the countries where armed struggle exists, and the Peruvian army, trained and advised by the Yankees, apparently carried out a successful action against the revolutionaries in that country. But if the foci [*focos*] of war grow with sufficient political and military wisdom, they will become practically invincible, obliging the Yankees to send reinforcements. In Peru itself many new figures, practically unknown, are now tenaciously and firmly reorganizing the guerrilla movement. Little by little the obsolete weapons which are sufficient for the repression of small armed bands will be exchanged for modern armaments and the United States military "advisers" will be substituted by United States soldiers until at a given moment they will be forced to draft increasingly greater numbers of regular troops to ensure the relative stability of a government whose national puppet army is disintegrating before the attacks of the guerrillas. It is the road of Vietnam; it is the road that will be followed in our America, with the special characteristic that the armed groups may create something like coordinating councils to frustrate the repressive efforts of Yankee imperialism and contribute to the revolutionary cause.

America, a forgotten continent in the world's more recent liberation struggles, which is now beginning to make itself heard through the Tricontinental in the voice of the vanguard of its peoples, the Cuban Revolution, has before it a task of much greater relevance: to create a second or a third Vietnam, or the second and third Vietnam of the world.

We must bear in mind that imperialism is a world system—the last stage of capitalism—and it must be defeated in a great world confrontation. The strategic end of this struggle must be the destruction of imperialism. Our part, the responsibility of the exploited and underdeveloped world, is to eliminate the foundations of imperialism—our oppressed nations, from which they extract capital, raw materials, cheap technicians, and common labor, and to which they export new capital (instrument of domination), arms, and every kind of article, submerging us in absolute dependence.

The fundamental element of this strategic end is then the real liberation of all peoples, a liberation that will be brought about in most cases through armed struggle and will, in our America, almost certainly have the characteristic of becoming a socialist revolution.

In envisaging the destruction of imperialism, it is necessary to identify its head, which is none other than the United States of America.

We must carry out a general task which has as its tactical purpose drawing the enemy out of his natural environment, forcing him to fight in places where his living habits clash with the existing reality. We must not underrate our adversary; the U.S. soldier has technical capacity and is backed by weapons and resources of such magnitude as to render him formidable. He lacks the essential ideological motivation which his most bitter enemies of today—the Vietnamese soldiers—have in the highest degree. We shall only be able to triumph over such an army by undermining its morale—and that is accomplished by causing it repeated defeats and repeated punishment.

But this brief scheme for victory implies immense sacrifice by the people, sacrifice that should be demanded beginning today, in plain words, and which perhaps may be less painful than what they would have to endure if we constantly avoided battle in an attempt to have others pull our chestnuts from the fire.

It is probable, of course, that the last country to liberate itself will accomplish this without armed struggle and that its people may be spared the sufferings of a long and cruel war against imperialism. But perhaps it will be impossible to avoid this struggle or its effects in a global conflagration and the last country's suffering may be the same, or even greater. We cannot foresee the future, but we should never give in to the defeatist temptation of being leaders of a nation that yearns for freedom but abhors the struggle it entails and awaits its freedom as a crumb of victory.

It is absolutely just to avoid all useless sacrifice. For that reason, it is necessary to study carefully the real possibilities that dependent America may have of liberating itself through peaceful means. For us, the answer to this question is quite clear: The present moment may or may not be the proper one for starting the struggle, but we cannot harbor any illusions, we have no right to do so, that freedom can be obtained without fighting. And the battles will not be mere street fights with stones against tear-gas bombs, nor pacific general strikes; neither will they be those of a furious people destroying in two or three days the repressive superstructure of the ruling oligarchy. The struggle will be long, harsh, and its battlefronts will be the guerrillas' refuge, the cities, the homes of the fighters—where the repressive forces will go seeking easy victims among their families, among the massacred rural population in the villages or cities destroyed by the bombardments of the enemy. They themselves impel us to this struggle: There is no alternative other than to prepare it and decide to undertake it.

The beginnings will not be easy; they will be extremely difficult. All of the oligarchies' power of repression, all of their brutality and demagoguery will be placed at the service of their cause. Our mission, in the first hours, will be to survive; later, we shall follow the perennial example of the guerrilla carrying out armed propaganda (in the Vietnamese sense, that is, the propaganda of bullets, of battles won or lost—but fought—against the enemy). The great lesson of the invincibility of the guerrillas will take root in the dispossessed masses: the galvanizing national spirit, preparation for harder tasks, for resisting even more violent repression; hatred as an element of struggle, relentless hatred of the enemy that impels us over and beyond the natural limitations of man and transforms us into effective, violent, selective, and cold killing machines. Our soldiers must be thus; a people without hatred cannot vanquish a brutal enemy. We must carry the war as far as the enemy carries it—to his home, to his centers of entertainment, in a total war. It is necessary to prevent him from having a moment of peace, a quiet moment outside his barracks or even inside; we must attack him wherever he may be, make him feel like a cornered beast wherever he may move. Then his morale will begin to fall. He will become still more savage, but we shall see the signs of decadence begin to appear.

And let us develop a true proletarian internationalism, with international proletarian armies; let the flag under which we fight be the sacred cause of redeeming humanity so that to die under the flag of Vietnam, of Venezuela, of Guatemala, of Laos, of Guinea, of Colombia, of Bolivia, of Brazil—to name only a few scenes of today's armed struggle—will be equally glorious and desirable for an American, an Asian, an African, or even a European.

Each drop of blood spilled in a country under whose flag one has not been born is an experience for those who survive to apply later in the liberation struggle of their own countries. And each nation liberated is a step toward victory in the battle for the liberation of one's own country.

The time has come to settle our discrepancies and place everything we have at the service of the struggle.

We all know that great controversies agitate the world now fighting for freedom; no one can hide it. We also know that these controversies have reached such intensity and such bitterness that the possibility of dialogue and reconciliation seems extremely difficult, if not impossible. It is useless to search for means and ways to propitiate a dialogue which the hostile parties avoid. But the enemy is there; it strikes every day and threatens us with new blows and these blows will unite us today, tomorrow, or the day after. Whoever understands this first and prepares for this necessary union will earn the people's gratitude.

Because of the virulence and the intransigence with which each cause is defended, we, the dispossessed, cannot take sides with one or the other form of these discrepancies even if we at times coincide with the contentions of one party or the other or in a greater measure with those of one part than with those of the other. In time of war, the expression of current differences constitutes a weakness; but as things stand at this moment, it is an illusion to hope to settle these differences by means of words. Time will erase them or give them their true explanation.

In our struggling world, all discrepancies regarding tactics and methods of action for the attainment of limited objectives should be analyzed with the respect that the opinions of others deserve. Regarding our great strategic objective, the total destruction of imperialism via armed struggle, we should be uncompromising.

Our aspirations to victory may be summed up: total destruction of imperialism by eliminating its firmest bulwark—imperialist domination by the United States of America; carrying out, as a tactical method, the gradual liberation of the peoples, one by one or in groups; forcing the enemy into a difficult fight far from its own territory; liquidation of all of its sustaining bases, that is, its dependent territories.

This means a long war. And, we repeat once more, a cruel war. Let no one fool himself at the outset and let no one hesitate to begin in fear of the consequences it may bring to his people. It is almost our sole hope for victory. We cannot elude the call of this hour. Vietnam is pointing it out with its endless lesson of heroism, its tragic and everyday lesson of struggle and death for the attainment of final victory.

There the imperialist soldiers encounter the discomforts of those who, accustomed to the vaunted U.S. standard of living, must face a hostile land, the insecurity of those who are unable to move without being aware of walking on enemy territory, death to those who advance beyond their fortified encampments, the permanent hostility of an entire population. All this provokes internal repercussions in the United States and precipitates the resurgence of a factor which was attenuated in the full vigor of imperialism: class struggle even within its own territory.

What a luminous, near future would be visible to us if two, three, or many Vietnams appeared throughout the world with their share of death and immense tragedies, their everyday heroism and repeated blows against imperialism, obliging it to disperse its forces under the attack and the increasing hatred of all the peoples of the earth!

And if we were all capable of uniting to make our blows more solid and infallible so that the effectiveness of every kind of support given to the struggling peoples were increased—how great and how near that future would be!

If we, those of us who on a small point of the world map, fulfill our duty and place at the disposal of this struggle whatever little we are able to give—our lives, our sacrifice—must someday breathe our last breath in any land not our own yet already ours, sprinkled with our blood, let it be known that we have measured the scope of our actions and that we consider ourselves no more than elements in the great army of the proletariat, but that we are proud to have learned from the Cuban Revolution and from its maximum leader the great lesson emanating from Cuba's attitude in this part of the world: "What do the dangers or the sacrifices of a man or of a nation matter when the destiny of humanity is at sake?"

Our every action is a battle cry against imperialism and a call for the people's unity against the great enemy of mankind: the United States of America. Whenever death may surprise us it will be welcome, provided that this, our battle cry, reach some receptive ear, that another hand be extended to take up our weapons, and that other men come forward to intone our funeral dirge with the staccato of machine guns and new cries of battle and victory.

Communique of the National Army
of Liberation of Bolivia

ЛЛЛЛЛЛЛЛЛЛЛЛЛЛЛЛЛЛЛЛЛЛЛ

We, the natives of this land, have lived and are now living as foreigners in our own country. Any Yankee imperialist enjoys more rights than we do in our national territory, which he calls "his concession." He may destroy, raze, and burn Bolivian dwellings, crops, and property.

Our land does not belong to us. Our natural wealth has served and is now serving to enrich foreigners, leaving us only holes in the ground and extensively damaged lungs. There are neither schools nor hospitals for our children. Our living conditions are miserable. We are paid starvation wages. Every year thousands of men, women, and children die of starvation. Our peasants live and work under conditions of extreme poverty.

Although this is the picture of our life, we are a people who struggle, who have never allowed ourselves to be dominated. How many heroes shoulder to shoulder with miners, peasants, factory workers, teachers, and our glorious youth, the students, have written the finest pages of our history with their own blood!

Still fresh in our minds is the memory of the massacres, murders, and insults to which the Bolivian people have been subjected. Hirelings, generals, and Yankee imperialists: Your hands are red with the blood of the Bolivian people, but the hour of reckoning has come. Today the Army of National Liberation (ELN) is rising from the pools of blood you have spilled, from the ashes of the thousands of patriots you have persecuted, jailed, exiled, and murdered. Courageous men from the countryside, the cities, mines, factories, schools, and universities now carry rifles.

The vigorous start of our struggle has put fear into the hearts of the ruling clique and their boss, Yankee imperialism. Like cornered animals, they strike out wildly; the persecution increases as they are driven to commit ever greater crimes, violating the pseudo-democratic constitution which they swore to respect. Any attempt

Leaflet issued by the Ejército de Liberación Nacional in Bolivia in April 1967. It is generally known in revolutionary circles in Bolivia that this leaflet was prepared by Guevara.

they make to smother the guerrillas or to remain in power will be in vain. Their end, as a ruling clique, is in sight.

We call on all patriotic officers and soldiers to lay down their arms, and we urge our country's youth to refuse to serve in the army.

The Army of National Liberation calls on the people of Bolivia to close ranks, to establish an iron-clad unity regardless of shades of political opinion, to join the ranks of the ELN. It is also possible to furnish aid from the outside. There are a thousand ways of doing so, and the people's ingenuity will find the most varied forms.

We hereby announced that the Army of National Liberation will see to it that the people's ideals are fulfilled. It will punish the oppressors, torturers, informers, and traitors as well as those who commit injustices against the poor. Organizations of civil defense are now being formed. People's revolutionary courts will soon go into action to judge and punish the guilty. In conclusion, the Army of National Liberation expresses its faith, confidence, and firm belief in the victory over the Yankees and invaders disguised as advisers, be they Yankee or not.

Death rather than life as slaves! Long live the guerrillas!

Death to Yankee imperialism and its military clique!

Freedom for all patriots now under arrest or in prison!

To the Miners
of Bolivia

ᴸᴸᴸᴸᴸᴸᴸᴸᴸᴸᴸᴸᴸᴸᴸᴸᴸᴸᴸᴸᴸᴸᴸᴸᴸᴸ

Compañeros:

Once more the blood of the proletariat has been shed in our mines. This age-old exploitation—alternating the bleeding of the enslaved miner with the spilling of his blood whenever great injustice causes violent outbursts of protest—has been repeated without variation in cycles covering hundreds of years.

In recent times this pattern was temporarily broken, and workers in rebellion played a major role in the April 9 victory.[1] This event gave rise to hopes that new horizons were opening up and that finally the workers would become masters of their own destiny. But the machinery of the imperialist world shows to those who wish to see it that in the matter of social revolution there are no halfway solutions: either seize complete power or lose advances gained through so much sacrifice and bloodshed.

The armed militia of the miner proletariat—the only strong factor in the initial stage—was joined by militia from other sectors of the working class, by the destitute and the farmers, whose members were not able to see the essential over-all interests involved and entered into conflict among themselves, manipulated as they were by demagogy aimed against the people. And, in the end, the professional army came on the scene, a true wolf in sheep's clothing. And that army, small and insignificant at the beginning, was transformed into the armed instrument against the proletariat, into the most reliable accomplice of imperialism. That is why imperialism approved of a military coup d'état.

We are now recovering from a defeat brought about by repeated tactical errors on the part of the working class, and patiently preparing the country for a deep revolution to change the system completely.

We should not insist on false tactics, heroic in themselves but use-

Granma (Havana), July 14, 1968, p. 4. A call to arms written by Guevara in 1967.

[1] The April 9, 1952, uprising in La Paz and other cities and mining areas which overthrew a traditional elite and began a national revolution aborted in 1964 when Paz Estenssoro was overthrown. Eds.

less, which plunge the proletariat in a bloodbath and decimate its ranks, thus depriving us of its best fighting elements.

In long months of struggle the guerrillas have caused an upheaval in the country, have killed a large number of soldiers, and have demoralized the army almost without suffering any losses. On the other hand, in a battle lasting only a few hours that same army scored a complete victory, and like peacocks the soldiers strutted in front of the workers' bodies. The thin line between correct and erroneous tactics accounts for the difference between victory and defeat.

Comrade miner: Do not listen again to the false apostles of the mass struggle who interpret this struggle as a compact frontal attack of the people against the weapons of the oppressors. Let us learn from experience! Bare chests, no matter how strong, are useless against machine guns and barricades, are useless against modern demolition methods. The mass struggle in the underdeveloped countries, with a large peasant population and extensive land area, must be undertaken by a small mobile vanguard, the guerrillas, established within the people. This organization will grow stronger at the cost of the enemy army and will serve as the catalyzing agent for the revolutionary fervor of the masses until a revolutionary situation is created in which state power will crumble under a single effective blow, dealt at the right moment.

Understand this well: This is not a call to total inactivity, but rather a recommendation not to risk forces in any action where success is not guaranteed. But the working masses must, at all times, exert pressure on the government because this is a class struggle without limited fronts. Wherever there is a proletarian, he is under the obligation to struggle within the limit of his power against the common enemy.

Comrade miner: The guerrillas of the ELN await you with open arms and invite you to join the workers of the subsoil now fighting at our side. Here we shall rebuild the worker-farmer alliance once destroyed by demagogy aimed against the people. Here we shall turn defeat into victory and the lament of the workers' widows into a paean of victory. We await you.

ELN

Instructions for Cadres
Who Work in Urban Areas

⊓⊔⊓⊔⊓⊔⊓⊔⊓⊔⊓⊔⊓⊔⊓⊔⊓⊔⊓⊔⊓⊔⊓⊔⊓⊔⊓⊔⊓⊔

The formation of a supporting network of the kind that we want should be guided by a series of norms, a generalization of which follows.

Action will be fundamentally underground but it will alternate with certain kinds of work in which contact with individuals or organizations will be necessary, thus forcing certain cadres to come out into the open. This demands strict sectioning off, isolating every front engaged in this work.

The cadres should be strictly governed by the general line of conduct laid down by the army command through the various levels of authority, but they will have complete liberty in the practical form this line will take.

In order to carry out the difficult tasks assigned him and survive, the underground cadre should have highly developed discipline, complete secrecy, guile, self-control, and sang-froid, and should use work methods which will keep him from becoming entangled in unforeseen contingencies.

All the comrades who work partially in the open will be governed by higher echelons—also clandestine—which will issue and control their work.

Whenever possible, both the leader of the network and the various persons in charge will have only one function, and horizontal contacts will be made through the leader. Every organized network will have at least the following officials—the chief and a person in charge of each of the following:

    I. supplies
   II. transportation
 III. information
  IV. finances
   V. urban action
  VI. contacts with sympathizers

On its being developed, the network will need a person in charge of communications, who will take his general orders from the leader.

Granma (Havana), July 14, 1968, p. 5. Written as an outline plan for underground work in the urban areas of Bolivia in 1967.

The leader will receive his instructions from the army command and will pass them on to the various persons in charge. He should be known only to this small directing nucleus so as to avoid endangering the whole network if he should be captured. If those persons responsible for certain functions know each other, in any case each one's work should be concealed from the others, and any change will not be communicated.

Measures will be taken so that if an important member of the network should be arrested, the leader and all those who knew the one arrested will change their places of residence and/or methods of contact.

The person in charge of supplies will have the job of providing supplies for the army but his task is organizational: Starting at the center, he will create smaller supporting networks which will extend throughout the ELN, whether they be purely rural organizations or receive the support of businessmen or other individuals or organizations.

The person in charge of transportation will see to the transporting of supplies from receiving points to the points where the smaller networks will take them or directly to liberated territory, as the case may be.

These two comrades should do their work under good cover, for example, organizing small businesses which will allay the suspicions of the repressive authorities when the magnitude and goals of the movement are made public.

The person in charge of information will gather all military and political information received through the proper contacts. He will work partially in the open, gathering information from sympathizers in the army or government. This makes his post a particularly dangerous one. All the information gathered will be sent to the person in charge of information in our army. The former must obey two commands: the network leader and our intelligence service.

The person in charge of finances will control the organization's expenses. This comrade must be fully aware of the importance of his post, for—despite being in great danger, exposed to an obscure death—he is to live in the city, will not suffer the physical hardship of the guerrilla, and may grow careless in handling the funds and supplies, thus running the risk of lowering his revolutionary standards as a result of constant exposure to temptation. This comrade should check how every cent is spent and see to it that not a single cent is spent without justification. He will also be in charge of the money from collections and taxes and will organize the collection of the latter.

The person in charge of finances will be under the direct orders of the network leader, but he will also act as his inspector in financial matters. It is thus to be understood that the person in charge of finances must have unshakable ideological conviction. The work of the person in charge of urban action covers all types of armed action in the city: the execution of informers, notorious torturers, and high officials of the regime; the kidnapping of some persons with the aim of obtaining ransom; the sabotage of centers of economic activity, and so forth. All action will be ordered by the network leader; the person in charge of urban action is not allowed to act on his own except in cases of extreme urgency.

The person in charge of contacts with sympathizers will be the one to work most in the open and will be in contact with weaker elements, those who clear their consciences by giving certain sums of money or other aid without committing themselves. These are people one can work with only as long as one keeps in mind that their support is conditional on their not running any risks. Taking this into account, an effort must be made to transform them gradually into active militants, urging them to make substantial contributions to the movement not only in the form of money but also in the form of medicines, hideouts, information, and so on.

In this type of network there must be some people who work very closely together; for example, the person in charge of transportation should be closely united with the person in charge of supplies, who will also be his immediate chief; the person in charge of contacts with sympathizers will take orders from the person in charge of finances; action and information will work in direct contact with the leader of the network.

The networks will be subject to inspection by cadres sent directly by the army. These have no executive function, but will simply check that instructions are carried out and norms observed.

The networks should "move" toward the army as follows: the high command issues orders to the network leader; he, in turn, will organize the network in the important cities, from which branches will extend toward the towns and from there to hamlets or individual houses occupied by peasants who will make contact with our army and where the actual delivery of supplies, money, or information will take place.

As our army's sphere of influence extends, our contact points will advance toward the city, and the area under direct control of the army will grow proportionately. This is a long process, with its inevitable ups and downs, whose development, as that of this war, must be measured in years.

The network headquarters will be established in the capital; branches will be organized in other cities, which at the moment are more important to us—Cochabamba, Santa Cruz, Sucre, and Camiri, that is, the rectangle encompassing our zone of operations. The men in charge of these four cities should be tested men—insofar as is possible; they will be in charge of similar but simplified organizations. Supplies and transportation will be under one leadership, and finance and sympathizers under another leadership; the third will be urban action—we can do away with information, leaving the local leader in charge of that. Urban action will be tied in with the army as army territory reaches the cities, and finally its members will become suburban guerrillas, acting under the orders of the military commander.

The network already described will branch out from these cities.

We must not overlook the development of the network in cities which today are removed from our field of action. We should ask for the support of the population and get ready in time for future action in these cities. Oruro and Potosí are the most important of these cities.

Special attention should be given to the border spots of Villazón and Tarija for contact and supplies from Argentina; Santa Cruz, from Brazil; Huaqui or some other place on the Peruvian border; and some other place on the Chilean border.

For the organization of a supply network it would be convenient to have staunch members who have formerly engaged in some activity similar to that which is needed now. For example, the owner of a warehouse could organize the matter of supplies or participate in some other way in this section of the network; the owner of a transportation company would be in charge of organizing transportation, and so forth.

If this cannot be done, an effort must be made to set up the organization patiently, without forcing events, thus avoiding the pitfall of installing an advance post without taking sufficient precautions, only to lose it and place others in jeopardy.

Shops or businesses that should be set up: grocery stores (in La Paz, Cochabamba, Santa Cruz, and Camiri), transportation services (La Paz–Santa Cruz, Santa Cruz–Camiri, La Paz–Sucre, and Sucre–Camiri), shoe factories (in La Paz, Santa Cruz, Camiri, and Cochabamba), clothing stores (in La Paz, Santa Cruz, Camiri, and Cochabamba) and machine shops (in La Paz and Santa Cruz). Land should be obtained in Chapare and Caranavi.

The first two will take care of the reception of supplies and the transportation of same—which will include war matériel—without raising suspicion. The shoe factories and clothing stores will meet two needs. They can buy material and manufacture shoes and clothing for us without raising suspicion. The machine shop can do the same with the war matériel, and the lands will serve as a base of support for future transfers and also for the settlers' propaganda among the peasants.

Once again we must emphasize that the cadres must have unshakable ideological conviction, for the revolutionary movement gives them what is strictly necessary for meeting their basic needs, while they give all their time and, if necessary, their freedom and/or their lives. Only thus shall we achieve the formation of the effective network needed for the success of our ambitious plan: the total liberation of Bolivia.

SPEECHES

Honoring the
Labor Movement

ЛЛЛЛЛЛЛЛЛЛЛЛЛЛЛЛЛЛЛЛЛЛЛЛЛЛЛЛЛ

I have not come here to be paid homage, but to pay tribute in the name of the Rebel Army to the Cuban working class. Under the leadership of men of dignity, the working class courageously struggles to recuperate from so many horrors perpetrated by the defeated tyranny.

I am sorry to come armed and with bodyguards to the Workers' Palace [1] because this should be a place where one can find peace while men work to build new institutions. The circumstances, nonetheless, force us to be armed in order to secure the Revolution which has begun. The struggle ended with the defeat of the dictatorship, but much remains to be done. Today I am a guerrilla fighter, I am no longer a professional physician. I will continue to be a guerrilla fighter until Cuba is totally free from threats from abroad or from inside the island.

We have begun a Revolution but we should remember that we are not alone in this world. The peoples of Latin America also suffer from dictatorship and they should be free. They need our aid. At the same time, there are vested interests that do not want us to be free. The North American press attacks our Revolution and demands clemency for those who should be shot. When the United States sent weapons to Batista to murder more than 20,000 Cubans, then the North American press did not express alarm. They do so now when 300 criminals have been punished justly. That press campaign is paid for by the powerful interests of Wall Street, but we have nothing to fear. We have made this Revolution without the aid of anyone from abroad.

To end let me say that our people owe a large debt to the Rebel Army. That debt should be paid with a true agrarian reform for our peasantry. Most of the bulk of our Rebel Army comes from the peasantry. Our people know what they want. They should express their thoughts in the mass meeting that will be held tomorrow in support of our Revolution, our president, Doctor Urrutia, and our commander in chief, Fidel Castro.

Speech made at the meeting in honor of Ernesto Guevara by the Cuban working class on January 19, 1959. *El Mundo* (Havana), January 20, 1959, p. A8.

[1] The Workers' Palace is the headquarters of the Cuban Confederation of Labor. Eds.

Social Ideals
of the Rebel Army

Tonight it is necessary to invoke Martí, as was pointed out by the gentleman introducing me. I think when we speak of the social ideals of the Rebel Army, we are basically referring to the dream which Martí hoped to realize.

As this is a night of remembrance, we shall briefly outline the past development of our Revolution before we discuss the topic and its historical significance.

I shall not begin with the attack on the Moncada Barracks on July 26, 1953. I shall refer only to those events in which I participated and which resulted in the Revolution of January first of this year.

Let us begin this story in Mexico, where it began for me.

It is very important for us to know the actual thinking of those who constitute our Rebel Army, the thinking of that group who embarked on the *Granma* adventure, the evolution of that thinking which was born from the very heart of the 26th of July Movement and its successive changes through the revolutionary process, reaching the final stage of this last chapter, of which the insurrectional part has just ended.

In Mexico I met several members of the 26th of July Movement. The social ideals of those men were very different prior to sailing on the *Granma*, prior to the first schism of the 26th of July Movement, when it was made up of the entire surviving nucleus of the attack on the Moncada Barracks. I recall an intimate discussion in a home in Mexico where I spoke of the need to offer the people of Cuba a revolutionary program; and a member of the 26th of July Movement who had participated in the Moncada Barracks assault —who fortunately left the Movement—answered me in a way I shall always remember: "The matter is simple. What we want to accomplish is a coup d'état. Batista pulled off a coup and took power in one day. We must make another coup to get him out.... Batista has made a hundred concessions to the Americans and we must give them a hundred and one." To him the main objective was to achieve power. I argued that a coup must be based on principles for it was

Speech made at the Sociedad Nuestro Tiempo on January 27, 1959. *Humanismo* (Mexico), January/April 1959, pp. 346-382.

important to know what we were going to do once we had taken over the government. This was the thinking of a member of the 26th of July Movement in its first stage. Those who held these criteria, fortunately for us, have left our revolutionary movement and have taken other paths.

From that time on the group which constituted the *Granma* crew began to take shape and it went through many difficult periods. We suffered the continuous persecution of Mexican authorities who at one point almost endangered the whole expedition. In addition, certain individuals who at first wanted to participate in the adventure later under one pretext or another left us and thus limited the number of the expeditionaries. In the end, eighty-two men boarded the *Granma*. The rest is well known by the Cuban people.

What I am concerned with and what I believe to be primarily important is the social thought of those who survived Alegría de Pío. This was the first and only disaster which the rebels suffered throughout the insurrection. Fifteen men, physically and morally destroyed, regrouped afterward. We were able to move forward only because of the enormous confidence which Fidel Castro, with the strong personality of a revolutionary caudillo, gave us in those decisive moments. We were a group with civilian origins attached but not grafted onto the Sierra Maestra. Thus we went from hut to hut; we touched nothing which did not belong to us, nor did we eat unless we could pay for it, and many a time we went hungry for this principle. Our group was looked on with tolerance but not joined by the peasants, and in this situation a great deal of time went by. For a few months we led a nomadic life in the high Sierra Maestra mountains. We made sporadic attacks. We went from one mountain to the next. Most of the time there was no water and living conditions were extremely difficult.

Bit by bit the peasants began to change their attitudes toward us, propelled by the actions of the repressive forces of Batista, who dedicated themselves to assassination and destruction of the houses of the peasants. Batista's men were hostile to all those who came into contact with the Rebel Army. This change in attitude was translated into the incorporation of peasants into our guerrillas; thus an army of civilians was beginning to change into an army of peasants. Simultaneously, as the peasants were incorporated into the armed struggle to attain liberty and social justice, the magic word began to spread to the oppressed masses of Cuba in their struggle for land: Agrarian Reform.

In that manner the first great social issue was established; later agrarian reform became the predominant banner of our movement even though we went through a stage of much restlessness due to our natural preoccupation with the policy and conduct of our neighbor to the north. At the time, the presence of foreign reporters, preferably North American, was more important to us than a military victory. More important than the incorporation in the struggle of the peasantry (who gave the Revolution their ideals and faith) was to have North American fighters who served to export our revolutionary propaganda.

At that time a tragic event occurred in Santiago de Cuba, the assassination of *compañero* Frank País. This marked a complete change in the structure of the revolutionary movement. The people of Santiago de Cuba, responding to the emotional impact of the assassination, went to the streets spontaneously, producing the first attempt at a general political strike, which even though it had no direction completely paralyzed Oriente Province, with repercussions in Las Villas and Camagüey provinces. The dictatorship liquidated this movement that began without preparation or revolutionary control. This popular phenomenon made us aware of the need to incorporate the workers into our liberation struggle. Immediately thereafter clandestine work began to prepare a general strike which would aid the Rebel Army in gaining power.

This gave rise to the creation of underground organizations with an insurrectional philosophy, yet those who encouraged these movements did not really know the meaning or the tactics of a people's war. The masses were led down false paths because their leaders did not create a revolutionary spirit and unity. They attempted to direct the strike from above without effective ties with the workers at the base.

The victories of the Rebel Army and the great efforts of the underground created within the country such a state of unrest that a general strike was called in April 9, 1958. It failed precisely because of organizational errors primarily due to the lack of contact between the leaders and the working masses and their mistaken attitude. The experience taught us a lesson. An ideological struggle developed within the 26th of July Movement which brought about a radical change in the analysis of the country's realities and in its activist sectors. The 26th of July Movement was strengthened by the failure of the strike, and the experience taught us a precious truth—mainly that the Revolution did not belong to any one group in particular but to all the Cuban people. Consequently all the energies of our militants in the mountains and cities were aimed toward that end.

Precisely at this time the Rebel Army took its first steps to develop the theory and doctrine of the Revolution; this demonstrated that the insurrectional movement had grown and achieved political maturity. We moved from an experimental stage to a constructive one, from trials to definite deeds. Immediately we initiated "small industries" in the Sierra Maestra: Like our ancestors, we moved from nomadic life into a settled life; we created centers of production in accord with our most basic needs. Shoe and weapons shops appeared and we began to build land mines from the bombs which Batista dropped on us.

The men and women of the Rebel Army did not forget that their fundamental mission in the Sierra Maestra and elsewhere was the betterment of the peasantry and their incorporation in the struggle for land. We formed schools in the mountainous regions of Oriente. There we made our first trial at distributing land through an agrarian code written by Dr. Humberto Sorí Marín, Fidel Castro, and myself, drawn up for the redistribution of the land. In a revolutionary manner, the land was given to peasants. Great farms of Batista's advocates were occupied, and all state lands in the region were given to the peasants. We were now fully identified as a peasant movement closely bound to the land and with agrarian reform as our emblem.

Later we reaped the consequences of the ill-fated strike of April 9 as the dictatorship increased its repression by the end of May, provoking in our cadres a loss of morale which could have had catastrophic consequences for our cause. The dictatorship began its most furious offensive. On May 25 of last year [1958], 10,000 well-equipped soldiers attacked our position, centering their offensive on Column Number One led personally by our commander in chief, Fidel Castro. At the time the Rebel Army controlled a very small area. And it is incredible that we faced a force of 10,000 soldiers with 300 rifles; those were the only rifles in the Sierra Maestra at the time. Suitable tactical leadership resulted in the end of the Batista offensive by July 30. From then on the rebels moved from defense into the offensive. We captured more than 600 new arms, more than twice the number of rifles we had when the action was begun. The enemy suffered more than 1,000 casualties in dead, wounded, deserters, and prisoners.

The Rebel Army came out of this campaign prepared to initiate the offensive in the lowlands. This was a tactical and psychological offensive because our armaments could not compete in quality or quantity with those of the dictatorship. This was a war in which we always counted on that imponderable: the extraordinary courage of the people. Our columns were able to constantly fool the enemy and place themselves in better positions not only because of our tactical advantage and the high morale of our militiamen, but also because of the generous support given by the peasants. The peasant was the invisible collaborator who did everything the rebel soldier could not do: he gave us information, watched the enemy, found the enemy's weaknesses, rapidly brought us urgent messages, and spied within the ranks of the Batista army. None of these was a miracle but a product of our energetic agrarian policy. Due to the attacks made on the Sierra Maestra and the hunger encirclement established by all the landowners in the surrounding areas, 10,000 head of cattle were sent to the mountains. They were sent to supply the Rebel Army and the peasants. For the first time the peasants of that region ate meat and the children drank milk. Also for the first time the peasants there were given the benefits of education. Our Revolution brought in its hand, schools. That is why the peasants reached a positive conclusion about our regime.

On the other hand the dictatorship burned the peasants' houses systematically; they were removed from their land or murdered. Death came sometimes from the skies in the form of napalm that the democratic neighbors to the north gave graciously to Batista to terrorize civilian populations; they gave 1,000-pound bombs which destroyed everything within a 100-meter circumference. A napalm bomb dropped over a coffee grove means the destruction of that wealth—and all the years of labor; what is destroyed in a minute will take five or six years to rebuild. At this time we began our march to Las Villas. This is important to point out, not because I participated in it, but because on our arrival in Las Villas we found a new sociopolitical panorama of the Revolution.

When we arrived at Las Villas with the flag of the 26th of July, the Directorio Revolutionario, groups of the Segundo Frente of Escambray, groups of the Partido Socialista Popular, and smaller ones of the Organización Auténtica were already there fighting against the dictatorship.[1] It was necessary to begin to work to achieve unity—an important factor in any revolutionary struggle. The 26th of July, with the Rebel Army at its head, had to promote unity among the different elements that were disgruntled with one another and who had as their only unifying element the work done

[1] Directorio Revolutionario was a student group; Segundo Frente was partly formed by social democratic groups; Partido Socialista Popular was the name of the Communist Party at the time; Organización Auténtica was a splinter section of the Partido Auténtico. Eds.

in the Sierra Maestra. First it was necessary to plan the unity of these groups of fighters not only in the hills but also in the plains. Thus, we had to perform the very important task of classifying all the sections of workers which were found in the province. This task was carried out amid opposition, even within our own movement, which still suffered from the disease of sectarianism.

We had just arrived in Las Villas and our first governmental edict —before establishing the first school—was a revolutionary law establishing an agrarian reform that ordered, among other things, owners of small parcels of land to pay no more rent until the Revolution considered each case separately. The agrarian reform was the spearhead with which the Rebel Army advanced. It was not a demagogic maneuver but it was simply that after one year and eight months of revolution, the close understanding existing between the leaders and the peasant masses was so great that many times it propelled the Revolution to do things it had not even conceived of doing before. We did not invent agrarian reform, it was an idea that came from the peasants; they pushed for it. We convinced the peasants that with the weapons at hand, with organization, and without fear of the enemy, victory was assured. And the peasantry, which had good reasons to do so, compelled the Revolution to make an agrarian reform, compelled the confiscation of cattle and all the other social measures adopted in the Sierra Maestra.

In the Sierra Maestra, Law Number Three was decreed on the day of the November 3 [1958] electoral farce. It established a true agrarian reform and, though incomplete, it contained very positive arrangements: State lands were to be distributed as well as land of those who served Batista and land obtained by fraudulent means, like that of the land-grabbers who swallowed thousands of acres of borderlands. It gave small *colonos* [2] plots not exceeding two *caballerías* [3] if they paid rent. Everything was free. The principle was very revolutionary. The agrarian reform will benefit over 200,000 families. Yet the agrarian revolution is not complete with Law Number Three. To complete it, it is necessary to establish a law that will proscribe large landholdings as stated by the Constitution. We must define exactly the concept of latifundio which characterizes our agrarian structure and is the source of the nation's backwardness and of all the miseries of the majority of the peasantry; this has not been touched yet.

[2] *Colonos:* individuals who rented land from the sugar mills and depended on the mill to sell their production. Tenant farmers. Eds.

[3] *Caballería:* 33.16 acres. Eds.

The organized peasant masses now have the task of demanding a law that will prohibit latifundia just as they once compelled the Rebel Army to establish Law Number Three. There is another aspect which must be considered. The Constitution states that land expropriation must be paid for in advance. If the agrarian reform is to follow that precept, it may be a little slow and expensive. The collective action of the peasantry, who have won their right to freedom since the triumph of the Revolution, is needed in order to demand the democratic derogation of that precept so they can advance toward a true and full agrarian reform.

Now we begin to consider the social ideals of the Rebel Army. Today we have an armed democracy. When we plan the agrarian reform and observe the new revolutionary laws that complement it, making it viable and immediate, our main concern is the social justice that land redistribution brings about. The creation of an extensive internal market and agricultural diversification, two of the fundamental and inseparable objectives of the revolutionary government, cannot be postponed because the interests of the people are implied in it.

All economic activities are related. We must increase the industrialization of the country without ignoring the many problems that this process creates. But a policy to encourage industrialization requires certain tariff measures, which protect our new industries, and an internal market capable of absorbing the new products. This market can only be increased by adding to it the peasant masses, the *guajiros*, who until now have had no buying power though remaining needy.

We are aware that our goals demand an enormous responsibility on our part, and these responsibilities are not the only ones. We must await the reaction of those who dominate more than 75 percent of our commercial trade and our market. We must prepare ourselves before this danger by applying countermeasures such as tariffs and the diversification of our markets abroad. We need to build a Cuban merchant fleet to transport sugar, tobacco, and other products because its existence will have a favorable influence on the type of cargoes on which to a large degree the progress of underdeveloped countries like Cuba depends.

If we are going to undertake an industrialization program, what is most important to achieve it? First, the raw materials which the Constitution wisely protected but which have been surrendered to foreign enterprises by the Batista dictatorship. We must rescue our subsoil, our minerals. Another element of industrialization is electricity. We have to rely on it. We are going to make sure that electric power returns to Cuban hands. We also have to nationalize the telephone company because of the poor service it has rendered and the high rates it maintains.

Which tools do we possess to carry out a program of this sort? We have the Rebel Army, and it must be our first instrument in the struggle, our most vigorous and positive weapon. What is left of Batista's army must be destroyed. Let it be understood that this is not done for revenge or only for the love of justice, but to assure that all those achievements made by the people be attained in the shortest time possible.

We defeated, with the support of the people, an army which was numerically superior to ours. We did so with suitable tactics and a revolutionary morale. But now we must face the fact that our Rebel Army is not yet capable of performing newly acquired responsibilities such as the integral defense of Cuban territory. We have to restructure the Rebel Army rapidly because we formed an armed force of workers and peasants, many of them illiterate and without technical preparation. We must educate this army culturally and technically for the demanding task they must face.

The Rebel Army is the vanguard of the Cuban people and when we refer to its technical and cultural development we should know the contemporary meaning of this. We have symbolically begun its education with a reading presided over almost exclusively by the spirit and teachings of José Martí.

The process of national reconstruction must destroy many privileges and that is why we must be on the alert to defend the nation from its real or hidden enemies. That is why the new army has to adapt to the new modes that have arisen in this war of liberation. We know that if Cuba suffers external aggression from a small island, it would be with the support of a nation that occupies almost an entire continent. We would have to face on our soil an immense aggressive force. That is why we must anticipate and prepare our vanguard with a guerrilla spirit and strategy—so that our defenses will not disintegrate with the first attack and will maintain their cohesive unity. All the Cuban people must become a guerrilla army because the Rebel Army is a growing institution whose capacity is only limited by our population of 6 million people. Each and every Cuban must learn to handle and if necessary use firearms in the defense of the nation.

Briefly I have outlined the social ideals of the Rebel Army after victory and its role as it moves the government toward verifying its revolutionary aspirations.

There is a most interesting thing to tell you before I end this talk.

The example our Revolution has set in Latin America and the teachings implied in it have destroyed all coffee-shop theories. We have demonstrated that a small group of determined men with the support of the people and without fear of death if necessary can defeat a regular and disciplined army. This is the fundamental lesson. There is another lesson that should be learned by our brothers in America because they find themselves economically in the same agrarian category in which we find ourselves. The lesson is that agrarian revolutions must be made; we must struggle in the countryside, in the mountains, and from there take the revolution to the cities. One cannot pretend to make revolution in the cities devoid of any social substance.

Now, with all the experiences we have had, we are faced with the question of what our future will be, a future very closely related to that of all the underdeveloped countries of Latin America. The Revolution is not limited to the Cuban nation because it has touched the consciousness of Latin America and has also alerted the enemies of our peoples. For this reason, we have warned that any aggression will be repelled with arms in hand. The example of Cuba has provoked more unrest in all of Latin America, in all oppressed countries. The Revolution has placed the dictators of Latin America on death row because they, like foreign monopolies, are the enemies of popular government. As we are a small country, we need the support of all democratic countries and especially of Latin America.

We have to truthfully inform the entire world of the noble goals of the Cuban Revolution. We have to call on the friendship of North Americans and Latin Americans. We have to create a spiritual unity among all of our countries, a unity that will transcend superfluous words and bureaucracy, a friendship that will transform itself in effective aid to our brothers by sharing with them our experience.

Finally, we must open new roads that will identify our common interests as underdeveloped countries. We must be aware of all efforts to divide us and struggle against those who would try to sow the seed of discord among us, those who, hiding behind well-known designs, aspire to profit from our political disagreements and incite impossible prejudices in this country.

Today the people of Cuba are standing up to the struggle and must continue to do so. Their victory against dictatorship is not transitory but rather the first step toward Latin America's victory.

Revolution and
University Reform

ᒥᒪᒥᒪᒥᒪᒥᒪᒥᒪᒥᒪᒥᒪᒥᒪᒥᒪᒥᒪᒥᒪᒥᒪᒥᒪᒥ

It is an honor to come here to speak at this revolutionary university. My topic is rather broad and, as you are probably aware, different themes could be developed on revolution and university reform. I am a revolutionary fighter and that is why my interest is mainly in the revolutionary duties of university students.

To consider this theme it is necessary to analyze carefully the social background of students. We also have to look at the relationship that exists between the actions of students and their social class.

Students are a reflection of their universities. No doubt there are different types of conditions facing students, but the essential factor is that the student belongs to a relatively well-to-do class. In general, students are middle class—not only in Cuba, but all over Latin America. Needless to say, there are exceptions. There are individuals who, due to their outstanding capacity, struggle against adverse conditions and succeed in acquiring a university degree. The majority, however, belong to the middle class and university students reflect the thinking of that class. Although sometimes, at times of great enthusiasm, the university students have moved into revolutionary positions.

We are trying to consider the main trends within the university and how they relate to the social bases from which students originate. Also, we have to analyze the revolutionary duties of students in relation to the whole community. This is important because the success or failure of the application of technology lies mainly with those attending universities.

We have established laws that have totally changed the social system. The large landholdings have been done away with. We have changed the tax structure. Prices and duties have been changed. Cooperatives have been created. A whole series of new institutions has appeared in Cuba. We are doing all these with very good intentions and without the professionals our Revolution requires. Our universities produced lawyers and doctors for the old social system, but did not create enough agricultural extension teachers, agrono-

Speech delivered at a symposium on university autonomy on October 17, 1959. Recorded by the authors.

mists, chemists, or physicists. In fact, we do not even have mathematicians. Consequently we have had to innovate.

In many cases our universities do not even offer the required resources. On a few occasions a very small number of students go into such fields. We have found a technological vacuum because there was no planning, no direction on the part of the state that considered the needs of our society.

We believe that the state is capable of understanding the needs of the nation; as such, then, the state must participate in the administration and direction of the university. Many people oppose this vehemently. Many consider it a destruction of university autonomy.

This is a mistaken attitude. The university cannot be an ivory tower, far away from the society, removed from the practical accomplishments of the Revolution. If such an attitude is maintained, the university will continue giving our society lawyers that we do not need.

There are two possible paths that the university can take. A number of students denounce state intervention and the loss of university autonomy. This student sector reflects its class background while forgetting its revolutionary obligation. This sector has not realized that it has an obligation to workers and peasants. Our workers and peasants died beside the students in order to attain power.

It is dangerous to maintain this attitude. The fact is that larger questions are involved here. Great strategic links are being developed abroad to destroy our Revolution. Those forces are trying to attract all those who have been hurt by the Revolution. We do not refer to the embezzlers, criminals, or the members of the old government; we are thinking of those who have remained on the margin of this revolutionary process, those who have lost economically but support the Revolution in a limited way.

All these people are dispersed throughout different social classes. Today they can express their discontent with freedom. National and international reactionaries want to strengthen their forces by attracting these people and making a front to bring economic depression, an invasion, or who knows what.

The issue of autonomy which is being fought so furiously is creating the very conditions that we should avoid. Those are the conditions that reactionaries can use effectively against the Revolution. The university, vanguard of our struggling people, cannot become a backward element, but it would become so if the university did not incorporate itself into the great plans of the Revolution.

The problem faced here is not new. It is not a theoretical question. The same thing has occurred in all of Latin America. There are multiple examples. I remember the pathetic example of the University of Guatemala which, like Cuban universities, was at the front of the struggle. They carried out a large part of the popular struggle when dictators were in power, and later during the Arevalo government. But, during the Arbenz government, the universities became opposition centers against the democratic regime. The universities defended their autonomy, just as is being done in Cuba. At this time, university autonomy is against the very interests of the nation.

In this blind and futile struggle, the universities became the instrument of reaction. The invasion of Castillo Armas, the public burning of books that ensued under the sponsorship of the little Guatemalan dictator, brought the universities back to their senses. The universities made a great mistake in Guatemala, and that country is still in a chaotic situation today. They are still searching for democracy. This is a vivid example that all of you should remember because it is recent history.

We could analyze the conquest of university autonomy more deeply by the University Reform Movement in 1918—a movement that originated in Córdoba, Argentina, that is, in the province of my birth. It is possible to look at the personalities of all of those militant students who fought hard to get university autonomy in the face of conservative governments ruling Latin America at the time. It is not my desire to mention names; I do not want to engage in international polemics. I ask you, instead, to read the book by Gabriel del Mazo where he studies carefully the University Reform Movement.[1] In that book you will find names. Then look at the political attitudes of those leaders of university autonomy in their respective countries and you will be quite surprised.

You will be surprised as I was, because once I thought like many of you do today. Once I thought that university autonomy was a progressive factor in Latin America; then I found that the most outright reactionaries, the biggest hypocrites, were the fountainheads of the idea of university autonomy.

I am addressing the majority of you today, all those who comprise this university. A few months ago I recommended that some of you get in touch with the people. Go to the masses, but do not go with

[1] Gabriel del Mazo, *Estudiantes y gobierno universitario* (Buenos Aires: Editorial El Ateneo), 1946. Eds.

airs of superiority; go to the people as a revolutionary, as a member of those who rule our country today.

Let each professional add to the knowledge he acquired in the classroom the knowledge he should acquire in the real battlefield of building a country. It is clear that one of the great duties of the university is to send its professionals to the people. It is also evident that in order to do so, organizationally, a state body has to plan and direct the activities of the university.

Nevertheless, the Revolution has not intervened in the university. It is illogical and dishonorable to do so. The Revolution simply shows reality to the student; we rely on reasoning and discussion. Thank you.

Honoring
José Martí

Dear fellow men, children, and adolescents of today, men and women of tomorrow, heroes of tomorrow, heroes if necessary in the rigors of armed struggle if not heroes in the peaceful construction of our sovereign nation.

Today is a special day, a day which calls for an intimate conversation among those who in some way have contributed directly to the Revolution.

Today is a new anniversary of the birth of José Martí, and before I approach the topic, I would like to warn you that I heard a few moments ago "Viva Che Guevara!" But none of you shouted, "Viva Martí!"—and this is not correct.

This is not correct for many reasons. Before Che Guevara was born and before the men who today have fought for today's liberation, Martí was born; he suffered and died for the ideal which we are realizing today.

Martí is the direct precursor of our Revolution, the man whose thoughts aid us in interpreting the historical process in which we are living and whose example we have to remember every time we wish to say something of importance about the fatherland. José Martí is more than simply Cuban, he is American; he belongs to the twenty nations of our continent and his voice is heard and respected not only in Cuba but in all America.

We have been given the honor of materializing the words of José Martí in his own fatherland, in the place where he was born. We could honor him by religiously participating in the ceremonies which mark his birth each year or remembering that nefarious nineteenth of May, 1895, when he died. We could honor Martí by quoting his phrases, which were perfect and beautiful and just. But we can and should honor Martí in the way he most wanted when he said, "The best way of telling is by doing."

This is why we are trying to honor him by doing what he wanted

Speech made on the 107th anniversary of José Martí's birth, January 28, 1960. *Revolución* (Havana), January 30, 1960, p. 16. José Martí (1835–1895) was Cuba's independence leader and outstanding intellectual.

to do but was prevented from doing because of political circumstances and colonial bullets.

None of us could be Martí, but all of us can take Martí's example and follow it according to our own efforts. To understand and revive him, we have to follow him in our daily conduct because that war of independence, which was a long war of liberation, has its own replica today in many modest and hidden heroes who followed correctly the precepts and thoughts of Martí.

I want to introduce today a young man that many of you might know already. Then I will give a short summary of our difficult days in the Sierra Maestra.

Do you know him? It is Major Joel Iglesias of the Rebel Army and chief of the Association of Young Rebels. Now I will explain why he occupies that post and why I proudly introduce him to you today.

Major Joel Iglesias is seventeen years old. He was fifteen when he went to the Sierra Maestra. When he came to me I did not want to admit him into our forces. At the time there was a sack full of machine gun rounds and no one wanted to carry it. Joel was given the task of carrying it through the high Sierra Maestra mountains. It was a test. The fact that he is here with us today indicates that he did not fail.

But there is more. Probably you have not noticed that he limps and his voice is hoarse. He was wounded ten times, and his voice and leg were damaged by enemy bullets because he was always the first in battle and in responsible posts.

I remember that a major of ours died by a tragic mistake. Cristino Naranjo was his name. He was forty years old when he was a simple soldier under the command of fifteen-year-old Lieutenant Joel Iglesias. Cristino always spoke to Joel with a friendly "you"; but Joel always ordered Cristino in terms of "sir." [1] Cristino Naranjo, nonetheless, always obeyed his orders, because in our Rebel Army—following Martí's ideas—we were not concerned with age, past accomplishments, political past, religion, or the prior ideology of a fighter. We were concerned only with the facts of the moment and devotion to the revolutionary cause.

We knew well, because of Martí, that what counts is not how many weapons one has, but the purity of ideals. And Joel Iglesias at that time was one of those with many pure ideals in his mind. I want to introduce him to you so that you may know that the Rebel Army is concerned with our youth. We want to give our youth our

[1] The familiar *tu* in Spanish as opposed to the formal *usted*.

best men, our best fighters, and our best workers because this is how Martí is honored.

I would like to tell you many things like this, to explain so that you will understand well and feel deeply in your hearts why we fought and why we struggle today against imperialist powers—a struggle that will be fought tomorrow in the economic field or on the battlefield.

Of Martí's phrases, there is one that summarizes the spirit of the apostle of our independence; it says, "A real man should feel on his own cheek the blow given to another man's cheek." This is what the Rebel Army and the Cuban Revolution are all about: an army and a revolution that feel the effrontery of witnessing a man being slapped in the face anywhere in the world.

This is a revolution made for the people through the people's efforts. The Revolution began from below and its ranks were filled by peasants and workers; it demanded the sacrifice of workers and peasants in the countryside and cities of the island. It has not forgotten them after victory.

"With the poor of the earth I will cast my lot," Martí said, and that is what we have done. We have been put in our posts by the people and here we shall remain as long as they want, destroying all injustice and establishing a new social order.

We do not fear words or accusations; Martí never feared them either. On May 1, I think, of 1872, when heroes of the American working class were killed for defending the people's rights, Martí pointed out that date with courage and emotion as he denounced those who disregarded the human rights of working-class leaders. May 1, Martí pointed out at the time, is the same date that the working class the world over—except that of the United States, who are afraid to remember that date—and all world capitals celebrate as their day. Martí was the first in mentioning that day as a proletarian day, just as he was always the first in denouncing injustices. He revolted with our patriots and at fifteen was imprisoned; his entire life was one of sacrifice. He always thought in those terms, knowing that his sacrifice was essential to creating the revolutionary reality in which you live today.

Martí taught us that a revolutionary and a ruler can have neither a private life nor pleasures. He must give everything to the people that choose him, and this places him in a position of responsibility and combat.

This is why when we devote all hours of the day and night to work for our people we think of Martí and believe we are making his thought come true.

If something is to remain of this conversation between you and me, if it does not disappear into thin air, then I wish you all would think about José Martí. Think about him as if he were alive, not as a god or a dead object, but rather as something which is ever-present in Cuba's life. He is with us as our comrade Camilo Cienfuegos is with us.[2] The people's heroes cannot be separated from the people; they cannot become statues, something outside the life of the people for whom they died. The popular hero must be alive and present in every moment of our people's history.

Just as you remember Camilo today, Martí should be remembered, a Martí who speaks and talks today in our language, because this is one greatness in outstanding revolutionaries and thinkers: their language does not age. Martí's words are our fighting standard.

This is my final recommendation: Be close to Martí without thinking you are approaching a god, but rather a man greater than most men. And keep in mind that of all of Martí's loves, his greatest was for the children and youth to whom he dedicated his most tender and heartfelt pages.

To conclude, I beg of you to bid me farewell as you began, but in a different order—with a "Viva Martí," who is alive!

[2] Major Camilo Cienfuegos disappeared mysteriously at the end of 1959 in Cuba. Eds.

Political Sovereignty
and Economic Independence

ЛЛЛЛЛЛЛЛЛЛЛЛЛЛЛЛЛЛЛЛЛЛЛЛЛЛЛ

Naturally, when a lecture of this type [1] begins one has to salute our Cuban listeners. Let us repeat the statements made by our comrade [2] to the effect that this type of popular education is of great importance because it directly reaches our peasants and workers and explains to them the truths of the Revolution. We tell the truth in simple language because that is the best way to present it to the people.

I have the honor of beginning this series of lectures even though our comrade Raúl Castro was to be the one to talk today. Because the topic deals with economic matters he declined and asked me to do so. As soldiers of the Revolution, we willingly perform the task that duty imposes on us. Sometimes we have to perform tasks for which we do not have the ideal capacity, at the least. Perhaps this is one of those tasks—to explain in simple words, in concepts that everyone well knows and understands, the great importance of the problem of political sovereignty and economic independence and to explain also the close unity between these two terms. It is possible, as happened in Cuba, that one antecedes the other; but they necessarily go together. And after awhile they come together as a positive statement, as in Cuba which achieved its political independence and immediately dedicated itself to acquiring its economic independence. At other times, in the negative case, countries achieve or begin the road toward political independence but because economic independence is not assured, political independence progressively weakens until it is lost. Our revolutionary task today is not only to think about the future full of threats, but also to think about a better future.

The order of the moment is planning, the conscious and intelligent restructuring of all the problems that will face the people of

Speech delivered on the television program "Universidad Popular" on March 20, 1960. *Revolución* (Havana), March 21, 1960, pp. 1, 8.

[1] In 1960 the revolutionary government started a series of televised lectures in which the major revolutionary leaders spoke on the goals of the Revolution. Eds.

[2] The man who introduced Guevara to the audience. A moderator of the program whose name was not made available. Eds.

Cuba in the coming years. We cannot think only about the reply or the counterblow to a more or less immediate aggressive act; we have to begin an effort to elaborate a plan that will permit us to predict the future. The men of the Revolution must go consciously to their destiny, but this is not sufficient; it is necessary that all the people of Cuba understand exactly all the revolutionary principles so that they will know that beyond these times of uncertainty for some there is a future—a happy and glorious future because Cuba has taken the first step toward Latin America's liberty. That is why a program like this is so important. This is a program that allows everyone who has a message to our people to express it. Of course it is not new, for every time our prime minister speaks on television he teaches us authoritatively, as only a pedagogue of his kind can do. But here we have planned our lesson and divided it into specific topics so it is more than responding only to the question of an interview. Let us then begin our discussion of political sovereignty and economic independence.

Before we refer to the tasks that the Revolution is carrying out in order to make these two terms reality—these two concepts that should always go together—it is necessary to define and explain their meaning. Definitions are always defective. They always freeze terms and make them dead, but it is necessary at least to give a general conceptualization of these twin terms. There are some that do not understand, or do not want to (which is the same), what sovereignty consists of. They are scared when our country signs a commercial agreement (in which I had the honor of participating) with the Soviet Union and receives credit from this nation. This struggle has antecedents in the history of Latin America. Precisely two days ago was the anniversary of the expropriation of Mexican oil companies during the government of General Lázaro Cárdenas. At the time, we were children. More than twenty years have gone by, and we cannot exactly determine the commotion that it produced in America, but the terms and the accusations were exactly the same as those that Cuba endures today; as the ones that not too long ago, and experienced by myself, Guatemala had to bear; as the ones that in the future all countries that choose freedom will have to bear. We can say today without simplifying that the companies or the big newspaper enterprises and the United States opinion makers set the tone of honesty and importance of a ruler by simply inverting terms. The more a ruler is attacked the better he undoubtedly is, and today we have the privilege of being the country and the government most attacked perhaps in all the history of Latin America, much more than Guatemala and perhaps even more than Mexico when General Cárdenas ordered expropriation in 1936 or 1938. Oil at that time played a major role in Mexican life; in our country today sugar has the same role—the role of one product that goes to only one market.

"Without sugar there is no country," yell the spokesmen of reaction, and they believe that if the present market does not buy sugar from us we shall have absolute ruin, as if the country that buys sugar from us does so only with the desire of aiding us. For centuries political power was in the hands of slaveholders, then in the hands of feudal lords. To facilitate carrying on wars against enemies and against the rebellion of the oppressed they delegated their powers to one of them, the one who united them, the most determined, the cruelest of them all perhaps became king, sovereign, and despot, who as time went by imposed his will through historic epochs until absolutism was reached.

Of course, we are not going to relate the whole historical process of humanity, and anyway the time of kings has gone by. Only a few samples are left in Europe. Fulgencio Batista never thought of calling himself Fulgencio I. For him it was enough that a certain powerful neighbor recognized him as president and that the army officials followed his orders, that is, those who controlled physical power, material power, the instruments of murder. They followed and supported him because he was the strongest among them, the cruelest, and the friendliest to those abroad. Today we have kings without crowns; they are the monopolies, the true masters of entire countries and on occasion of continents, as the African continent, sections of Asia, and, sadly, our America have been up to now. At times they have tried to dominate the world. Hitler was first, a representative of the great German monopolies, who in the name of racial superiority tried to rule over the world by waging a war that left 40 million dead.

The importance of monopolies is immense, so great that it makes the political power of many republics disappear. Some time ago we read an essay by Papini, whose main character, Gog, bought a country and then stated that the people of that country thought that they had presidents, legislatures, armies, and that it had sovereignty; but in reality, he had bought them all. And this caricature is exact. There are some republics that depend on the omniscient will of the United Fruit Company, for example, whose well-hated director was a lawyer; others depend on Standard Oil Company or some other monopolist petroleum company. There are still others that depend on the kings of tin or coffee to mention American examples and not those of Asia or Africa. In other words, political sovereignty is a term that should not be defined formalistically for one has to go to its roots. All the treatises and codes of law and all the politicians of the world maintain that national sovereignty is an idea indivisible from the sovereign state. If it were not so, world powers would not have to call their colonies free associated states,[3] which hides the fact of colonization behind the phrase. Whether an internal regime will permit in a greater or lesser degree, will permit complete, or will not permit the exercise of sovereignty to its people is a matter that concerns only that people. National sovereignty signifies first of all the right of a nation to have no other nation interfere in its internal affairs, the right of the people to have the government of their choosing and the way of life which they consider best. This depends on the will of the people and only they can determine whether a government should change or not. But all these concepts of political sovereignty are fictitious if there is no economic independence.

We have stated that political sovereignty and economic independence go hand in hand. If there is no national economy, if the economy is penetrated by foreign capital, one is not free from the tutelage of the country on which one depends. Much less can one carry out the national will if it goes against the great foreign interests that dominate the economy. This idea is not absolutely clear to the people of Cuba, and it is necessary to restate it. The pillars of political sovereignty that were built on January 1, 1959, can only be consolidated when absolute economic independence is achieved. We have made some progress by the daily measures that have been taken to assure our economic independence. At the moment when government measures hinder our progress along this road or make the nation move backward—even if by only one step—everything is lost and colonial systems will return under the new façade that each country and social situation give them.

These concepts should be known today. Now it is very difficult to crush the political sovereignty of a nation through pure and simple violence. The last two examples that we have witnessed are the cruel and unexpected attack launched by English and French colonialists on Port Said in Egypt and the landing of North American troops in Lebanon. Nonetheless, the marines are not sent now with the same impunity as before. Now it is easier to establish a curtain

[3] Refers to Puerto Rico. Eds.

of lies than to invade a country simply because it has hurt the economic interests of a large monopoly. To invade a country that demands its right to exercise its sovereignty at this time in which the peoples can state their views at the United Nations is difficult. It is difficult to misinform the entire world public opinion. To do so a great propagandistic effort is necessary which will prepare the conditions that will make intervention less hateful.

This is precisely what is being done to us. The conditions are being prepared to reduce Cuba by any means necessary and it depends on only us to prevent that aggression from taking place. They could carry out economic aggression, but we have to be sure that our country is conscious of this so that if they want to send soldiers of monopolies and mercenaries from other nations they will find it so costly that they would not do so. They are trying to drown this Revolution in blood if necessary only because we are moving toward economic liberation, because we are setting the example with the measures that will liberate our country, and because we seek to achieve a degree of economic freedom similar to our present political freedom and maturity.

We have taken political power and begun our fight for liberation with this power which is firmly held by the people. The people cannot even dream about sovereignty if there is no power that responds to the people's interests and aspirations. Popular power does not mean merely that the people control the council of ministers, the police, the courts of law, and all the governmental machinery, but it also means that the economic institutions are beginning to be controlled by the people. Revolutionary power or political sovereignty is the instrument to conquer economic independence and to make a reality of national sovereignty. In terms of Cuba, this means that the revolutionary government is the instrument which will allow only Cubans to rule in Cuba, from politics to the wealth of our land and our industry. We cannot proclaim yet before the tombs of our martyrs that Cuba is economically independent. Cuba cannot be independent when a single ship detained by the United States makes a factory in Cuba stop operations, when a simple order of a monopoly paralyzes a labor center here. Cuba will be independent when it develops all its natural resources and when it is assured through treaties and trade with all the world that the unilateral move of no foreign power can impede the rate of production and it can maintain all factories and rural production at optimum rates within the context of the planning we are carrying out. We can state that political sovereignty was achieved the day that popular power triumphed, the day that the Revolution triumphed, January 1, 1959.

That day marks not only the beginning of an extraordinary year in the history of Cuba but also the beginning of an era. And we believe that it is not only the beginning of a new era in Cuba, but also in Latin America. For Cuba January 1 is the culmination of July 26, 1953, and of August 12, 1933, just as it is the end of a struggle that began on February 24, 1895, and on October 10, 1868.[4] January 1 is also a glorious date for America; it might mark the continuation of May 25, 1809, when Morillo revolted in Alto Peru, or it could be May 25, 1810, when the Cabildo Abierto [5] in Buenos Aires revolted, or any other date that marks the beginning of the struggle of Latin America for its political independence in the early nineteenth century. This date, January 1, conquered at an enormously high price for the Cuban people, culminates the struggles of generations of Cubans ever since the formation of our national identity to attain complete sovereignty, for the fatherland, for freedom, and for the complete political and economic independence of Cuba.

January 1 can be reduced to a bloody, spectacular, and (if you like) decisive event, but as well to hardly a moment in Cuban history. January 1, 1959, marks the death of the despotic regime of Fulgencio Batista, that little Weyler [6] of our own, but it marks as well the establishment of the true republic, politically free and sovereign, guided by the supreme law of man's total dignity.

This January 1 signifies the triumph of all the martyrs who preceded us, starting from José Martí, Antonio Maceo, Máximo Gómez, Calixto García, Moncada, or Juan Gualberto Gómez, who were preceded by Narciso López, Ignacio Agramonte, and Carlos Manuel de Céspedes, as well as by all the martyrs of our republican era—Mella, Guiteras, Frank País, José Antonio Echeverría, and Camilo Cienfuegos.[7]

[4] July 26, 1953, was the day on which Castro attacked the Moncada Barracks in Oriente Province. August 12, 1933, was the date on which a revolutionary strike overthrew the dictatorship of Gerardo Machado. February 24, 1895, marks the reinitiation of the war of independence that began in Cuba on October 10, 1868. Eds.

[5] A sort of town-meeting organization that became important during the revolts against Spain in Latin America. Eds.

[6] The Spanish general Weyler was responsible for the establishment of concentration compounds in Cuba in the 1890's. Eds.

[7] Martí, Maceo, Máximo and Juan Gualberto Gómez, García, and Moncada were independence leaders in the 1880's and 1890's; López, Agramonte, and Céspedes were independence leaders in the period from 1868 to the 1870's; Mella and Guiteras were revolutionary leaders in the 1930's; País, Echeverría, and Cienfuegos fought against the Batista dictatorship. Eds.

Fidel has been aware, as always, since he began to fight whole-heartedly for his people, of the magnitude of the revolutionary forti-tude, of the greatness of the time that made the collective heroism of the people possible: this marvelous people from which the glo-rious Rebel Army arose, a continuation of the Mambí army.[8] That is why Fidel likes to compare the tasks to be fulfilled with the tasks facing the handful of survivors from the legendary *Granma* landing.[9] There we left, when the *Granma* was abandoned, all individual hopes, and the struggle in which an entire people had to triumph or be de-feated began. That is why, due to the great faith and unity of Fidel with his people, we were never dismayed—not even at the most dif-ficult moments of the campaign. We knew that we were not iso-lated in the Sierra Maestra mountains, and that the struggle was going on all over Cuba, everywhere a man or a woman had dignity.

As Fidel knew, and all of us learned later, that was a struggle like the one now in which the entire Cuban people would achieve victory or be defeated. Today he insists on this: Either we are all saved or we all drown. You are acquainted with the phrase. All the diffi-culties that have to be overcome are as difficult as in those days of the *Granma* landing, but now the combatants are not a few units or dozens but millions. All of Cuba has become a Sierra Maestra to fight the enemy on any ground, the definitive battle for the liberty, fu-ture, and honor of our fatherland and of America because, sadly, it is the only representative of our peoples standing up.

The battle of Cuba is the battle of America but not a definitive battle, at least in one sense. Even if we suppose that Cuba loses the battle, America will not lose it; but if Cuba wins this battle, the whole of America will have won the struggle. That is the importance of our island and that is why they want to suppress this "bad exam-ple" we are making. In 1956, the strategic objective, that is, the gen-eral objective of our war, was the overthrow of Batista's dictator-ship, in other words, the re-establishment of all of the concepts of democracy, sovereignty, and independence taught to us by foreign monopolies. Since March 10, 1952,[10] Cuba had been a barracks with the same characteristics as the barracks we are turning into schools today. All Cuba was a barracks then. However, March 10, 1952, was not the work of a single man but the product of a caste, a group of men united by a series of privileges of which one of them, the most

[8] Mambí army refers to the rebels that fought against Spain in the nineteenth century in Cuba. Eds.

[9] December 2, 1956. Eds.

[10] The day on which Fulgencio Batista led a military coup. Eds.

ambitious and bold, the Fulgencio I of our story, was the leader. This caste was accountable to the reactionary class of our country, the landowners and the parasitical capitalists, and was allied to foreign colonialism. They were quite a few, a whole series of characters who have disappeared today as if by magic: everything from *manengues* [11] to the president's newspapermen, everything from strikebreakers to the czars of gambling and prostitution. On January 1, 1959, the fundamental strategic objective of the Revolution was achieved: the destruction of the tyranny that for almost seven years had spilled blood all over Cuba. However, our Revolution, which is a conscious revolution, knows that political sovereignty is closely related to economic sovereignty.

This Revolution does not want to repeat the mistakes made in the decade of the thirties, that is, to simply liquidate a man without realizing that that man represents a class and a state of affairs, and that if that state of affairs is not destroyed, the enemies of the people create another man. That is why the Revolution had to destroy the root of the illness Cuba suffered. It is necessary to imitate Martí and to repeat over and over again that a radical is one who goes to the root of things; if one does not go to the root, one cannot be called a radical. If one does not want the security and happiness of man, one cannot be called a man. This Revolution has the goal of pulling all injustices out by the roots. Fidel has said so using different terms, but the idea comes from Martí. Now that the great strategic objective of Batista's downfall and revolutionary power that arose from the people, whose armed instrument is now an army synonymous with the people, is established, the new strategic objective is the conquest of economic independence, that is, the conquest of complete national sovereignty. Yesterday the tactical objectives of the struggle were in the mountains, the plains, Santa Clara, the presidential palace, Camp Columbia, [12] production centers, all of which had to be taken by frontal attack, encirclement, or through underground activity.

Our tactical objectives today are the triumph of the agrarian reform which creates the basis for the industrialization of the country, diversification of foreign trade, raising the standard of living of the people in order to achieve the great strategic objective of liberating our national economy. The economic front is today the main scene of the struggle, even if we consider other fronts such as education

[11] *Manengues:* Cuban slang for those who hold sinecures. Eds.
[12] Camp Columbia in Havana was the headquarters of the Cuban armed forces under Batista.

of great importance. Not long ago I referred to the importance of education because it would permit us to have the technicians required to win this battle. But this indicates that in the struggle the economic front is the most important and education is destined to produce the officers that will enable us to wage this battle under the best possible conditions. I can call myself a military man, but one who arose from the people and fought as many others simply obeying a call, fulfilling his duty at a moment when it was necessary. Today I am in another post. I do not pretend to be an economist; I am simply a revolutionary fighter placed in a new trench and, as such, I have to be concerned as few are with the future of the economy on which the destiny of the Revolution depends. But this battle on the economic front is different from those we fought in the mountains; these are battles for positions, battles where the unexpected almost never occurs. Troops are concentrated, and the attacks are prepared with care. The victories are the result of work, endurance, and planning. It is a war where collective heroism and the sacrifice of all is demanded. This war will not last a day, a week, or a month; it is a long struggle. The more isolated we are, the less we have studied all the characteristics of the terrain in which the fight will take place, the longer the struggle will be. The enemy must be analyzed completely.

This war is waged with many weapons, from the 4 percent contribution by the workers [13] for the industrialization of the country to the work in every cooperative and the establishment of new branches of the national economy such as petrochemicals or steel. It has as its main strategic objective, and this must be emphasized constantly, the conquest of national sovereignty.

To conquer something, we have to take it away from someone else. It is necessary to speak clearly and not to hide behind concepts that could be misinterpreted. We have to conquer our national sovereignty, and we have to take it away from foreign monopolies. Even though monopolies in general do not have a fatherland, they have at least a common denominator. All the monopolies that have exploited Cuba, that have profited from our land, have very close ties with the United States. In other words, our economic war will be against the great power of the north. This is not a simple war. Our liberation will be achieved if we defeat the monopolies in general and North American monopolies in particular. The control of a nation's economy by another reduces, undoubtedly, the economy of that country.

[13] Made from the salaries of the workers. Eds.

Fidel said on February 24, 1960, that it is inconceivable that a revolution would wait for foreign private capital to solve the problems of the nation. How can anyone conceive that a revolution that arose from the need of the workers, sought for many years, could wait for a solution to the problem from private foreign capital investments when those interests invest in sectors not essential to the country, but instead invest in those that assure a profit? The Revolution could not go along that road because that was the road of exploitation. It was necessary to find another path. We had to hit the most irritating of all monopolies, that which controlled our land; we had to destroy it and give the land to the people and then initiate the true fight, because despite everything this was the first contact between the two enemies. The battle was not waged at the agrarian reform level, that is a fact. The battle will be fought now and in the future because despite the fact that monopolies had large extensions of land here, those were not the most important. The important ones are in chemistry, engineering, oil, and it is there that the example of Cuba—the bad example, as they call it—really hurts.

Nonetheless we had to start with the agrarian reform. One and a half percent of landowners in Cuba owned 46 percent of the national territory whereas 70 percent of all landowners owned only 12 percent of the land area. There were 62,000 farms with less than three fourths of a *caballería* [14] but the necessary minimum for a family of five was two *caballerías* in lands without irrigation as established in our agrarian reform. In Camagüey Province, five or six sugar companies controlled 56,000 *caballerías*, that is, 20 percent of the land area of Camagüey.

In addition, the monopolies controlled our nickel, cobalt, iron ore, chrome, manganese, and all the oil concessions. In oil, for instance, the concessions covered three times our land area. That is, they had the oil concessions of our entire land area, of every small isle, and the Cuban continental platform. Moreover, some companies fought each other to get the same concession. We also moved to abolish the property relations that the North American companies had. Housing speculation suffered a great blow when rents were reduced, and the INAV [15] plans to make cheap housing. There were many housing monopolies here. Even though not all were North American, they were parasitical capitalists allied to the North Americans—at least in the ideological concept of private property at the service of

[14] 1 caballería = 33.16 acres. Eds.
[15] Instituto Nacional de Ahorro y Vivienda, a government institution in charge of the Cuban lottery and housing at the time. Eds.

one person to exploit the people. With the intervention [16] of large supermarkets and the creation of people's stores—we have 1,400 of them in the countryside—we stopped speculation (or took the first steps to do so) and the monopoly over our internal market.

You know how expensive some products are; if there are any peasants listening you know of the large gap that exists between the actual prices and the prices charged by loan sharks in the past in our countryside. At least we have stopped the unbridled actions of public service monopolies. The electric and telephone monopolies are good examples. Those monopolies participated in every aspect of the life of the Cuban people, not only economically but politically and culturally as well.

We had to take measures in our liberation struggle in order to end the foreign trade monopoly. Already a number of commercial treaties have been signed with diverse countries and new countries come here constantly to seek our internal market on the basis of absolute equality. Undoubtedly, the agreement with the Soviet Union is the most important we have signed. It is good to emphasize this because we have already sold an unusual amount: we have sold all of our quota without anything left for the world market, and we still have some orders that can be estimated between 800,000 to 1 million tons, if new contracts are not made. Also, we have secured a market of 1 million tons for five years. It is true that we will not get dollars for all of it. Only 20 percent of the sugar will be paid in dollars. But the dollar is merely an instrument to buy with; it has no other value than its purchasing power and because we use our sugar to acquire manufactured products or raw materials, we are simply using sugar as a dollar substitute. Someone told me that an agreement of this nature would bring ruin to us because the transportation cost between the Soviet Union and Cuba would notably increase the prices of all imported goods. Our oil agreement demonstrates these predictions to be false. The Soviet Union has promised to supply Cuba with different types of oil at a price 33 percent cheaper than that of the North American monopolists, which are only a step from us. That is called economic liberation.

Naturally some people say that all these agreements from the Soviet Union are political in nature. Some affirm that all this is done to bother the United States. We can admit that it might be true. If the Soviet Union—a sovereign nation—wants to bother the United States, and sells us cheap oil and buys our sugar in order to do so,

[16] Intervention: when the government takes control of an enterprise but profits are received by the owner.

we do not mind. We are not concerned with their intentions. We simply trade; we are selling our sugar and not our national sovereignty, as we were doing before. We are simply going to talk in a language of equality. Every time a representative of a new nation comes here, it comes to talk a language of equality. It does not matter how large the country is or the power of their cannons. In terms of independence we are a nation equal to any other. Cuba has one vote at the United Nations just like the United States and the Soviet Union. It is in that spirit that all agreements have been made. All of our commercial treaties will be made on that basis. We must insist on what Martí some time ago made clear: the nation that buys is the nation that orders and the nation that sells is the one that obeys. When Fidel Castro explained that the trade agreement with the Soviet Union was very beneficial to Cuba, he was simply summarizing the Cuban people's sentiments. In fact, we all felt a little bit freer when we found that Cuba could sign trade agreements with anyone it wanted to. Today everyone should feel even freer, not just because our sovereignty was used to sign a commercial agreement, but it is also one of the most beneficial agreements signed by Cuba. When the onerous loans made by the North American companies are analyzed and compared with the credit Cuba received from the Soviet Union at 2½ percent interest for a twelve-year period—one of the lowest interest rates in the history of international commercial relations—the importance of the agreement becomes even clearer.

It is true that this credit is to buy Soviet merchandise, but it is not less true that the loans given by the Export-Import Bank—a supposedly international organization—are made to buy United States products. Furthermore, those loans are given to purchase specific merchandise made by foreign monopolies. The Export-Import Bank lends 8, 10, or 15 million (of course this does not mean real) pesos to the electric company of Burma—a company very similar to the Cuban Electric Company. An electric plant is installed and electricity is supplied to the nation at a very high price with very bad service. Enormous profits are made and then the nation pays. That is how international credit systems work. It is enormously different from receiving a credit that will benefit the people of the country. It would have been something else if the Soviet Union had given 100 million pesos to one of its subsidiaries here and if profits were repatriated to the Soviet Union. Through the credit Cuba has received, a steel mill and an oil refinery will be built which will belong to the nation and will serve the people.

In other words, we will pay back what we have received; this is a correct and fair agreement, as we have seen in the case of oil. I am not saying that as new contracts are signed, the people will be informed with the same openness that the Revolution explains all its actions, of all the extraordinarily cheap merchandise produced in the Soviet Union. The *Diario de la Marina* [17] believe it or not, once again, opposes all this. Unfortunately, I do not have with me a very interesting article that gave at least seven reasons why this agreement is harmful to Cuba. All the reasons are false, of course. But they are not only mistaken in interpretation, which is quite bad in itself, they are wrong even in terms of hard facts. They are false, for example, when they say that it means a compromise by Cuba through which it would support Soviet maneuvers at the United Nations. It is very different that in a declaration absolutely without connection to the trade agreement, a declaration written by common consent, Cuba agrees to struggle for peace within the United Nations. In other words, Cuba is condemned, as Fidel has explained, for doing that for which the United Nations was created according to its constitution. Other economic questions have been well refuted by our Minister of Commerce. The most important refers to prices. As you know, the price of sugar in the world market follows the law of supply and demand. *Diario de la Marina* says that if the one million tons that Cuba has sold are resold by the Soviet Union on the world market, Cuba would make no money. That is a lie, because of the simple fact that is clearly stated in the agreement that the Soviet Union can only export its sugar to those countries to which she has traditionally sold it. The Soviet Union imports sugar, but it also exports refined sugar to border states that lack refining capacity such as Iran, Iraq, and Afghanistan. To those countries to which the Soviet Union traditionally exports, it will keep selling sugar, but our sugar will be consumed entirely by the planned increase in consumption of the people of the Soviet Union.

If the North Americans are very worried—because now they are saying in Congress that the Soviet Union is catching up—and if they believe what the Soviet Union says, why shouldn't we? When they tell us, and they have signed a document stating it, that the sugar we sell them will be consumed in the Soviet Union, we believe them. Why should any newspaper spread doubt, a doubt made international which might harm the price of sugar in the world? Simply because it is carrying out counterrevolutionary activity. It is the work

[17] *Diario de la Marina:* the oldest conservative daily in Cuba. It was closed down in mid-1960. Eds.

of those who have not resigned themselves to losing their privileges.

With reference to the price of Cuban sugar, we made a statement a few days ago that received the undeserved comment of U.S. spokesman Lincoln Price; [18] they insist that the 150 million pesos the United States pays for our sugar is a gift to Cuba. That is not so. Cuba has had to sign tariff agreements in return which have forced us to spend $1.15 more or less in the United States for every $1.00 they spend here. This means that in a ten-year period our people have given one billion dollars to the North American monopolies. We do not have to give anyone gifts, but if our money went to the North American people we would be a little more satisfied with the whole arrangement, but our money goes to the vaults of the monopolies. That money serves as an instrument of oppression used to prevent the enslaved peoples of the world from initiating their liberation. Cuba has paid 61 cents in interest for every single dollar loaned by the United States and this is only short term—just imagine what it would be over a long term if we had received a loan similar to that of the Soviet Union. That is why we have followed Martí's advice and tried to diversify our foreign trade as much as possible. We do not want to be tied to any one buyer. Our goal is to diversify our foreign trade and internal production in order to get more markets abroad.

Cuba is moving forward. We are living at a glorious moment in our history, a moment in time when all the countries of Latin America look up to this island and reactionary governments accuse Cuba of every burst of popular indignation that takes place in any corner of America. It has been made very clear that Cuba does not export revolutions; revolutions cannot be exported. Revolutions occur at the instant in which a series of insurmountable contradictions appear inside a country. Cuba only exports its example, that "bad example" mentioned before. It is the example of a small nation that challenges the laws of a false science called "geopolitics" and at the very doorsteps of the monster, as Martí once said, it cries for freedom. That is our crime and the example the imperialists fear, the North American colonialists. They want to crush us because we are the standard-bearers of Latin America; they want to apply the Monroe Doctrine to us.[19] There is a new version of the

18 Guevara refers to a statement made on March 5, 1960, by State Department spokesman Lincoln White. Eds.
19 Established in 1823 by the United States, it stated that European powers could not colonize Latin America. Eds.

Doctrine in the Senate of the United States; I think that luckily for them it was not accepted or did not pass a certain commission.

I had the opportunity of reading the version and it showed their prehistoric mentality, so extraordinarily colonialist that I think it would have constituted a disgrace to the North American people if it had been approved. The motion revived the Monroe Doctrine, but it was much more clear. One of its paragraphs, I remember perfectly well, read as follows: "The Monroe Doctrine establishes clearly that no nation outside this hemisphere can enslave the American nations." That is to say, nations inside this hemisphere can do so. And then it continued: "It is natural to have a new version of the Doctrine in order to be able to intervene without calling the OAS"—and then present the consummated fact to the OAS. Well, these are some of the political dangers we have to face because of our economic liberation campaign.

Finally we have another problem: how to invest our earnings, how to invest the nation's effort to achieve our economic aspirations rapidly. On February 24, 1960, Fidel Castro told the workers when he received the symbolic 4 percent [20] that, "When the Revolution achieved power, our reserves could not become any lower but we had a people accustomed to consumption by imports more than exports."

In such a situation a country has to serve or receive capital from abroad. Well then, our thesis was to save and to save mainly foreign exchange in order to develop our own industry. Then there was the thesis of importing private capital. Private national capital is in the country, but when we deal with the importation of capital (because capital is needed and to resolve the issue the formula of foreign capital investment is advised) such capital does not move through generosity or charity nor is it mobilized through a desire to aid the people. Foreign capital only acts to help itself. Private foreign capital is the surplus capital of a nation that is sent to another country where salaries are much lower, living conditions are worse, and raw materials are cheaper in order to obtain higher profits. What moves foreign capital investments is not generosity but profits; and the thesis defended for a long time in our country was just that, to benefit the foreign capital investments here so that it would solve the problems of industrialization.

We shall invest 300 million pesos in the agricultural and industrial sectors. That is the battle to develop our country economically and

[20] Workers donated 4 percent of their salaries to create more jobs. Eds.

solve our problems. It is clearly a difficult road. You know that we are threatened—you know that they talk of economic reprisals and maneuvers, of taking away our quotas, etc., etc., while we try to sell our products. Does this mean that we have to retreat? Does it mean that we have to abandon all hope of improvement because they threaten us? What is the correct road of the people? Whom do we harm if we want to progress? Is it that we are trying to live off the labor of other peoples? Is it that we want to live off other peoples' wealth? What do we want? What do Cubans want? What we want is to live from our own efforts and not from the sweat of others.

We do not want to live on the wealth of others, but from our own wealth in order to satisfy all the material needs of our people. On that basis we want to solve the problems of the country. We talk in economic terms but not for purely economic reasons; we talk of economics as a basis to satisfy all the needs of the country, of education, health, and hygiene, the need for a life in which one can work and find some rest. How all these millions will be spent will be explained by another *compañero* in a future talk. He will explain why, not only how, this money will be spent in the road we have chosen.

Now for those who are weak, for those who are afraid, for those who think that we are in a unique situation in history and that this situation cannot be solved, I want to cite an anecdote of Jesús Silva Herzog, Mexican economist and author of the petroleum expropriation law. This anecdote refers precisely to a time lived by Mexico when international capital hovered against the spiritual and cultural values of the people. This is a synthesis of what is said of Cuba today.

Of course, it was said that Mexico was a communist country. The specter of communism appeared. Ambassador Daniels, in the book that I have already cited in previous conferences, tells us that he went to Washington in those difficult days and an English gentleman discussed with him the problem of Mexican communism. Mr. Daniels stated, "In Mexico I only know one communist, Diego Rivera. But what is a communist?" Daniels asked the English gentleman. The man sat down, meditated, arose, tried one definition, was not satisfied, then another definition, but it was not satisfactory either. Then at last, desperately, he told Daniels, "Sir, a communist is a person we dislike."

You can see how historical situations repeat themselves; I am sure that we all displease those people. But it seems that I have the honor along with Raúl [21] of being one of the most disliked.

21 Raúl Castro, Fidel's brother. Eds.

Historical situations have their counterparts. Just as Mexico nationalized its oil and continued to move ahead and Lázaro Cárdenas is recognized today as one of the great presidents of that republic, we shall also continue moving ahead. Those on the other side will call us different names, but all that matters is that we work to benefit the people. We shall not retreat and those who have lost their privileges shall not return.

The Working Class and the
Industrialization of Cuba

ꓴꓶꓴꓶꓴꓶꓴꓶꓴꓶꓴꓶꓴꓶꓴꓶꓴꓶꓴꓶꓴꓶꓴꓶꓴꓶꓴꓶꓴꓶ

A revolution like ours, a popular revolution made by the will of the people and for the people, cannot move ahead if every step is not made by all the people. In order to take those steps with enthusiasm, it is necessary to know the revolutionary process; it is necessary to know the need to take those steps and to take them gladly. If one sacrifices, one should know why. The road to industrialization, a road that ends in collective well-being, is a difficult one.

Moreover, as contradictions in the world increase and the popular movements in the underdeveloped regions of the world replace the aggressive economic imperialism of the United States, North American aggressiveness moves home to its *mare nostrum*—the Caribbean. In other words, the great awakening we are witnessing everywhere engenders threats to Cuba. It is now necessary to be aware of the fact that we are partly responsible for all those events.

There is an evident awakening in the underdeveloped countries and to some extent the Cuban example has contributed to it. Needless to say, in Latin America our example has been much stronger than in Japan. Nevertheless, it has been demonstrated that the colonial powers are not so strong as they were once presumed to be.

On our road toward industrialization, this is the positive side which creates international solidarity if any aggression is committed against us. When I mention aggression, I mean real aggression and not mere economic aggression such as that which will take place shortly in the U.S. House of Representatives with respect to our sugar quota.

We have to go down a difficult road. Our power lies in the unity of workers and peasants, all our needy classes who have to march toward the future.

This lecture is aimed directly at the workers and not at the peasants. This is so for two reasons. First, the peasants have fulfilled all of their first historic phase; they fought energetically to conquer their right to the land and they are already receiving the fruits of that victory. Our peasantry is completely behind the Revolution.

Speech of June 18, 1960. *Obra Revolucionaria* (Havana), June 19, 1960, pp. 3–15.

The working class, in contrast, has not yet received the fruits of industrialization. There is a clear answer for that: We had to create a base for industrialization first and that base required change in the agricultural structure. Agrarian reform created the base for industrialization.

Now we begin the road to industrialization. The role of the working class has become very important. The workers should understand all their duties and the importance of the moment in which we live or we shall fail in achieving an industrial society.

I want to make this clear; one does not need to beat around the bush when one talks to revolutionaries. It is good to know all our weaknesses and to try to overcome them. One cannot hide the fact that the revolutionary movement was based first in the peasants and later in the working class. There are a number of reasons for this. First, the strongest insurrectional movement took place in peasant regions. The insurrectional leader with greatest prestige, Fidel Castro, was in a peasant region. But there are also socioeconomic reasons of great relevance: Cuba, like all underdeveloped countries, did not have a strong proletariat.

In some industries, mainly in the new ones linked to monopolist capital, the workers were sometimes privileged individuals. The sugar worker had to sweat for hours under the sun for three months, then suffer hunger for the remaining nine months, while other workers had a job for the entire year and received six times more. This is a great difference and establishes divisions within the working class. In fact, this is exactly what the colonialist powers sponsor; they try to divide the working class by giving privileges to a few who will want to preserve the status quo. The worker is told that he can move up personally through his own efforts and not by collective action. In this manner the solidarity of the proletariat is broken.

That is why since the Revolution achieved power we have had arduous fights against Mujal's representatives.[1] Those representatives blocked the development of the labor movement. Today we cannot say that those representatives from the past have been totally annihilated, but they will be destroyed soon.

There remains within the working class, however, some of that spirit that divided issues according to employer and employee—a very simplistic analysis of reality. So today, when we begin our

[1] Eusebio Mujal was a labor leader during the Batista dictatorship who worked out an agreement with Batista through which the workers would increase their well-being economically while remaining aloof from politics. Eds.

industrialization process and give a major role to the state, we see that many workers consider the state another employer. Our state is precisely the opposite of a patron-state; [2] consequently, long dialogues are being carried on with the workers to point this out. Workers are changing their attitudes, but for awhile they put a brake on development.

I could mention a few examples, but there is no need to discuss individual cases and point the finger at anyone because I am convinced that in most cases the problem is not the product of evil intent, but arises from an old mentality that has to be rooted out. The workers do not want to interfere with the Revolution. What Fidel said recently should be clear to everyone: The best labor leader is not the one who seeks the daily bread of workers. The best labor leader is the one who fights for everyone's daily bread, the one who understands the revolutionary process perfectly and who, analyzing it and comprehending it deeply, will support the government and convince his comrades by explaining the reasons for certain revolutionary measures. But this does not mean that a labor leader should be transformed into a parrot who would simply repeat everything that is said by the Ministry of Labor, or by any other government agency.

Obviously, there will be mistakes made by the government and the labor leader will have to call attention to those mistakes. If the mistakes are repeated, the labor leader will have to call attention to them forcefully. This is merely a problem of procedure. There are many people's representatives in the government; they want to serve the people and they are ready to rectify any mistake we might make. There is no exception. Naturally mistakes are made by a group of young men who, without prior experience, have taken over an accelerated process of development while facing the greatest economic and military power of this continent, of the so-called "Western world." The task of the labor leader is to show to the people's representatives their mistakes, convince them if necessary and keep doing so until steps are taken to rectify those mistakes. The labor leader has to show his comrades the mistakes made and how they should be fought, how things must be changed, but this must be done through discussion.

It is inadmissible, and it would be the beginning of our end, for the workers to have to go on strike because the employer state— and I refer to the process of industrialization, that is, of the ma-

2 Patron-state: *estado patrono* in the original refers to a state that owns the means of production and does not listen to its workers. Eds.

jority participation in the state—adopted an intransigent and absurd position that forced the workers to strike. The day this happens it will be the beginning of the end of the people's government. It would be the negation of everything that we have upheld. Sometimes the government will have to ask certain labor sectors to sacrifice. Already the sugar workers have made great sacrifices on two occasions; they are—and I say this in all sincerity—the most combative and class-conscious sector of the working class. They are very conscious of their revolutionary obligations. In the future all of us will have to fulfill our revolutionary duties and temporarily renounce some of our privileges and rights in order to benefit the collectivity. That is another task of the labor leader: He has to recognize the moment when this sacrifice will be necessary, he has to analyze it and make sure that the workers' sacrifice is the smallest possible, but at the same time convince his comrades of the necessity of the sacrifice. The workers will have to be convinced of the justice of the demand; the labor leader has to explain and make sure that everyone is convinced. A revolutionary government cannot demand sacrifices from above; sacrifices have to be the product of everyone's will.

Industrialization is built on sacrifice. One cannot enter a process of accelerated industrialization as if one were going to a dance. This will be very clear in the future. Meanwhile the monopolist companies have already struck a blow (or rather have shown their claws, because they have not struck yet) in the case of oil. They have tried to leave us without oil. A few years ago our revolutionary government would have perished without oil. Fortunately, today there are powers that have oil and have absolute independence in selling it; moreover, they have the power to deliver that oil to us, no matter who might oppose the transaction. The present division of power in the world has permitted Cuba to escape from colonialism and gain control of its resources.

Our subsoil is worthless if we do not know if there is any oil in it. To find that out we need to prospect and that is quite expensive. In the meantime we had to find enough power to run our industries. You know that almost 90 percent of our country's power depends on electricity, and more than 90 percent of our electricity depends on oil. Oil plays a strategic role in our economy; that is why a great battle was waged on that issue. We knew that it was just a matter of time before the battle was launched. We approached the foreign companies through legal channels; they replied with their monopolistic arrogance, trying to create a problem.

Today there is a power that has oil; it has the ships to deliver the oil and the power to bring it here. If we did not have that source of oil, we would be facing a great dilemma today: to allow the Revolution to be destroyed or to return to a primitive state, with a minor advance—no more—because we would have horses and mules, which our aborigine ancestors did not have. That would have meant the complete paralysis of our industries. Naturally, it would have been a very difficult situation. Luckily there is a third alternative, and we must continue moving ahead.

This does not mean that we have achieved a definite victory and all danger is over. There is a reason why most of you are wearing militia uniforms today. Vigilance and training are now more necessary than ever. Perhaps many of us will have to die defending the Revolution. But the important thing is to work while knowing that that moment might come, foreseeing it, but working as if that moment would never come, always thinking of building our country in peace. We have to think this way, it is the ideal solution, we have a right to it. If they attack us, we shall defend ourselves. If enemy bombs destroy what we have built it will not matter, we shall build it again after victory. Today we have to think only about constructing.

This leads us to the analysis of what we have today politically and economically. Today we have, without doubt, a revolutionary government. I do not think anyone questions that; this is a government of the people whose goal is to raise the standard of living of the population and to create the conditions which make the happiness of our people possible. Another thing that we have done is to destroy the traditional armed forces.

It is essential for the people to have a people's government. Today we have a government of the people. But a government needs to base itself, unfortunately, on the army. It is necessary to have an army but we have to escape from making it a parasitical institution. Ours has largely escaped this. If we had not destroyed the traditional army, today we would be in prison if not dead. That is why the Rebel Army is so important today. Our revolutionary government is based on the Rebel Army. They are one and the same.

We also have a good geographic location and an exuberant nature that allow us extraordinary economic development. We have unknown mineral resources. We are the second largest producer of nickel in the world—or at least the second largest in the Western world. Nickel is used in the heads of missiles and rockets. It is also used in the armor of every tank and, until recently, in delicate weldings for aircraft. It is a strategic mineral that will be used even more in the future. Maybe we have oil. It is known that we have iron ore—difficult to process, but we have it. We do not have coal, but we are looking for a way to get it. In addition we have sugar cane, an extraordinary source of abundant wealth.

Those are our assets, but we also have some liabilities.

First of all, we have uneven development. We are a monoproducer, like all underdeveloped countries. We produce mainly sugar; all our development has gravitated around that product. We have developed only our sugar mills and a group of importers of manufactured goods purchased with the money from those mills. To this it must be added that our past governments never tried hard to sell our sugar in an adequate manner; instead they sold out to a colonialist economic system dominated by the United States. They never tried to establish new markets. Although many countries ate less sugar than they might, although a large part of the world was increasing its buying power and was ready to buy sugar, our country did not seek new markets. They were blind to reality.

We had a quota system. That system allowed landowners to have more land than needed. Consequently our agricultural development stagnated. A rich country like Cuba had a primitive agricultural technology. Land was left alone and cut once a year. On the average the fields were renewed every seven years. That is why Cuba had very poor yields.

There is another problem. We all know it—to put it mildly.

Ninety miles from our territory there is an air base, a base full of war criminals, a potential base of aggression. They have everything from diplomatic aggression here to paid assassins in other countries. Today aggression against Cuba is reaching high levels. We are in the strategic heart of the Caribbean. We have an enemy base on our territory which is constantly provoking friction with us. They want to cause a war. Above all we have the dangerous honor of being a "bad example" for Latin America. Eisenhower, as you know, goes to Latin America and ends up crying from the tear gas. In other words, the situation of the poor president is very critical.

Our president went to Latin America. The governments' functionaries treated him coldly, but he received warm support from the people. Our example is an honor, and also a threat. That is why the colonialists try to isolate us; but it is impossible to isolate us from the people. They are trying to isolate us gradually. First they will try to isolate the dictator of the Dominican Republic; then they will argue that there is another dictator in Latin America that should be isolated. As Fidel pointed out, they will try to surround us and then commit aggression.

This is the external threat we face. Now we must continue moving forward. The political dangers do not matter; we have to measure our economic possibilities and then move ahead gradually until we accomplish our industrialization. We have to set certain goals. What are our main goals? Our greatest goals? From the political standpoint, we first want to be the masters of our own destiny, we want to be an independent nation. We want to find our system of development without foreign interference. We want to trade freely with the world. Also, we want to improve the standard of living of the people.

We should not worry about the political problem. We have the support of the people and no one can force us to our knees because of a political problem. Our development, however, should not cost the people more than necessary. We realize that some people are unhappy because there is a shortage of many consumer goods. We were taught by colonialism to use just these articles. Chewing gum is a case in point. We were taught to consume chewing gum; then when there is none, people wonder whether this government is really going to raise the standard of living of the people.

It should be clear that we can make mistakes; but it must also be realized that there are many items that we do not need—they are not essential. Today there are 300,000 people unemployed. And that means hunger, misery, and disease. We cannot—and we say so with all frankness—import chewing gum or peaches and other items and at the same time create jobs for the unemployed and underemployed. This is a very great task.

Today our labor force amounts to 2,300,000. One third of our population constitutes our labor force. Thirteen percent of the labor force is unemployed, that is, 300,000 persons, and another thirteen percent is underemployed. A tragic example of underemployment is the sugar workers, almost 300,000, who work only three months a year.

The main duty of the revolutionary government in economic terms is to take care of the unemployed first and the underemployed second. That is why many of us have fought hard against salary increases. A salary increase means another person without a job. The capital of this nation is finite; we cannot create it with a machine. The more money we would make, the less value it would have. We have to develop with the capital we have. We have to plan carefully so that the industries we create offer as much employment as possible. It is our duty, first of all, to see that everyone earns his daily bread. Our first goal is to assure that no one goes hungry, then to see that everyone eats daily. Afterward we should assure decent living conditions for everyone. This would be followed by free medical assistance and education.

Now our main problem is unemployment. That is what we have to think about. Saving foreign exchange is not a hobby but an overriding necessity. Every cent saved will be used to create jobs. But let us return to our theme of how to achieve our economic development.

There are two ways through which we can develop. One is the free enterprise system, also called in French *laissez faire,* which means to let it be, to let it alone, to allow all economic forces to act freely. These economic forces are supposed to be equal and would freely compete with one another to develop the country. We had this system in Cuba in the past and it led us nowhere. I have emphasized on a number of occasions examples that show how our people were enslaved through economic means without even realizing it.

At the time there was a dictatorship, but all this could have happened without that dictatorship. For example, there is a company—now state-controlled—called Cubanitro. The company is worth 20 million pesos and we shall have to expand it. It is a valuable company. That company was formerly owned by a group of stockholders who invested only 400,000 pesos in it. The group got a loan for 400,000 pesos from a bank and overnight a man with an idea and some initiative became a millionaire.

There are other cases where the investments were not made in the factory, in production. It would not be so bad if a man got 20 million pesos and created jobs and developed the nation's industry. There are cases in which 20 million pesos were not invested in industry; instead, half was spent in buying machinery and the difference was pocketed. They had no desire to create an industrial plan; it could go bankrupt for all they cared.

A classic example of this is Técnica Cubana, a paper factory that was created only to steal money from loans. These are two examples in which the state lent money to free enterprise. This of course is not the picture of all industrial enterprises, but as they acquired strength most enterprises began to make deals with the soldiers or politicians who controlled power at the time. In this way they gained more advantages.

Another good example of the free enterprise system is the letter that Fidel read once from Radio Cremata in which he made clear his services to the Compañía Cubana de Electricidad [3] while he was a representative of the Cuban people. That is another example of the free enterprise system.

In addition to that desire to steal on the part of owners is the sad example of so many idle factories. Why? There are two reasons. First, those small factories owned by small Cuban capitalists had to compete with large monopolist enterprises which, when they had a competitor, reduced their prices and the competitor went out of business. In worldwide terms, and that is how these big concerns function, the lowering of prices costs them very little. But a small enterprise goes bankrupt in six months.

Another reason is that anarchy that can be found in the free enterprise system. When a producer starts a business and is doing well, three more producers go into the same business, but the market potential allows for only one producer. Consequently they go out of business.

Another product of the free enterprise system is the fact that the worker has to sell himself as merchandise that works because of unemployment and the struggle among economic forces. The workers have to compete among themselves in order to find a job. They all sell themselves because they do not want to go hungry. The capitalist, needless to say, buys the cheapest worker. Sometimes workers sell themselves more cheaply because they are hungry and by doing so they betray the interests of the working class. That is, the one who gets the job clears the path for the others to follow and accept the same conditions. That is the other result.

Sometimes the opposite occurs. The foreign enterprise pays higher salaries than the state or a national capitalist enterprise and turns the workers into privileged persons. The worker develops a loyalty to that "good" company while the enterprise gets enormous profits yearly out of the country. The oil companies, for example, were taking 30 million dollars out of Cuba yearly. I just complained about a Cuban who pocketed 20 million pesos, but the oil companies made a yearly profit of 34 million. This goes for all the large international enterprises—the telephone company, the electric company. They have developed a system: They pay high salaries and get large profits. Through that system they divide the working class. Also, they tell their workers that they are special people because they work for foreign companies. They have their own club; Negroes are not allowed to work there. A whole series of divisionist instruments is

[3] Cuban Electric Company—U.S.-owned. Eds.

used. These are visible examples that can be seen in Cuba because that system functioned here for a long time. Now they tell us that it is the only system that develops a nation democratically. They are trying to sell us that now.

There is another system. Our system states that we are revolutionaries and our revolutionary government represents the people. For whom should we build industries? Whom should we benefit? We have to benefit the people. We are representatives of the people, that is why the industrialization of the country has to be directed by the government. In this way there will be no anarchy. If we need a screw factory, there will be one; if we need a machete factory somewhere else, we shall build one. There will be no chaos and the nation's capital will be saved.

If the need for a basic industry arises, even if it functions at a loss, it will be built because it will create the foundations for our industrialization. Besides, we shall never have to break a strike or break up a workers' demonstration with tricks or maneuvers. We shall not divide the working class. We should never pay more than a just salary to the worker or the professional in order to gain an advantage, or to destroy someone, because those are not revolutionary methods. We shall try, nonetheless, to give the worker the highest salary possible in any industry, always keeping in mind that our essential goal is to assure a job for everyone; and after jobs for the unemployed, more work for the underemployed.

There are great differences between free enterprise development and revolutionary development. In one of them, wealth is concentrated in the hands of a few, the friends of the government, the best connivers. In the other, the nation's wealth belongs to everyone. Every enterprise functions to serve the entire nation. Through revolutionary development our wealth will not be controlled by foreign monopolies. Revolutionary development even assures the progressive rescuing of our national wealth from the foreign monopolies.

Those are the fundamental differences between the two systems. Our people have chosen the revolutionary road of development. Our enterprises, as Fidel once said, will be called "People's Company, Inc."

If you analyze what we have done so far, you will see that we have been consistent with this type of development. We began, as we were supposed to begin, with the most timid laws which could effectively benefit the people. Electric rates were reduced, rents lowered, public administration cleaned up. Then came the law that marked the turning point on our road because until then, when we lowered the electric and telephone rates, the rents, and cleaned up public administration, this was what the defenders of the free enterprise system proposed as well. Some had apartment buildings and were not too happy. The electric company did not like our measures, nor the telephone company. But the large foreign monopolies supported our moves. This is what they wanted, a government with a good reputation that improved the standard of living of the people a little. That was the perfect government for them. The ideal was to have a government representing Western democracy like Figueres's; [4] it does not matter if he is a large landowner as well as other things. After this came the agrarian reform and things got complicated. In the first place, there is the United Fruit Company, which you all know is directly related to the State Department of the United States.

It became clear then that the revolutionary government was going to carry out reforms and not just talk about them demagogically. Bit by bit our national wealth was increasing and with it our ability to act. We distributed land to the peasants; our sugar cooperatives created factories at the agrarian reform level. We were creating the necessary conditions to incorporate the people into the revolutionary process so that we could all advance at the same time. We acquired more strength through small things such as the confiscation of the property of war criminals and swindlers.

Then aggression began. We were attacked by small planes. Havana was bombed. We replied to the aggression with new revolutionary laws: the oil law, the mining law. We kept moving along that path. The United States threatened to cut our sugar quota and we signed an agreement with the Soviet Union. They cut off our credits with their banks and we signed more profitable agreements with communist countries and Japan. We diversified our foreign trade and awaited their blow, because anyone who knows how these people operate should know that sooner or later they will strike. Monopolies never play a fair game. When they realize that their possibilities for profit in a nation are gone, they attack that country. Sometimes the attack is direct, as in times of Big Stick diplomacy; at others, it is economic. This is the case now with the sugar quota. We foresaw the problem and were faced with a dilemma: either to do what had to be done and face aggression or to become the most representative "Figuereses" of this continent. We have always avoided becoming new "Figuereses" because that is the very negation of the people's

---

[4] José Figueres was president of Costa Rica (1953–1958) and has been one of the leaders of the "democratic left" in Latin America. He is very friendly to the United States. Eds.

aspirations. It is a very bad joke to disguise oneself as a democrat. It is better to be a Somoza,[5] for we all know what he is. To disguise oneself as a patriot, as a revolutionary, a "moderate" leftist, is a sad betrayal of the people. We could never do that. No, we could not talk the language of revolution to the people while behind closed doors we negotiated with the large monopolies. We chose a difficult road, one that we believe to be just, and the people have supported us.

Now we have to fight on two fronts. We may have to defend our coasts physically and we have to wage the battle of industrialization. After analyzing the problems we face, it is necessary to define the fundamental duties of the working class.

There are many duties, but economically there are three great obligations to be fulfilled. These three obligations sometimes even conflict with the common denominator the working class has made of its aspirations and its struggle against employers. One of the great obligations of the working class today is to produce well. When we say "produce" and workers might think that we are telling them exactly the same thing the private employers told them, that is, that they should work more and produce more wealth but that this would mean unemployment for another worker as well as a greater concentration of wealth for the employer. There is an apparent contradiction, it is true; but today we have to produce more wealth in order for the state to create more sources of work—so that everyone can work. The time has come to invent constantly; new jobs must be created, sources of work that will demand the greatest development possible.

As you know, there are several ways to evaluate an investment. There are investments of a high concentration of capital, of approximately 10,000 pesos per worker employed. As a rule, they yield very high earnings. There are also investments of a low concentration of capital, about 2,000 pesos per worker. This type of investment yields much lower earnings, but it is this which better suits our present needs. We have to employ as many people as possible at a minimum cost. We need this first because it eliminates unemployment while creating the technical base necessary for complete industrialization.

I wanted to save this document. The workers of CMQ Television gave it to me and it clearly shows what should be done by the working class. It is merely an idea to save the spools of all the country's typewriter ribbons to avoid the importation of that item. This is another duty of the working class which is related to the obligation

[5] The Somoza family has ruled over Nicaragua in a dictatorial manner for more than twenty years. Eds.

to produce: to save, to think of ways in which we can save money. We have to save as much as possible; we cannot spend a single cent unnecessarily. Every cent should be spent effectively to benefit the people. Each cent saved is put into our foreign trade, or into the national treasury. It allows the creation of another source of work.

Production and savings are the foundations of economic development, production and savings to benefit the workers and not a few people. We could not ask you for great sacrifices, to be more careful, to work harder, if the benefits would go to someone else. It would be unjust to make such demands. We ask these sacrifices to benefit the entire people. We ask for greater production in those factories controlled by the state. More and more the large factories—the ones we will build, of course—will be state controlled. State control will increase in time and the duty of the working class will increase too. But even in all the privately owned industries, waste must be avoided and care taken of the machinery. . . .[6]

A third obligation of the working class besides producing and saving is to organize: not to organize along the traditional lines of one class against another, but to organize in such a manner as to better serve the Revolution, the people, and the working class because, for example, the difference between peasants and workers has to disappear. There is already a group of 300,000 agricultural workers that will begin to work the land with more mechanized methods. They are becoming more technical in their labor and this is how everyone is transformed into a worker, everyone who is directly related to production.

We have to do exactly the opposite of what we have been used to doing. Our immediate circle has been the most important—the labor union, the neighborhood, the family, and the individual. Previously the individual has been considered the most important. Today the nation, the entire people, is more important than the individual. We have to consider ourselves the least important, the least important part in the machinery, but we should function well. We have to be ready to sacrifice any individual benefit for the collective good. Each human grouping is more important than the individual. A labor sector is more important than a factory labor union. All workers are more important than one worker. This is something that has to be understood. We have to organize to change a mentality created in the past.

[6] At this point Guevara mentions that many have learned in an irresponsible way. He cites the case of brand-new Cadillacs taken over from the hierarchy of the old regime which are already dented, scratched, and broken. Eds.

It is necessary to change the way of thinking of labor union leaders. Their function is not to shout louder than the boss or to impose absurd measures within the production system such as getting wages for people that do not work. If a worker gets pay without earning it, he conspires against the nation and against himself.

These are the three duties of the working class. To fulfill them you need to understand the development of the revolutionary process and then add specific knowledge of the factory in which you work; you need to know the entire production system. This is a duty and a right that should be demanded by every worker: to know his machine perfectly, to repair it and improve it if possible. You should know your machine, your section, and the entire production process. This is a duty and a right to be demanded of your administration.

A close relationship should be established between the workers and the administrators of state-controlled factories. It is not the same thing to direct a large factory and be a worker in that factory. Problems are seen from a different perspective. Workers and administrators even today see problems from a different perspective. The administrator should go to the workbench or the worker should go to the administrator's office; the worker and the administrator have to exchange viewpoints so that both will see the process in the same light. Then they would see the process from all sides and problems would be solved—and you would see how many of the demands made on labor today would be withdrawn.

There are some factories already controlled by the state. In one of them a worker, for example, found a more efficient system of production and his foreman prohibited him from producing more. I would not consider that treason, but it *is* a false interpretation of the situation, a false interpretation of the revolutionary movement. It should be clear that old modes of thinking have been made obsolete by history. We have to think anew. We have to use our brains and analyze every problem that arises. We have to analyze each and every one of our problems with a clear mind.

The labor leader and the rank-and-file worker will participate then in the productive process and will be responsible for it. We have not been able to advance further because there are hostile labor unions or the workers have failed to understand the problem. Sometimes a labor union leader talks to the administrator and the rank and file considers that a sellout. Those attitudes have to disappear because our great task of industrializing the nation cannot be accomplished if they remain with us. Our task is to see the best road and explain it. The duty of the people is to aid us in seeing that road and to contribute with all their efforts in marching rapidly along that road. The people should correct our mistakes in a constructive manner.

Up to now we have outlined very moderate goals in order to be able to fulfill them. We are not yet certain if the working class has understood the problems we face or how much they will help. We have proposed to double in ten years the yearly income of each Cuban. Today the per capita income of every Cuban is about 415 pesos a year. If you divide that by the twelve months of the year, you will see that each person really earns very little monthly. Of course, many women and children do not work, but it is still little. We hope that in ten years we can increase per capita income to about 900 pesos. That amount, twice today's income per capita, is one of the major efforts we ought to make for it is something that has never been done in Latin America. This would mean a yearly increment of 7 percent in the buying power of the people. In Latin America the rate of growth in annual per capita income is between 1 and 2 percent and in some countries the rate is decreasing. In other words, our development would be highly accelerated and it would be even more so if everyone absolutely understood his duties. I am not complaining; certainly, to achieve that goal would be a fabulous triumph. We will achieve it and it will be a fabulous triumph. . . .[7]

Another goal we have set for ourselves demands more attention and it is that by the end of 1962, that is within exactly two and a half years, we want to eradicate unemployment in Cuba. You can not applaud that; that is nothing but a goal, and we can all applaud ourselves if we reach it, or hiss at ourselves if we fail. But it is everyone's job, the job of the government and of the people united, and the great obligation of solidarity of everyone who has enough to eat with those who have nothing or almost nothing.

[Someone in the audience says that in the four days of government intervention the number of hotel guests has increased by four thousand.]

Naturally, one of so many collective jobs is the joint administration, by workers and the government, of each enterprise. For example, the ability of the working class and its democratically elected leaders is being tested by the hotel problem. Of course this initial victory is not the definitive victory. The hotels are a difficult problem, because they were built and operated in Cuba with a colonial mentality, for the tourist who came here to leave his dollars at the gambling table or in some other pleasant place. That is, they were

---

[7] Guevara here summarizes all the points he has made before and concludes. The following paragraphs are in response to questions from the audience. Eds.

built for the great master who came to his Caribbean possessions to drop off a little of what those possessions gave him during the year. We should not forget that.

Now we have to change completely the system, the mentality, and the structure of the tourist trade. The tourists that come, if they come from the United States, will be the ones with enough sensitivity and courage to withstand all of their more or less fraudulent threats. In addition, Latin American tourists who want to see the revolutionary process close at hand will come, and moreover, those hotels should be filled with our citizens—with Cubans from all over the island, who travel across her, learning about her. That is, we must overturn the tourist system entirely, and it is not an easy job. Now, I am sure that those who will do that job best are the leaders the workers have elected, in collaboration with the revolutionary government.

Development of a
Marxist Revolution

ЛЛЛЛЛЛЛЛЛЛЛЛЛЛЛЛЛЛЛЛЛЛЛЛЛ

Compañeros of America and the world over:

It would take too long to enumerate the individual greetings that our fatherland gives each of you and the countries you represent. We want, nonetheless, to salute the representatives of some countries that have suffered natural catastrophes or the catastrophe of imperialism. We would like to salute this evening especially the representative of the Chilean people, Clotario Bletz, whose young voice you heard a few minutes ago, but whose maturity can serve as example and guide to our brother workers from that suffering country which has been castigated with one of the worst earthquakes in history.

We want to especially salute Jacobo Arbenz,[1] president of the first Latin American nation that raised its voice, without fear, against colonialism and expressed through a profound and courageous agrarian reform the aspirations of the peasant masses. We also want to thank him and the democracy which succumbed there because its example correctly taught us the weaknesses his government could not overcome so that we could go to the root of the problem and behead with a single slash all those who had power, as well as their henchmen.

We also want to greet the two delegations that possibly have suffered the most in our hemisphere: the delegation from Puerto Rico which even today, 150 years after the first declaration of liberty still struggles to take the first step (perhaps the most difficult one to attain, at least formally) toward a free government. I hope the Puerto Rican delegates will salute Pedro Albizu Campos [2] in my name and that of all Cuba. Transmit to him all of our honest friendship, our recognition of the courageous example he has set, all of our fraternity as free men to another free man, even though he is in a dungeon of the so-called North American democracy. I also want to welcome, even though it might seem paradoxical, the delegation representing

Speech made at the First Congress of Latin American Youth on July 28, 1960. *Obra Revolucionaria* (Havana), August 25, 1960, pp. 13–20.
[1] President of Guatemala (1951–1954), overthrown with the aid of the United States government. Eds.
[2] Leader of Puerto Rican independence who died in 1965. Eds.

the purest of the North American people. I would like to welcome it because not only are the North American people not responsible for the barbarism and injustices of their rulers, but also because they are innocent victims of the wrath of people the world over—who often confuse a social system with the people.

To the distinguished people I have mentioned, and to all the delegations of our brother peoples, I give my individualized greetings. My arms and those of Cuba are stretched open to receive you and show you what is good and bad here, what has been accomplished and what is to be accomplished, the road we have traveled and what remains to be traveled. Because, even though all of you came here to discuss the problems of our continent in this Latin American Youth Congress, each of you—and I am sure of that—is also curious and wants to know exactly what this phenomenon is that has appeared on this Caribbean island, namely, the Cuban Revolution.

Many of you, of diverse political tendencies, have asked, What is the Cuban Revolution? What is its ideology? And immediately the question arises, whether among followers or the opposition, is the Cuban Revolution communist? Some will wishfully state this is so, or that it is moving in that direction. Others, perhaps feeling disappointed, will also answer in the affirmative, and still others with disappointment will think that this is not a communist revolution. Others, still hoping, will answer no. And if someone asks me if this Revolution before your eyes is a communist revolution, I would reply (after asking the traditional question of what communism is and leaving aside all the accusations made by imperialism and the colonial powers who try to bring confusion to everything) that we realize that this Revolution, if it happens to be Marxist—and listen carefully, I say Marxist—is thus because it discovered by its own means the path that Marx pointed out.

Recently one of the important representatives of the Soviet Union, Vice-Prime Minister Mikoyan, a life-long Marxist, toasting the happiness of the Cuban Revolution, acknowledged that this was a phenomenon not foreseen by Marx. He pointed out then that life teaches more than the greatest books and the wisest thinkers.

This Cuban Revolution, without worrying about adjectives or concerning itself with what others considered it but rather constantly looking for what the Cuban people wanted, moved forward. Suddenly it realized what it had already done, or was about to do, for the happiness of the people, as everyone began to look at us in a curious manner, friends and foes. There were the glances of a hopeful continent, and the angry looks of the kings of the monopolies.

But this did not happen from one day to the next, so allow me to recall some of my experience—an experience that might serve many people in similar circumstances—in order that you may have a dynamic idea as to how the revolutionary thought of today appeared. The Cuban Revolution of today, even though it has been continuous, is not the same as the Cuban Revolution of yesterday—even after victory was achieved—and still less the same as that of the insurrectional period before victory. There is a great difference between those eighty-two young men who crossed the rough sea of the Gulf of Mexico to reach the Sierra Maestra coast and the Cuban representatives of today. This distance cannot be measured in years, that is, it cannot be measured correctly in terms of years, with days of twenty-four hours and hours of sixty minutes.

All of the members of the Cuban government, young in age, character, and hopes, have matured rapidly in the extraordinary school of experience, in close contact with the people, their needs and aspirations. We all thought about arriving at some place in Cuba and after a few cries, several heroic battles, a few radio broadcasts and several deaths, we would expel dictator Batista and achieve power. Yet history taught us that it was much more difficult to defeat a government backed by an army of assassins, who in addition to being assassins were partners with and were backed by the most powerful colonial power on earth.

That is why little by little our concepts changed. We city people began to respect the peasant, to respect his sense of independence, his loyalty, to recognize his century-old aspirations for the land which was grabbed from him, and we began to recognize his experience through the thousand paths of the forest. The peasant learned from us the power of a man when he has a rifle in his hands and is ready to shoot another man, regardless of how many rifles accompany the other man. The peasant taught us wisdom, and we taught him our sense of rebellion. Since then and forever the Cuban peasants, the rebel forces, and the revolutionary government march united.

The Revolution continued to progress and expelled the dictator's forces from the rough canyons of the Sierra Maestra. Then we were faced with a new reality, the worker. The rural and industrial workers taught us and we taught them in return that in a given moment a well-aimed bullet is more powerful and positive than any peaceful demonstration. We learned the value of organization. We taught the value of rebellion once again and from this arose organized rebellion all over Cuba.

Much time had gone by and many deaths of fighters and innocent people marked our victorious path. The imperialist forces began to see in the Sierra Maestra something more than a group of bandits or a group of ambitious power seekers. They generously offered the Batista dictatorship bombs, bullets, planes, and tanks. With all that they tried to move once again, and for the last time, into the Sierra Maestra. In spite of the time which went by and although columns of the Rebel Army had already begun to invade other regions and the Segundo Frente Oriental Frank País had been formed under the command of Major Raúl Castro, despite all that, despite all of our public opinion backing (for we were in the headlines of every major newspaper), we had only 200 rifles, not 200 men, to withstand the regime's last offensive. The enemy had accumulated 10,000 soldiers and all types of instruments of death. The history of each of those 200 rifles is full of sacrifice and blood; those were the rifles of imperialism taken with the blood and decision of our martyrs which they dignified and turned into the people's rifles. And this is how the last phase of the great army offensive developed: they called it "encirclement and annihilation."

This is why I tell you today, studious youth of Latin America, that if we do that which is called Marxism it is because we discovered it here. Because at that time, after defeating the dictator's troops and inflicting 1,000 casualties on the enemy, after causing five times more casualties than our total forces and taking 600 weapons, we got hold of a small pamphlet written by Mao Tse-tung that dealt precisely with strategic problems of the revolutionary war in China. In it was described the Chiang Kai-shek campaigns against the popular forces. The Chinese dictator called his campaigns "encirclement and annihilation." Moreover, not only did the dictators use the same terms in opposite places of the world but also similar campaigns were waged to destroy the popular forces. The popular forces, without knowing these manuals on strategy and tactics on guerrilla war beforehand, written in China, carried on our guerrilla war in a similar manner. Naturally, when someone explains his own experience it can be studied by anyone, but it is also possible that the experience could be repeated without knowing the prior experience.

We did not know the experiences of the Chinese troops in twenty years of struggle in their territory, but we knew our territory, our enemy, and we used something that every man has on his shoulders. We used our heads to fight the enemy. This is why he was defeated. Afterward a history of invasions to the west followed, communications were ruptured, and the dictatorship fell unexpectedly. Then January 1, 1959, arrived. The Revolution, once again, without thinking about what it had read but listening to what the people said had to be done, decided to punish all those guilty and they were punished.

The colonial powers immediately made this a headline story, called it assassination and tried to sow—as imperialists always do—division. They stated that "Cuba has Communist assassins but the innocent patriot Fidel Castro has nothing to do with this and could be saved." They tried with pretexts and trivial arguments to divide the men who had fought together for the same cause and for a time they maintained that hope. Yet one day they were faced with an agrarian reform law which was more violent and thorough than had been advised by the brainy and self-appointed advisers of the government —all of whom, by the way, are today in Miami or some other city of the United States—such as Pepín Rivero in *Diario de la Marina* or Medrano in *Prensa Libre*.[3] There was even a prime minister in our government who advised great moderation, because "all these things have to be dealt with moderation."[4]

"Moderation" is another word that the agents of colonialism love to use. "Moderates" are all those who are afraid, all those who want to commit some kind of treason. . . .[5] The people are never moderate.

The moderates advised distribution of land with marabu, a shrub that grows in the countryside; the peasants would cut down the marabu or settle in a swamp or grab some state land which had escaped the landowners' voracity. But to touch the large landowners' land was a sin beyond which they thought was possible. But it was possible.

I remember that at the time, in a conversation with one gentleman, he told me he had no problem with the revolutionary government because he had only 900 *caballerías; 900 caballerías* is over 10,000 hectares.[6] Of course that gentleman had problems with the revolutionary government. The land was taken and distributed. Land ownership was given to the small individual peasant; and cooperatives were created on the land on which the agricultural laborers were accustomed to work as a community for a salary.

Here resides one of the peculiarities that has to be studied in the Cuban Revolution. This Revolution made an agrarian reform for the first time in Latin America, attacking property relations that were

[3] Pepín Rivero and Humberto Medrano were the main writers for these conservative and liberal newspapers respectively. Eds.

[4] Guevara refers to José Miró Cardona who was prime minister of the revolutionary government in the first weeks in 1959. Cardona, in April 1961, was the civilian leader of the Bay of Pigs invasion sponsored by the United States. Eds.

[5] Original appears edited. Eds.

[6] About 25,000 acres. Eds.

not feudal. It is true that there were a few feudal sectors in the tobacco and coffee industries. The coffee and tobacco lands were given to those individual small producers who for a long time had been on that land and wanted it, but the sugar, rice, and cattle lands are now worked collectively by workers who own them in common. They do not own any single part of the land in those cooperatives. This has allowed us to move rapidly in our agrarian reform. One thing that should stay with you, a truth which cannot be refuted in any way, is the fact that a government in America cannot be called revolutionary if it states that it will make an agrarian reform that does not change the property relations of land. It is not enough to give the unused land to the peasant; the land that should be distributed is that owned by large landlords because that is the best land and was stolen from the peasant in the past.

That is agrarian reform and it should be the first measure of every revolutionary government. On the basis of agrarian reform will come the great battle for the industrialization of the country, which is very complicated and in which we will have to struggle against great phenomena. We could have failed very easily in past times, but today there are powerful friendly forces that aid small nations; this fact has to be noted by all, by those who are friendly and those who hate us. That is, in this moment countries like Cuba which are revolutionary countries and not very moderate can pose the question of whether the Soviet Union and China are friends of ours, and they cannot answer in a lukewarm manner. They must respond with the strength of the Soviet Union, China, all the socialist countries, and many other colonial or semicolonial countries which are liberated. They are our friends; on that friendship, in friendship with those governments of the whole world, is the realization of the American revolution. Because if the Soviet Union had not existed to give us oil and buy sugar from us when the sugar and oil aggressions were made, all the strength, all the faith, and all the devotion of this country, which are enormous, would be needed to withstand the blow that it would have meant. The forces of disunity would have worked afterward, protected by the effect on the standard of living of the Cuban people of the measures taken by "North American democracy" against this threat to the free world, because they attacked us openly. After all this there are still Latin American rulers who advise us to lick the hands of those who persistently want to hit us and to spit on those who wish to defend us. Our reply to the leaders of those countries which preach humiliation in the midst of the twentieth century is that Cuba, in the first place, will never humiliate itself before anyone. In the second place, Cuba knows through its own experience and her leaders know, they know very well, the weakness and the corruption of the governments that advise that measure. However, Cuba has not consented, has not permitted itself, does not believe it permissible up to this moment to advise the leaders of that country to execute all of its traitorous officers and to nationalize all the monopolist enterprises.

The people of Cuba executed its assassins and dissolved the dictatorship's army, but we have not told any American government to execute the people's assassins or liquidate the pillars of dictatorship. However, Cuba knows that there are assassins in each of those countries; and if Cuba does not know, those who can tell are the Cuban members of our own movement, assassinated in a friendly country by the dictatorship's henchmen who still remain.

We do not demand the firing squad for the assassin of our militants, even though we would have given him the firing squad in this country. We simply prefer, if one cannot express solidarity in America, that at least one should not be a traitor to America. Let it not be repeated any more in America that we are bound to a continental alliance with our great enslaver because that is the most cowardly and most denigrating lie that a ruler of America could profess. We, the members of the Cuban Revolution, the entire Cuban people, call our friends friends and our enemies enemies and we do not admit in-between positions: you are either a friend or you are an enemy. We, the people of Cuba, do not indicate to any country on earth what they must do about the International Monetary Fund, for example, nor do we permit any one to come here and advise us. We know what has to be done; if they want to do it, fine; if they do not want to do it, it is up to them. But we do not allow advice because we are here alone to the very end, waiting standing up the direct aggression of the strongest power in the capitalist world, and we ask help from no one and we are ready here to resist with our people until the final consequences of our rebellion.

That is why we can talk with our head held high and with a clear voice in all the congresses and in all councils where our brothers might gather. The Cuban Revolution speaks; it might be mistaken but it never tells a lie. The Cuban Revolution always expresses, in each podium from which it must speak, the truth of the children of her earth and expresses it always with face forward to friends and enemies. It never hides to throw a stone and never gives advice that carries a dagger within but which is lined with velvet.

We are attacked, we are attacked for what we are, but we are attacked even more for what we show all the people of America one can be. And imperialism is more concerned with this than with Cuba's nickel mines or the sugar mills, Venezuela's oil, Mexico's cotton, Chile's copper, Argentina's cattle, Paraguay's grasslands, and Brazil's coffee—and they care about the total sum of these raw materials which feed the monopolies.

This is why they place roadblocks in our way as often as they can. And when the roadblocks cannot be placed by them, there are, unfortunately, in America those who are willing to place them. Names do not matter because no one is guilty; we cannot say here that President Betancourt [7] is responsible for the death of our compatriot and peer. President Betancourt is not guilty; he is simply the prisoner of a regime that calls itself democratic. That democratic regime, that regime which could have been an example for Latin America committed the great mistake of not using the firing squad soon enough. And today the democratic government of Venezuela is a prisoner of the criminals whom Venezuela knew until not long ago, whom Cuba knew, and whom most of America has known.

We cannot blame President Betancourt for one death; we can only say, basing this on our history of revolutionaries and on our faith in revolutionaries, that if President Betancourt—elected by his people —one day feels so imprisoned that he cannot move ahead any more and wants the aid of a brother country, here is Cuba to show Venezuela some of the experiences in the revolutionary field; President Betancourt should know that it was not—that in no manner could it have been—our diplomatic representative who initiated all that row that ended up in one death. In the final analysis it was they, the North Americans or the North American government, a little bit here and there, Batista's followers, all those who were the reserve of the North American government in this country, who dressed up as anti-Batista but who wanted to overthrow Batista and preserve the system, the Mirós, Quevedos, Díaz Lanzes, Hubert Matoses . . . and, visibly, the forces of reaction which operate in Venezuela.[8] It is sad to say that the Venezuelan leader is at the mercy of his own troops who might assassinate him, as occurred not very long ago with a car loaded with dynamite. The Venezuelan president is today a prisoner of his own repressive forces.

It hurts, it is sad, because Venezuela gave the Cuban people the strongest and most solid help when we were in the Sierra Maestra. It hurts because Venezuela was able to get rid at least of the most

[7] Rómulo Betancourt, president of Venezuela, 1959–1963. Eds.
[8] Ellipses in original. Eds.

hated aspects of the oppressive system, represented by Pérez Jiménez, even before we did.[9] It saddens us because it received our delegation when it arrived there—first, Fidel Castro, followed later by our President Dorticós—with the greatest demonstrations of affection and love.

A people who have achieved the high degree of political consciousness and fighting spirit of the Venezuelan people will not remain prisoners of bayonets or bullets for long because the bayonets and bullets can change hands and the assassins can end up dead.

But it is not my mission to come here to enumerate the stabs we have received from governments of America in these last few days: We do not have to throw any more wood on the fire of rebellion. That is not my task because, first of all, Cuba is not free from danger and even today is the only center which is watched by imperialists in this part of the world and needs the solidarity of you all: the solidarity of Acción Democrática, as well as the URD or the Communists, or COPEI,[10] or any other party; the solidarity of the people of Mexico, Colombia, Brazil, and every other country of America.

It is true that the colonialists were scared. They also fear the rockets; [11] and they also like everyone else fear bombs, and they saw for the first time in their history that the destructive bombs could fall on their women and children, on everything they had built with so much love, as anyone loves his wealth. They began to make calculations; their electronic calculating machines began to function and they saw that the system was not good. But this does not mean that they have given up, by any means, suppression of Cuba's democracy. They are again obtaining laborious calculations in their multiplying machines, trying to learn which of the alternative methods is best to attack the Cuban Revolution. They have the Idígoras method,[12] the Nicaragua method, the Haiti method. Although they are not using the Santo Domingo method for the time being,[13] they also have mercenaries in Florida, and the OAS method; they have quite a few methods available. And the necessary force to improve them.

President Arbenz and his people know they have many methods and great strength. Unfortunately for Guatemala, President Arbenz

[9] Pérez Jiménez: Venezuelan dictator, 1950–1958. Eds.

[10] Political parties of Venezuela. Eds.

[11] A few weeks earlier the Soviet Union threatened the United States with nuclear war if Cuba was invaded. Eds.

[12] General Miguel Idígoras, president of Guatemala at the time. Weeks earlier he had assented to the training of Cuban exiles in his country to overthrow Castro. Eds.

[13] United States relations with the Dominican Republic were at a low ebb. Eds.

has a traditional army and he has not known entirely about the people's solidarity and their capacity to make any aggression retreat.

This is one of our great strengths: the forces which are moving throughout the world and which forget all the particular banners of struggle in national politics to defend the Cuban Revolution in a given moment. And permit me to say it is also the duty of Latin America's youth because this that we have here is something new and worthy of study. I shall not tell you what it has of value: you can see for yourselves.

I know that the Revolution has much that is wrong, that there is too much disorganization here . . . I know that. You would know it perhaps if you had gone to the mountains. There is *guerrillerismo* [14] still . . . I know that. We lack a fabulous number of technicians while having grandiose plans . . . I know that. Our army has not acquired the necessary maturity, and the militiamen have not achieved enough coordination to be transformed into an army . . . I know that. But what I know, and I would like all of you to know, is that this Revolution was made taking into account the will of the entire people of Cuba. If a peasant or a worker does not know how to use a rifle, he is trying every day to learn how to handle it better to defend his Revolution. And if at this moment he cannot understand the complicated mechanism of a machine whose technician has already left for the United States, he is studying daily to learn so that his factory will function better. And the peasant will study his tractor in order to solve any mechanical problem it might have so that the yields will increase in cooperative lands.

Every Cuban from the city or the countryside, united by a brotherly sentiment, moves toward the future thinking with absolute unity, led by a leader in whom he has absolute trust because he has demonstrated in a thousand battles and on a thousand different occasions his capacity for sacrifice as well as the power and clarity of his thought.

And this people, who today are before you, tell you that even if they were to disappear from the face of the earth due to an atomic conflict unleashed by him and they were the first target, even when the island and its inhabitants totally disappeared, they would be completely happy and fulfilled if each of you went back to your countries and said, "Here we are. The word still humid from the Cuban forests. We have climbed the Sierra Maestra and we have known the dawn, we have our minds and our hands full of the seeds of dawn,

[14] An attitude of disorganization transferred to the administrative level after the guerrilla fighters attained power. Eds.

and we are ready to sow them in this land and defend it so that it will be fruitful." And from all the sister countries of America and our land, if it still persists as an example, the voice of the people will answer from that moment and forever: "So be it: Freedom should be conquered in every corner of America!"

The Duty of a Revolutionary Doctor

ЛЛЛЛЛЛЛЛЛЛЛЛЛЛЛЛЛЛЛЛЛЛЛЛЛЛЛЛ

Compañeros:

This simple meeting, one more in the hundreds of meetings by which the Cuban people commemorate their freedom and the advances of all their revolutionary laws, a forward move on the road to total independence, is of great interest to me.

Almost everyone knows that I began my career as a doctor a few years ago. When I began to study medicine, most of the concepts that I now have as a revolutionary were absent from my store of ideals. I wanted to succeed just as everyone wants to succeed. I dreamed of becoming a famous researcher; I dreamed of working tirelessly to aid humanity, but this was conceived as personal achievement. I was —as we all are—a product of my environment.

After graduating, due to special circumstances and perhaps also to my personality, I began to travel throughout America. Except for Haiti and the Dominican Republic, I have visited all the countries of Latin America. Because of the circumstances in which I made my trips, first as a student and later as a doctor, I perceived closely misery, hunger, disease—a father's inability to have his child treated because he lacks the money, the brutalization that hunger and permanent punishment provoke in man until a father sees the death of his child as something without importance, as happens very often to the mistreated classes of our American fatherland. I began to realize then that there were things as important as being a famous researcher or as important as making a substantial contribution to medicine: to aid those people.

But I continued to be, as we always remain, a product of my environment and I wanted to aid those people with my personal effort. Already I had traveled much—at the time I was in Guatemala, Arbenz's Guatemala—and I began to make some notes on the norms that a revolutionary doctor should follow. I began to study the means of becoming a revolutionary doctor.

Then aggression came to Guatemala. It was the aggression of the United Fruit Company, the State Department, and John Foster

Speech made at the inauguration of an indoctrination course at the Ministry of Public Health on August 20, 1960. *El Mundo* (Havana), August 21, 1960, p. 6.

Dulles—in reality the same thing—and their puppet, called Castillo Armas. The aggression succeeded, for the Guatemala people had not achieved the degree of maturity that the Cuban people have today. One day I chose the road of exile, that is, the road of flight, for Guatemala was not my country.[1]

I became aware, then, of a fundamental fact: To be a revolutionary doctor or to be a revolutionary at all, there must first be a revolution. The isolated effort of one man, regardless of its purity of ideals, is worthless. If one works alone in some isolated corner of Latin America because of a desire to sacrifice one's entire life to noble ideals, it makes no difference because one fights against adverse governments and social conditions that prevent progress. To be useful it is essential to make a revolution as we have done in Cuba, where the whole population mobilizes and learns to use arms and fight together. Cubans have learned how much value there is in a weapon and in the unity of the people. So today one has the right and the duty of being, above everything else, a revolutionary doctor, that is, a man who uses his professional knowledge to serve the Revolution and the people.

Now old questions reappear: How does one actually carry out a work of social welfare? How does one correlate individual effort with the needs of society? To answer, we have to review each of our lives, and this should be done with critical zeal in order to reach the conclusion that almost everything that we thought and felt before the Revolution should be filed and a new type of human being should be created.

If each one is his own architect of the new man, it will be much easier for everyone to create the new man—who would be an example of the new Cuba. I should emphasize this idea for you, the inhabitants of Havana who are here today: In Cuba a new type of man is being created. This cannot be clearly perceived in the capital but can be seen in every corner of the country. Those of you who have gone to the Sierra Maestra have seen two completely unknown things: an army working with pick and shovel, an army whose greatest pride is to parade on patriotic holidays with picks and shovels raised, while their military comrades march with rifles. But you probably saw something even more important. You must have seen children whose bodies appear to be eight or nine years old, yet most of whom are thirteen or fourteen. They are the authentic children of the Sierra Maestra, the authentic children of hunger and misery, creatures of malnutrition.

[1] Guevara went to Mexico where he met Castro. Eds.

In this small Cuba, with four or five television channels and hundreds of radio stations, with all the advances of modern science, when those children went to school at night and saw the light bulbs they thought they were looking at the stars. And those children whom some of you have seen, are learning in collective schools today. They are learning everything from the alphabet to the difficult science of being revolutionaries.

Those are the new human types that are being born in Cuba. They are appearing in isolated areas, in distant corners of the Sierra Maestra, and also in the cooperatives and work centers. And all that has much to do with the theme of our talk today: the integration of the doctor or any other medical worker into the revolutionary movement because that task, the task of educating and feeding children, the task of educating the army, the task of distributing the land of absentee owners to those who worked it without reaping its fruits, that is the greatest task of social medicine in Cuba.

The fight against disease should be based on the principle of creating a robust body, but this cannot be done by the artistic work of a physician on a weak organism. Rather, the creation of a robust body is done with the work of the whole collectivity, with the entire social collectivity. Medicine will one day have to become a science that serves to prevent disease and orients the public toward carrying out its medical duties. Medicine should intervene only in extremely urgent cases, to perform surgery or something else which lies outside the skills of the people of the new society we are creating.

The Ministry of Health and similar organizations today are supposed to organize public health services to provide as much assistance as possible to the greatest number of people. They have to institute a program of preventive medicine and orient the public to methods of hygiene. For this organizational task, as for all revolutionary tasks, the individual is needed. The Revolution is not, as some people pretend, a standardization of the collective will, of the collective initiative, but the opposite; the Revolution liberates the individual capacity of man. The Revolution merely orients the capacities of the individual. Our task today is to orient the creative capacity of all medical professionals toward the tasks of social medicine.

We are at the end of an era, and not only in Cuba: capitalism— as we have known it, under which we developed and suffered—is being defeated all over the world today despite what some people say to the contrary. Monopolies are being defeated. Collective science is scoring more important victories daily. And we have had the honor and the demanding duty of being the vanguard of a liberation movement which began some time ago in Africa and Asia. This radical social change demands equally profound changes in the minds of the people.

Individualism as the isolated action of a person in society has to disappear in Cuba. In the future, individualism should be the fullest utilization of every individual for the absolute benefit of the collectivity. But even if this idea is understood today, even when you all comprehend what I am talking about and think a little about the present, the past, and what the future ought to be, even then in order to change our thinking it is necessary to undergo deep internal changes and to witness deep external changes, especially social ones.

These external changes occur in Cuba daily. One way to learn to know this Revolution, to understand the forces held in reserve by the people, so long asleep within the people, is to visit all of Cuba. This can be appreciated if one visits the cooperatives and the work centers that are being created. One way to get to the core of the medical question is not only to know and visit the people in the cooperatives and work centers, but also to find out the diseases they have, what their afflictions are, what have been their chronic miseries for years, and which hereditary diseases are the consequences of centuries of complete repression and submission.

The doctor, the medical worker, must go to the root of his work, which is the man in the collectivity. Always, no matter what, because the doctor is extremely close to his patient and knows his psyche, because he fights pain and reduces pain, he has great responsibility, he is an invaluable element in society.

A few months ago a group of new medical graduates here in Havana refused to go to the countryside and demanded remuneration before they would agree to go.[2] This is a logical demand if one has a traditional mentality. I can understand that perfectly. This situation is very similar to my own; it reminds me of what I was and what I thought a few years ago. It is the same story of the gladiator who revolts, the isolated fighter who wants to assure a better future, better conditions, and points out how much we need him.

What would have happened if instead of these boys, whose families were generally well-off and could afford to pay for a university education, others with less fortune had finished their schooling? What would have happened if instead of those students, two or three

[2] Medical degrees in 1960 stipulated that graduates had to serve at least two years in the countryside before they could practice in urban areas. Eds.

hundred peasants were the ones who, as if by magic, had graduated from the universities? They would have immediately run enthusiastically to help their brothers. They would have demanded the most difficult and responsible jobs in order to show that their years of study were not in vain. What would have happened will happen six or seven years from now when the children of workers and peasants receive professional degrees of all kinds.

We should not look at the future with fatalism, nor divide mankind into children of the working class, peasantry, or counter-revolutionaries, because it is simplistic and not true. There is nothing that educates an honest man more than to live in a revolution. None of us, none of those who came in the *Granma* and settled in the Sierra Maestra and learned to respect the peasant and the worker by living alongside them, none of us had a peasant or working-class background. Naturally, there were those who had had to work, who had known certain privations in childhood; but hunger, real hunger, was alien to us. We knew hunger in a transitory way during our two years in the Sierra Maestra. And then many things became clear. At first we severely punished anyone who touched the property of a rich peasant or landowner, but then one day we brought ten thousand head of cattle to the Sierra Maestra and told the peasants simply to eat. The peasants, some of them for the first time in their life, ate beef.

And the respect we had for the sacred right of property of those ten thousand cattle was lost in the course of armed struggle; we learned that a man's life is worth a million times more than the property of the richest man. We learned this, we who were not children of the working class or the peasantry. Are we going to say we are the chosen ones and that no one else in Cuba can also learn this? It can be learned. In fact, the Revolution demands that one learn it. The Revolution demands that the pride of serving another person is more important than receiving a material reward for doing so. Much more definitive and lasting than all the money in the world is the gratitude of the people; that is the most precious treasure one could accumulate. And each doctor, within the circle of his activities, can and must accumulate the people's gratitude.

We ought to begin to erase old concepts and begin to move closer to the people and be increasingly conscious as we do so. We should not go to the people as we did before, saying, "No, I am a friend of the people. I like to talk with the workers and the peasants; on Sundays I go to such and such a place to see such and such." Everyone has done that. But they have done so practicing charity, and what we have to practice is solidarity. We should not go to the people and say, "Here we are. We come to give you charity, to teach you our science, to make you aware of your illiteracy, your lack of elemental knowledge." We should go to the people with an inquiring mind, with a humble spirit ready to learn at that great source of wisdom that is the people.

Later we shall become aware of how mistaken we were about familiar concepts that were an automatic part of our thinking. We shall need to change all our concepts often, not only general ideas, the social or philosophical ones, but also our medical concepts. We shall see that diseases need not be treated as they are in the big city hospitals; we shall see that the doctor must be a farmer, and learn how to plant new foods and set through example the desire to consume new food; he has to diversify the nutritional structure of Cuba which is poor and limited in one of the richest countries of the world agriculturally. In those circumstances we shall have to be a little bit of a pedagogue, sometimes a full-time pedagogue. We shall have to be politically oriented as well because our first task will not be to teach the people but rather to demonstrate that we want to learn from them, that we are going to realize a great and beautiful common experience: the construction of a new Cuba.

Many steps have been taken. There is a great distance traveled between January 1, 1959, and today; this is a distance that cannot be measured by conventional means. Most people understood from the outset that a dictator had fallen and a social system ended. Now the people must learn that a new social system must be built on the ashes of the old one, a new system that will bring about the absolute happiness of our people.

I remember that in the early months of last year *compañero* Guillén [3] arrived from Argentina. He was as great a poet as ever, gaining new readers the world over for his books are being translated more. However, it was difficult for Guillén to read his poems, people's poems, here because that was a time when we were full of prejudices. No one ever thought that with unfaltering dedication he placed all his extraordinary poetic gift at the service of the people and the cause in which he believed. Guillén was seen as a representative of a political party that was taboo and not as a glorious son of Cuba.

Now all that has been forgotten. We have learned that there can be no divisions in our way of thinking of certain social structures

[3] Nicolás Guillén, well-known Cuban communist poet and member of the Partido Socialista Popular. Eds.

of our country if we have a common enemy and a common goal. We have to agree on whether we have a common enemy and are trying to achieve a common goal. If not, you all know what will happen. By now we are definitely convinced that there is a common enemy. No one looks around to see if anyone might hear, to see if any embassy informer [4] might transmit his opinion; now everyone says without fear: "Our enemy and the enemy of all of America is the monopolist government of the United States of America." If everyone knows who is the enemy and that anyone fighting against that enemy has something in common with us, then we come to the second part. What are Cuba's goals today? Do we want the people's happiness? Do we fight for the absolute economic liberation of Cuba? Do we struggle to be a free country among the free without belonging to any military bloc, without having to consult the embassy of any great power of the world on our internal or external measures? If we plan to redistribute the wealth of those who have too much to those who have too little, if we intend to make creative work a daily and dynamic source of happiness, then we have definite goals. Anyone with those goals is our friend. If he has other ideas besides, or belongs to some kind of organization, that is a minor matter.

In times of great danger, in times of great tension, in times of great creation, what counts is great enemies and great goals. If we all agree, if we all know where we are going, then we have to begin our work regardless of who might oppose it.

To be a revolutionary one needs, first of all, a revolution. We already have it. Next we need to know the people with whom we shall work. I think that we still do not know each other well; we have to work on this. If someone asked me what are the vehicles to know the people, besides going to the countryside, knowing, living, and working in cooperatives (and not everyone can do this, even if in many places the presence of medical workers is of great importance), in those cases I would tell them that one of the great manifestations of solidarity with the people is to join the revolutionary militias. The militias give the doctor a new function and prepare him for what was until recently a sad and almost fatal reality for Cuba, that is, to be a prey, or at least a victim of threat of a large armed attack.

And I should say that the doctor in his militia and in his revolutionary function should also be a doctor. Do not make the same mistake we made in the mountains. Perhaps it was not a mistake, but all our medical comrades at the time know about it. We thought

[4] Refers to the U.S. embassy. Eds.

that it was dishonorable to aid a wounded or sick man; instead we all wanted to grab a rifle and fight in the front lines. Now conditions are different; the new armies being formed to defend the country should have different techniques, and the doctor should have a major role within the techniques of that new army. He must continue being a doctor, one of the most beautiful tasks in the world and also an important one in wartime. Also of utmost importance are nurses, laboratory technicians—all those who dedicate their lives to this humane profession. But all of us must, even when knowing the latent danger and even when preparing to repel the threat of aggression, quit thinking about it because if we make it the center of our worries to prepare for war, we cannot build what we want and dedicate ourselves to creative work.

All work, all capital invested in preparing for war is wasted labor, wasted money. Sadly, we have to do it because others are preparing themselves—and I say with honesty and the honor of a soldier that I see with sadness the money that leaves the National Bank to buy weapons of destruction.

The militias, however, have a function in peacetime; the militias should be in the populated centers, the instrument that unites and makes the people known. Extreme solidarity, as I am told is practiced by doctors in the militias, should be generalized. In dangerous times the militias should immediately solve problems in all of Cuba of our poor people. But, as well, they offer the opportunity to live together, to know one another, joined and made equal by a uniform with men of all social classes.

If we medical workers—and allow me to use a title I had forgotten for some time—are successful, if we use this new weapon of solidarity, if we know our goals, our enemy, and know in which direction we must move, then all that is left for us to know is the road to be traveled daily. And that part we have to learn by ourselves, no one can travel it for us; we have to learn it in the daily exercise of our profession.

Now that we have all the required elements to march toward the future, let us remember Martí's advice. Although at this moment I am ignoring it, one should constantly follow it: "The best way of telling is by doing." Let us march toward Cuba's future.

The Alliance
for Progress

ЛПЛПЛПЛПЛПЛПЛПЛПЛПЛПЛПЛПЛ

Mr. Chairman, fellow delegates:

Like all other delegations, we must begin by thanking the government and the people of Uruguay for the warm welcome we have received on this visit.

I should also like to express my personal thanks to the chairman of the meeting for his gift of the complete works of Rodó,[1] and to explain to him that I am not beginning these remarks with a quotation from that great American for two reasons. The first is that I went back after many years to *Ariel*, looking for a passage that would represent at the present time the ideas of a man who is more than a Uruguayan, a man who is our American, an American from south of the Rio Grande; but throughout his *Ariel*, Rodó speaks of the violent struggle and opposition of the Latin American countries against the nation that fifty years ago was also interfering in our economy and in our political freedom, and it is not proper to mention this, since the host is involved.

And the second reason, Mr. Chairman, is that the chairman of one of the delegations here present gave us a quotation from Martí to begin his statement. We shall, then, reply to Martí with Martí. To Martí with Martí, but with the anti-imperialistic and antifeudal Martí who died facing Spanish bullets, fighting for the freedom of his country and by Cuba's freedom trying to prevent the United States from spreading over Latin America, as he wrote in one of his last letters.

At that international monetary conference recalled by the president of the Inter-American Bank when he spoke of the seventy years of waiting, Martí said:

Statement as chairman of the Cuban delegation at the Fifth Plenary Session of the O.A.S. Special Meeting of the Inter-American Economic and Social Council, on August 8, 1961, Punta del Este, Uruguay. O.A.S. Official Documents, OEA/ SER. H/X.1 (English).
[1] José Enrique Rodó (1872–1917), Uruguayan, is widely known throughout Latin America for his work *Ariel* (1900), in which he called for an intellectual elite that would withstand the materialistic power and influence of the United States. Eds.

He who speaks of economic union speaks of political union. The nation that buys commands, and the nation that sells serves; it is necessary to balance trade in order to ensure freedom; the country that wants to die sells only to one country, and the country that wants to survive sells to more than one. The excessive influence of one country on the trade of another becomes political influence. Politics is the work of men, who surrender their feelings to interests, or who sacrifice part of their feelings to interests. When a strong nation gives food to another, it makes use of the latter. When a strong nation wants to wage war against another, it forces those who need it to ally themselves with it and to serve it. The nation that wants to be free must be free in commerce. Let it distribute its trade among other equally strong countries. If it is to show preference for any, let it be for the one that needs it least. Neither unions of American countries against Europe, nor with Europe against a country of the Americas. The geographic fact of living together in the Americas does not compel political union except in the mind of some candidate or some babbler. Commerce flows along the slopes of the land and over the water and toward the one who has something to trade, be it a monarchy or a republic. Union with the world, and not with a part of it; not with one part of it against another. If the family of republics of the Americas has any function, it is not to be herded behind any one of them against the future republics.

That, Mr. Chairman, was Martí seventy years ago.

Now, having performed the basic duty of recalling the past and reciprocating the delegate's courtesy to us, I shall pass on to the fundamental part of my statement, an analysis of why we are here and the characteristics of this conference. And I must say, Mr. Chairman, that in the name of Cuba I disagree with almost all of the statements that have been made, although I do not know if I disagree with the speakers' innermost thoughts.

I must say that Cuba interprets this as a political conference; Cuba does not acknowledge a separation of economic matters from political ones; it understands that they always go hand in hand. That is why there can be no experts speaking of technical matters when the fate of the peoples is at stake. I shall explain why this is a political conference. It is political because all economic conferences are political, but it is also political because it was conceived against Cuba and against the example represented by Cuba in the entire Western hemisphere.

Let us see if this is not true. On the tenth, in Fort Amador, Canal Zone, General Decker, instructing a group of Latin American military personnel in the art of repressing peoples, spoke of the Montevideo Technical Conference and said that it is necessary to help it. But that is nothing. In his message of August 5, 1961, read at the inaugural session, President Kennedy said the following:

Those of you at this conference are present at an historic moment in the life of this hemisphere. For this is far more than an economic discussion or a technical conference on development. In a very real sense it is a demonstration of the capacity of free nations to meet the human and material problems of the modern world.

I could continue with a quotation from the prime minister of Peru, when he was referring to political subjects; but in order not to tire the delegates, since I foresee that my statement will be some-what lengthy, I shall refer to some of the statements made by the "experts," and here I use quotation marks, taken from Topic V of the agenda. As a definitive conclusion, it says:

... Establishing, both at the hemisphere and the national levels, regular procedures for consultation among labor union advisory committees, in order that they may play an influential role in the policy development of the programs that may be agreed upon at the Special Meeting.

And to reinforce my statement, so that there may be no doubt about my right to talk politics, which is what I plan to do in the name of the government of Cuba, here is a quotation of that same report concerning the same Topic V:

Any delay on the part of democratic information media in assuming their duty to defend, unflaggingly and without material compromise, the essential values of our civilization, would be of irreparable damage to democratic society and would put those same media in imminent danger of losing the freedoms they now enjoy, as has been the case in Cuba [Cuba, spelled out in full] where today the press, radio, television and motion pictures are all under the absolute control of the Government.[2]

That is to say, fellow delegates, that in the report under discussion Cuba is judged from the political standpoint. Very well. Cuba will speak the truth from the political standpoint, and from the economic standpoint, too.

We are in agreement with only one thing in the report on Topic V prepared by the experts, with one single sentence which describes the present situation:

Relationships among the peoples of the Americas are entering upon a new phase

it says, and that is true. It is just that this new phase is beginning under the sign of Cuba, Free Territory of the Americas, and this conference and the special treatment given to all of the delegations, and the credits that are approved, all bear the name of Cuba, whether

2 Remark in brackets is Guevara's. Eds.

the beneficiaries like it or not, because there has been a qualitative change in the Americas, a change that has enabled a country to rise up in arms, destroy an oppressive army, form a new people's army, stand up to an invincible monster, await the monster's attack, and defeat it also.

And that is something new in the Americas, that is what has led to this new language and to the fact that relations are easier among all, except, naturally, between the two great rivals of this conference.

At this moment Cuba cannot even speak of the Americas alone. Cuba is part of a world that is under anguishing tension, because it does not know if one of the parties—weaker but the more aggressive—will commit the clumsy blunder of unleashing a conflict which necessarily will be atomic. And Cuba is watchful because it knows that imperialism will succumb, wrapped in flames, but it knows that Cuba would also pay with its blood the price of the defeat of imperialism, and it hopes that this defeat may be achieved by other means. Cuba hopes that its children may see a better future and that they will not have to pay the price of victory with the lives of millions of human beings destroyed by atomic fallout.

The world situation is tense. Our meeting here is not only because of Cuba, not in the least. Imperialism has to make sure of its rear guard, because the battle is being waged on all sides, at a time of deep anguish.

The Soviet Union has reaffirmed its decision to sign a German peace treaty, and President Kennedy has announced that he would even go to war over Berlin. But it is not Berlin alone, it is not Cuba alone; there is Laos, and the Congo, where Lumumba was murdered by imperialism; there is divided Vietnam and divided Korea; Formosa in the hands of Chiang Kai-shek's gang; there is Argentina, prostrate, and now they want to divide it, too; and Tunisia, whose people the other day were machine-gunned for committing the "crime" of wanting to recover their territory.

That is the way it is in the world today, and that is how we have to see it in order to interpret this conference and be able to arrive at the conclusions that will permit our countries to move toward a happy future and orderly development, for otherwise they may become appendages of imperialism in the preparation of a new and terrible war; or they may also be bled by civil strife when their peoples—as almost all of you have said—tired of waiting, tired of being deceived again, start on the path that Cuba once started on: to take up arms, to fight on their own soil, to take away the weapons of the foreign army that represents reaction, and to destroy to its very foundations an entire social order that was made to exploit the people.

The history of the Cuban Revolution is short in years, but rich in deeds, rich in positive facts, and rich, also, in the bitterness of the aggressions it has suffered.

We shall spell out some of them, so that it may be clearly understood that it was a long chain of events that led us here.

In October 1959, only the agrarian reform had been carried out as a basic economic measure by the revolutionary government. Pirate airplanes coming from the United States flew over Havana and, as a result of the very bombs they dropped, plus the fire from our anti-aircraft batteries, two persons were killed and half a hundred wounded. Later, there was the burning of the cane fields, which is economic aggression, aggression against our wealth, and which was denied by the United States until an airplane—pilot and all—exploded, and the evidence proved beyond the shadow of a doubt the source of the pirate aircraft. This time the American government was kind enough to apologize. The España sugar mill was also bombed by one of these aircraft in February 1960.

In March of that year, the steamship *Le Couvre*, which was bringing arms and ammunition from Belgium, exploded at the docks of Havana, causing a hundred dead, in an accident which the experts classified as intentional.

In May 1960, the conflict with imperialism became open and acute. The oil companies operating in Cuba, invoking the right of might and ignoring the laws of the Republic that clearly specified their obligations, refused to refine the petroleum purchased from the Soviet Union, in the exercise of our free right to trade with the whole world and not with one part thereof, as Martí put it.

Everybody knows how the Soviet Union responded, sending us, with real effort, hundreds of ships to carry 3,600,000 tons per year—our total imports of crude petroleum—to keep in operation all of the industrial machinery which works on the basis of petroleum today.

In July 1960, there was the economic aggression against Cuban sugar, which some governments have not yet perceived. The differences became more acute, and the O.A.S. meeting took place in Costa Rica in August of 1960. There—in August 1960—it was declared that the meeting,

... Condemns energetically the intervention or threat of intervention, by an extracontinental power in the affairs of the American republics and declares that the acceptance of a threat of extracontinental intervention by any American state endangers American solidarity and security, and that this obliges the Organization of American States to disapprove it and reject it with equal vigor.

That is to say, the American republics, meeting in Costa Rica, denied us the right to defend ourselves. This is one of the strangest denials ever made in the history of international law. Naturally, our people are a little refractory with respect to the voice of technical meetings and they met in the Assembly of Havana and approved unanimously—more than a million hands raised to the skies, one sixth of the country's total population—the Declaration of Havana, which states in part as follows:

The People's National General Assembly reaffirms—and is sure that in doing so it is expressing the common criterion of the peoples of Latin America—that democracy is incompatible with financial oligarchy, with the existence of discrimination against the Negro and the excesses of the Ku Klux Klan, and with the persecution that deprived scientists such as Oppenheimer of their jobs, that for years prevented the world from hearing the wonderful voice of Paul Robeson, a prisoner in his own country, and that led the Rosenbergs to their death, in the face of the protests and the horror of the whole world and despite the appeals of the leaders of various countries and of Pope Pius XII. The People's National General Assembly of Cuba expresses the Cuban conviction that democracy cannot consist merely in the exercise of an electoral vote which is nearly always fictitious and is directed by large landowners and professional politicians, but rather in the right of the citizens to decide their own destinies, as this People's Assembly is now doing. Furthermore, democracy will exist in Latin America only when its peoples are really free to choose, when the humble are no longer reduced—by hunger, by social inequality, by illiteracy, and by the judicial systems—to the most hopeless impotence.

And further, the People's National General Assembly of Cuba condemned "the exploitation of man by man, and the exploitation of the underdeveloped countries by imperialist financial capital."

That was a declaration of our peoples, made before the world, to show our determination to defend with arms, with blood, with our lives, our freedom, and our right to control the destinies of the country in the way that our people deem most advisable.

Later came many skirmishes and battles, sometimes verbal, sometimes otherwise, until in December 1960, the Cuban sugar quota in the United States market was definitively cut. The Soviet Union responded in a way which you already know, other Socialist countries did likewise, and contracts were signed to sell 4 million tons throughout the socialist area at a preferential price of 4 cents, which naturally saved the situation for Cuba, which unfortunately is still a single-crop country (like the majority of the American nations) and which was as dependent on one market and one product—at that time—as the other republics are today.

It seemed that President Kennedy had inaugurated the new era which had been spoken of so much. In spite of the fact that there had also been a rough verbal exchange between President Kennedy and the prime minister of our government, we hoped that things would improve. President Kennedy gave a speech in which he gave clear warning of a series of positions to be taken in the Americas, but he seemed to be announcing to the world that Cuba's case should be considered as something that had already taken shape, as a "fait accompli."

We were then mobilized. The day after Kennedy's speech, we ordered demobilization. Unfortunately, on March 13, 1961, President Kennedy spoke of the Alliance for Progress. On that same day, there was a pirate attack against our refinery in Santiago de Cuba, which endangered the installations and took the life of one of the defenders. So once again we were faced with a de facto situation.

In that speech, which I have no doubt will be memorable, Kennedy also said that he hoped that the people of Cuba and the Dominican Republic, for whom he expressed great friendship, might rejoin the society of free nations. One month later the events at Playa Girón took place, and a few days later [former] President Trujillo was mysteriously assassinated. We were always the enemies of President Trujillo, and we are just establishing the bare facts of the case, which to this date has not been clarified in any way.

Later, there came a true masterpiece of belligerency and political ingeniousness, which wound up under the name of the White Paper. According to the magazines, which say so much in the United States, even provoking President Kennedy's anger, its author was one of the distinguished advisers of the United States delegation with us today. It is an accusation full of misrepresentations of Cuba's real situation, conceived in preparation for what was forthcoming.

"The revolutionary regime betrayed their own revolution," so said the White Paper, as if it were the judge of revolutions and how to make revolutions, and the great evaluator of the revolutions of the Americas.

"The Castro regime offers a clear and present danger to the authentic ... revolution of the Americas," because the word "revolution," as one of the members of the presidential staff said, also needs to clean up once in a while.

"The Castro regime refuses to negotiate on a friendly basis," despite the fact that many times we have said that we would sit down on an equal footing to discuss our problems with the United States, and I wish to take advantage of this opportunity, Mr. Chairman, to affirm once more on behalf of my government that Cuba is willing to sit down to discuss on equal footing anything that the delegation of the United States may wish to discuss, on a strict basis of nothing more than no previous conditions at all. That is to say, our position in this matter is very clear.

The White Paper called on the people of Cuba to engage in subversion and revolution "against the Castro regime"; however, on April 13, President Kennedy once more spoke and categorically affirmed that he would not invade Cuba and that the armed forces of the United States would never intervene in Cuba's internal affairs. Two days later, unidentified aircraft bombed our airports and made ashes out of most of our air force, an ancient remnant that the Batista people had left behind in their flight.

In the Security Council, Mr. Stevenson gave emphatic assurances that it was Cuban pilots, of our air force, "unhappy with the Castro regime," who had done this thing and he stated that he had talked with them.

On April 19, there was the unsuccessful invasion, when our entire people united and on a war footing showed once again that there are forces stronger than generalized propaganda, forces stronger than the brute force of arms, and values more important than the values of money. They crowded down the narrow ways that led to the battlefield, and many of them were massacred en route by the enemy's superior aircraft. Nine Cuban pilots with their old planes were the heroes of the day. Two of them gave their lives; seven are outstanding examples of the triumph of the arms of freedom.

Playa Girón was over, and to say nothing more about this, because "confession takes the place of evidence," President Kennedy took on himself the total responsibility for the aggression. Perhaps at that time he did not recall the words he had uttered a few days before.

We might have thought that the history of aggressions had ended; however, as the newspapermen say, "I've got news for you." On July 26 of this year, groups of armed counterrevolutionaries at the Guantánamo Naval Base lay in wait for Major Raúl Castro in two strategic places, in order to assassinate him. The plan was intelligent and macabre. They would shoot at Major Raúl Castro as he traveled down the highway from his house to the rally with which we were celebrating the anniversary of our Revolution. If they failed, they would dynamite the base, or rather, they would detonate the already dynamited bases of the box from which our *compañero* Raúl Castro was to preside over that patriotic rally. And a few hours later, North American mortars, located on Cuban soil, would open fire on the Guantánamo Naval Base. The world would then clearly explain the case to itself: The Cubans, exasperated because in one of their private quarrels one of those "Communists they have there" was assassinated, launched an attack on the Guantánamo Naval Base, and the poor United States had no choice but to defend itself.

That was the plan that our security forces, considerably more efficient than they were thought to be, discovered a few days ago.

So, because of all these things I have related, I believe that the Cuban Revolution cannot come to this assembly of distinguished experts to speak of technical matters. I know that you are thinking, "and furthermore, because they don't know," and perhaps you are right. But the basic thing is that politics and facts, so stubborn that they are constantly appearing in our midst, prevent us from coming to speak of figures or to analyze the perfect accomplishments of the I-A ECOSOC experts.

There are a number of political problems floating around. One of them is political and economic: the question of the tractors. Five hundred tractors is not an item of exchange. Five hundred tractors is what our government considers as possible reparations for the material damages caused by 1,200 mercenaries. They would not pay for a single life because we are not in the habit of measuring the lives of our citizens in terms of dollars or equipment of any kind— and much less the lives of the children and the women who died there in Playa Girón.

But we would like to add that if this seems to be an odious transaction stemming from the days of the pirates, that is, to exchange human beings—whom we call worms—for tractors, we could exchange human beings for human beings. We address ourselves to the gentlemen from the United States. We wish to remind them of the great patriot, Pedro Albizu Campos, dying now after years and years spent in the dungeons of the empire, and we offer them anything they want for the freedom of Albizu Campos; and we wish to remind the countries of the Americas who have political prisoners in their jails that we could make a trade. No one responded.

Naturally, we cannot force this trade. It is simply in the hands of those who believe that the freedom of the "brave" Cuban counter-revolutionaries—the only army in the world that ever surrendered completely, almost without casualties—who believe that these people should go free. Then let them free their political prisoners, and all the Americas will have shining jails, or at least the political jails will cause no worries.

There is another problem, also of a political and economic nature. It is, Mr. Chairman, that our air transport fleet, plane by plane, is being kept in the United States. The procedure is simple: Some ladies get on board with weapons hidden in their clothing; they hand these to their accomplices; the accomplices shoot the guard, put a pistol to the pilot's head, the pilot makes a beeline for Miami, a company—legally of course, because everything is done legally in the United States—files a claim for debts against the Cuban state, and then the plane is confiscated.

But it so happens that one of many patriotic Cubans—and there was also a patriotic North American, but he is not one of ours—a patriotic Cuban who was traveling around there, and without anybody's telling him anything, he decided to amend the record of twin-engine plane thieves, and he brought a beautiful four-engine plane to Cuban shores. Naturally, we are not going to use that four-engine plane, for it is not ours. We respect private property, but we also demand the right to be respected ourselves, gentlemen; we demand the right of having no more farces, the right of having American agencies that can speak up and tell the United States: "Gentlemen, you are committing a vulgar abuse; you cannot take planes away from a state, even though it is against you; those airplanes are not yours; return them or you will be punished." Naturally, we know that unfortunately there are no inter-American agencies having that much strength.

We appeal, however, to this august gathering, to the sentiments of fairness and justice of the delegation of the United States, to normalize the situation of the respective airplane robberies.

It is necessary to explain what the Cuban Revolution is, what this special affair is that has made the blood of the empires of the world boil, and has also made the blood of the dispossessed of the world— or at least of this part of the world—boil, but with hope.

It is an agrarian, antifeudal, and anti-imperialist revolution, transformed by its internal evolution and by external aggression into a socialist revolution, and it so proclaims itself before the Americas; it is a socialist revolution.

It is a socialist revolution that took land from those who had much and gave it to those who worked on that land as hired hands, or distributed it in the form of cooperatives among other groups of persons who had no land to work, not even as hired hands.

It is a revolution that came to power with its own army and on the ruins of the army of oppression; that took possession of this power, looked round about, and undertook systematically to destroy all of the previous forms of the structure maintained by the dictatorship of an exploiting class over the exploited class.

It completely destroyed the army as a caste, as an institution, but not as men, except for the war criminals, who were shot, also in the face of public opinion of the hemisphere, and with a very clear conscience.

It is a revolution that reaffirmed national sovereignty, and for the first time raised the issue, for itself and for all countries of the Americas and for all peoples of the world, of the recovery of territories unjustly occupied by other powers.

It is a revolution with an independent foreign policy; Cuba comes here to this meeting of the American states as one among many Latin American countries; it goes to the meeting of the nonaligned countries as one of their important members; and it sits in on the deliberations of the socialist countries and these look on it as a brother.

It is a revolution with humanistic characteristics. It feels solidarity with the oppressed peoples of the world; solidarity because, as Martí also said, "Every true man ought to feel on his cheek the blow given to the cheek of any man." And every time an imperial power enslaves any territory, it is striking a blow at all of the inhabitants of that territory.

That is why we fight, indiscriminately, without asking questions about the political system or the aspirations of countries that are fighting for their independence; we fight for the independence of those countries; we fight for the recovery of occupied territory. We support Panama that has a strip of its territory occupied by the United States. We say Malvinas Islands, not Falkland Islands, speaking of those that lie south of Argentina; and we say Isla del Cisne when speaking of the island that the United States snatched away from Honduras and from which vantage point it is committing aggression against us by telegraph and radio.

We fight constantly here in the Americas for the independence of the Guianas and the British West Indies; we accept the fact of an independent Belize, because Guatemala has already renounced its sovereignty over that part of its territory; and we fight also in Africa, in Asia, anywhere in the world where the powerful oppress the weak, so that the weak may gain their independence, their self-determination, and their right to govern themselves as sovereign states.

Our country—and excuse my mentioning this—on the occasion of the earthquake that devastated Chile, assisted that nation as far as it was able with its only product, sugar. Small assistance, but nonetheless it was help given that demanded nothing in return; it was simply a gift to a friendly people, of something to eat to carry them through those difficult hours. That country does not have to thank us, and much less does it owe us anything. Our duty led us to give what we gave.

Our Revolution nationalized the national economy; it nationalized the basic industries, including mining; it nationalized our foreign trade, which now is in the hands of the state and we began to diversify, trading with all the world; it nationalized the banking system in order to have in its hands an effective instrument for the technical control of credit according to the needs of the country.

Our workers now participate in the direction of our planned national economy, and a few months ago the Revolution carried out its urban reform, which gave each inhabitant of our country the house in which he lived, to be his property, the one condition being that he would continue paying the same amount he had been paying, in accordance with a table, for a certain number of years.

It took many steps to affirm human dignity, one of the first having been the abolition of racial discrimination—because racial discrimination did exist in our country, in a more subtle form, but it did exist. The beaches in our island formerly could not be used by the Negro or the poor, because they belonged to private clubs and because the tourists who came from other places did not like to go swimming with Negroes.

Our hotels, the large hotels of Havana, built by foreign companies, did not permit Negroes to sleep in them, because the tourists from other countries did not like Negroes.

That is what our country was like. Women had no equal rights; they were paid less for the same work, they were discriminated against, as is the case in most of our American countries.

The cities and the rural areas were two zones in permanent struggle against each other, and the imperialists obtained from this struggle sufficient manpower to be able to pay the working man poorly and sporadically.

All of these were subject to our Revolution, and we also accomplished a true revolution in education, culture, and health.

This year illiteracy will be ended in Cuba. One hundred and four thousand instructors of all ages are traveling through rural Cuba teaching 1,250,000 illiterates to read—because there were illiterates in Cuba, many more than the official statistics of previous times had indicated.

This year we have extended compulsory primary education to nine years, and free and compulsory secondary education for all of the school population. We have carried out university reform, giving all the people free access to higher culture, to modern science and technology. We have greatly emphasized our national values as opposed to the cultural deformation produced by imperialism, and the expressions of our art are applauded all over the world—not by all, for in some places our art is not admitted; we are emphasizing the cultural heritage of our Latin America, giving annual prizes to writers from all parts of the Americas, the prize for poetry, Mr. Chairman, having been won by the distinguished poet, Roberto Ibañez, in the last contest; the social function of medicine is being extended for the benefit of humble farm and city workers; there are sports for all the people, as reflected in the 75,000 who paraded on July 25 in a sports festival held in honor of Major Yuri Gagarin, the world's first cosmonaut; the beaches have been opened to all without distinction as to color or ideology, and also free of charge; and there are the Workers' Social Centers, converted out of all the exclusive clubs in the country—and there were many.

So then, fellow delegates, the time has come to speak of the economic part of the agenda. Topic I, very broad, also prepared by very brainy experts, deals with planning for the economic and social development of Latin America.

The first inconsistency that we see in the paper is contained in the following sentence:

The view is often expressed that an increase in the level and diversity of economic activity brings in its wake improvements in health conditions; it is the conviction of the Group that such improvements are desirable in themselves, that they are an essential prerequisite for economic growth, and that, therefore, they must be an integral element in any meaningful development program for the region.

This is also reflected in the structure of the loans of the Inter-American Development Bank, for in the analysis we made of the first 120 million loaned, we found that 40 million, that is, one third, was directly for loans of this kind: for dwellings, water systems, sewers.

This is a little . . . I don't know, but I would almost call it a colonial condition. I get the impression that what is intended is to make the outhouse a fundamental thing. This improves the social conditions of the poor Indian, the poor Negro, the poor man who leads a subhuman existence. "Let's build him an outhouse and then, after we build him an outhouse, and after he is educated to keep it clean, then he can enjoy the benefits of production." It should be noted that the subject of industrialization does not appear in the analysis made by the experts. To the experts, to plan means to plan outhouses. For the rest, who knows how it will be done?

If the chairman will permit, I want to express deep regrets, on behalf of the Cuban delegation, at having lost the services of an expert as efficient as the one who headed this First Group, Dr. Felipe Pazos. With his intelligence and his capacity for work, and with our revolutionary activity, in two years Cuba would be the paradise of the outhouse, even though we would not have even one of the 250 factories we have begun to build, even though we would not have agrarian reform.

I ask myself, fellow delegates, are they trying to pull somebody's leg? Not Cuba's—Cuba is not in this, for the Alliance for Progress is not made for Cuba but against it and there is no provision for giving it a cent—but the legs of the other delegates. Don't you get a slight feeling that your leg is being pulled? Dollars are given to build highways, dollars are given to build sewers. Gentlemen, what are highways and roads built with, what are sewers built with, what are houses built with? You don't have to be a genius to answer that. Why don't they give dollars for equipment, dollars for machinery, dollars so that all of our underdeveloped countries, all of them, may become industrial-agricultural countries at one and the same time? It really is sad.

On page 10, speaking of the elements of development planning, in Point 6, it shows who is the real author of this plan.

Point 6 states, "It can furnish a sounder basis for the provision and utilization of external financial assistance, particularly inasmuch as it provides more efficient criteria for judging individual projects."

We are not going to furnish sounder bases for the provision and utilization because we are not the ones who provide; you are the ones who receive, not those who provide; we—Cuba—are the ones who look on, and the United States is the one that provides. This Point 6, then, was drafted directly by the United States; it is a recommendation of the United States; and this is the spirit of this whole bungling thing called Topic I.

Now I wish to state one thing for the record: We have spoken a great deal about politics; we have charged that this is a political confabulation and in our conversations with other delegates we have emphasized Cuba's right to express these opinions, because Cuba is attacked directly in Topic V.

Cuba has not come here to sabotage the meeting, as has been asserted by some newspapers or by some spokesmen of foreign news agencies. Cuba has come to condemn what is subject to condemnation from the standpoint of principles, but it has also come here to work harmoniously, if that is possible, to try to straighten this out, this thing that was born misshapen, and it is willing to cooperate with all the delegates to straighten it out and make it a nice project.

The Honorable Douglas Dillon mentioned financing in his speech; that is important. In gathering together to speak of development we have to speak of financing, and we all have gathered here to speak with the only country that has capital for financing.

Mr. Dillon has said,

Looking toward the coming years and toward all sources of external financing—international institutions, Europe, and Japan, as well as the United States, new private investments, and investments of public funds [if Latin America takes the necessary internal measures it can logically expect that its efforts—it isn't even that "if it takes the measures, the funds will be granted," but rather that "it can logically expect"] that its efforts will be met by an inflow of capital of at least 20 billion dollars in the next ten years. And most of these funds will come from public resources.[3]

Is this what there is? No, there are 500 million dollars approved, that is what is being spoken of. This must be clearly emphasized, because it is the heart of the question. What does it mean?—and I assure you that I am not asking this for ourselves, but rather for the good of everybody—what is meant by "if Latin America takes the necessary internal measures," and what is meant by "it can logically expect"?

I believe that after the work of the committee or whenever the United States representative deems it appropriate, it will be necessary to pinpoint this part a little, because 20 billion is an interesting figure. It is nothing more than two thirds of the figure that our prime minister announced as being necessary for the development of America; a little push more and we get to the 30 billion mark. But we have to get those 30 billion cash on the barrelhead, one by one, in the national treasuries of each of the countries of America, except for this poor Cinderella, who will probably get nothing.

This is where we can help, not by blackmail, as is being looked for, because it has been said, "No, Cuba is the goose that lays the golden eggs; Cuba is there, and as long as Cuba is there, the United States will give." No, we have not come here like that; we have come here to work, to try to fight on the level of principles and of ideas, so that our countries may develop, because all or almost all

[3] Remarks in brackets are Guevara's. Eds.

of the delegates have said that if the Alliance for Progress fails, nothing can halt the wave of popular movements—I use my own terms, but this is what was meant—nothing can halt the waves of popular movements, if the Alliance for Progress fails, and we are interested in not having it fail, insofar as it may mean for the Americas a genuine improvement in the standard of living of their 200 million inhabitants. I can make this statement here in honesty and all sincerity.

We have diagnosed and foreseen the social revolution in the Americas, the real revolution, because events are shaping up otherwise, because an attempt is being made to halt the people with bayonets, and when the people realize that they can take the bayonets and turn them against those who hold them, those who hold them are lost. But if it is wished to lead the people along the path of logical and harmonious development, by long-term loans up to fifty years at a low interest rate, as Mr. Dillon announced, we are also in agreement.

The only thing, fellow delegates, is that we must all work together so that this figure may be made firm here and to make sure that the Congress of the United States will approve it, because you must not forget that we are faced with a presidential and legislative system, not a "dictatorship" like Cuba, where a representative of Cuba stands up and speaks in the name of the government, and is responsible for his actions. But things have to be ratified there, and the experience of many of the delegates has been that often the promises made have not been ratified there.

Well, I have a lot to say on each of the topics, so I shall hasten along here and then discuss them in a fraternal spirit in the committees. Just a few general figures, some general comments:

The rate of growth that is advanced as a very fine thing for all the Americas is 2.5 percent net. Bolivia announced 5 percent for ten years, and we congratulate the representative of Bolivia and tell him that with a little effort and mobilization of popular forces, he could say 10 percent. We speak of 10 percent development with no fear whatsoever; 10 percent is the rate of development foreseen by Cuba for the coming years.

What does this mean, fellow delegates? It means that if all countries continue on the road they are now following, when all the Americas, which at present have a per capita income of around 330 dollars, obtain an annual growth of 2.5 percent in their net product, somewhere around 1980 they will have 500 dollars per capita. Of course, for many countries this will be really phenomenal.

What does Cuba expect to have in 1980? A per capita net income of 3,000 dollars, more than the United States has now. And if you don't believe us, that's all right too; we're here to compete. Leave us alone, let us develop, and then we can meet again twenty years from now, to see if the siren song came from revolutionary Cuba or from some other source. But we hereby announce, with full responsibility, that rate of annual growth.

The experts suggest the replacement of inefficient *latifundia* and *minifundia* with well-equipped farms. We say: Do you want to have agrarian reform? Take the land from those who have a lot and give it to those who have none. That is the way to conduct agrarian reform. The way to do it, whether you give land divided into parcels in accordance with all the rules of private property, whether you give it as collective property, or whether you have a mixed system—as we do—depends on the individual characteristics of each country. But agrarian reform is carried out by liquidating the latifundia, not by settling some far away place.

And I could talk like this about redistribution of income, which in Cuba was effectively achieved, because you take from those who have more and permit those who have less or have nothing to have more, I can talk like this because we have carried out an agrarian reform; we have carried out our urban reform; we have reduced electricity and telephone rates—which, parenthetically, was our first skirmish with the foreign monopolistic companies—we have made workers' social centers and child centers where the workers' children go to get food and live while their parents work; we have made popular beaches; and we have nationalized education, which is absolutely free. In addition, we are working on a comprehensive health plan.

I shall speak of industrialization later, because it is the fundamental basis of development, and that is how we interpret it. But there is a very interesting point—that is, the filter, the purifier, the experts, seven of them, I believe. Once again, gentlemen, there is the danger of "outhouse-ocracy" stuck in the middle of the plans by which the countries want to improve their standard of living; another case of politicians dressed up as experts and saying *yes* here and *no* there; *yes*, this and that—but in reality because you're an easy tool of the one who furnishes the means; and you, *no*, because you've done this wrong—but in reality because you're not a tool of the one furnishing the means, because you say, for example, that you cannot accept aggression against Cuba as the price of a loan.

This is the danger, without counting the fact that the small countries, as is the case everywhere, receive little or nothing. Fellow delegates, there is only one place where the small ones have a right to "kick," and that is here, where each vote is a vote. This matter has to be voted, and the small countries—if they are ready to do so—can count on Cuba's militant vote against the idea of the "seven," meant to "sterilize," to "purify," and to channel the credit, with technical disguises, along different lines.

What is the position that will really lead to genuine planning, fully coordinated but not subordinated to any supranational agency?

We believe—and that is how we did it in our country—that the prior condition for true economic planning is that the political power be in the hands of the working class. This is the sine qua non of true planning for us. Furthermore, it is necessary that the imperialistic monopolies be completely eliminated and that the basic activities of production be controlled by the state. With these three ends well tied together, one can begin planning for economic development; if not, everything else is lost in words, speeches, and meetings.

In addition, there are two requisites which will make it possible or not for this development to take advantage of the latent potentialities lying within the people, who are waiting for them to be awakened. These are, on the one hand, rational central direction of the economy by a single power with authority to make decisions—I am not speaking of dictatorial powers, but decision-making powers—and, on the other, the active participation of all the people in the job of planning.

Naturally, in order to have all the people participate in planning, the people must own the means of production; otherwise, it will be difficult for them to participate. The people will not want to, and the owners of the companies where they work will not either, it seems to me.

We can speak for a few minutes about what Cuba has obtained by following its path, trading with the world, "flowing along the slopes of commerce," as Martí put it.

Up to this time we have contracted for loans amounting to 357 million dollars with the socialist countries, and we are engaged in conversations—which really are conversations—for a hundred and some million dollars more, with which we shall have reached 500 million dollars in loans during these five years. These loans, which give us possession and control over our economic development, amount to 500 million dollars, as we just said—the amount that the United States is giving to all the Americas—just for the small republic alone. This, divided by the population of Cuba and transferred to the Americas, would mean that to furnish equivalent amounts, the United States would have to give 15 billion pesos in five years, or 30 billion dollars—I speak of pesos or dollars, because in my country they are both worth the same—30 billion dollars in ten years, the amount of the economic process. Then Latin America would be something altogether different in only five years.

Let us go on now to Topic II of the agenda. And, naturally, before analyzing it, we shall state a political question.

Our friends in these meetings—and there are many of them, even though it may not seem so—ask us if we are willing to come back into the family of Latin American nations. We have never left the Latin American nations, and we are fighting against our expulsion, against being forced to leave the family of Latin American republics. What we do not want is to be herded, as Martí said. Just that.

We denounce the dangers of economic integration of Latin America because we know the examples of Europe and, furthermore, Latin America has already learned to the depths of its being what European economic integration cost it. We denounce the danger of having the processes of trade within free trade associations completely vested in the hands of international monopolies. But we also wish to announce here in this conference, and we hope our announcement will be accepted, that we are willing to join the Latin American Free Trade Association, as just another member, criticizing what ought to be criticized but complying with all the requisites, just as long as respect is given to Cuba, to its particular economic and social organization, and provided that its socialist government is accepted as an already consummated and irreversible fact.

And in addition, Cuba must be given equality of treatment and a fair share in the advantages of the international division of labor. Cuba must participate actively and it can contribute a great deal to improve many of the great "bottlenecks" that exist in the economies of our countries, with the help of planned economy, centrally directed and with a clear and well-defined goal.

However, Cuba also wishes to propose the following measures: It proposes the initiation of immediate bilateral negotiations for the evacuation of bases or territories in member states occupied by other member states, so that there may be no more cases like the one denounced by the delegation of Panama, where Panama's wage policies cannot be applied in part of its territory. The same thing happens with us, and we should like this anomaly to cease, speaking from the economic viewpoint.

We propose the study of rational plans for the development and coordination of technical and financial assistance from all of the industrialized countries, without ideological or geographical distinctions of any kind; we also propose that guarantees be requested to safeguard the interests of the weaker countries; we propose the prohibition of acts of economic aggression by some member states against other member states, guarantees to protect Latin American businessmen against the competition of foreign monopolies, the reduction of United States tariffs on industrial products of the integrated Latin American states. And we state that, as we see it, external financing would be good only if it took the form of indirect investments that met the following conditions: the investments should not be subject to political requirements and should not discriminate against state enterprises; they should be applied in accordance with the interests of the receiving country; the interest rates should not exceed 3 percent and the amortization period should be not less than ten years and subject to extension in case of balance of payments difficulties; the seizure of or confiscation of ships and aircraft of a member country by another should be prohibited; and tax reforms should be initiated, removing the tax burden from the working masses and providing protection against the action of foreign monopolies.

Topic III has been dealt with just as delicately as the others by the experts; they have approached this matter with a gentle pair of tweezers, lifted the veil slightly, and let it drop immediately, because this is a tough subject.

It might have been desirable—and it was tempting—for the Group to formulate broad and spectacular recommendations. But it was impossible to do so because of the numerous and intricate technical problems which would have had to be resolved first. Therefore, the recommendations actually set forth were confined to those considered technically feasible.

I do not know if I am overly perspicacious, but I think that I can read between the lines. Because there have been no verdicts, the delegation of Cuba specifically presents what should be achieved by this meeting: a guarantee of stable prices, without any "could" or "might," without any "we would examine" or "we shall examine," but just guarantees of stable prices; expanding or at least stable markets; guarantees against economic aggression, against the unilateral suspension of purchases in traditional markets, against the dumping of subsidized agricultural surpluses, and against protectionism for the production of basic commodities; creation of conditions in the industrialized countries for the purchase of primary products that have been subject to a higher degree of processing.

Cuba declares that it would be desirable for the delegation of the United States to state in the committee whether it will continue to subsidize its production of copper, lead, zinc, sugar, cotton, wheat, or wool. Cuba asks whether the United States will continue pressuring to stop member countries from selling their primary product surpluses to socialist countries, thus increasing its own market.

And now we come to Topic V of the agenda. Topic IV is nothing more than a report, but this Topic V is the other side of the coin.

On the occasion of the Costa Rica Conference, Fidel Castro said that the United States had attended "with a bag of gold in one hand and a club in the other." Here today the United States comes with a bag of gold—fortunately a larger bag—in one hand and the barrier to isolate Cuba in the other. It is, in any case, a victory of historic circumstances.

In Topic V of the agenda, a program of measures is established for Latin America for the regimentation of thought, the subordination of the labor movement, and, if it can be done, the preparation of military aggression against Cuba.

Three steps are foreseen in reading it: mobilization, as of now, of Latin American media of information and publicity against the Cuban Revolution and against the struggles of our countries for their freedom; the formation, at a later conference, of an Inter-American Press, Radio, Television, and Motion Picture Federation that will enable the United States to direct the public opinion organs of Latin America, all of them—right now there are not many outside its sphere of influence but it seeks them all—to exercise monopolistic control over new information agencies, and to absorb as many of the old ones as possible.

All of this is something extraordinary, which was announced here in all calmness and which in my country gave rise to deep discussion when something similar was done in a single instance. This is an attempt, fellow delegates, to establish a common market for culture, organized, directed, paid, mastered; the culture of all the Americas at the service of imperialistic propaganda plans, to show that the hunger of our peoples is not hunger but laziness. Magnificent!

The organs of public opinion of Latin America must be exhorted to support the ideals of national liberation of each Latin American country. An exhortation must be made for the exchange of information, cultural media, press organs, and for the direct visits between peoples without discrimination, because a United States citizen who goes to Cuba nowadays faces five years of prison on returning to his country. The Latin American governments must be exhorted to guarantee the labor movement freedom to organize independently, to defend the interests of the workers, and to struggle for the true independence of their countries. We call for a total and absolute condemnation of Topic V as an imperialistic attempt to domesticate the only thing that our countries have been saving from disaster: national culture.

I shall take the liberty, fellow delegates, of presenting an outline of the objectives of Cuba's first plan for economic development during the next four years. The general growth rate will be 12 percent, that is, more than 9.5 percent per capita, net. In the industrial field, the plan calls for the transformation of Cuba into the most highly industrialized country of Latin America in relation to its population, as may be seen from the following figures:

First place in Latin America in the per capita production of steel, electric power, and, except for Venezuela, in petroleum refining; first place in' Latin America in tractors, rayon, shoes, textiles, and so forth; second place in the world in the production of metallic nickel —nickel production in 1965 will amount to 70,000 metric tons, which is about 30 percent of world production, and in addition, it will produce 2,600 metric tons of metallic cobalt; sugar production of 8.5 to 9 million tons; and the commencement of the transformation of the sugar industry into a sugar-chemical industry.

In order to do this, which is easy to say but which will require an enormous amount of work and the effort of an entire people and a very large amount of external financing furnished from the standpoint of aid not spoliation, the following measures have been adopted: more than one billion pesos are going to be invested in industry—the Cuban peso is equivalent to the dollar—in the installation of 800 megawatts of electric power. In 1960, the installed capacity—except for the sugar industry, which operates seasonally—amounted to 621 megawatts. The installation of 205 industries, of which the 22 more important ones are the following: a new plant for refining nickel ore, which will raise the total to 70,000 tons; a petroleum refinery for 2 million tons of crude petroleum; the first steel mill, with a capacity of 700,000 tons of steel, which in this four-year period will reach 500,000 tons; the expansion of our plants to produce seamed steel tubes, amounting to 25,000 metric tons; tractors, 5,000 units per year; motorcycles, 10,000 units per year; three cement plants and expansion of the existing ones for a total of 1.5 million metric tons, which will raise our production to 2.5 million per year; metal containers, 291 million units; expansion of our glass plants by 23,700 metric tons per year; one million square meters of flat glass; a new plant for making bagasse fiberboard, 10,000 cubic meters; a bagasse cellulose plant, 60,000 cubic meters, in addition to a wood cellulose plant for 40,000 metric tons per year; an ammonium nitrate plant, 60,000 metric tons; a plant for simple superphosphate, for 70,000 tons, and 81,000 metric tons of triple superphosphate; 132,000 metric tons of nitric acid; 85,000 metric tons of ammonia; eight new textile plants and expansion of existing ones with 451,000 spindles; a kenaf bag plant for 16 million bags; and so on to others of lesser importance, going as high as 205 at the present time.

These credits have been contracted for thus far as follows: 200 million dollars with the Soviet Union; 60 million dollars with the Chinese People's Republic; 40 million with the Socialist Republic of Czechoslovakia; 15 million with the Rumanian People's Republic; 15 million with the Hungarian People's Republic; 12 million with the Polish People's Republic; 10 million with the German Democratic Republic; and 5 million with the Democratic Republic of Bulgaria. The total amount contracted for the time is 357 million dollars. The new negotiations that we hope to conclude soon are basically with the Soviet Union which, as the most highly industrialized country of the socialist area, is the one that has given us the most support.

As for agriculture, Cuba intends to achieve self-sufficiency in the production of foodstuffs, including fats and rice, but not in wheat; self-sufficiency in cotton and hard fibers; production of exportable surpluses in tropical fruits and other agricultural products which will triple the present levels of exports.

With respect to foreign trade, the value of exports will be increased by 75 percent over the 1960 figure. There will be a diversification of the economy, with sugar and sugar by-products amounting to around 60 percent of exports and not 80 percent as at the present time.

With respect to construction; the plan calls for elimination of 40 percent of the present housing deficit, including *bohios*, which are our rural shacks, and a rational combination of building materials so that use of local materials may be increased without sacrificing quality.

There is a point that I should like to dwell on for a moment, and that is education. We have laughed at the group of experts who placed education and health as sine qua non conditions to starting on the road to development. To us this is an aberration, but it is no less true that once the road to development is started, education should progress parallel to it. Without adequate technological education, development is slowed down. Therefore, Cuba has carried out a complete reform of education; it has expanded and improved educational services and has prepared over-all educational plans.

At the present time Cuba ranks first in Latin America in the allocation of funds to education; we devote 5.3 percent of our national income to it. The developed countries allocate between 3 percent and 4 percent, and the Latin American countries between 1 percent and 2 percent of their national income. In Cuba, 28.3 percent of the state's current expenditures are for the ministry of education, and including other agencies that spend money for education, this figure increases to 30 percent. The Latin American country that ranks second in this respect allocates 21 percent of its budget to this purpose.

The increase in our budget for education from 75 million in 1958 to 128 million in 1961 represents an increase of 7 percent. Total expenditures for education, including the campaign against illiteracy and school construction amount to 170 million, or 25 pesos per capita. In Denmark, for example, 25 pesos per capita per year are spent on education; in France, 15; in Latin America, 5.

In two years, 10,000 schoolrooms have been provided and 10,000 new teachers appointed. Ours is the first country in Latin America fully to satisfy all primary instruction needs of the school-age population, an aspiration of the UNESCO Principal Project for Latin America by 1968, which has already been fulfilled in Cuba.

These measures and these really marvelous and absolutely accurate figures we present here, fellow delegates, have been made possible by the following actions: nationalization of teaching, making it secular and free, and making possible the total utilization of its services; establishment of a system of scholarships to guarantee the satisfaction of all the needs of the students, in accordance with the following plan: 20,000 scholarships for basic secondary schools, grades seven to nine; 3,000 scholarships for preuniversity institutes; 3,000 for art instructors; 6,000 for the universities; 1,500 for courses in artificial insemination; 1,200 for courses on agricultural machinery; 14,000 for courses in sewing and dressmaking and basic domestic science training for farm women; 1,200 for training of teachers for the mountain areas; 750 for beginners' courses for primary school teachers; 10,000 including both scholarships and study grants for students preparing for technological teaching; and in addition, hundreds of scholarships for the study of technology in the socialist countries; establishment of 100 centers of secondary education, so that each municipality will have at least one.

This year in Cuba, as I already stated, illiteracy is being wiped out. It is a wonderful sight. Up to the present time, 104,500 brigade members, almost all of them students between the ages of ten and eighteen, have flooded the country from one end to the other, going directly to the cabins of the farm people and the homes of workers, to convince the old people who no longer want to study and thus to eliminate illiteracy.

Whenever a factory eradicates illiteracy among its workers, it raises a flag announcing this fact to the people of Cuba; whenever a farm cooperative becomes free of illiteracy among its members, it hoists a similar pennant; and there are 104,500 young students, who have as their insignia a book and a lamp, to carry the light of education into the backward areas, and who belong to the "Conrado Benitez" Brigades, named in honor of the first martyr of education of the Cuban Revolution, who was hanged by a group of counter-revolutionaries for the serious crime of being in the mountains of our country teaching the people how to read.

This is the difference, fellow delegates, between our country and those that are fighting against it.

One hundred and fifty-six thousand volunteer fighters against illiteracy, workers and professionals, work part-time in this teaching field; 32,000 teachers head this army, and only with the active cooperation of all the people of Cuba could figures of such magnitude have been achieved.

This has all been done in one year, or rather, in two years: seven regimental headquarters have become school campuses; twenty-seven barracks have become schools; and all of this while there was danger of imperialistic aggression. The Camilo Cienfuegos School campus at the present time has 5,000 pupils from the Sierra Maestra and is building units for 20,000 pupils; we intend to build a similar campus in every province; each school campus will be self-sufficient in food, thus initiating the farm children in agricultural practices.

In addition, new teaching methods have been instituted. Primary school enrollment increased from 602,000 in 1958 to 1,231,700 in 1959; secondary school enrollment from 21,900 to 83,800; business schools, from 8,900 to 21,300; technological schools, from 5,600 to 11,500.

Forty-eight million pesos have been invested in school construction in just two years.

The National Printing Office guarantees textbooks and other printed material for all school children free of charge.

Two television networks, covering the whole country, make possible the use of this powerful medium for mass education. Likewise, the entire national radio system is at the disposal of the Ministry of Education.

The Cuban Institute of Motion Picture Art and Industry, the National Library, and the National Theater, with representatives throughout the whole country, complete this great system for the dissemination of culture.

The National Institute of Sports, Physical Education, and Recreation, whose initials are INDER, promotes physical development on a massive scale.

This, fellow delegates, is the cultural picture in Cuba at this time.

Now we come to the final part of our statement, the part containing definitions, because we want to establish our position very clearly.

We have denounced the Alliance for Progress as an instrument designed to separate Cuba from the other countries of Latin America, to sterilize the example of the Cuban Revolution, and then to bend the other countries to the wishes of the imperialists.

Permit me to offer full proof of this.

There are many interesting documents in the world. We shall distribute to the delegates some documents which came into our hands and which show, for example, the opinion held by the imperialists of the government of Venezuela, whose foreign minister attacked us harshly a few days ago, perhaps because he understood that we were violating laws of friendship with his people or his government.

However, it is interesting to point out that friendly hands sent us an interesting document. It is a report on a secret document addressed to Ambassador Moscoso in Venezuela by his advisers, John M. Cates, Jr., Irvin Tragen, and Robert Cox.

This document, in one of its paragraphs, states, speaking of the measures Venezuela must take in order to have a real Alliance for Progress, directed by the United States:

"Reform of the Bureaucracy. All plans that are made"—speaking of Venezuela—"all programs initiated for the economic development of Venezuela, either by the Venezuelan Government or by United States technicians, will have to be implemented through Venezuela's bureaucracy. But as long as the civil service of that country is characterized by ineptitude, indifference, inefficiency, formalism, party favoritism in the granting of jobs, corruption, duplication of functions, and the building of private empires, it will be practically impossible to have dynamic and effective projects go through the government machinery. Therefore, a reform of the administrative structure is possibly the most basic need, since not only would it be directed toward correcting a basic economic and social imbalance, but would also imply a reconditioning of the very instrument which should shape all of the other basic reforms and development projects."

There are many interesting things in this document which we shall place at the disposal of the delegates; for example, where it speaks of the natives. After the natives are taught, the natives can be permitted to work. We are natives, and nothing more. But there is something interesting, fellow delegates, and that is the recommendation made by Mr. Cates to Mr. Moscoso as to what has to be done. It reads as follows:

"The United States will be forced, probably sooner than is expected, to point out to the right wings, the oligarchy, the nouveau riches, and the national and foreign economic circles in general, the military, and the clergy that in the long run they will have to make a choice between two things: either contribute to the establishment in Venezuela of a society based on the masses, maintaining at the same time their status quo and their wealth, or face the loss of both (and perhaps death itself before the firing squad)"—this is a report by Americans to their ambassador—"if the forces of moderation and progress are displaced in Venezuela."

Then this is completed, giving the picture and all the machinations by which this conference began to develop, with other reports of secret instructions sent to Latin America by the United States Department of State concerning the "Cuban case."

This is very important, because it shows where the lamb's mother was. It says—and I shall take the liberty of quoting a few extracts from it, though we shall distribute it later, in deference to the brevity that I have already violated somewhat:

From the beginning, it was generally understood in Latin America that the United States backed the invasion, and that it would therefore be successful. The majority of the governments and the responsible sectors of the people were prepared to accept a fait accompli, although there were misgivings about violation of the principle of nonintervention. The Communists and other strongly pro-Castro elements immediately took the offensive with demonstrations and acts of violence directed against United States agencies, especially in Argentina, Bolivia, and Mexico. However, these anti-American and pro-Castro activities received limited backing and produced less results than might have been expected.

The failure of the invasion discouraged the anti-Castro sectors, who considered that the United States should do something dramatic to restore its damaged prestige, but it was received with glee by the Communists and other pro-Castro elements.

It continues:

In most cases, the reactions of the Latin American governments were not surprising. With the exception of Haiti and the Dominican Republic, the republics that had already broken or suspended relations with Cuba expressed their understanding of the United States' position. Honduras joined the anti-Castro camp, suspending relations in April and proposing the formation of an alliance of Central American and Caribbean nations to have it out with Cuba by force. The proposal—which was also suggested independently by Nicaragua—was quietly dropped when Venezuela refused to back it up. Venezuela, Colombia, and Panama expressed serious concern over the penetration of the Soviets and of international communism in Cuba, but favored some sort of collective action by the O.A.S. ["collective action by the O.A.S." brings us into familiar ground] to deal with the Cuban problem. A similar opinion was expressed by Argentina, Uruguay, and Costa Rica. Chile, Ecuador, Bolivia, Brazil, and Mexico refused to support any position that would imply intervention in Cuba's internal affairs. This attitude was probably very strong in Chile, where the government found strong opposition in all circles to open military intervention by any state against the Castro regime. In Brazil and in Ecuador the matter provoked serious splits in the cabinet, in congress, and in the political parties. In the case of Ecuador, the intransigent pro-Cuban position adopted by President Velasco was shaken but not altered by the discovery of the fact that Ecuadorean Communists were being trained in that country in guerrilla tactics by pro-Castro revolutionaires. [Parenthetically, and this is my comment, that is a lie.]

Likewise, there are few doubts that some of the previously uncommitted elements in Latin America have been favorably impressed by Castro's capacity to survive a military attack, supported by the United States, against his regime. Many of those who had previously hesitated to commit themselves, assuming that the United States would in time eliminate the Castro regime, may now have changed their minds. Castro's victory has shown them the permanent and workable nature of the Cuban revolution [this is a report by the United States]. In addition, his victory has no doubt aroused the latent anti-United States attitude that prevails in a large part of Latin America.

In every respect, the member states of the O.A.S. are now less hostile toward United States intervention in Cuba than before the invasion, but a majority of them—including Brazil and Mexico, which accounted for more than half the population of Latin America—are not willing to intervene actively or even to join a quarantine against Cuba. Nor can it be expected that the Organization would give its prior approval to direct intervention by the United States, except in the event that Castro were to be involved beyond a doubt in an attack against a Latin American government.

Even if the United States were successful—which seems improbable—

in persuading a majority of the Latin American states to join in a quarantine against Cuba, the attempt would not be completely successful. It is certain that Mexico and Brazil would refuse to cooperate and would serve as a channel for travel and other communications between Latin America and Cuba.

Mexico's long-standing opposition to intervention of any kind would not be an unsurmountable obstacle to collective action by the O.A.S. against Cuba. The attitude of Brazil, however, which exercises strong influence over its South American neighbors, is decisive for hemisphere cooperation. As long as Brazil refuses to act against Castro, it is probable that a number of other nations, including Argentina and Chile, will not wish to risk adverse internal repercussions to please the United States.

The magnitude of the threat represented by Castro and the Communists in other parts of Latin America will probably continue to depend basically on the following factors: (a) The ability of the regime to maintain its position; (b) its effectiveness in showing the success of its way of dealing with the problems of reform and development; and (c) the ability of non-Communist elements in other Latin American countries to furnish feasible and popularly accepted alternatives. If, by means of propaganda, etc., Castro can convince the disaffected elements existing in Latin America that basic social reforms are really being made [that is to say, if the delegates become convinced that what we are saying is true] that will benefit the poorer classes, the attractiveness of the Cuban example will increase and it will continue to inspire leftist imitators in this entire area. The danger is not so much that a subversive apparatus, based in Havana, may export the revolution, but that increasing poverty and unrest among the masses of the Latin American people will give the pro-Castro elements an opportunity to act.

After considering whether we intervene or not, they reason as follows:

It is probable that the Cubans will act cautiously in this regard for some time. They probably are not desirous of risking the interception or discovery of any acts of piracy or military supplies coming from Cuba.

Such an eventuality would result in a greater stiffening of Latin American official opinion against Cuba, perhaps to the point of giving tacit backing to United States intervention, or at least of providing possible reasons for sanctions by the O.A.S. For these reasons, and because of Castro's concern over the defense of his own territory at this time, the use of Cuban military forces to support insurrection in other areas is extremely improbable.

And so, for any of you delegates who have any doubts, the government of the United States announces that it would be very difficult for our troops to intervene in the national affairs of other countries.

As time goes by, and in view of the absence of direct Cuban intervention in the internal affairs of neighboring states, present fears of

Castroism, of Soviet intervention in the regime, of its "Socialist" nature [the quotation marks are theirs] and the repugnance against Castro's police-state repression will tend to diminish and the traditional policy of non-intervention will be reaffirmed.

It goes on to say:

Aside from its direct effect on the prestige of the United States in that area—which undoubtedly has dropped as a result of the failure of the invasion—the survival of the Castro regime might have a profound effect on American political life in the coming years. It is preparing the scene for a political stuggle on the terms promoted by Communist propaganda for a long time in this hemisphere, with the "popular" [in quotation marks] anti-American forces on the one hand and the dominant groups allied with the United States on the other hand. The governments that promise evolutionary reforms for a period of years, even at an accelerated pace, will be faced with political leaders who will promise an immediate remedy for social ills through the confiscation of property and the overturning of society. The most immediate danger of Castro's example for Latin America might well be the danger to the stability of those governments that are at present attempting evolutional social and economic changes rather than for those that have tried to prevent such changes, in part because of the tensions and awakened hopes accompanying such social changes and economic development. The unemployed city-dwellers and landless peasants in Venezuela and Peru, for example, who have been waiting for Acción Democrática and APRA to make reforms, are an easy source of political strength for the politician who convinces them that the change can be made more quickly than has been promised by the Social Democratic movements. The popular support at present enjoyed by groups seeking evolutionary changes, or the potential support they might normally obtain as the Latin American masses become more politically active, would be lost to the extent to which extremist political leaders, using Castro's example, might arouse support for revolutionary change.

And in the last paragraph, gentlemen, our friend present here says:

The Alliance for Progress might well furnish the stimulus to carry out more intensive reform programs, but unless these programs are started quickly and soon begin to show positive results, it is probable that they will not be enough of a counterweight to increasing pressure from the extreme left. The years ahead of us will almost certainly witness a race between those forces that are attempting to initiate evolutionary reform programs and those that are trying to generate support by the masses for fundamental economic and social revolution. If the moderates lag behind in this race, they might in time be deprived of the support of the masses and caught in an untenable position between the extremes of the right and the left.[4]

[4] Comments in brackets are Guevara's. Eds.

These, fellow delegates, are the documents that the delegation of Cuba wanted to present to you, to make an unvarnished analysis of the "Alliance for Progress."

We all know the innermost feelings of the Department of State of the United States: "We have to get the Latin American countries to grow because otherwise we shall get a phenomenon called 'Castroism,' which is awful for the United States."

Well, then, gentlemen, let us have the Alliance for Progress on these terms: Let there be a genuine growth in the economies of all of the member countries of the Organization of American States; let them grow, so that they may consume their products, not to become a source of wealth for United States monopolies; let them grow to ensure social peace, not to create new reserves for a future war of conquest; let them grow for us, not for outsiders. And to all of you, fellow delegates, the delegation of Cuba wishes to say with all frankness: We, with our own conditions, want to be a part of the Latin American family; we want to live together with Latin America; we want to see it grow, if possible, at the same pace we are growing, but we are not opposed to its growing at a different pace. What we do demand is a guarantee of nonaggression against our borders.

We cannot stop exporting an example, as the United States wishes, because an example is something intangible that transcends borders. What we do give is a guarantee that we shall not export revolutions, we guarantee that not a single rifle will leave Cuba, that not a single weapon will leave Cuba for battle in any other country of America.

What we cannot assure is that Cuba's ideas will not be applied in any other country of America, and what we do assure you in this conference is that if urgent measures of social improvement are not adopted, the example of Cuba will take fire in various countries, and then that comment which gave so much food for thought, uttered by Fidel on a certain 26th of July, and which was interpreted as aggression, will again be true. Fidel said that if social conditions remained as they were, "the cordilleras of the Andes would be the Sierra Maestra of the Americas."

We, gentlemen, call the Alliance for Progress the alliance for our progress, the peaceful alliance for the progress of all. We are not opposed to being left out in the distribution of credits, but we are opposed to being left out of participation in the cultural and spiritual life of our Latin American peoples, of which we are a part.

What we shall never accept is a curtailment of our freedom to trade and to have relations with all countries of the world, and what we shall defend ourselves against with all our strength is any attempt of foreign aggression, whether it comes from an imperial power or from any Latin American organization that incorporates the desires of some to see us wiped out.

To conclude, Mr. Chairman, fellow delegates, I want to tell you that some time ago we held a meeting of the staff of the Revolutionary Forces of my country, a staff to which I belong. The matter concerned aggression against Cuba, which we knew was coming although we did not know when or where. We thought it would be large, indeed it would be very large. This took place before the famous warning by the premier of the Soviet Union, Nikita Krushchev, that his rockets could reach beyond Soviet borders. We had not requested that aid and were not aware of that willingness to aid us. That is why we held our meeting, knowing that an invasion was coming, to face our final fate as revolutionaries. We knew that if the United States invaded Cuba, there would be a blood bath, but in the end we would be defeated and expelled from all inhabited areas of the country.

Then we, the members of the staff, proposed that Fidel Castro withdraw to a mountain redoubt, and that one of us take charge of the defense of Havana. Our prime minister and chief, speaking in words that ennoble him—as do all of his acts—then answered that if the United States invaded Cuba and if Havana were defended as it should be, hundreds of thousands of men, women, and children would die under the thrust of Yankee weapons, and that the leader of a people in revolution could not be asked to hide in the mountains, that his place was there with the beloved fallen, and that there, with them, he would fulfill his historic mission.

The invasion did not materialize but, fellow delegates, we maintain that spirit. That is why I can predict that the Cuban Revolution is invincible, because it has a people and because it has a leader like the one who is ruling Cuba.

That is all, fellow delegates.

Technology
and Society

Comrade students and professors of architecture the world over:

It is my duty to conclude this International Congress of Students. First of all, I have to make a very embarrassing statement: I confess my great ignorance of architecture, an ignorance that goes to the extreme of not realizing that this International Congress was apolitical. I thought it was a students' conference, without knowing that it was an organization dependent on the International Union of Architects. Therefore, as political men—that is, as students who participate in the active life of your country—and after reading the resolutions of this meeting (which show that the ignorance was collective because the resolutions are very political also), I wish to state, first of all, that the resolutions of this conference have my fullest support. They are logical conclusions, scientific and revolutionary at the same time. But now I want to make a small political speech even though I really do not know if this is the appropriate time to talk about political matters. At any rate you should decide because I cannot talk about technology.

I am not trying to sell you cheap demagoguery or elude your bylaws. I did not know your regulations and simply came to make a resumé in my political capacity, a new politician, one that belongs to the people, but a politician nonetheless, due to my functions. Also, I am impressed by the ample majority that supported the conclusions. I am wholeheartedly in agreement with most of the resolutions because they outline the role of the student and the technician in society.

The resolutions of this conference surprised me to some extent because I have seen here people from every country of the world. The socialist nations are few in number but in number of people are strongly represented.

The countries struggling for their liberation, under diverse regimes and at different stages of their fight, are many but they also have different governments and above all their professionals do not

Speech delivered at the First International Meeting of Architecture on September 29, 1963. *El Mundo* (Havana), October 1, 1963, pp. 5–6.

always respond to the same interests. The capitalist countries, naturally, have their own ideologies. That is why we were amazed by the tone of the discussions. I thought, perhaps a little bit mechanically, that the majority of the students of the capitalist, colonial, and semicolonial countries would not be concerned with the problems of the proletariat because they do not come from their ranks. I thought the students' ideology would be far from the revolutionary ideology that we defend and maintain in Cuba. Nevertheless, I did not forget in my mechanistic thinking that in Cuba a group of students came from other social groups than the proletariat and, notwithstanding, that group of students participated in the recent revolutionary struggle in Cuba. They gave the liberation some of the most beloved martyrs of our people. Many of them are committed to the Revolution today while others are in the process of integrating themselves into it.

I forgot that there is something more important than social class that belongs to the individual: that is, youth, freshness of ideals, culture that the moment it emerges from adolescence is put into the service of the highest ideals.

As time goes by, the student might change his mind due to the social mechanisms created by oppressive regimes. Nonetheless, students tend to be revolutionary. Students might have more or less awareness of a scientific revolution, they might be more or less conscious of what they want or how to achieve their goal. But students are, by nature, revolutionaries because they are young and acquiring new knowledge daily. This has happened in our country.

Even though it is evident that students and professionals have left, we have seen with satisfaction, and sometimes with surprise, that the majority of students and professionals remained in Cuba in spite of all the temptations offered by imperialism. The reason is logical: even if we are aware that under exploiting social systems the students cannot choose their career, follow their real vocation, there is always a meeting point between vocation and career; the frustrated cases are only a few. As a rule, the choice of most careers is influenced by a series of economic pressures, but the choice is made mainly because the career is appealing.

In our country the professionals and students have been given the opportunity that a true professional should seek: the opportunity to have all the instruments required to realize his work. The professionals, for the first time in Cuba, are true builders of our society. They participate in it, they are responsible to society. They are no longer wage-earners, hiding behind diverse forms of exploitation.

They no longer work for others, interpreting the desires of others, always creating wealth for others by their own work.

It is true that in this beginning stage the limitations have been great. Our scientists cannot carry out their investigations. Sometimes we lack the chemical materials necessary to make certain experiments. Our architects cannot design with all the taste and beauty they know how to use because we lack some of the building materials. It is necessary to distribute to the maximum what we have to those who do not have anything. At this stage it is essential to redistribute wealth so that everyone will have a little.

The creative spirit of man is put to a test in the exercise of his profession. The problem is posited by the lack of materials, but the solution has to be found by our professionals. This has to be fought as one battles nature, against means external to man's will, in order to fulfill as well as possible the desire to give more to our people. One also finds personal satisfaction in building a new society with one's own knowledge, talents, and hands.

Our revolution has been open-minded. We have not suffered the great problems that other countries building socialism had with professionals and their differences over art. We have been open-minded even though we do not agree with everything that our professionals and artists believe. Often we have discussed heatedly with them, but even those who are not socialist or who hate socialism and dream about the old days have stayed in Cuba, fighting, discussing, working, and building. And, in fact, they are practically socialistic, which is what interests us.

We have never refused confrontation or discussion. We are always ready to discuss all ideas, and the only thing we do not permit is blackmail through ideas, or sabotage of the Revolution. In this respect we are absolutely inflexible.

In terms of principles, our country has what is scientifically called the dictatorship of the proletariat. At this stage we do not permit the dictatorship of the proletariat to be attacked, but within it there exists a wide margin of discussion and expression of ideas. The only thing we demand is that the general lines of the state in this stage of socialist construction be respected.

Some professionals have gone to prison because of their counterrevolutionary activities, but even they have been rehabilitated in prison working first there and after their release in our industries. We trust them as we trust any of our technicians, and they entrust themselves to the Revolution—even though they have known the hardest and gloomiest side of it, that is, repression. A triumphant revolution has to use repression because with its triumph the class struggle does not end and, in our case, the class struggle became much worse after the victory of the Revolution. Sabotage, assassination attempts—you probably noticed that yesterday we were welcomed to a meeting with a bomb—become part of the counterrevolution. It has always been that way.

We have no mercy for those who take weapons against us; it does not matter if they are weapons of destruction or ideological weapons. The rest, those who disagree, the honestly unhappy, those who state that they are not and will never be socialist, to them we simply say: good, before, nobody ever asked you if you were a capitalist or not, you had a contract and you fulfilled it; now you should do the same—go ahead and work, we do not care about your ideas, we are not concerned with them.

That is how we keep on building, with many problems, with many jumps backward. A revolution never moves forward on a continuous basis. There are times when we fall into an impasse, when the revolutionary momentum is lost. Then our forces have to be reorganized, problems anaylzed, and then we march forward.

That is how revolutions are made and consolidated. One begins as we began: a group of men supported by the people in an adequate guerrilla zone. Now we reach the time in which we presently find ourselves and I am supposed to be the theoretician of something I do not know. With my limited knowledge I will try to define what I understand to be an architect.

I think that an architect—and practically every professional—is a man who unites the general culture of humanity reached at a given moment with the general technology of humanity or a specific people.

The architect, like every professional, is a man living in society. He can meet in international apolitical meetings—and this is correct—to maintain peaceful coexistence, but I cannot understand how as a man he can maintain his apolitical position.

To be apolitical is to turn one's back on every movement in the world, to turn one's back on who will be president or leader of a nation, to turn one's back on the construction of society or the struggle to build a new society. In any of these cases, one has taken a political position. In the present society every man is by nature political.

Every architect is a political man because he unites the culture of all humanity and its technology. He lives in a real world.

Culture is something that belongs to the world; like language, it belongs to *homo sapiens*. But technology is a weapon and should be used as such, and everyone uses it as a weapon. We can show you that mural over there, for instance; there is a weapon. It is an American M-1, a Garand rifle. That weapon in the hands of Batista's soldiers when firing on us was ugly, but that same weapon was extraordinarily beautiful when we captured it, when we snatched it from a soldier's hands, when it became a people's weapon. Without changing its structure or function of killing men, the weapon became dignified. The weapon acquired a new quality: now it was used to liberate the people.

Technology is the same. Technology can be used to dominate the people or it can be used to help liberate them. That is the conclusion one can reach from the document you approved.

To use the weapon of technology to society's benefit, one has to control society. To control society, the elements of oppression must be destroyed, the social conditions of the country must be changed, and the weapon of technology must be given to the people. That is the function of all of us who believe that change is required in certain regions of the world.

We cannot have technicians who think like revolutionaries but do not act as such. Revolution is an urgent need on most of our continents, in most of Latin America, in all of Africa and Asia, wherever exploitation has reached inconceivable depths.

Whoever pretends that a technician, an architect, a physician, an engineer, or any type of scientist should merely work with his instruments in a specific field while his people die of starvation, or die fighting in battle, has already chosen sides with the enemy. He is not apolitical, he is political but opposed to liberation movements.

Naturally, I respect the opinions of all who are present. Evidently there must be young men and professionals here who think that a socialist regime—what is known of it up to now—is a regime of oppression, misery, and mediocrity. This is what is stated in a vulgar way by propagandists, who add that man achieves self-realization when there is free enterprise, freedom of thought, and all those opinions that imperialism throws at us. Many of these people honestly believe these statements and I do not intend to argue. One cannot argue on these problems. Many people have been influenced by propaganda to a great degree over generations. Capitalism, through collective education, has created this mode of thinking which has allowed it to survive. But capitalism has begun to fall because the world is awakening. Today all the old and accepted capitalist statements are being questioned. People demand practical ratification of that which is asserted; they want a scientific analysis of all statements. From that restlessness, revolutionary ideas are born and spread more and more over the world, based on the examples set by the socialist countries which have shown what can be achieved when technology is used to serve man. That is what I can tell you.

Now I want to speak to the Cuban students. Because all of my statements will be about a specific subject matter, a little bit provincial for many of you, I beg you to simply disregard it if it holds no interest for you. But our students have to be considered every single day. Our youth was born in the midst of great turmoil. A few years ago North American marines performed their bodily functions on the head of Martí's statue, but today our people stand firm against North American imperialism. An extraordinary phenomenon has occurred: a total change in the consciousness of the masses in a few years of revolutionary work. But many things have been left unclear with the many drastic and abrupt changes that have taken place. Our students' minds are not exempt from a great many doubts, as is the case with our people.

This is why we want to insist once more that at this moment of struggle we are threatened daily by Yankee imperialism. Its aggressiveness is clear and the students' task is today more important than ever. They have to accelerate their studies in order to become the true builders of the new society. At the same time, students should also deepen their consciousness so that they know where they are going and how they are getting there. They should not be mere builders without ideas. They must put their hands, their head, their heart, at the service of the society being born. And at the same time they must be ready with rifle in hand, because the defense of our society is not a job that falls to one or another class. The defense of the Cuban Revolution is the continuous task of every Cuban at all times, in every trench.

Your task, comrade students, is to follow Lenin's advice to the fullest: "Every revolutionary ought to be in his place of work, of struggle, the best." And your place of struggle is today the university, your main task is to study and become professionals in order to fill the vacuum left us by imperialism when our cadres were taken. Your task is to move the nation away from backwardness and hasten the building of a new society.

That is the essential, but not the sole, task, because one should never leave aside the conscientious study of theory or the possibility of having to seize a rifle at any moment and the permanent necessity of defending the Revolution with ideological weapons every minute of our lives. These are hard tasks, but this is a generation of sacrifice.

This generation, our generation, will not have even remotely the goods of the generations that follow. We have to be aware of this, conscious of our role, because we have had the immense glory of being the revolutionary vanguard of Latin America, and today we have the glory of being the country most hated by imperialism.

We are in the vanguard at every moment of the struggle. We have not renounced one of our principles, nor sacrificed one of our ideals. We have not left unfulfilled one of our obligations. That is why we are at the head, that is why we feel the glory that each Cuban feels in each corner of the world that he visits. But all this demands effort.

This generation has made a reality of the apparent miracle of establishing a socialist revolution a few steps from North American imperialism. This honor has to be paid for with sacrifice. This generation must sacrifice daily in order to build a better future, the one you dream about, a future in which every single material, every means, all technology, will be at your disposal so that you can transform them and give them life—this might sound idealistic—and put them in the service of the people.

To do that, consumer goods must be created, imperialism must be repelled and all difficulties fought. For this, our generation will have a place in the history of Cuba and Latin America. We cannot disappoint the faith that all revolutionary comrades, all oppressed peoples in Latin America and perhaps in the world, have in the Cuban Revolution.

Also, it must not be forgotten that the Cuban Revolution, through the power of its example, has duties beyond its borders: the duty to spread the ideology of revolution to every corner of Latin America, to every corner of the world; the duty to fight exploitation and unjustice the world over; the duty that Martí synthesized in a phrase we have used often, and which we should put at the head of our bed in the most visible place, "Every true man ought to feel on his own cheek the blow given to the cheek of any man."

That is in synthesis the ideas of the Revolution toward every country of the world. Our youth must be free, always discussing, sharing ideas, concerned over what is happening the world over, open to technology, receiving from anyone whatever they might offer us. You must be sensitive to the people's struggle, to the sufferings and hopes of oppressed people everywhere.

In this way the future will be built.

Today—to arrive at a real and practical day of today—you have much work ahead. Congresses with technology the prime concern will begin to be held and politics will disappear from human relations. But you, students of the world, never forget that behind technology there is always someone controlling it; society controls technology and one can favor or oppose that society. In this world some people think that exploitation is good and others think it bad and want to end it. And, even when no one talks of politics any longer, political man cannot renounce this aspect of his human condition. Technology is a weapon, and if you feel that the world can be improved, then you must struggle to put technology at the service of the people; that is why society must be rescued before that can be accomplished. Then we can construct a future society—the name does not matter. The society that we dream of was called by the founder of scientific socialism, "communism."

Patria o muerte! Venceremos!

Volunteer Labor

ЛЛЛЛЛЛЛЛЛЛЛЛЛЛЛЛЛЛЛЛЛЛЛ

[In his opening statement, Guevara reads the names of those workers who are to be awarded diplomas in recognition of their volunteer labor. He also mentions that the Vice-Ministry for Light Industries has accumulated 774,344 hours of volunteer work. Eds.]

Now I want to refer briefly to the meaning of this meeting which the CTCR [1] and the Ministry of Industries have convoked. The importance of volunteer work lies not in economics, but rather its importance lies in the consciousness that is acquired through this type of work and the stimulus and example that this attitude represents for all the comrades of the various work units. The vanguard volunteer workers are men who fulfill the ideals of the true communist better than anyone else, the ideals of the true communist who from his place of work or center of production—which is his place of struggle, his front line—tells the rest, "Follow me along this road." We have always insisted on this.

The communist's attitude toward life is to show with his example the road to follow, to lead the masses by his own example regardless of the difficulties which must be overcome in the process. The one who can show with his example day after day without expecting from society anything but recognition of his merits as a builder of the new society has the right to demand sacrifice of others when the time comes. The construction of our society cannot be done except on the basis of sacrifice.

Many and powerful are our enemies and they are very close. Cuba means much as the lighthouse for America, the example to be followed by our sister countries of America, and even Asia and Africa (where other shining examples are found) so that imperialism gives up its prey, so that it cannot destroy Cuba's example—which teaches the people of America the road to liberation—the example they all look to. Our enemies dream daily of showing a destroyed Cuba, with

Speech made on January 11, 1964, at the issuing of communist certificates. *El Mundo* (Havana), January 12, 1964, pp. 1, 10.

[1] Confederación de Trabajadores Cubanos Revolucionarios, Cuban Confederation of Revolutionary Workers. Eds.

all the leaders dead or in prison, with its people crushed by the imperialist boot in order to show what would happen to the people who dare oppose Yankee imperialism.

This is why they try to drown us once and again even though the international climate is not ripe for the maneuvers which they carry out at this moment. First they tried economic pressures. They failed. They tried Playa Girón and failed. Again they applied economic pressures and again they failed. They tried to blackmail us with an atomic war and failed again. Even with their might and all their threats this country stood before imperialism and once again came out victorious.

During those October days, all those who occupied the production trenches worked harder than ever. During October 1962, the chart from our ministry points out the increase in production due to the patriotic feelings of our people to counter with everything they had the imperialists' objective of liquidating us. The same happened during this last October when hurricane Flora struck: Our production jumped upward. Almost spontaneously, in all units, brigades were formed to give hours and hours of labor voluntarily (and in some cases, not voluntarily, that is, not without retribution, but always at the service of production at a time in which our society needed it).

We are trying to create the "October spirit" for the whole year—every month, every day—in all comrades. This is the spirit that considers all labor, regardless of how simple or humble, as fundamental. But when we are not reminded by imperialism or by a natural phenomenon, the people's consciousness falls asleep a bit.

Our bureaucrats also let the paper work lie around. But during those October days the papers were flying everywhere and an infinite number of problems, which for a long time had been shifted from discussion to discussion, from committee to committee, from drawer to drawer, were solved. Among the good things the crisis left us was to have seen how rapidly the papers—as if they had legs—moved from one place to another and how the problems were solved.

This is the spirit with which we would like to infect everyone. This is the spirit that you should infect in all those near you; the spirit to place legs and wings on everything; the spirit to fly in production; the spirit to move forward doing away with all the obstacles that block fulfillment of our social duty.[2]

I want to give a small warning. This act, the enthusiasm of the comrades present here, is precisely what mobilizes all those who

_____

[2] Guevara calls on several workers and supervisors who are to receive special awards for having excelled in their work. Eds.

belong to these units. We have to guard ourselves against the tendency of compulsion. Do you understand well? Moral compulsion, yes, if realized in a good manner. But we should not rub someone's nose on the volunteer worker certificate. Do not ask the administrator on Monday: "Listen, I didn't see you yesterday around here, why haven't you come?" Volunteer labor is labor volunteered and nothing else, and it serves the whole society but fundamentally the development of the consciousness of each individual. Only those who want to do it should do it, and this does not mean that those who do not want to do it have not fulfilled their duty. They have simply failed in their extra duty which only the most enthusiastic in society impose on themselves.

Having made this clear, allow me a few more words. Let it be clear, so that no one will be upset by these certificates and in order that no one feels too haughty by them, that they are an indication of having fully contributed to society, as well as giving to it everything we can give for its development.

We began to talk not long ago, but we are relatively young in the communist revolution which today is our goal. Our revolution is almost five years old. It is not yet three years since we proclaimed the socialist character of the Revolution. Now we are fully in a transitional period, a first stage of construction before entering socialism and from then into building communism. But we already have the communist society as our main objective. We have had a glimpse—it does not matter that it is very far away and that the long road will not be covered in a year or two, as we all know. Already this is a new society, absolutely new, without classes and, therefore, without class dictatorship.

How does one arrive at communism? We have spoken of this many times: Communism is a social phenomenon which we can only reach by developing our productive forces, by suppressing the exploiters, by increasing the number of goods available to the people, and by creating the awareness that a new society is being forged.

After the October Revolution of 1917, Lenin's revolution, man acquired a new consciousness. The men of the French Revolution, who gave so many beautiful things to mankind, gave us so many examples, and whose traditions are preserved, were however simple instruments of history. The economic forces were moving and they interpreted the popular mood, the feelings of the people of that epoch, and some intuitively saw even further, but they were not yet able to direct history, to construct their own history consciously.

After the October Revolution, this was achieved and since World

War II, the bloc of nations that forms the camp of peace and socialism has grown very strong. There are a thousand million men who direct and construct history, who know what they are doing. Within those thousand million, as a drop but as a differentiated drop with its own characteristics and pride, are seven million Cubans.

Now our task is to develop production in order to give the people all the goods they need. But to do so we have to create heavy industry, develop agriculture, harmonize different sectors of our society, sacrifice ourselves at certain times, think constantly about working and, more important yet, we must acquire consciousness in order to be aware that we leaders of society, all of us, the people of Cuba, must learn more, know more to go more profoundly into various phenomena and into the intimate meaning of labor with the great creative force of work.

Marx, in his genial vision of all that was to occur, spoke of work under communism as a moral necessity of man and this, for example, is already found in the Soviet Union's communist party program for the building of communism. That is, work acquired a new quality unknown until now, an quality unknown in the epoch in which man had to sell his labor to the machine owner or landlord in order to bring his children a crumb of bread. Now the means of production are owned by the people, and yet the people are the same who yesterday criticized the boss and damned their work.

The conditions of labor in many cases have not changed, but we have to change the workers' consciousness rapidly so that they understand clearly the new nature of their work, the new nature of sacrifice, which at times will mean work under difficult conditions for the Cuban proletariat. We must create a new awareness that will permit us to enormously accelerate our transition to communism.

Besides, when work becomes for each Cuban a vital necessity, an expression of human creation, technology and inventions will succeed one another by the thousands. Each unit will be changed year after year, rejuvenated and modernized. Everyone will participate with unrestrained strength in the building of the new society. This is why we salute you, *compañeros*, for your vanguard character as men and women who go happily to work, who identify with their labor and with the responsibility necessary today to occupy that front line.

Let us never forget and let us always insist on the fact that our duty is not only toward Cuban society. Our duty lies also in the unified defense of the great socialist camp, in contributing to its victorious advance. In America our duty lies in maintaining higher and clearer than ever, brighter than ever, our torch of liberation, our example of liberation for all the countries which today is one form or another are readying to conquer their liberty.

We must maintain that torch very high. We must show ourselves not only as an example of what a people are capable of doing when they take up arms to liquidate the puppet of the day, but also of what a people are capable of doing when they take up arms and the instruments of production to reject all their enemies regardless of how strong they are, to annihilate the internal counterrevolution strong as it may be, and to speedily create the new society. All of this constitutes our example.

You know—our prime minister has explained it and it has been explained at the United Nations—that we could not sign the agreement with Moscow. We explained why. We explained how the aggressive nature of Yankee imperialism considered that there could be peace everywhere except in those places of the world where its interests were directly threatened.

This is why we welcomed the positive aspects which the signing of the agreement would have had for international relations, but we pointed out that Cuba would not sign it as long as the present conditions continue to exist.

The whole world understood us. The imperialists too, for they know well what they want and they are thinking about how to get it. They attempt to continue narrowing the circle. We break them one after another, but they find new forms, new formulas of aggression, and thus constantly show their bestial nature. Now suddenly Panama—something which no one foresaw; in an innocent patriotic demonstration, a flag, which is nothing more than a symbol, was raised; but it is a symbol without sovereignty in a land occupied by the invaders, although raising it had, however, been already recognized as one of the rights of the Panamanians. There are twenty-seven deaths already according to the news this morning and hundreds of wounded in the hospitals of Panama. This is how aggressive imperialism is. And this is nothing more than a sample of what they will do to all of the peoples of America. But they also say that there is a Yankee soldier stoned or dead; and we can answer that this is nothing more than a sample of what is going to happen to imperialism in America.

If imperialism decides to attack the countries which liberate themselves—the Dominican Republic or Guatemala or Venezuela or Nicaragua or Honduras or Paraguay or Panama, which today has given its first signal of struggle—then North American mothers also will begin to receive telegrams in which it will be indicated that some relative "died honorably in the fulfillment of his duty by assassin hordes" in some place in America.

And the day will come when the telegrams will be abundant and the moment will arrive when the North American people will know through their own flesh and blood what it means to have homes without fathers, without brothers, or homes with orphans, hungry homes where there is no one to support them. We all see that day coming; it is drawing near and not only cautiously by the winding paths of the mountains. It is drawing near at the sound of the drums, it was announced in Caracas, it has been permanent in Guatemala for the last two years, it is all over the Andean mountains—the Sierra Maestra of America as Fidel called it one day.

These are our responsibilities and this is the example and the hope to obtain a country where the people will really become the creator and leader of their history, where their own happiness will be built by their own hands.

The peoples of America are struggling just as the oppressed peoples of the world on three continents are. This is why our responsibility is great. These are not vain words, *compañeros*. They are real and true.

Every time that visitors from the world come with humbleness, we speak even of our own defects, of all the problems that a nation which is building socialism without a strong base faces; and nevertheless, we create a great impression on them. If they did not know it before, they begin to learn that there are other truths in the world and they begin to see the true image of a free, happy, and courageous people who are not ostentatious, a working people with joy who are there before their eyes and there is nothing which can resist that proof. This is also why the imperialists encircle us—because our example is contagious even from afar, but it is much more dangerously contagious when one is right here. They know this well.

For our future and the future of America, which is also ours, for the future of the entire world, of all men and women who are still in the United States and all imperialist countries, let us make, *compañeros*, the firm decision to heed the advice of Fidel of which *Compañero* Roca [3] reminded us: to do our work every day, analyze it, see

---

[3] Blas Roca is a member of the Cuban Communist Party and belongs to the old guard of the Cuban communists which has been, and continues to be, pro-Moscow oriented. Eds.

where it is bad and whether we have done enough, and promise to correct it for the following day.[4]

Let our example be better than words. Let each of us be a flag to be followed by our comrades in the construction of communism.

In this manner, all united, marching with the gigantic and sustained steps which our fatherland needs, we shall have realized the great aspiration of humanity and we shall have fully fulfilled our greatest duty: that all of our people be the flag of struggle for the peoples of the entire world.

[4] In the brief part omitted here, Guevara strongly urges that this idea be applied to every phase of Cuban society. Eds.

On Trade
and Development

⊓⊔⊓

This is the delegation of Cuba, an island country situated at the mouth of the Gulf of Mexico in the Caribbean Sea, speaking. It is addressing you under the protection of its right to come to this forum and proclaim the truth about itself. It addresses you, first of all, as a country which is making the vast experiment of building socialism. It does so also as a country belonging to the group of Latin American nations, even though illegal decisions have temporarily severed it from the regional organization owing to the pressure exerted and the action taken by the United States of America. From the geographical standpoint, it is an underdeveloped country which addresses you, one which has suffered from colonialist and imperial exploitation and which knows from bitter experience the subjection of its markets and its entire economy or, what amounts to the same thing, the subjection of its entire governmental machinery to a foreign power. Cuba also addresses you as a country under attack.

All these features have given our country a prominent place in the news throughout the world in spite of its small size, its lack of economic importance, and the small size of its population.

At this conference, Cuba will express its views from the various angles which reflect its special situation in the world, but it will base its analysis on its most important and positive attribute: that of a country which is building socialism. As a Latin American and underdeveloped country, it will support the main demands of its sister countries, and as a country under attack it will denounce from the very outset all the underhanded activities set in train by the coercive machinery of that imperialist power, the United States of America.

We preface our statement with these words of explanation because our country considers it imperative to define exactly the scope of the conference, its meaning, and its possible importance.

We come to this meeting seventeen years after the Havana Conference, where the intention was to create a world order that suited the competitive interests of the imperialist powers. Although Cuba

Speech at the United Nations Conference on Trade and Development, March 25, 1964. *Proceedings of the United Nations Conference on Trade and Development, Policy Statements* (New York: United Nations), 1964, vol. 2, pp. 161–171.

was the site of that conference, our revolutionary government does not consider itself bound in the slightest by the role then played by a government subordinated to imperialist interests, nor by the content or scope of the so-called Havana Charter.

At that conference, and at the previous meeting at Bretton Woods, a number of international bodies were set up whose activities have been harmful to the interests of the dependent countries of the contemporary world. And even though the United States of America did not ratify the Havana Charter because it considered it too "daring," the various international credit and financial bodies and the General Agreement of Tariffs and Trade—the tangible outcome of those two meetings—have proved to be effective weapons for defending its interests and, what is more, weapons for attacking our countries.

These are subjects which we must deal with at length later on.

Today the conference agenda is broader and more realistic because it includes, among others, three of the crucial problems facing the modern world: the relations between the camp of the socialist countries and that of the developed capitalist countries; the relations between the underdeveloped countries and the developed capitalist powers; and the great problem of development for the dependent world.

The participants at this new meeting far outnumber those who met at Havana in 1947. Nevertheless, we cannot say with complete accuracy that this is the forum of the peoples of the world. The result of the strange legal interpretations which certain powers still use with impunity is that countries of great importance in the world are missing from this meeting: for example, the People's Republic of China, the sole lawful representative of the most populous nation on earth, whose seats are occupied by a delegation which falsely claims to represent that nation and which, to add to the anomaly, even enjoys the right of veto in the United Nations.

It should also be noted that delegations representing the Democratic Republic of Korea and the Democratic Republic of Vietnam, the genuine governments of those nations, are absent, while representatives of the governments of the southern parts of both those divided states are present; and to add to the absurdity of the situation, while the German Democratic Republic is unjustly excluded, the Federal Republic of Germany is attending this conference and is given a vice-presidency. And while the socialist republics I mentioned are not represented here, the government of the Union of South Africa, which violates the Charter of the United Nations by the inhuman and fascist policy of apartheid embodied in its national laws, and which defies the United Nations by refusing to transmit information on the territories which it holds in trust, makes bold to occupy a seat in this hall.

Because of all these anomalies, the conference cannot be defined as the forum of the world's peoples. It is our duty to point this out and draw it to the attention of those present because, so long as this situation persists and justice remains the tool of a few powerful interests, legal interpretations will continue to be tailored to the convenience of the oppressor powers and it will be difficult to relax the prevailing tension: a situation which entails real dangers for mankind. We also stress these facts in order to call attention to the responsibilities incumbent upon us and to the consequences that may flow from the decisions taken here. A single moment of weakness, wavering, or compromise may discredit us in the eyes of history, just as we state members of the United Nations are in a sense accomplices and, in a manner of speaking, bear on our hands the blood of Patrice Lumumba, prime minister of the Congolese, who was wretchedly murdered at a time when United Nations troops supposedly guaranteed the stability of his regime. What is worse, those troops had been expressly called in by the martyr, Patrice Lumumba.

Events of such gravity or of a similar nature, or which have negative implications for international relations and which jeopardize our prestige as sovereign nations, must not be allowed to happen at this conference.

We live in a world that is deeply and antagonistically divided into groupings of nations very dissimilar in economic, social, and political outlook. In this world of contradictions, that existing between the socialist countries and the developed capitalist countries is spoken of as the fundamental contradiction of our time. The fact that the cold war, conceived by the warmongering West, has shown itself lacking in real effectiveness and in political realism, is one of the factors that have led to the convening of this conference. But while that is the most important contradiction, it is nevertheless not the only one; there is also the contradiction between the developed capitalist countries and the world's underdeveloped nations; and, at this Conference on Trade and Development, the contradictions existing between these groups of nations are also of fundamental importance. In addition there is the inherent contradiction between the various developed capitalist countries, which struggle unceasingly among themselves to divide up the world and to gain a firm hold on its markets so that they may enjoy an extensive development based, unfortunately, on the hunger and exploitation of the dependent world.

These contradictions are important; they reflect the realities of the world today, and they give rise to the danger of new conflagrations which, in the atomic age, may spread throughout the world.

If, at this egalitarian conference—where all nations can express, through their votes, the hopes of their peoples—a solution satisfactory to the majority can be reached, a unique step will have been taken in the history of the world. However, there are many forces at work to prevent this from happening. The responsibility for the decisions to be taken devolves upon the representatives of the underdeveloped peoples. If all the peoples who live under precarious economic conditions and who depend on foreign powers for some vital aspects of their economy and for their economic and social structure are capable of resisting the temptations made in cold blood, although in the heat of the moment, and impose a new type of relationship here, mankind will have taken a step forward.

If, on the other hand, the groups of underdeveloped countries, lured by the siren song of the vested interests of the developed powers which exploit their backwardness, contend futilely among themselves for the crumbs from the tables of the mighty of this world, and break the ranks of numerically superior forces; or if they are not capable of insisting on clear agreements, free from escape clauses open to capricious interpretations; or if they rest content with agreements that can simply be violated at will by the mighty, our efforts will have been to no avail and the lengthy deliberations at this conference will result in nothing more than innocuous documents and files for international bureaucracy zealously to guard: tons of printed paper and kilometers of magnetic tape recording the opinions expressed by the participants. And the world will stay as it is.

Such is the nature of this conference. It will have to deal not only with the problems involved in the domination of markets and the deterioration in the terms of trade but also with the main cause of this state of world affairs: the subordination of the national economies of the dependent countries to other more developed countries which, through investment, hold sway over the main sectors of each economy.

It must be clearly understood, and we say it in all frankness, that the only way to solve the problems now besetting mankind is to eliminate completely the exploitation of dependent countries by developed capitalist countries, with all the consequences that implies. We have come here fully aware that what is involved is a discussion between the representatives of countries which have put an end to the exploitation of man by man, of countries which maintain such exploitation as their working philosophy, and of the majority group of the exploited countries; and we must begin our discussion by affirming the truth of these statements.

But though our convictions are so firm that no arguments can change them, we are ready to join in constructive debate in a setting of peaceful coexistence between countries with different political, economic and social systems. The difficulty lies in making sure that we all know how much we can hope to get without having to take it by force and where to yield a privilege before it is inevitably wrung from us by force. The conference has to proceed along this narrow, craggy pass; if we stray, we shall find ourselves on barren ground.

We announced at the beginning of this statement that Cuba would speak here also as a country under attack. The latest developments which have made our country the target of imperialist wrath and the object of every conceivable kind of repression and violation of international law, from before the time of the Bay of Pigs till now, are known to all. It was no accident that Cuba was the main scene of one of the incidents that have most gravely endangered world peace, as a result of legitimate action taken by Cuba in exercise of its right to adopt principles of its own devising for the development of its own people.

Acts of aggression by the United States against Cuba began virtually as soon as the Revolution had been won. In the first stage they took the form of direct attacks on Cuban centers of production.

Later, these acts took the form of measures aimed at paralyzing the Cuban economy; about the middle of 1960, an attempt was made to deprive Cuba of the fuel needed to operate her industries, transport, and power stations. Under pressure from the Department of State, the independent United States oil companies refused to sell petroleum to Cuba or to provide Cuba with tankers to ship it in. Shortly afterward, efforts were made to deprive Cuba of the foreign exchange needed for its external trade; a cut of 700,000 short tons in the Cuban sugar quota in the United States was made by the then President Eisenhower on July 6, 1960, and the quota was abolished altogether on March 31, 1961, a few days after the announcement of the Alliance for Progress and a few days before Bay of Pigs. In an endeavor to paralyze Cuban industry by cutting off its supplies of raw materials and spare machine parts, the United States Department of Commerce issued on October 19, 1960, an order prohibiting the shipment of a large number of products to our island. This ban on trade with Cuba was progressively intensified until on February 3, 1962, the late President Kennedy placed an embargo on all United States trade with Cuba.

After all these acts of aggression had failed, the United States went on to subject our country to economic blockade with the object of stopping trade between other countries and our own. First, on January 24, 1962, the United States Treasury Department announced a ban on the importation into the United States of any article made wholly or partly from products of Cuban origin, even if it was manufactured in another country. A further step, equivalent to setting up a virtual economic blockade, was taken on February 6, 1963, when the White House issued a communiqué announcing that goods bought with United States Government funds would not be shipped in vessels flying the flag of foreign countries which had traded with Cuba after January 1 of that year. This was the beginning of the blacklist, which now includes over 150 ships belonging to countries that have not yielded to the illegal United States blockade. A further measure to obstruct Cuba's trade was taken on July 8, 1963, when the United States Treasury Department froze all Cuban property in United States territory and prohibited the transfer of dollars to or from Cuba, together with any other kind of dollar transaction carried out through third countries. Obsessed with the desire to attack us, the United States specifically excluded our country from the supposed benefits of the Trade Expansion Act. Acts of aggression have continued during the current year. On February 18, 1964, the United States announced the suspension of its aid to the United Kingdom, France, and Yugoslavia because these countries were still trading with Cuba. Dean Rusk, the Secretary of State, said that there could be no improvement in relations with Communist China while that country incited and supported acts of aggression in Southeast Asia, or in those with Cuba while it represented a threat to the Western hemisphere. That threat, he went on, could be ended to Washington's satisfaction only with the overthrow of the Castro regime by the Cuban people; they regarded that regime as temporary.

Cuba summons the delegation of the United States Government to say whether the actions foreshadowed by this statement and others like it, and the incidents we have described are or are not at odds with coexistence in the world today, and whether, in the opinion of that delegation, the successive acts of economic aggression committed against our island and against other countries which trade with us are legitimate. I ask whether that attitude is or is not at odds with the principle of the organization that brings us together—that of practicing tolerance between states—and with the obligation laid by that organization on countries which have ratified its charter to settle their disputes by peaceful means. I ask whether that attitude is or is not at odds with the spirit of this meeting in favor of abandoning all forms of discrimination and removing the barriers between countries with different social systems and at different stages of development. And I ask the conference to pass judgment on the explanation, if the United States delegation ventures to make one. We, for our part, maintain the only position we have ever taken in the matter: We are ready to join in discussions provided that no prior conditions are imposed.

The period which has elapsed since the Havana Charter was signed has been marked by events of undeniable importance in the field of trade and economic development. In the first place, we have to note the expansion of the socialist camp and the collapse of the colonial system. Many countries, covering an area of more than 30 million square kilometers and with one third of the world's population, have chosen as their system of development the construction of a communist society and as their working philosophy Marxist-Leninism. Others, without directly embracing the Marxist-Leninist philosophy, have stated their intention of laying the foundations on which to build socialism. Europe, Asia, and now Africa and America are continents shaken by the new ideas abroad in the world.

The countries in the socialist camp have developed uninterruptedly at rates of growth much faster than those of the capitalist countries in spite of having started out, as a general rule, from fairly low levels of development and of having had to withstand wars of extermination and rigorous blockades.

In contrast with the rapid rate of growth of the countries in the socialist camp and the development taking place, albeit much more slowly in the majority of the capitalist countries, is the unquestionable fact that a large proportion of the so-called underdeveloped countries are in total stagnation and that in some of them the rate of economic growth is lower than that of population increase.

These characteristics are not fortuitous; they correspond strictly to the nature of the developed capitalist system in full expansion, which transfers to the dependent countries the most abusive and barefaced forms of exploitation.

Since the end of the last century, this aggressive expansionist trend has been manifested in countless attacks on various countries in the more backward continents. Today, however, it mainly takes the form of control exercised by the developed powers over the production of and trade in raw materials in the dependent countries. In general it is shown by the dependence of a given country on a single primary commodity which sells only in a specific market in quantities restricted to the needs of that market.

The inflow of capital from the developed countries is the essential condition for the establishment of economic dependence. This inflow takes various forms: loans granted on onerous terms; investments which place a given country in the power of the investors; almost total technological subordination of the dependent country to the developed country; control of a country's foreign trade by the big international monopolies; and, in extreme cases, the use of force as an economic power in support of the other forms of exploitation.

Sometimes this inflow takes very subtle forms, such as the use of international financial credit and other types of organizations. The International Monetary Fund, the International Bank for Reconstruction and Development, GATT,[1] and, on the American continent, the Inter-American Development Bank are examples of international organizations placed at the service of the great capitalist colonialist powers—essentially at the service of United States imperialism. These organizations make their way into domestic economic policy, foreign trade policy, and domestic and external financial relations of all kinds.

The International Monetary Fund is the watchdog of the dollar in the capitalist camp; the International Bank for Reconstruction and Development is the instrument for the infiltration of United States capital into the underdeveloped world, and the Inter-American Development Bank performs the same sorry function on the American continent. All these organizations are governed by rules and principles which are represented as safeguards of equity and reciprocity in international economic relations, whereas in reality they are merely fetishes masking the subtlest kinds of instruments for the perpetuation of backwardness and exploitation. The International Monetary Fund, which is supposed to watch over the stability of exchange rates and the liberalization of international payments, merely denies the underdeveloped countries even the slightest means of defense against the competition and penetration of foreign monopolies.

While launching so-called austerity programs and opposing the forms of payment necessary for the expansion of trade between countries faced with a balance-of-payments crisis and suffering from severe discriminatory measures in international trade, it strives desperately to save the dollar from its precarious situation, without going to the heart of the structural problems which afflict the international monetary system and which impede a more rapid expansion of world trade.

[1] General Agreement on Tariffs and Trade. Eds.

GATT, for its part, by establishing equal treatment and reciprocal concessions between developed and underdeveloped countries, helps to maintain the status quo and serves the interests of the former group of countries, and its machinery fails to provide the necessary means for the elimination of agricultural protectionism, subsidies, tariffs, and other obstacles to the expansion of exports from the dependent countries, for all that it now has its so-called "Program of Action" and, by a rather suspicious coincidence, the "Kennedy Round" is just about to begin.

In order to strengthen imperialist domination, the establishment of preference areas has been adopted as a means of exploitation and neocolonial control. We can speak in full knowledge of this, for we ourselves have suffered the effects of Cuban-United States preference agreements which shackled our trade and placed it at the disposal of the United States monopolies.

There is no better way to show what those preferences meant for Cuba than to quote the views of Sumner Welles, the United States ambassador, on the reciprocal trade agreement which was negotiated in 1933 and signed in 1934:

> ...the Cuban Government in turn would grant us a practical monopoly of the Cuban market for American imports, the sole reservation being that in view of the fact that Great Britain was Cuba's chief customer for that portion of sugar exports which did not go to the United States the Cuban Government may desire to concede certain advantages to a limited category of imports from Great Britain.
> ...Finally, the negotiation at this time of a reciprocal trade agreement with Cuba along the lines above indicated, will not only revivify Cuba but will give us practical control of a market we have been steadily losing for the past ten years not only for our manufactured products but for our agricultural exports as well as notably in such categories as wheat, animal fats, meat products, rice and potatoes.
> [Telegram from Ambassador Welles to the Secretary of State of the United States, sent on May 13, 1933, at 6 P.M. and reproduced on pages 289 and 290 of Volume V (1933) of the official publication *Foreign Relations of the United States*.]

The results of the so-called reciprocal trade agreement confirmed the view of Ambassador Welles.

Cuba had to hawk its main product, sugar, all over the world in order to obtain foreign currency with which to achieve a balance of payments with the United States, and the special tariffs which were imposed prevented producers in European countries, as well as our own national producers, from competing with those of the United States.

It is necessary only to quote a few figures to prove that it was

Cuba's function to seek foreign currency all over the world for the United States. During the period 1948–1957, Cuba had a persistently unfavorable balance of trade with the United States totalling 382.7 million pesos, whereas its trade balance with the rest of the world was consistently favorable, totalling 1,274.6 million pesos. The balance of payments for the period 1948–1958 tells the story even more eloquently: Cuba had a positive balance of 543.9 million pesos in its trade with countries other than the United States, but lost this to its rich neighbor, with which it had a negative balance of 952.1 million pesos, with the result that its foreign currency reserves were reduced by 408.2 million pesos.

The so-called Alliance for Progress is another clear demonstration of the fraudulent methods used by the United States to maintain false hopes among nations while exploitation grows worse.

When Fidel Castro, our prime minister, indicated at Buenos Aires in 1959 that a minimum of $3,000 million a year of additional external income was needed to finance a rate of development which would really reduce the enormous gap separating Latin America from the developed countries, many thought that the figure was exaggerated. At Punta del Este, however, $2,000 million a year was promised. Today, it is recognized that merely to offset the loss caused by the deterioration in the terms of trade in 1961 (the last year for which figures are available), 30 percent a year more than the hypothetical amount promised will be required. The paradoxical situation now is that, while the loans are either not forthcoming or are made for projects which contribute little or nothing to the industrial development of the region, increased amounts of foreign currency are being transferred to the industrialized countries. This means that the wealth required by the labor of peoples who live for the most part in conditions of backwardness, hunger, and poverty is enjoyed in United States imperialist circles. In 1961, for instance, according to the figures given by the Economic Commission for Latin America, there was an outflow of $1,735 million from Latin America, in the form of interest on foreign investments and similar payments, and of $1,456 million in payments on foreign short-term and long-term loans. If we add to this the indirect loss of purchasing power of exports (or deterioration in the terms of trade), which amounted to $2,660 million in 1961, and $400 million for the flight of capital, we arrive at a total of $6,200 million, or more than three "Alliances for Progress" a year. Thus, assuming that the situation has not deteriorated further in 1964, the Latin American countries participating in the Alliance for Progress will lose directly or indirectly, during the three months of this conference, almost $1,600 million of the wealth created by the labor of their peoples. On the other hand, of the $2,000 million pledged for the entire year, barely half can be expected, on an optimistic estimate, to be forthcoming.

Latin America's experience of the real results of this type of "aid," which is represented as the surest and most effective means of increasing external income, better than the direct method—that of increasing the volume and value of exports, and modifying their structure—has been a sad one. For this very reason it may serve as a lesson for other regions and for the underdeveloped world in general. At present our region is virtually at a standstill so far as growth is concerned; it is also afflicted by inflation and unemployment, is caught up in the vicious circle of foreign indebtedness, and is racked with tensions which are sometimes discharged by armed conflict.

Cuba has drawn attention to these facts as they emerged, and has predicted the outcome, specifying that it rejected any solution other than those inspired by its example and enjoying its moral support; and events have proved it to be right. The Second Declaration of Havana is proving its historical validity.

These phenomena, which we have analysed in relation to Latin America but which are valid for the whole of the dependent world, have the effect of enabling the developed powers to maintain trade conditions that lead to a deterioration in the terms of trade between the dependent countries and the developed countries.

This aspect—one of the more obvious ones, which the capitalist propaganda machinery has been unable to conceal—is another of the factors that have led to the convening of this conference.

The deterioration in the terms of trade is quite simple in its practical effect: The underdeveloped countries must export raw materials and primary commodities in order to import the same amount of industrial goods. The problem is particularly serious in the case of the machinery and equipment which are essential to agricultural and industrial development.

We submit a short tabulation indicating, in physical terms, the amount of primary commodities needed to import a 30–39 horsepower tractor in the years 1955 and 1962. These figures are given merely to illustrate the problem we are considering. Obviously, there are some primary commodities for which prices have not fallen and may indeed have risen somewhat during the same period, and there may be some machinery and equipment which has not risen in relative cost as substantially as that in our example. What we give here is the general trend.

**Quantity of Primary Commodities
Needed to Purchase a 30–39 h.p. Tractor**
(Sources: FAO *Production Yearbook;* Financial Statistics)

Commodity and share in national exports	Country	Quantity needed (in metric tons) 1955	Quantity needed (in metric tons) 1962	Increase (metric tons)	(percentage)
Cocoa 67 percent	Ghana	3.06	7.14	4.08	133
Coconut oil 35 percent	Philippines	11.21	13.63	2.42	21
Coffee 46 percent	Brazil	2.38	4.79	2.41	101
Copper 58 percent	Rhodesia	4.23	5.45	1.22	28
Cotton (Karnak) 71 percent	United Arab Republic	2.11	3.41	1.30	61
Petroleum 92 percent	Venezuela	938*	1118*	180*	19
Rice 71 percent	Burma	26.35	32.57	6.22	23
Rubber 66 percent	Malaysia	3.27	5.55	2.28	70
Tea 60 percent	Ceylon	1.89	2.93	1.04	55
Tobacco 26 percent	Turkey	1.77	2.90	1.13	63
Wool 55 percent	Uruguay	1.94	2.52	0.58	30

* Barrels

We have taken several representative countries as producers of the raw materials or primary commodities mentioned. This does not mean, however, that they are the only producers of the item or that they produce nothing else.

Many underdeveloped countries, on analyzing their troubles, arrive at what seems a logical conclusion. They say that the deterioration in the terms of trade is an objective fact, is the underlying cause of most of their problems, and is attributable to the fall in the prices of the raw materials which they export and the rise in the prices of the manufactures which they import—I refer here to world market prices. If, however, they trade with the socialist countries at the prices prevailing in those markets, they benefit from the state of affairs there because they are generally exporters of manufactures and importers of raw materials. In all honesty, we have to recognize that this is the case, but in equal honesty we must recognize that the socialist countries did not cause the present situation—they absorb barely 10 percent of the underdeveloped countries' primary commodity exports to the rest of the world—and that for historical reasons, they have been compelled to trade under the conditions prevailing in the world market which is the outcome of imperialist domination over the internal economy and external markets of the dependent countries. This is not the basis on which the socialist countries organize their long-term trade with the underdeveloped countries. There are many examples to bear this out including, in particular, Cuba. When our social organization changed and our relations with the socialist camp attained a new level of mutual trust, we did not cease to be underdeveloped, but we established a new type of relationship with the countries in that camp. The most striking example of this new relationship are the sugar price agreements we have concluded with the Soviet Union, under which that sister power has undertaken to purchase increasing amounts of our main product at fair and stable prices which have already been agreed up to the year 1970.

Furthermore, we must not forget that there are underdeveloped countries in a variety of circumstances and that they maintain a variety of policies toward the socialist camp. There are some, like Cuba, which have chosen the path of socialism; there are some which are developing in a more or less capitalist manner and are beginning to produce manufactures for export; there are some which have neocolonial ties; there are some which have a virtually feudal structure; and there are others which, unfortunately, do not participate in conferences of this type because the developed countries have not granted the independence to which their peoples aspire. Such is the case of British Guiana, Puerto Rico, and other countries in Latin America, Africa, and Asia. Except in the first of these groups, foreign capital has made its way into these countries in one way or another, and the demands that are today being directed to the socialist countries should be placed on the correct footing of negotiation. In some cases this means negotiation between underdeveloped and developed country; almost always, however, it means negotiation between one country subject to discrimination and another in the same case. On many occasions, these same countries demand unilateral preferential treatment from all the developed countries without exception, i.e., including in this category the socialist countries. They place all kinds of obstacles in the way of direct trading with these states. There is a danger that they may seek to trade through national subsidiaries of the imperialist powers—thus giving the latter the chance of spectacular profits—by claiming that a given country is underdeveloped and therefore entitled to unilateral preferences.

If we do not want to wreck this conference, we must abide strictly by principles. We who speak for underdeveloped countries must stress that we have right on our side; in our case, as a socialist country, we can also speak of the discrimination that is practiced against us, not only by some developed capitalist countries but also by underdeveloped countries which, consciously or otherwise, are serving the interests of the monopolist capital that has taken over basic control of their economy.

We do not regard the existing terms of world trade as fair, but this is not the only injustice that exists. There is direct exploitation of some countries by others; there is discrimination among countries by reason of differences in economic structure; and, as we already pointed out, there is the invasion of foreign capital to the point where it controls a country's economy for its own ends. To be logical, when we address requests to the developed socialist countries, we should also specify what we are going to do to end discrimination and at any rate the most obvious and dangerous forms of imperialist penetration.

We all know about the trade discrimination practiced by the imperialist metropolitan countries against the socialist countries with the object of hampering their development. At times, it has been tantamount to a real blockade, such as the almost absolute blockade maintained by United States imperialism against the German Democratic Republic, the People's Republic of China, the Democratic Republic of Korea, the Democratic Republic of Vietnam, and the Republic of Cuba. Everyone knows that that policy has failed, and that other powers which originally followed the lead of the United States have gradually parted company from it in order to secure their own profits. The failure of this policy is by now only too obvious.

Trade discrimination has also been practiced against dependent and socialist countries, the ultimate object being to ensure that the monopolies do not lose their sphere of exploitation and at the same time to strengthen the blockade of the socialist camp. This policy, too, is failing and the question arises whether there is any point in remaining bound to foreign interests which history has condemned or whether the time has come to break through all the obstacles to trade and expand markets in the socialist area.

The various forms of discrimination which hamper trade, and

which make it easier for the imperialists to manipulate a range of primary commodities and a number of countries producing those commodities, are still being maintained. In the atomic era, it is simply absurd to classify such products as copper and other minerals as strategic materials and to obstruct trade in them; yet this policy has been maintained, and is maintained to this day. There is also talk of so-called incompatibilities between state monopoly of foreign trade and the forms of trading adopted by the capitalist countries, and on that pretext discriminatory relations, quotas, and so forth, are established—maneuvers in which GATT has played a dominant role under the official guise of combating unfair trade practices. Discrimination against state trading not only serves as a weapon against the socialist countries but is also designed to prevent the underdeveloped countries from adopting any of the most urgent measures needed to strengthen their negotiating position on the international market and to counteract the operations of the monopolies.

The suspension of economic aid by international agencies to countries adopting the socialist system of government is a further variation on the same theme. For the International Monetary Fund, to attack bilateral payments agreements with socialist countries and impose on its weaker members a policy of opposition to this type of relations between peoples has been a common practice in recent years.

As we have already pointed out, all these discriminatory measures imposed by imperialism have the dual object of blockading the socialist camp and strengthening the exploitation of the underdeveloped countries.

It is incontrovertible that present-day prices are unfair; it is equally true that those prices are conditioned by monopolist limitation of markets and by the establishment of political relationships that make free competition a term of one-sided application; free competition for the monopolies; a free fox among free chickens. Quite apart from the agreements that may emanate from this conference, the opening up of the large and growing markets of the socialist camp would help to raise raw material prices. The world is hungry but lacks the money to buy food; and paradoxically, in the underdeveloped world, in the world of the hungry, possible ways of expanding food production are discouraged in order to keep prices up—i.e., in order to be able to eat. This is the inexorable law of the philosophy of plunder, which must cease to be the rule in relations between peoples.

Furthermore, it would be feasible for some underdeveloped countries to export manufactured goods to the socialist countries and even for long-term agreements to be concluded so as to enable some nations to make better use of their natural wealth and specialize in certain branches of industry that would enable them to participate in world trade as manufacturing countries. All this can be supplemented by the provision of long-term credits for the development of the industries, or branches of industry, we are considering; it must always be borne in mind, however, that certain measures in respect of relations between socialist countries and underdeveloped countries cannot be taken unilaterally.

It is a strange paradox that, while the United Nations is forecasting in its reports adverse trends in the foreign trade of the underdeveloped countries, and while Mr. Prebisch, the Secretary-General of the conference, is stressing the dangers that will arise if this state of affairs persists, there is still talk of the feasibility—and in some cases, such as that of the so-called strategic materials, the necessity—of discriminating against certain states because they belong to the socialist countries' camp.

All these anomalies are possible because of the incontrovertible fact that, at the present stage of human history, the underdeveloped countries are the battleground of economic systems that belong to different historical eras. In some of these countries, feudalism still exists; in others, a nascent, still weak bourgeoisie has to stand the dual pressure of imperialist interests and of its own proletariat, who are fighting for a fairer distribution of income. In the face of this dilemma, the bourgeoisie in some countries has maintained its independence or adopted some forms of joint action with the proletariat, while elsewhere it has made common cause with imperialism; it has become its appendage, its agent, and has imparted the same character to the governments representing it.

We must sound a warning that this type of dependence, skillfully used, may endanger the possibility of solid progress at the conference; but we must also point out that such advantages as these governments may gain today, at the price of disunity, will be repaid with interest tomorrow, when in addition to facing the hostility of their own peoples, they will have to stand up alone to the monopolist offensive for which the only law is maximum profit.

We have made a brief analysis of the causes and results of the contradictions between the socialist camp and the imperialist camp and between the camp of the exploited and that of the exploiting countries; here are two clear and present dangers to the peace of the world. It must also be pointed out, however, that the growing boom in some capitalist countries and their inevitable expansion in search of new markets have led to changes in the balance of forces among them and set up stresses that will need careful attention if world peace is to be preserved. It should not be forgotten that the last two world conflagrations were sparked off by clashes between developed powers that found force to be the only way out. On every hand we observe a series of phenomena which demonstrate the growing acuteness of this struggle.

This situation may involve real dangers to world peace in time to come, but it is exceedingly dangerous to the smooth progress of this conference meeting here today. There is a clear distribution of spheres of influence between the United States and other developed capitalist powers, embracing the backward continents and, in some cases, Europe as well. If these influences grow so strong as to turn the exploited countries into a field of battle waged for the benefit of the imperialist powers, the conference will have failed.

Cuba considers that, as is pointed out in the joint statement of the underdeveloped countries, the trade problems of our countries are well known and what is needed is that clear principles would be adopted and practical action taken to usher in a new era for the world. We also consider that the statement of principles submitted by the U.S.S.R. and other socialist countries forms the right basis on which to start discussion, and we endorse it fully. Our country also supports the measures formulated at the meeting of experts at Brasilia, which would give coherent effect to the principles we advocate, and which we shall go on to expound.

Cuba wishes to make one point clear at the outset: We are not begging for aid. We are demanding justice, but not a justice subject to the fallacious interpretations we have so often seen prevail at international meetings; a justice which, perhaps, the peoples cannot define in legal terms but the desire for which is deeply rooted in spirits oppressed by generations of exploitation.

Cuba affirms that this conference must produce a definition of international trade as an appropriate tool for the speedier economic development of the underdeveloped people and of those subjected to discrimination, and that this definition must make for the elimination of all forms of discrimination and all differences, even those emanating from allegedly equal treatment. Treatment must be equitable, and equity, in this context, is not equality; equity is the inequality needed to enable the exploited peoples to attain an acceptable level of living. Our task here is to lay a foundation on which a new international division of labor can be instituted by making full use of all a country's natural resources and by raising the degree of processing of those resources until the most complex forms of manufacture can be undertaken.

In addition, the new division of labor must be approached by restoring to the underdeveloped countries the traditional export markets that have been snatched from them by artificial measures for the protection and encouragement of production in the developed countries; and the underdeveloped countries must be given a fair share of future increases in consumption.

The conference will have to recommend specific methods of regulating the use of primary commodity surpluses so as to prevent their conversion into a form of subsidy for the exports of developed countries to the detriment of the traditional exports of the underdeveloped countries, or their use as an instrument for the injection of foreign capital into an underdeveloped country.

It is inconceivable that the underdeveloped countries, which are sustaining the vast losses inflicted by the deterioration in the terms of trade and which, through the steady drain of interest payments, have richly repaid the imperialist powers for the value of their investments, should have to bear the growing burden of indebtedness and repayment, while more rightful demands go unheeded. The Cuban delegation proposes that, until such time as the prices for the underdeveloped countries' exports reach a level which will reimburse them for the losses sustained over the past decade, all payments of dividends, interest, and amortization should be suspended.

It must be made crystal clear that foreign capital investment dominating any country's economy, the deterioration in terms of trade, the control of one country's markets by another, discriminatory relations, and the use of force as an instrument of persuasion, are a danger to world trade and world peace.

This conference must also establish in plain terms the right of all peoples to unrestricted freedom of trade, and the obligation on all states signatories of the agreement emanating from the conference to refrain from restraining trade in any manner, direct or indirect.

The right of all countries freely to arrange the shipment of their goods by sea or air and to move them freely throughout the world without let or hindrance will be clearly laid down.

The application of economic measures, or the incitement to apply economic measures, used by a state to infringe the sovereign freedom of another state and to obtain from it advantages of any nature whatsoever, or to bring about the collapse of its economy, must be condemned.

In order to achieve the foregoing, the principle of self-determination embodied in the Charter of the United Nations must be fully implemented and the right of states to dispose of their own resources, to adopt the form of political and economic organization that suits them best, and to choose their own lines of development and specialization in economic activity, without incurring reprisals of any kind whatsoever, must be reaffirmed.

The conference must adopt measures for the establishment of financial, credit, and tariff bodies, with rules based on absolute equality and on justice and equity, to take the place of the existing bodies, which are out of date from the functional point of view and reprehensible from the standpoint of specific aims.

In order to guarantee to a people the entire disposal of its resources, it is necessary to condemn the existence of foreign bases, the presence—temporary or otherwise—of foreign troops in a country without its consent, and the maintenance of the colonial regime by a few developed capitalist powers.

For all these purposes, the conference must reach agreement and lay a firm foundation for the establishment of an international trade organization, to be governed by the principle of the equality and universality of its members, and to possess sufficient authority to take decisions binding on all signatory states, abolishing the practice of barring such forums to countries which have won their liberation since the establishment of the United Nations and with social systems which are not to the liking of some of the mighty ones of this world.

Only the establishment of an organization of the type mentioned, to take the place of existing bodies that are mere props for the status quo and for discrimination, and not compromise formulas which merely enable us to talk ourselves to a standstill about what we already know, will guarantee compliance with new rules of international relations and the attainment of the desired economic security.

At all relevant points, exact time limits must be laid down for the completion of the measures decided on.

These are the most important points which the Cuban delegation wished to bring to the attention of the conference. It should be pointed out that many of the ideas which are now gaining currency through being expressed by international bodies, by the precise analysis of the present situation of the developing countries submitted by Mr. Prebisch, the Secretary-General of the conference, and many of the measures approved by other states—trading with socialist countries, obtaining credits from them, the need of basic social reforms for economic development, and so forth—have been formulated and put into practice by Cuba during the revolutionary government's five years in office, and have exposed it to unjust censure and to acts of economic and military aggression approved by some of the countries which now endorse those ideas.

Suffice it to recall the criticism and censure aimed at Cuba for having established trade relations and cooperation with countries outside our hemisphere, and its "de facto" exclusion, to this day, from the Latin American regional group which meets under the auspices of the Charter of Alta Gracia, namely the Organization of American States, from which Cuba is barred.

We have dealt with the basic points concerning foreign trade, the need for changes in the foreign policy of the developed countries in their relations with the underdeveloped countries, and the need to reconstruct all international credit, financial, and similar bodies; but it must be emphasized that these measures are not sufficient to guarantee economic development and that other measures—which Cuba, an underdeveloped country, has put into practice—are needed as well. As a minimum, exchange control must be established, prohibiting remittances of funds abroad or restricting them to an appreciable degree; there must be state control of foreign trade, and land reform; all natural resources must be returned to the nation; and technical education must be encouraged, together with other measures of internal reorganization which are essential to a faster rate of development.

Out of respect for the wishes of the governments represented here, Cuba has not included among the irreducible minimum measures the taking over by the state of all the means of production, but it considers that this measure would contribute to a more efficient and swifter solution to the serious problems under discussion.

And the imperialists? Will they sit with arms folded? No!

The system they practice is the cause of the evils from which we are suffering, but they will try to obscure the facts with twisted statements, of which they are masters. They will try to compromise the conference and sow disunity in the camp of the exploited countries by offering them crumbs.

They will try everything in an endeavor to keep in being the old international bodies which serve their ends so well, and will offer reforms but not basic reforms. They will seek a way to lead the conference into a blind alley, so that it will be suspended or adjourned; they will try to rob it of importance by comparison with other meetings convened by themselves, or to see that it ends without achieving any tangible results.

They will not accept a new international trade organization; they will threaten to boycott it, and will probably do so.

They will try to show that the existing international division of labor is beneficial to all, and will refer to industrialization as a dangerous and excessive ambition.

Lastly, they will allege that the blame for underdevelopment rests with the underdeveloped.

To this last we can reply that to a certain extent they are right, and that they will be all the more so if we show ourselves incapable of banding together, in wholehearted determination, so as to present a united front of victims of discrimination and exploitation.

The questions we wish to ask this assembly are these: Shall we be able to carry out the task history has laid on us? Will the developed capitalist countries have the political acumen to accede to the minimum demands?

If the measures here indicated cannot be adopted by this conference and all that emerges once again is a hybrid document crammed with vague statements and escape clauses; and unless, at the very least, the economic and political barriers to trade among all regions of the world and to international cooperation are removed, the underdeveloped countries will continue to face increasingly difficult economic situations and world tension may mount dangerously. A world conflagration may be sparked off at any moment by the ambition of some imperialist country to destroy the socialist countries' camp, or, in the not too distant future, by insolvable contradictions between the capitalist countries. In addition, moreover, the feeling of revolt will grow stronger every day among the peoples subjected to various degrees of exploitation, and they will take up arms to gain by force the rights which reasoning alone has not won them.

This is happening today among the peoples of so-called Portuguese Guinea and Angola, who are fighting to free themselves from the colonial yoke, and with the people of South Vietnam who, weapons in hand, stand ready to shake off the yoke of imperialism and its puppets.

Let it be known that Cuba supports and applauds those peoples who, having exhausted all possibilities of a peaceful solution, have called a halt to exploitation, and that their magnificent showing has won our militant solidarity. Having stated the essential points on which our analysis of the present situation is based, having put forward the recommendations we consider pertinent to this conference and our views on what the future holds if no progress is made in trade relations between countries—an appropriate means of reducing tension and contributing to development—we wish to place on record our hope that the constructive discussion we spoke of will take place. The aim of our efforts is to bring about such a discussion, from which everyone will gain and to rally the underdeveloped countries of the world to unity, so as to present a cohesive front. We place our hopes also in the success of this conference, and we unite them in friendship to those of the poor of this world and to those of countries in the socialist camp, putting all our meager powers to work for its success.

Colonialism
Is Doomed

ЛЛЛЛЛЛЛЛЛЛЛЛЛЛЛЛЛЛЛЛЛЛЛЛЛЛЛ

The delegation of Cuba to this Assembly has pleasure in first of all performing the agreeable duty of welcoming three new nations to the already large number of those which discuss world problems in this forum. We welcome the peoples of Zambia, Malawi, and Malta in the persons of their presidents and prime ministers and express the hope that these countries will from the outset join the group of nonaligned nations which are fighting against imperialism, colonialism, and neocolonialism.

We likewise extend our congratulations to the president of this Assembly. His elevation to this high post is particularly significant, since it reflects this new historic period of resounding triumphs for the peoples of Africa that were until yesterday subject to the colonial system of imperialism but have today, in their vast majority and in lawful exercise of their self-determination, become sovereign states. The hour of doom for colonialism has struck, and millions of inhabitants of Africa, Asia, and Latin America are rising up to face a new life and making good their unrestricted right to self-determination and the independent development of their nations. We wish you, Mr. President, the greatest success in the task entrusted to you by the member states.

Cuba comes here to state its position on the most important controversial issues. It will do so with a full sense of the responsibility which use of this rostrum implies, while at the same time performing its inescapable duty of speaking with all clarity and frankness.

We wish to see this Assembly stretch its limbs and march forward; we want the committees to begin their work, which should not stop at the first confrontation. Imperialism seeks to convert this meeting into a pointless competition in oratory, to prevent it from solving the serious problems of the world; that design we must frustrate. This Assembly must be remembered, in the future, not merely by the number "nineteen" which serves to identify it. Such will be the purpose of our efforts.

Speech at the United Nations General Assembly, December 11, 1964. United Nations, *Official Records of the General Assembly, 19th Session, Plenary Meetings* (New York: United Nations), 1966, vol. 1, pp. 7–14.

We feel that we have the right and the duty to take this line, because our country constitutes a point of constant friction. It is one of the places where the principles buttressing the right of small countries to their sovereignty are put to the test day by day and minute by minute. At the same time our country is one of the trenches of the fighters for world freedom, situated only a stone's throw from United States imperialism and showing by the action issuing from it and by its daily example that the peoples can in fact be liberated and remain free in the present circumstances of mankind. Of course, there is now a socialist camp that is daily growing stronger and equipping itself with ever more powerful weapons with which to make a response; but more is necessary for survival—internal unity, faith in one's own destiny, and unswerving resolution to fight to the death in defense of one's country and of the revolution. All this Cuba possesses.

Of all the burning problems to be dealt with by this Assembly, one which for us Cubans is particularly important and must, we feel, be posed in a way that leaves no doubt in anyone's mind, is peaceful coexistence between states with different economic and social systems. Much progress has been made in this regard, but imperialism—particularly United States imperialism—has tried to make people believe that peaceful coexistence is reserved for the great powers alone. We repeat here what was stated by our president at Cairo and was later embodied in the Declaration of the Second Conference of Heads of State or Government of Nonaligned Countries: there cannot be peaceful coexistence between powerful nations only, if world peace is to be ensured; there must be peaceful coexistence between all states, regardless of their size, their previous historical relationship, and the problems arising among some of them at any particular moment.

Today, the kind of peaceful coexistence to which we aspire has, in many instances, failed to materialize. The kingdom of Cambodia has been subjected to every type of treacherous and brutal attack from United States bases in South Vietnam, simply because it has maintained a neutral attitude and refused to lend itself to the machinations of United States imperialism. Laos, a divided country, has also been the target of imperialist aggression of every kind. Its people have been attacked from the air; the agreements signed at Geneva have been violated, and part of its territory is in constant danger of being attacked with impunity by the imperialist forces. The Democratic Republic of Vietnam, which is more familiar than most other countries with this type of aggression, has once again seen its frontiers violated, its installations blasted by enemy bombers and fighter aircraft, and its naval stations attacked by United States warships violating its territorial waters. At this very moment the Democratic Republic of Vietnam is faced with the threat that United States warmongers may openly extend to its territory and people the war which they have been waging for several years now against the people of South Vietnam. The Soviet Union and the People's Republic of China have issued stern warnings to the United States. We are faced here with a case in which world peace is in danger; but, in addition, the lives of millions of human beings throughout this part of Asia are under constant menace, depending on the whim of the United States invaders.

Peaceful coexistence has also been put to a brutal test in Cyprus because of pressure from the Turkish government and NATO, which has compelled the people and government of Cyprus to make a vigorous and heroic effort in defense of their sovereignty.

In all these places, imperialism is trying to impose its version of what coexistence should be. It is the oppressed peoples, in alliance with the socialist camp, who should show what genuine coexistence is, and the United Nations has an obligation to support them.

We should also point out that the concept of peaceful coexistence is to be defined only in terms of relations between the sovereign states involved. As Marxists, we have maintained that peaceful coexistence between nations does not include coexistence between exploiters and exploited, between oppressors and oppressed.

Moreover, a principle has been proclaimed in this organization—namely, the right of a people to complete independence and freedom from all forms of colonial oppression. That is why we express our solidarity with the peoples—now colonial—of so-called Portuguese Guinea, Angola, and Mozambique, who are attacked and massacred for the crime of asking for their freedom; we are prepared to help them, to the best of our ability, in accordance with the Cairo Declaration.

We express our solidarity with the people of Puerto Rico and their great leader, Pedro Albizu Campos, who, by another act of hypocrisy, has been released at the age of seventy-two, hardly able to speak and in a paralytic condition, after a lifetime spent in prison. Albizu Campos is a symbol of a still unredeemed but indomitable America. Years and years of imprisonment, almost intolerable pressure while in prison, mental torture, solitude, complete isolation from his people and his family, and the insolence of the conquerors and their lackeys in the land of his birth—none of these things broke his will. The delegation of Cuba, on behalf of the Cuban people, pays a tribute of admiration and gratitude to a patriot who lends dignity to our America.

For years the United States has tried to turn Puerto Rico into a mirror of hybrid culture—Spanish-speaking but with English inflections, Spanish-speaking but with a hinged backbone to make it bow down before the North American soldier. Puerto Rican soldiers have been used as cannon fodder in imperialist wars, as in Korea, and have even been made to fire on their own brothers, as during the massacre perpetrated some months ago by the United States Army against the defenseless people of Panama—one of the most recent misdeeds of United States imperialism.

Nevertheless, despite such tremendous violence done to its will and historic destiny, the people of Puerto Rico has preserved its culture, Latin character, and national feelings—which in itself is proof of the implacable determination of the mass of the population of this Latin American island to be, some day, independent.

We must also observe that the principle of peaceful coexistence does not imply the right to flout the people's will, as in the case in so-called British Guiana. There, the government of Prime Minister Cheddi Jagan has been the victim of every kind of pressure and maneuver, and the date for his country's independence has been postponed while methods are devised to flout the people's wishes and secure the docility of a different government, installed by devious manipulations, with a view to some sort of emasculated freedom being granted to this piece of American soil. The people of Guiana can count on Cuba's moral and militant support, whatever the course that Guiana is obliged to take in order to obtain its freedom. We must likewise mention the islands of Guadeloupe and Martinique, which have been fighting for independence for some time, without obtaining it; such a state of affairs must not continue.

Once again we raise our voice to warn the nations of what is happening in South Africa. The brutal policy of apartheid is being applied before the eyes of the entire world, the peoples of Africa compelled to tolerate the continued application, in their continent, of an official doctrine of the superiority of one race over another, and murders, perpetrated with impunity in the name of that racial superiority. Will the United Nations do nothing to prevent it?

I would refer specifically to the tragic case of the Congo—a case which is without parallel in the modern world, and which shows how the rights of peoples can be flouted with absolute impunity and the most insolent cynicism. The direct cause of all this is the Congo's vast resources, which the imperialist nations wish to keep under their control. In the speech which he made on the occasion of his first visit to the United Nations, our comrade Fidel Castro pointed out in the General Assembly (872nd meeting) that the whole problem of coexistence between nations turned upon the misappropriation of other people's wealth. He made this observation: "When this philosophy of despoilment disappears, the philosophy of war will have disappeared." Yet not only has the philosophy of despoilment not disappeared, it is more widespread than ever—which explains why those who used the name of the United Nations in order to perpetrate the assassination of Lumumba are today murdering thousands of Congolese, in the name of the defense of the white race.

How can we forget the way in which Patrice Lumumba's hopes in the United Nations were betrayed? How can we forget the machinations and maneuvers that followed the occupation of the Congo by United Nations troops, under whose auspices the assassins of the great African patriot acted with impunity? How can we forget that the man who flouted the authority of the United Nations in the Congo—and not precisely for patriotic reasons, but rather under cover of conflicts between imperialists—was none other than Moise Tshombe, who initiated the secession of Katanga with Belgian support? And how can one justify or explain the fact that, after the entire United Nations action had been completed, Tshombe, ousted from Katanga, was able to return as lord and master of the Congo? Who can deny the sorry role that the imperialists forced the United Nations to play?

In short, spectacular military movements were made to avert the secession of Katanga; yet today Katanga is in power, the riches of the Congo are in imperialist hands, and . . .[1] the costs of all this are to be paid by the decent nations. What good business is done by the merchants of war! For this reason the government of Cuba supports the just attitude of the Soviet Union in refusing to pay the cost of crime.

And now, as a crowning insult, the recent actions that have filled the world with indignation are flung in our faces. Who are the perpetrators? Belgian paratroopers, transported by United States aircraft which took off from British bases. We remember, as if it were yesterday, seeing a small, industrious, and civilized country of Europe, the kingdom of Belgium, invaded by Hitler's hordes. We thought bitterly of that small nation being attacked and mas-

[1] Ellipses in official text. Eds.

sacred by German imperialism, and our hearts went out to its people. But many of us did not see this other face of the imperialist coin.

It may be that sons of Belgium patriots who died in defense of their country's freedom murdered with impunity thousands of Congolese in the name of the white race, just as they had suffered under the German heel because their blood was not sufficiently Aryan.

Our eyes, looking today in freedom on new horizons, can see what our status as colonial slaves had prevented us from seeing— that "Western civilization" conceals behind its showy façade a picture of hyenas and jackals. For such are the only names merited by those who went out to fulfill these "humanitarian" tasks in the Congo. A carnivorous animal feeding on the helpless—that is what imperialism does to man, that is the distinguishing mark of the "white" imperialist. All free men throughout the world must make ready to avenge the Congo crime.

It may be that many of these soldiers, transformed into subhuman creatures by imperialist machinations, honestly believe that they are defending the rights of a superior race; but in this Assembly the peoples whose skins are tanned by a different sun and colored by different pigments are in the majority, and they have completely grasped the fact that the difference between men resides, not in the color of their skin, but in the forms of ownership of the means of production, the production relationships in which they are involved.

The Cuban delegation sends its greetings to the peoples of Southern Rhodesia and Southwest Africa, oppressed by white colonialist minorities; to Basutoland, Bechuanaland, and Swaziland, to French Somaliland; to the Arab people of Palestine, to Aden and the Protectorates, to Oman and to all the peoples struggling against imperialism and colonialism; it reaffirms its support for them. We also hope for a just solution of the conflict which faces our sister republic of Indonesia in its relations with Malaysia.

One of the basic agenda items for this session is general and complete disarmament. We express our support for general and complete disarmament; we also advocate the complete destruction of thermonuclear devices, and favor the convening of a conference of all nations of the world to give effect to these aspirations of their peoples. In his statement before this Assembly (872nd meeting), our prime minister issued the warning that arms races have always led to war. New atomic powers have appeared in the world, and the possibility of a confrontation is increasing.

We believe that such a conference is necessary in order to obtain the total destruction of thermonuclear weapons and, as a first step, the total prohibition of nuclear testing. At the same time, it must be clearly established that all states are under an obligation to respect the present frontiers of other states, and to refrain from all aggressive action, even with conventional weapons.

In adding our voice to the chorus of the world's peoples that demand general and complete disarmament, the destruction of all atomic weapons, and a complete ban on the production of new thermonuclear devices and on atomic tests of any kind, we believe it is necessary to stress that, in addition, the territorial integrity of nations must be respected and the mailed fist of imperialism restrained, for the latter is just as dangerous when it holds only conventional weapons. Those who murdered thousands of defenseless Congolese did not use atomic weapons; the deaths were caused by conventional weapons, wielded by imperialism.

Although implementation of the measures advocated here would render this statement unnecessary, it must be stressed that we cannot accede to any regional denuclearization agreement so long as the United States maintains aggressive bases in our own territory, in Puerto Rico, in Panama, and in other American states where it feels it is entitled to have both conventional and nuclear weapons, without any restriction, at its disposal. Moreover, the latest resolutions of the Organization of American States directed against our country, according to which Cuba could be attacked on the basis of the Treaty of Rio de Janeiro,[2] make it necessary for us to possess all the means of defense open to us.

We believe that if the conference of which we have spoken could attain all these objectives—a difficult task, unfortunately—it would represent one of the most important developments in the history of mankind. If this goal is to be reached, the People's Republic of China must be represented, and that is why a meeting of this type is imperative. But it would be much simpler for the peoples of the world to recognize the undeniable truth that the People's Republic of China exists and that its rulers are the only representatives of its people, and to give it its rightful place, at present usurped by the clique which with United States support controls the province of Taiwan.

The problem of the representation of China in the United Nations

[2] Inter-American Treaty of Reciprocal Assistance and Final Act of the Inter-American Conference for the Maintenance of Continental Peace and Security, signed at Rio de Janeiro on September 2, 1947. Eds.

can in no way be regarded as involving a new admission to the organization; it is a case of restoring the lawful rights of the People's Republic of China. We must emphatically reject the "two Chinas" plot. The Chiang Kai-shek clique of Taiwan cannot remain in the United Nations. It is, we repeat, a question of expelling the usurper and installing the lawful representative of the Chinese people.

Furthermore, we issue a warning against the United States government's insistence on presenting the question of the lawful representation of China in the United Nations as "an important question," with the aim of making it subject to the rule of the two thirds majority of members present and voting.

The entry of the People's Republic of China into the United Nations is certainly an important question for the world as a whole, but not for the purposes of the machinery of the United Nations, where it should constitute a simple question of procedure. In this way justice would be done, and—what is equally important—it would be demonstrated once and for all that this Assembly has eyes to see, ears to hear, its own tongue to speak with, and the right standards whereby to take decisions.

The proliferation of atomic weapons among the NATO countries, and especially the possession of these devices of mass destruction by the Federal Republic of Germany, would make the possibility of a disarmament agreement even more remote. And associated with such agreements is the problem of the peaceful reunification of Germany. So long as no clear understanding has been reached, the existence of two Germanies—the German Democratic Republic and the Federal Republic of Germany—must be recognized. The German problem cannot be solved unless the German Democratic Republic takes a direct part in the negotiations, with full rights.

We shall touch but lightly on the questions of economic development and international trade, which are amply represented in the Assembly's agenda. This year of 1964 witnessed the holding of the United Nations Conference on Trade and Development, at which very many points connected with these aspects of international relations were discussed. Unfortunately for the economically dependent countries, the warnings and predictions of our delegation were fully confirmed.

We merely wish to point out that, so far as Cuba is concerned, the United States has not complied with the explicit recommendations of this conference. Recently, indeed, the United States government prohibited the sale of medicaments to Cuba, thus throwing away once and for all the humanitarian mask behind which it was trying to conceal the aggressive nature of its blockade against the Cuban people.

Moreover, we would say once again that the faults of colonialism which impede the people's development are not confined to the political field. The so-called deterioration in the terms of trade is simply the result of the unequal exchange between primary producing countries and the industrialized countries which dominate the markets and impose the apparent justice of trade which is equal in value. So long as the economically dependent peoples do not free themselves from the capitalist markets and, in firm solidarity with the socialist countries, impose new trade relations between the exploiters and the exploited, there will be no sound economic development and in certain cases there will be retrogression, the weak countries falling once more under the political domination of the imperialists and the colonialists.

Finally, it must be clearly realized that maneuvers and preparations for aggression against Cuba are taking place in the Caribbean area. Particularly on the littoral of Nicaragua, but also in Costa Rica, the Panama Canal Zone, the Puerto Rican island of Vieques, Florida, and probably other parts of United States territory, as well as possibly in Honduras, Cuban mercenaries and mercenaries of other nationalities are training, with a purpose that cannot be peaceful.

As the result of a notorious scandal, the government of Costa Rica is said to have ordered the closing of all training camps for Cuban exiles in that country. No one knows whether this attitude is sincere, or whether what we have here is merely a pretense dictated by the consideration that the mercenaries trained there are about to commit some villainy. We hope that there will be clear realization of the existence of bases for aggression, which we have long denounced, and that consideration will be given to the international responsibility of a government which authorizes and facilitates the training of mercenaries for an attack against Cuba. We must point out that reports on the training of mercenaries at various places in the Caribbean and the participation of the United States government in such acts appear openly in United States newspapers. We know of no official Latin American protest against this.

It reveals the cynicism with which the United States manipulates its pawns. The subtle ministers for foreign affairs of O.A.S., who had eyes to see Cuban emblems and find "irrefutable" proof in the Yankee weapons exhibited by Venezuela, do not see the obvious preparations for aggression in the United States, just as they did not hear the voice of President Kennedy, who explicitly declared himself to be the aggressor against Cuba at Playa Girón. In some instances, it is a case of blindness provoked by the hatred felt by the ruling classes in Latin American countries for our Revolution; in others, which are even sadder, it is a case of being dazzled by the glint of mammon.

As is well known, after the tremendous flurry of the so-called "Caribbean crisis," the United States reached with the Soviet Union certain agreements culminating in the withdrawal of a certain type of armament which continued acts of aggression by the United States—such as the mercenary attack at Playa Girón and the threats to invade our country—had compelled us to install in Cuba, in implementation of our inalienable right of self-defense. The United States also claimed that the United Nations should inspect our territory—a claim which we emphatically rejected, since Cuba does not recognize the right of the United States, or of any one else in the world, to determine what weapons Cuba should possess within its frontiers.

In this connection, we would respect only multilateral agreements, containing equal obligations for all the parties. As Fidel Castro has said, so long as sovereignty is a prerogative of independent nations and peoples, and a right of all peoples, we shall not allow our own people to be deprived of that right; so long as the world is governed by these principles, so long as the world is governed by these concepts, which have universal validity because they are universally accepted and sanctioned by the peoples, we shall not allow ourselves to be deprived of any of those rights, we shall not renounce a single one of them.

The Secretary-General of the United Nations, U Thant, understood our reasons. Nevertheless, the United States sought to establish a new, arbitrary, and illegal prerogative—that of violating the air space of any small country. Thus, there have been streaking through our country's air space, with impunity, U-2 aircraft and other types of espionage apparatus. We have issued all the necessary warning that an end should be put to violations of air space, as well as to provocative actions by Yankee sailors against our sentry-posts in the Guantánamo area, to the "buzzing" of our ships and ships of other nationalities by aircraft in international waters, to piratical attacks on ships sailing under various flags, and to the clandestine introduction of spies, saboteurs, and arms into our island.

We want to build socialism; we have declared ourselves supporters of those who are fighting for peace; and although we are Marxist-Leninists, we have said that we belong to the group of nonaligned countries, because those countries, like ourselves, are struggling against imperialism. We want peace, we wish to build a better life for our people, and we therefore do our best not to respond to the provocations engineered by the Yankees; yet we know the mentality of their rulers—they hope to force us to pay a very high price for that peace. We reply that that price cannot exceed the limits dictated by honor.

And Cuba once again reaffirms both its right to maintain on its territory whatever arms it sees fit and its refusal to recognize the right of any power on earth, no matter how mighty, to violate our soil, our territorial waters, and our air space. If at any Assembly Cuba assumes obligations of a collective nature, it will fulfill them to the letter. Until that happens, it will maintain its rights to the full, just like any other nation.

In the face of imperialist demands, our prime minister laid down the five points essential to a well-established peace in the Caribbean. These are,

1. Cessation of the economic blockade and of all the measures of commercial and economic pressure brought to bear by the United States in every part of the world against our country.

2. Cessation of all subversive activities, the dropping and landing of weapons and explosives by air and sea, the organization of invasions by mercenaries, and the clandestine introduction of spies and saboteurs—all of which are actions carried out from the territory of the United States and of certain collaborating countries.

3. Cessation of the piratical attacks launched from bases in the United States and in Puerto Rico.

4. Cessation of all violations of our air space and territorial waters by aircraft and warships of the United States.

5. Evacuation of the Guantánamo naval base, and return of Cuban territory occupied by the United States.

None of these elementary requirements has been complied with, and our troops are still the object of harassment from the naval base at Guantánamo. This base has become a hideout for malefactors and a springboard for their introduction into our territory.

We should weary this Assembly if we gave an even moderately detailed account of all the provocations of this type which have been committed. Suffice it to say that in 1964 alone, including the first days of December, there have been 1,323 of these incidents. The list includes minor provocations such as violations of the boundary line, the throwing of objects from the territory controlled by the North Americans, acts of sexual exhibitionism by North Americans of both sexes, and oral insults. Others of a more serious nature are the firing of small arms, the aiming of weapons at our territory, and insults to our national flag. Much more serious provocations include: the crossing of the boundary line in order to start fires in installations on the Cuban side, and the firing of rifles—repeated seventy-eight times throughout the year and causing the sad death of Ramón López Pena, a soldier killed as a result of two shots fired from a United States army post three and a half kilometers from the coast on the northeastern sector of the boundary.

This last and extremely serious provocation took place at 7:42 P.M. on July 19, 1964; and our prime minister publicly declared, on July 26, that if there was any repetition of such an incident, he would give orders for our troops to repel the aggression. At the same time Cuban troops were ordered to withdraw from their forward positions further from the boundary line, and an order for the construction of adequate casements was given.

A total of 1,323 provocations in 340 days means approximately four per day. Only a perfectly disciplined army with a high morale, such as ours, can resist such an accumulation of hostile acts without loss of calm.

Forty-seven countries, meeting at Cairo for the Second Conference of Heads of State or Government of Nonaligned Countries, unanimously agreed on the following:

Noting with concern that foreign military bases are in practice a means of bringing pressure on nations and retarding their emancipation and development, based on their own ideological, political, economic, and cultural ideas, the Conference declares its full support to the countries which are seeking to secure the evacuation of foreign bases on their territory and calls upon all States maintaining troops and bases in other countries to remove them forthwith.

The Conference considers that the maintenance at Guantánamo (Cuba) of a military base of the United States of America, in defiance of the will of the Government and people of Cuba and in defiance of the provisions embodied in the Declaration of the Belgrade Conference, constitutes a violation of Cuba's sovereignty and territorial integrity.

Noting that the Cuban Government expresses its readiness to settle its dispute over the base of Guantánamo with the United States on an equal footing, the Conference urges the United States Government to negotiate the evacuation of this base with the Cuban Government.

(A/5763, Section VIII.)

The United States government has not responded to this request of the Cairo Conference, and proposes to maintain indefinitely its forcible occupation of a piece of our territory from which it carries out acts of aggression such as those I have already described.

The Organization of American States, also popularly known as the United States Ministry of the Colonies, "strongly" condemned us—although it had already excluded us from its membership—and ordered its member countries to break off diplomatic and trade relations with Cuba. The Organization authorized aggression against our country, at any time and on any pretext—thus violating the most elementary international laws and completely disregarding the United Nations.

Uruguay, Bolivia, Chile, and Mexico voted against these measures, and the government of the United Mexican States refused to comply with the sanctions when they were approved; since that time we have had no relations with any Latin American country except Mexico, and one of the preliminary steps toward direct imperialist aggression has thus been taken.

We would explain once more that our concern for the countries of Latin America is based on the ties which unite us: the language we speak, our culture, and the master we formerly shared. We have no other reason for desiring the liberation of Latin America from the colonial yoke of the United States. If any of the Latin American countries here today decided to re-establish relations with Cuba, we should be ready to act in that sense on a basis of equality and not on the assumption that recognition of Cuba as a free country was an act of generosity toward our government, for we won that recognition with our blood during our struggle for liberation; we achieved it with our blood in defending our shores against the Yankee invasion.

Although we reject any attempt to charge us with interference in the domestic affairs of other countries, we cannot deny that we sympathize with the peoples who are fighting for their freedom; and we must conform with the obligation of our government and people to proclaim aloud, to the world, our moral support of and solidarity with the peoples that are anywhere struggling to achieve the rights of sovereignty proclaimed in the United Nations Charter.

The United States, for its part, is certainly intervening; it has a long history of intervention in America. Cuba has been aware of it since the end of the last century; but Colombia, Venezuela, Nicaragua, and Central America as a whole, Mexico, Haiti, and Santo Domingo are also aware of it.

In recent years direct aggression has been experienced, not only by our own people, but by Panama, where marines stationed in the

Canal opened fire with impunity on the defenseless population; by Santo Domingo, whose coasts were violated by the Yankee fleet with a view to preventing a justifiable outburst of popular fury after the murder of Trujillo; [3] and by Colombia, whose capital was taken by storm immediately after the rebellion which the assassination of Gaitán had provoked.[4] Underhanded intervention is being carried out through military missions which take part in internal repression —by organizing armed forces for that purpose in a number of countries—and in all the coups d'état known as *"gorilazos,"* [5] which have occurred so frequently on the American continent in recent times.

Specifically, United States forces are intervening to aid in the repression of the peoples of Venezuela, Colombia, and Guatemala that are carrying on an armed struggle for freedom. In the first-named country, they not only advise the army and the police, but carry out genocidal attacks from the air against the peasant population of large rebel-held areas, and the Yankee troops stationed there exert every kind of pressure with a view to increasing direct interference. The imperialists are preparing to repress the American peoples and are creating an "International" of crime.

The United States is intervening in America on the pretext of defending free institutions. The day will come when this Assembly will acquire even greater maturity and will demand from the United States government guarantees for the lives of the Negro and Latin American people living in this country, most of them native-born or naturalized United States citizens.

How can a country which murders its own children and discriminates between them daily because of the color of their skins, a country that allows the murderers of Negroes to go free, actually protects them and punishes the Negroes for demanding respect for their lawful rights as free human beings, claim to be a guardian of liberty? We realize that today the Assembly is not in a position to

[3] Leónidas Trujillo (1891–1961) was a Dominican Republic dictator for about thirty years. Eds.

[4] Jorge Eliecer Gaitán was the leftwing leader of the Liberal Party of Colombia. He was a charismatic figure who called for a social restructuring of the society in order to improve the welfare of the poor. His shooting on April 9, 1948, triggered a violent upheaval in that country which has not ended yet. Eds.

[5] *Gorilazo:* the term refers to military coups. It seems that the term arose in the early 1960's when a foreign reporter asked a military leader of a Latin American country whether there were any guerrillas in the mountains; the military man understood "gorillas" and showed the reporter some apes in the jungle. From then on, the Latin American left has called the military men *gorilas* and a military coup is termed a *gorilazo*. Eds.

demand explanations for these acts; yet it must be clearly established that the government of the United States is not the guardian of liberty, but rather that it is perpetuating the exploitation and oppression of many of the world's peoples and of many of its own citizens.

Our reply to the ambiguous language with which certain representatives have described the case of Cuba and O.A.S. is a forthright proclamation that the peoples of America will make the treacherous governments pay for their treason.

Cuba, a free and sovereign country with no chains binding it to anyone, with no foreign investments in its territory, with no proconsuls to "direct" its policy, can hold its head high in this Assembly and prove its title to the name "Free Territory of America" with which it will be baptized.

Our example will bear fruit on the continent, as it has already borne fruit to a certain extent in Guatemala, Colombia, and Venezuela. There is no small enemy, nor any contemptible little army, because there are no longer any isolated peoples. As is set forth in the Second Declaration of Havana,

No one people of Latin America is weak, because all are part of a family of 200 million brothers who suffer the same miseries, harbor the same feelings, and face the same enemy. All dream alike of a happier fate and can count on the solidarity of all honorable men and women through the world.

This epic which lies before us will be written by the hungry masses of Indians, of landless peasants, of exploited workers. It will be written by the progressive masses, the honest and brilliant intellectuals of whom there are so many in our suffering lands of Latin America. A struggle of masses and of ideas, this epic will be borne forward by our peoples who have been maltreated and despised by imperialism, by our peoples, who, slighted until today, are now beginning to awaken from their sleep. We were regarded as an impotent, submissive herd; but now they are beginning to fear that herd, a gigantic herd of 200 million Latin Americans who will dig the grave of Yankee monopoly capital, as that capital already senses.

...The hour of their vindication is striking, the hour they themselves have chosen. The bell is sounding clearly from one end of the continent to the other. This anonymous mass, this colored America, sombre and taciturn, which is singing throughout the continent the same sad, disillusioned song, is now beginning to take its history into its own hands, to write it with its own blood, to suffer and to die. For now, in the fields and mountains of America, on the slopes of its "sierras," in its plains and in its forests, in solitude or amid the bustle of cities, on the shores of the ocean and the bank of the river, these valiant hearts are beginning to stir hot with the desire to die for what is theirs, to gain and hold their rights which have been flouted for nearly five hundred years.

Yes, history must now reckon with the poor people of America, with the exploited and scorned of Latin America, who have decided that henceforth they will write their own history. Day after day they can be seen on the roads, on foot, marching endlessly, for hundreds of miles, to reach their "Olympian" rulers and to secure their rights. Day after day they can be seen, here, there, and everywhere, armed with stones, sticks, and matches, occupying the land, digging their hooks into the soil which is theirs and defending it with their lives. They can be seen bearing their banners, flags, and slogans, letting them blow in the wind amid the mountains or across the plains. And this wave of shaking fury, of justice demanded, of rights withheld, which is beginning to engulf the countries of Latin America, will not recede. It will mount with every day that passes because it consists of the masses, those who are in a majority in all things, those whose labor produces the wealth, who create the values, who turn the wheels of history, and are now awakening from the long benumbing sleep to which others had consigned them.

For this great mass of humanity has said "Enough!" and has begun to move. And its march, its march of giants, will not stop until that true independence, for which lives have more than once been lost in vain, has been won. Now at least those who die will die as the Cubans did at Playa Girón—for their own, true, and inalienable independence.

This new structure of a continent, of America, is rising and taking shape in the daily asseveration by our people of their irrevocable determination to fight and to paralyze the mailed fist of the invader. This proclaimed determination has the understanding and support of all peoples of the world, and especially of the socialist camp headed by the Soviet Union. The proclamation is: "Fatherland or Death."

Revolution and
Underdevelopment

ЛГЛГЛГЛГЛГЛГЛГЛГЛГЛГЛГЛГЛГЛГЛГЛГЛ

Dear brothers:

Cuba comes to this conference to speak for the peoples of America; and, as we have emphasized on other occasions, it also does so as an underdeveloped country which at the same time is building socialism. It is not by accident that our delegation is permitted to express its opinion within the circle of Asian and African peoples. A common aspiration, the defeat of imperialism, unites us in our march toward the future; a common history of struggle against the same enemy has united us along this path.

This is an assembly of peoples in struggle; it is waged on two fronts of equal importance and demands our total effort. On one front is the struggle against imperialism to free ourselves from colonial or neocolonial ties, which is being carried out by means of political weapons or firearms or a combination of both. This struggle is inseparably tied to the struggle against backwardness and poverty. Both are stages of the same path that leads to the creation of a new, rich, and just society. It is imperative to obtain political power and liquidate the oppressing classes, but afterward the second stage of the struggle must be faced, whose characteristics are, if that is possible, even more difficult than the preceding one.

Ever since monopolistic capital appropriated the world, it has maintained most of humanity in poverty, dividing up the profits among the group of the most powerful countries. The standard of living of those countries is based on the misery of ours; therefore to raise the standard of living of the underdeveloped peoples, it is necessary to fight against imperialism. Every time a country splits off from the imperialist tree, not only a partial victory against the fundamental enemy is won, but it also contributes to the real weakening of imperialism and is taking a step toward final victory.

There are no frontiers in this struggle to the death. We cannot remain indifferent in the face of what occurs in any part of the world. A victory for any country against imperialism is our victory, just as any country's defeat is a defeat for all. The practice of pro-

Speech at the Second Economic Seminar of Afro-Asian Solidarity in Algiers on February 24, 1965. *El Mundo* (Havana), February 25, 1965, pp. 1, 5.

letarian internationalism is not only a duty for the peoples who struggle for a better future, it is also an inescapable necessity. If the imperialist enemy, North American or any other, carries out its action against the underdeveloped peoples and the socialist countries, elemental logic determines the need for an alliance of the underdeveloped peoples and the socialist countries. If there were no other basis for unity, the common enemy should constitute one.

Of course these alliances cannot be made spontaneously, without discussions, at times painful, as a prelude to a pact.

Each time a country liberates itself, as we have said, it is a defeat for the world imperialist system, but we should agree that the splitting off does not occur by the mere proclamation of independence or by winning an armed victory in a revolution. It occurs when the imperialist economic domination over a people ends. Therefore, the socialist countries are vitally interested in making these separations effective, and it is our international duty, a duty determined by the ideology that guides us, to contribute our efforts to make this liberation as rapid and thorough as possible.

From all this a conclusion must be drawn: The development of the countries which now begin the road of liberation must be underwritten by the socialist countries. We say it in this manner without the least desire to blackmail anyone or to be spectacular. Nor do we say it in an easy search for greater closeness with the ranks of the Afro-Asian peoples. It is a profound conviction. There can be socialism only if there is change in man's consciousness that will provoke a new fraternal attitude toward humanity on the individual level in the society which builds or has built socialism and also on a world level in relation to all the peoples who suffer imperialist oppression.

We believe that with this spirit the responsibility of aiding dependent countries ought to be faced and that there should be no more talk of developing mutually beneficial trade based on prices that the law of value and unequal international trade relations imposed on backward countries. How can "mutual benefit" mean selling at world market prices raw materials which cost unlimited sweat and suffering to the backward countries and buying at world market prices the machines produced in the large automated factories of today?

If we establish that type of relationship between the two groups of nations, we must agree that the socialist countries are, to a certain extent, accomplices to imperialist exploitation. It can be argued that the amount of trade with the underdeveloped countries constitutes an insignificant part of the foreign trade of the socialist countries. It is a great truth, but it does not do away with the immoral character of the exchange.

The socialist countries have the moral duty of liquidating their tacit complicity with the exploiting countries of the West. The fact that the trade is small today means nothing: in 1959, Cuba occasionally sold sugar to a given country of the socialist bloc, most of it through British or other foreign channels; today 80 percent of Cuba's trade is with that area. All of its vital supplies come from the socialist camp, and in fact it has joined that camp. We cannot say that this entry was produced by the mere increase in trade nor that the increase in trade developed by the destruction of the old structures and choosing the socialist form of development. Both extremes meet and both are interrelated.

We did not embark on the path that would end in communism with all our steps foreseen; it was not a logical product of a predetermined ideology. The truths of socialism and the crude facts of imperialism forged our people and taught them the path which we have now consciously adopted. The peoples of Africa and Asia who move toward their definite liberation will have to take the same path sooner or later, even though today they qualify their socialism. There is only one valid definition of socialism—the abolition of exploitation of man by man. So long as this is not achieved, we find ourselves in the period of socialist construction; and if instead of achieving this goal, the task of suppressing exploitation stagnates, or worse yet regresses toward exploitation, it is not valid to speak even of socialist construction.

We must prepare the conditions that will allow our brothers to enter the path of definite abolition of exploitation directly, but we cannot invite them to enter if we are accomplices of that exploitation. If we were asked, "What are the methods that will establish just prices?" we could not answer. We do not know the practical magnitude of the question. All we know is that after political discussions between Cuba and the Soviet Union an agreement was signed which is advantageous to us. We shall sell up to 5 million tons of sugar at fixed prices above the normal price of the world sugar market. The People's Republic of China also maintains these purchasing prices.

This is only a precedent; the real task consists of fixing the prices that will permit development. There must be a great change of concepts on the level of international relations. Foreign trade must not determine politics, but on the contrary, it must be subordinated to a fraternal policy toward the people.

Let us briefly analyze the problem of long-term credits for developing basic industries. Frequently we find that beneficiary countries attempt to create industrial bases disproportionate to their actual capability whose products will not be consumed domestically. In addition, the nation's reserves will be committed by the effort.

Our reasoning is that investments by socialist states in their own territory pass directly to the state budget and are only recovered through the use of what is produced by the investment in the entire manufacturing cycle, until the very end of production. We propose that some thought be given to the possibility of making this kind of investment in the underdeveloped countries.

In this manner an immense force—miserably exploited but never helped in its development—could be placed in motion and a new era of authentic international division of labor begun, based not on the history of what has been done up to now but rather on the history of what could be done.

The states in whose territories the new investments are to be made will have all the inherent rights of sovereign property over them without any payment or credit due, but they will be obliged to deliver certain quantities of products to the investor countries for a certain number of years at fixed prices.

The method of financing local expenses incurred by the investor country is also deserving of study. One form of aid not requiring the expenditure of freely convertible foreign exchange could be supplying marketable goods to the governments of underdeveloped countries by means of long-term credit.

Another difficult problem to resolve is the mastering of technology. The shortage of technicians in the developing countries is a well-known fact. Educational institutions and teachers are lacking. Sometimes we lack a real understanding of our needs and of a determination to carry out a policy of technical, cultural, and ideological development to which top priority is assigned.

The socialist countries should supply the aid needed to organize the institutions for technical education; they should insist on the great importance of this and supply the technicians that we now lack. It is necessary to insist further on this last point. The technicians who come to our countries should be exemplary. They are *compañeros* who will find themselves in a strange environment often hostile to technology, they speak a different language and have totally different customs. The technicians facing this difficult task must be above all communists in the deepest and most noble sense of the word. With this single quality, a minimum of organization, and flexibility, they will accomplish wonders.

We know that it can be achieved because brother countries have sent us a certain number of technicians who have done more for the development of our country than ten institutes and have contributed to a closer friendship between our countries than ten ambassadors or a hundred diplomatic receptions.

If we could really practice effectively the points that we have noted and if all the technology of the developed countries could be placed at the disposal of the underdeveloped nations, without following the present patent procedures covering discoveries in both groups of nations, we could make much progress in our common task.

Imperialism has been defeated in many partial battles but remains a considerable force in the world, and we cannot aspire to its definite defeat except through the effort and sacrifice of all. However, the proposed steps cannot be taken unilaterally. The development of the underdeveloped countries must involve expense for the socialist countries; in this we agree. But also the underdeveloped countries must exert all their force and firmly embark on the path of building a new society—regardless of what we call it—in which the instruments of labor are no longer the instruments of exploitation of man by man.

Nor can we expect the confidence of the socialist countries if we play at balancing capitalism and socialism, trying to use both forces as countervailing elements in order to gain certain advantages from this competition. A new policy of absolute seriousness should govern the relations between the two groups of societies. It is convenient to emphasize once again that the means of production should preferably be in the hands of the state in order for the signs of exploitation to gradually disappear.

On the other hand, development should not be left to the most complete improvisation; the construction of the new society must be planned. Planning is one of the laws of socialism, and without it socialism will not exist. Without correct planning, there cannot be a sufficient guarantee that all the economic sectors of any country will combine harmoniously to take the leap forward which the present epoch demands. Planning is not an isolated problem of each of our countries—small, distorted in their development, possessors of some raw materials, or producers of some manufactured or semi-manufactured goods but lacking in most others. From the outset, planning should lean toward a certain regionalism in order to interrelate the national economies of various countries, thus achieving an integration on the basis of authentic mutual benefit.

The road ahead is full of dangers. These dangers are not invented or foreseen in the distant future by some superior mind; they are the palpable result of the realities that beset us. The fight against colonialism has reached its final stages, but in the present era colonial status is only a consequence of imperialistic domination. As long as imperialism exists, by definition it will exert its domination over other countries. Today that domination is called neocolonialism.

Neocolonialism developed first in South America, throughout the whole continent, and today it is felt with increasing intensity in Africa and Asia. Its forms of penetration and development have different characteristics. One is brutal, which we have known in the Congo. Brute force without any façade is its ultimate weapon. But there is another more subtle form: the penetration of the politically liberated countries, alliances with the rising indigenous bourgeoisies, development of a parasitic bourgeoisie in close alliance with the old metropolitan interests. This is based on a transitory rise in the popular standard of living, for in many backward countries the simple step from feudal to capitalist relations signals a great advance without consideration of the dire long-run consequences for the workers.

Neocolonialism has shown its claws in the Congo, a sign not of strength but of weakness. It had to resort to force—its extreme weapon as an economic argument. This has brought forth intense opposition, but at the same time a much more subtle form of neocolonialism is being rapidly created in the countries of Africa and Asia. This has been called the South Americanization of these continents, that is, the development of a parasitic bourgeoisie which adds nothing to the national wealth and even goes so far as to deposit its ill-gotten gains in capitalist banks abroad, and enters into agreements with foreigners with absolute disregard for the welfare of the people in order to reap more profits.

There are also other dangers such as competition between brother countries which are politically friendly and sometimes neighbors because both are trying to develop the same investments at the same time and in markets which often do not permit it. Such competition has the defect of wasting energies that could be utilized in much greater economic cooperation, and furthermore it permits the imperialist monopolies to play games with us.

On occasion when it has been impossible to obtain a certain investment with the aid of the socialist camp, it has been obtained through agreement with the capitalists. These capitalist investments not only have the disadvantage of the form in which the loans are made but also other disadvantages such as the creation of mixed economic enterprises with a dangerous partner. Because in general these investments are parallel to those made in other states, this tends to create divisions among friendly countries due to economic differences; and further, it establishes the danger of corruption that emanates from the constant presence of capitalism which is so skillful in the presentation of images of development and welfare that becloud the understanding of many people.

Later when the market prices decline due to overproduction of products of a similar nature, the countries affected are forced to ask for new loans or to permit additional investments for further competition. The fall of the economy into the hands of the monopolies and the slow but sure return to the past is the final consequence of such a policy.

As we see it, the only safe way of obtaining investments from the capitalist powers is when the state has direct control over the purchasing of goods, limiting imperialist participation to the supply of goods according to contracts while not allowing them to get past the street door of our house. Here it is legal to take advantage of interimperialist contradictions in order to secure the least onerous conditions. It is necessary to pay attention to the "disinterested" economic, cultural, and other types of aid that imperialism offers either directly or through puppet states which are more acceptable in certain parts of the world.

If all of the dangers pointed out are not seen in time, countries that have begun the task of national liberation with faith and enthusiasm may find themselves unwittingly moving into the neo-colonial road. They may find that domination by monopoly has gradually established itself within their territories in such a subtle manner that its effects are difficult to perceive until they are brutally felt.

There are many tasks to be performed—immense problems are faced by our two worlds, the world of the socialist countries and this so-called third world. They are problems that are directly related to man and his well-being and to the struggle against the main perpetrators of our backwardness.

All the countries and peoples who are conscious of our duties and of the dangers that such a position engenders must take concrete measures to solve these problems so that our friendship can be united on two planes, the economic and the political, which can never be separated. A large compact bloc must be formed that will in turn help other countries liberate themselves not only from imperialist political power but from imperialist economic power as well. The aspect of armed struggle to achieve liberation from the oppression of a political power must be approached according to the rules of proletarian internationalism. If it is absurd to imagine that in a socialist country which is at war a factory manager would demand a guarantee of payment before shipping the tanks his factory produces to the front lines, it is no less absurd to inquire about the possibility of payment by a people who fight for their liberation or need those arms to defend their liberty.

Arms cannot be merchandise in our world. They should be delivered without any cost whatsoever and in quantities determined by their need and availability to those people who ask for them in order to direct their fight against the common enemy. That is the spirit in which the U.S.S.R. and the People's Republic of China have offered us their military aid. We are socialists, and this constitutes the guarantee of the proper utilization of those arms; but we are not the only ones, and all must receive the same treatment. The ominous attack of North American imperialism against Vietnam or the Congo should be answered by supplying these sister countries with all the defense equipment they need and giving them our unconditional solidarity.

In the economic sphere, we must conquer the road to development with the most advanced technology possible. We cannot climb the entire long ascending path of humanity from feudalism to the atomic and automated era; that would be a path of immense and useless sacrifice. It is necessary to seize technology at its present level to make the great technological leap that will reduce the gap that exists today between the more developed countries and ourselves. This calls for large factories and a properly developed agriculture. And above all our basis of strength must be a technological and ideological culture with sufficient strength and a mass base to allow the continuous sustenance of our institutes and research organizations. These institutes will have to be created in each country as will the men to utilize the present technology and to adapt themselves to newly acquired technology.

These cadres must have a clear awareness of their duties to the society in which they live. We cannot have adequate technological culture if it is not complemented with an ideological culture. In most of our countries, a proper foundation for industrial development—which is what determines the growth of a modern society—

cannot exist if we do not begin by assuring the people necessary food, essential consumer goods, and an adequate education. It is necessary to spend a good part of our national income on so-called unproductive investments in education and special attention must be given to the development of agricultural productivity. The latter has reached incredible proportions in many capitalist countries, producing the senseless crisis of overproduction and a surplus of grain and other food products or industrial raw materials while the rest of the world suffers from hunger, although it has enough land and labor to produce several times over what the entire world requires to feed itself.

Agriculture must be considered a fundamental element of our development; therefore, changes in the agricultural structure and the adaptation of new technological possibilities as well as new obligations of eliminating the exploitation of man should constitute the fundamental aspect of our work.

Before making costly decisions that could cause irreparable damage, it is necessary to carefully study the national territory. This constitutes one of the preliminary steps in economic research, and it is an elemental requirement of correct planning.

We warmly support Algeria's proposal for institutionalizing our relations. We would like only to offer some supplementary suggestions. First: In order that the union be an instrument of the struggle against imperialism, the participation of Latin American peoples in the alliance of the socialist countries is necessary. Second: The revolutionary character of the union must be guarded, preventing admission to it of governments or movements not identified with the general aspirations of the peoples and creating mechanisms that would permit the separation from it of any government or popular movement that separates itself from the just path. Third: We must advocate the establishment of new relations based on equality between our countries and the capitalist countries, and the establishment of a revolutionary jurisprudence that would protect us in case of conflict and would give new meaning to the relations between us and the rest of the world.

We speak a revolutionary language and we honestly fight for the victory of that cause, but often we entangle ourselves in the nets of an international law created as a result of the confrontation between the imperialist powers and not by free and just people in the course of their struggle.

Our peoples, for example, suffer the painful pressures of foreign bases established in their territories, or they must bear the heavy burden of incredibly large foreign debts. The history of these trials is well known to all: puppet governments, governments weakened by a long struggle for liberation or by the development of capitalist laws of the market place, all have permitted the signing of agreements which threaten our internal stability and compromise our future.

It is time to throw off the yoke, impose renegotiation of oppressive external debts, and force the imperialists to abandon their bases of aggression.

I would not want to conclude these words, this repetition of concepts already known to you, without calling the attention of this seminar to the fact that Cuba is not the only American country; simply, it is the one that has the opportunity to speak to you today. Other countries are shedding their blood to acquire the rights we have now. From here and at all conferences wherever they may be held, we must simultaneously send greetings to the heroic peoples of Vietnam, Laos, "Portuguese" Guinea, South Africa, or Palestine, and extend our friendly voice, our hand, and our encouragement to all exploited countries struggling for their emancipation; to our brothers in Venezuela, Guatemala, and Colombia who, arms in hand, finally say "No!" to the imperialist enemy.

There are few places as symbolic as Algiers, one of the most heroic capitals of freedom, from which this can be said. Let the magnificent Algerian people, trained like few others in the sufferings to achieve independence, under the resolute leadership of their party, with our dear comrade Ahmed Ben Bella at their head, serve as an inspiration to us in this battle without quarter against world imperialism.

INTERVIEWS

ЛГЛЛЛЛЛЛЛЛЛЛЛЛЛЛЛЛЛЛЛЛЛЛЛЛ

Q: Why are you here?

A: I am here simply because I think that the only way to liberate America from dictators is by overthrowing them—helping their downfall in any way, the more directly the better.

Q: Are you not afraid that your participation in the internal affairs of a country that is not yours could be called meddling?

A: First of all, my fatherland is not only Argentina, but all America. I have antecedents as glorious as Martí and it is precisely in his land where I abide by his doctrine. Besides, I do not see how it could be called meddling when I offer my blood for a cause that I consider just and popular, to help a country liberate itself from a tyranny, a country that allows the meddling of a foreign power which aids it with weapons, planes, money, and official instructors. No country up to now has denounced North American meddling in Cuban affairs, and no newspaper accuses the Yankees of helping Batista massacre his own people. But many are concerned with me. I am the intruding foreigner who aids the rebels with his own life. Those who provide the weapons for an internal war are not intruders, but I am.

Q: What is the truth of Fidel Castro's communism?

A: Fidel is not a communist. If he were one, he would have at least a few more weapons. This revolution is exclusively Cuban. No, it is Latin American. Politically, Fidel and his movement could be defined as "national revolutionary." [1] Of course, it is anti-Yankee to the degree that the Yankees are antirevolutionary. But in fact we do not raise a proselytist anti-Yankeeism. We are against the United States because it is against our peoples.

I am the one most attacked with the communist argument. Every Yankee newspaperman who reached the Sierra [Maestra] always

This interview was made by the Argentine reporter, Jorge Masetti, in April 1958 in the Sierra Maestra mountains. Jorge Masetti, *Los que luchan y los que lloran; el Fidel Castro que yo vi* (Havana: Editorial Madiedo,) 1959, pp. 48–56; also in Jorge Ricardo Masetti, "Che en Guatemala," *Granma* (Havana), October 16, 1967, p. 8.

[1] Parties that consider social revolution a necessity while emphasizing parliamentary democracy—though not always practicing it. Recently they have become the major defenders of U.S. policy in Latin America. Eds.

began by asking me what was my role in the communist party of Guatemala—with the premise that I acted in the communist party of that country—only because I was, and still am, a wholehearted admirer of the democratic government of Colonel Jacobo Arbenz.

Q: Did you have any post in the government?

A: No, never; but when the North American invasion took place, I tried to form a group of young men like myself to fight the [United Fruit] adventurers. In Guatemala it was necessary to fight and yet almost no one fought. It was necessary to resist and almost no one wanted to do it.

From there I escaped to Mexico, when the FBI agents were already arresting and murdering directly all those who represented a danger to the government of the United Fruit. In Aztec land I met once again some members of the 26th of July Movement that I had known in Guatemala and struck up a friendship with Raúl Castro, Fidel's youngest brother. He introduced me to the chief of the Movement when they were already planning the invasion of Cuba.

Q: How did you join the Cuban revolutionaries?

A: I spoke with Fidel a whole night. At dawn I was already the physician of the future expedition. In reality, after the experience I went through, my long walks throughout all of Latin America and the Guatemalan closing, not much was needed to convince me to join any revolution against a tyrant; but Fidel impressed me as an extraordinary man. He faced and resolved the impossible. He had an unshakable faith that once he left he would arrive in Cuba, that once he arrived he would fight, that once he began fighting he would win. I shared his optimism. It was imperative to act, to fight, to concretize. It was imperative to stop crying and fight. It was necessary to demonstrate to the people of his fatherland that they could have faith in him, because he practiced what he preached. He said "In 1956 we shall be free or we shall be martyrs," and he announced that before the year ended he would land somewhere in Cuba leading his expeditionary army.[2]

Q: What happened when you landed?

A: When we arrived they disbanded us. We had an atrocious journey in the *Granma* yacht. There were eighty-two men in it, plus the crew. A storm forced us to change our course and most of us were seasick. Water and food ran out, and to top it off, when we arrived at the island the yacht ran aground. They shot at us persistently from the air and the coast; and after awhile only half of us were alive, or only

[2] Guevara refers to an interview Castro had with Francis L. McCarthy in August 1956. See *El Mundo* (Havana), August 7, 1956, pp. 1, A10.

half-alive if we take into consideration our condition. Of the eighty-two men only twelve were left with Fidel. At first our group was reduced to seven, for the other five had become separated. Of the ambitious invading army of the 26th of July Movement only that was left. Lying on the ground, without being able to shoot so that we would not be discovered, we awaited the final decision of Fidel, while far away the naval batteries and machine-gun rattle of planes could be heard.

What a man Fidel is! Do you know that he used the machine-gun sound to stand up and say "Listen how they fire at us. They are terrified. They fear us because they know we are going to finish them up." And without saying another word, he took his rifle and knapsack and headed our small caravan. We looked for the Turquino, the highest and most inaccessible peak in the Sierra, and there we established our first camp. The peasants saw us pass by without showing friendship. But Fidel was not disturbed. He would salute them and a few minutes later he would have a more or less friendly conversation going on. When they denied food to us, we kept on moving without protest. Little by little the peasantry realized that the bearded ones that had "revolted" constituted precisely the opposite of the guards looking for us. Whereas the Batista army appropriated all that they wanted from the peasants—even the women—Fidel Castro's men respected the property of the peasants and paid generously for everything that they consumed. We noticed with some astonishment that the peasants were confused with our behavior. They were accustomed to the treatment they received from Batista's army. Little by little they became our true friends and as we fought with guards that we could surprise in the mountains, many peasants expressed their desire to join us. But those first battles to get weapons, those ambushes that began to worry the guards, also gave rise to a most ferocious wave of terrorism imaginable. Every peasant was seen as a potential rebel and was killed. If they heard that we had passed through a given zone, they burned all the huts we visited. If they arrived at a farm and found no men—because they were working or had gone to town—they imagined the men had joined our ranks, which each day were more numerous, and shot all those that remained in the house. The terrorism established by the army of Batista was without doubt our best ally at the beginning; it was the most brutal and eloquent demonstration the peasantry needed for the necessity to end the Batista regime.

Interview in the
Escambray Mountains

⊓⊔⊓⊔⊓⊔⊓⊔⊓⊔⊓⊔⊓⊔⊓⊔⊓⊔⊓⊔⊓⊔⊓⊔⊓⊔⊓⊔⊓⊔⊓⊔⊓⊓

Q: Good evening, Major Guevara. How long have you been in this movement?

A: Approximately three years; I cannot say exactly how long but it was from the time that Fidel Castro visited Mexico. Once I knew the democratic ideals of the revolution led by Fidel Castro, I declared myself a partisan of it.

Q: What can you tell us about the invasion march led by you up to this province?

A: We began this march on August 31 and we moved by truck for four days; afterward we marched by foot because it was impossible for us to use the roads. We moved to the south of Oriente Province. We had a number of difficulties which we had not foreseen at the outset. We broke a number of encirclements; we made some kidnappings; we lost four comrades on two different occasions, and engaged the army a number of times and on each of them we inflicted heavy casualties on the enemy. Our most difficult situation was in Baragua, where we were completely surrounded and our health was very bad, but we were able to escape. Then we moved through Ciego de Avila and the Jatibonico River.

Q: What sort of welcome did you have in the towns of Las Villas.

A: Well, the welcome was fantastic. We could not have expected a better reception. We had some problems with the revolutionary sectors operating in the zone, but our behavior at the end did away with all the disagreements.

Q: What do you think, Major Guevara, about the situation of the despotic regime?

A: I think that it is at the age of collapse. If foreign elements intervene, it might remain in power for some time. Nevertheless, the popular forces are so strong that the collapse is inevitable. I believe that the interventionist element should not materialize at this moment due to the revolutionary spirit of all the people.

Q: Well, Major, in comparison with your prior battles in the Sierra Maestra, how do they compare with the struggle here?

   This interview was broadcast by Radio Rebelde in December 1958. "Cuba, Diciembre 1958," *Verde Olivo* (Havana), December 31, 1966, pp. 23, 24.

A: It is much easier for us. In the Sierra Maestra we began the struggle with a group of men who were almost unarmed, without bullets and almost without any peasant support. Our actions improved in time, but the Sierra Maestra is an inhospitable place with very few roads. In contrast, in Las Villas we find ourselves very close to the important cities and the national highway and we received a great amount of aid from our supply structure from the *llano*.[1] The conditions are much better.

Q: Then you like this better?

A: It is not a matter of liking it better. To be more comfortable does not mean that I like it better for I feel a great love for that region of the Sierra Maestra where we began our struggle and where we acquired revolutionary strength.

Q: What can you tell us in relation to the large offensive that was courageously repelled by you?

A: It was not only repelled by the men under my command, it was also humiliatingly lost by the dictatorship's army, which did not fight, retreating and leaving behind weapons and equipment.

Q: And what do you think about the offensive in this province?

A: It is necessary and vital to break communications between the east and the west, and I believe that the city of Santa Clara is virtually in our hands when all the revolutionary elements wage an offensive.

Q: What can you tell us about the Agrarian Reform Law?

A: Well, the Agrarian Reform Law, Law No. 3 decreed from the Sierra Maestra, has as a basis the elimination of the latifundia, distributing small parcels of land so that the peasant can live a dignified life; we should also give him easy credit terms and the necessary technical aid which, of course, we cannot now offer as a revolutionary army. That will follow later. The peasants will pay nothing for the land.

Q: Now a last question, Dr. Guevara. Do you think we shall be able to eat together on Christmas Eve?

A: We can all eat together, the question is where; at any rate, I hope that all of us here will dine in harmony.

Q: Thank you very much, Major Guevara, for your visit to 6F.V.[2]

---

[1] Even though it can be translated as *plain*, it refers mainly to the urban area.
[2] 6F.V was the name of the rebel radio station broadcasting the interview. Eds.

A New Old
Che Guevara Interview

GUEVARA: We have always looked up to Comrade Mao Tse-tung. When we were engaged in guerrilla warfare we studied Comrade Mao Tse-tung's theory on guerilla warfare. Mimeographed copies published at the front lines circulated widely among our cadres; they were called "food from China." We studied this little book carefully and learned many things. We discovered that there were many problems that Comrade Mao Tse-tung had already systematically and scientifically studied and answered. This was a great help to us.

REPORTER: Will you please tell us how Cuba achieved her revolutionary victory?

GUEVARA: Certainly. Let us begin at the time I joined the 26th of July Movement in Mexico. Before the dangerous crossing on the *Granma*, the views on society of the members of this organization were very different. I remember, in a frank discussion within our family in Mexico, I suggested we ought to propose a revolutionary program to the Cuban people. I have never forgotten how one of the participants in the attack on the Moncada army camp responded at the time. He said to me: "Our action is very simple. What we want to do is to initiate a coup d'état. Batista pulled off a coup and in only one morning took over the government. We must make another coup and expel him from power. . . .[1] Batista has made a hundred concessions to the Americans, and we will make one hundred and one." At that time I argued with him, saying that we had to make a coup on the basis of principle and yet at the same time understand clearly what we would do after taking over the government. That was the thinking of a member of the first stage of the 26th of July Movement. Those who held the same view and did not change left our revolutionary movement later and adopted another path.

From that time on, the small organization that later made the crossing on the *Granma* encountered repeated difficulties. Besides

This interview appeared in China's *Shih-chieh Chih-shih* on June 5, 1959. A translation was made by William E. Ratliff for the *Hispanic American Historical Review*, vol. 46, no. 2, August 1966, pp. 288–299. The interview was made on April 18, 1959, in Havana.
1 Omission made in original. Eds.

the never-ending suppression by the Mexican authorities, there was also a series of internal problems, like those people who were adventurous in the beginning but later used this pretext and that to break away from the military expedition. Finally at the time of the crossing on the *Granma* there remained only eighty-two men in the organization.

The adventurous thought of that time was the first and only catastrophe encountered within the organization during the process of starting the uprising. We suffered from the blow. But we gathered again in the Sierra Maestra. For many months the manner of our life in the mountains was most irregular. We climbed from one mountain peak to another, in a drought, without a drop of water. Merely to survive was extremely difficult.

The peasants who had to endure the persecution of Batista's military units gradually began to participate in our guerrilla units. In this way our rank and file changed from city people to peasants. At that same time, as the peasants began to participate in the armed struggle for freedom of rights and social justice, we put forth a correct slogan—land reform. This slogan mobilized the oppressed Cuban masses to come forward and fight to seize the land. From this time on the first great social plan was determined, and it later became the banner and primary spearhead of our movement.

It was at just this time that a tragedy occurred in Santiago de Cuba; our comrade Frank País was killed. This produced a turning point in our revolutionary movement. The enraged people of Santiago on their own poured into the streets and called forth the first politically oriented general strike. Even though the strike did not have a leader, it paralyzed the whole of Oriente Province. The dictatorial government suppressed the incident. This movement, however, caused us to understand that working class participation in the struggle to achieve freedom was absolutely essential! We then began to carry out secret work among the workers, in preparation for another general strike, to help the Rebel Army seize the government.

The victorious and bold secret activities of the Rebel Army shook the whole country; all of the people were stirred up, leading to the general strike on April 9 last year. But the strike failed because of a lack of contact between the leaders and the working masses. Experience taught the leaders of the 26th of July Movement a valuable truth: The Revolution must not belong to this or that specific clique —it must be the undertaking of the whole body of the Cuban people. This conclusion inspired the members of the movement to work their hardest both on the plain and in the mountains.

At this time we began to educate our forces in revolutionary theory and doctrine. This all showed that the rebel movement had already grown and was even beginning to achieve political maturity. Before long we began to construct "small-scale industry" in the Sierra Maestra. We passed from a life of wandering to a stationary existence. In order to fulfill our most pressing needs, we built our own shoe factories, arsenals, and bomb conversion factories. We took the bombs Batista dropped on us, converted them to land mines, and then turned them on the dictator.

Every person in the Rebel Army remembered his basic duties in the Sierra Maestra and other areas: to improve the status of the peasants, to participate in the struggle to seize land, and to build schools. Agrarian law was tried for the first time; using revolutionary methods we confiscated the extensive possessions of the officials of the dictatorial government and distributed to the peasants all of the state-held land in the area. At this time there rose up a peasant movement, closely connected to the land, with land reform as its banner.

As a consequence of the failure of the April 9 strike, Batista began his barbaric suppression at the end of May. On about May 25 an enemy army of ten thousand approached our military camp and focused its attack on the first column of troops led by our commander, Castro himself. Although it is hard to believe, at that time in the Sierra Maestra we had barely three hundred "Freedom" model rifles against a ten thousand-man army. By about July 30 this campaign had checked Batista's attack because of correct strategic leadership, and the Rebel Army turned from defense to the attack.

After this campaign the Rebel Army began to prepare to move down to the plains. This attack had strategic significance and psychological influence because at that time our weapons could in no way be compared to those of the dictatorial government either in quality or quantity. In this fight we had the best ally there is, but one that is hard to estimate—the people. None of our columns of troops could be stopped from molesting the enemy or from occupying the most advantageous military positions. This was not the result entirely of the excellent strategy of our military units; especially important was the great help of the peasants. They did all the things the Rebel Army could not do. They made secret reports, kept close watch over the enemy army, discovered the enemy's weak points, transmitted urgent correspondence, and acted as spies in the puppet army. It was no miracle that brought all of this cooperation, but our carrying out of policies that were beneficial to the peasants and ranchers. When the enemy attacked us in the Sierra Maestra and hunger overtook us, ten thousand head of cattle were chased up into the mountains from the border area of the landowners. We not only had enough cattle to supply the Rebel Army, but could also distribute some among the peasants. This was the first time especially poor *guajiros* [2] of this region had received livestock from anyone. It was also the first time they had received any education, because the Revolution provided them with schools.

Meanwhile, the dictatorial government was still treacherously raping, looting, killing, and throwing the peasants off of their land. It used a great quantity of napalm from its northern ally, the United States, to slaughter good and innocent people.

It was at this time that we began to move the army toward Las Villas Province. As soon as we arrived there we issued a revolutionary proclamation announcing the land reform. In the proclamation it was stated that small landowners did not have to pay land tax. Most surely the land reform was like the spearhead of the Rebel Army; we advanced holding high the banner of land reform. During the one year and eight months of revolutionary process, the leaders and the peasants have established harmonious relationships, making it possible for the Revolution to do things that before this time had been beyond imagination. This was not of our doing, but came from the strength of the peasants. This kind of strength caused us to believe firmly that if only we could arouse, organize, and arm the peasants, the victory would be assured.

On November 3, the day Batista held the rigged general elections, Law Number 3 of the Sierra Maestra was proclaimed. It determined the carrying out of the land reform: the free distribution and granting of right of ownership to any sugar cane farmers who did not have over two caballerías of land, to the land held by the state and officials of the dictatorial government, and to the land of those people who by shameless methods forcibly occupied territory sometimes in excess of several thousand caballerías. The land reform has benefited over two hundred thousand peasant households. But still the agrarian revolution enacted in Law Number 3 is not complete. It is necessary in the constitution of the state to stipulate rules opposing the latifundia system, the special characteristic of our agricultural structure. The latifundia system is the cause of the national backwardness and of all the miseries of the peasant masses. This cause has not been eliminated even down to the present.

To thoroughly carry out the law providing for the abolition of the latifundia system will be the concern of the peasant masses them-

[2] Peasants. Eds.

selves. The present state constitution provides for mandatory monetary compensation whenever land is taken away, and land reform under it will be both sluggish and difficult. Now after the victory of the Revolution, the peasants who have achieved their freedom must rise up in collective action and democratically demand the abolition of the latifundia system and the carrying out of a true and extensive land reform.

REPORTER: What problems does the Cuban Revolution now face, and what are its current responsibilities?

GUEVARA: The first difficulty is that our new actions must be accomplished on the old foundations. Cuba's antipeople regime and army are already destroyed, but the dictatorial social system and economic foundations have not yet been abolished. Some of the old people are still working within the national structure. In order to protect the fruits of the revolutionary victory and to enable the unending development of the Revolution, we need to take another step forward in our work to rectify and strengthen the government. Second, what the new government took over was a rundown mess. When Batista fled, he cleaned out the national treasury, leaving serious difficulties in the national finances. We must work very hard in order to keep intact the balance of foreign exchange, otherwise our national currency will be depreciated. Third, Cuba's land system is one in which latifundistas hold large amounts of land, while at the same time many people are unemployed. We cannot process our underground ore reserves ourselves, but must depend on foreign companies to ship the reserves abroad for processing. Ours is a monocultural economy in which it is essential for us to grow sugar cane. Our foreign trade is also monocultural. The United States controls Cuban trade; consequently, national industries are smothered because of United States competition. Smuggling is very serious. Commodity prices are very high. Fourth, there is still racial discrimination in our society which is not beneficial to efforts to achieve the internal unification of the people. Fifth, our house rents are the highest in the world; a family frequently has to pay over a third of its income for rent. To sum up, the reform of the foundations of the economy of the Cuban society is very difficult and will take a long time.

In establishing the order of society and in democratizing national life, the new government has adopted many positive measures. We have exerted great effort to restore the national economy. For example, the government has passed a law lowering rents by 50 percent. Yesterday a law regulating beaches was passed to cancel the privileges of a small number of people who occupy the land and the seashores. The price of real estate has fallen from the previous one thousand per square meter to four hundred pesos, and the income from the sales goes as an investment for the collective advantage of the country. When the government took control of the buildings and real estate of the old officials, and subsequently gave it to the people, this alone accounted for an immediate income of over twenty million pesos. Smuggling has already been cut off for all practical purposes, to the great benefit of this country's national industries and above all to the development of the tobacco and cotton cloth industries.

Other fundamental laws are now being enacted. Most important is the land reform law, which will soon be promulgated. Moreover, we will found a National Land Reform Institute. Our land reform here is not yet very penetrating; it is not as thorough as the one in China. Yet it must be considered the most progressive in Latin America.

When we propose land reform and enact revolutionary laws in order to achieve this goal quickly, we consider especially the redistribution of the land, the establishment of a vast national market, and the realization of a diversified economy. This is where the interest of the people is. As far as the land reform at the present time is concerned, the most important thing is the promotion of sugar cane production and efforts to improve production techniques. Second is to make it possible for the cultivator to have his own fields, to encourage the opening up of virgin lands, and to cultivate all cultivable land. Third is to fix output, to raise production and to decrease the import of food grains (the present import of food grains each year takes fifty million pesos in foreign exchange). Fourth is to establish people's coffee and tobacco stores, to fix reasonable prices, and to eliminate middle exploitation. Fifth is to promote animal husbandry.

We must work for national industrialization without neglecting any of the problems that arise therefrom. Industrialization requires the adoption of protective measures for new industries, and an internal market of consumers for the new products. For instance, if we do not open the main door of the market to the *guajiros* who have consumer needs but no buying power, there is no way to expand the internal market.

Events do not entirely depend on us; we will meet with the opposition of the people who control over 75 percent of our national trade. Facing this kind of danger, we must prepare to adopt countermeasures, like a doubly enlarged foreign market. We will need to establish a merchant marine fleet to transport sugar, tobacco, and other products, because transportation expenses of a merchant marine fleet in a large degree affect the progress of backward nations like Cuba.

What is the most important thing if we want to carry out our industrialization successfully? It is raw materials. Because of Batista's dictatorial government, the country's raw materials are all delivered over to the hands of his foreign coplotters. We cannot fail to redeem our country's raw materials, our ore reserves. Another element of industrialization is electric power. We pledge that electrical power will be returned to the people.

Where is our power to achieve the above-mentioned plan? We have a Rebel Army. We must quickly train the worker-peasant military units, arm them with modern techniques and doctrine, and make them able to shoulder the even greater responsibility of courageously killing the enemy. National regeneration will require the destruction of many privileges. For this reason we must immediately prepare to strike a blow against our disguised or open enemies in defense of the country. The new army must become a new style of army, formed in the fight for liberation, changed into a people's army, producing on the one hand and training on the other. This is necessary because we know that if a small country were to commit aggression against us, it would have the support of a large, strong country. At such a time we would have to resist large-scale aggression in our own territory. Thus we must prepare early.

REPORTER: How will Cuba struggle against domestic and foreign reactionary enemies? What are the prospects of the Revolution?

GUEVARA: The Cuban Revolution is not a class revolution, but a liberation movement that has overthrown a dictatorial, tyrannical government. The people detested the American-supported Batista dictatorial government from the bottoms of their hearts and so rose up and overthrew it. The revolutionary government has received the broad support of all strata of people because its economic measures have taken care of the requirements of all and have gradually improved the livelihood of the people. The only enemies remaining in the country are the latifundistas and the reactionary bourgeoisie. They oppose the land reform that goes against their own interests. These internal reactionary forces may get in league with the developing provocations of the foreign reactionary forces and attack the revolutionary government.

The only foreign enemies who oppose the Cuban Revolution are the people who monopolize capital and who have representatives in the United States Department of State. The victory and continuous development of the Cuban Revolution has caused these people to panic. They do not willingly accept defeat and are doing everything possible to maintain their control over the Cuban government and economy and to block the great influence of the Cuban Revolution on the people's struggles in the other Latin American countries.

I would like to take this opportunity to talk a little about the influence of the victory of the Cuban Revolution on the people of the other countries of Latin America. Today the Cuban people have all stood up to carry forward the fight. The Cuban people will retain their unity in order to prevent any miscarriage of the victory they achieved in overthrowing the dictatorial government and to make this victory the first step in the victory of all of Latin America. Our Revolution has set an example for every other country in Latin America. The experience and lessons of our Revolution have caused the mere talk of the coffee houses to be dispersed like smoke. We have proved that an uprising can begin even when there is only a small group of fearless men with a resolute will; that it is only necessary to gain the support of the people who can compete with, and in the end defeat, the regular disciplined army of the government. It is also necessary to carry out a land reform. This is another experience that our Latin American brothers ought to absorb. On the economic front and in agricultural structure they are at the same stage as we are.

The future of every economically underdeveloped country in Latin America is closely connected with our own future. The Revolution is not limited to Cuba. It has stimulated the heart of Latin America and has made the mutual enemies of the peoples of the various countries very nervous. The Cuban example has already penetrated deeply into the people's hearts in all of Latin America and in every oppressed country and signals the imminent downfall of all the Latin American dictators. Cuba is a small country and needs the support of the people of every country, every socialist country, and especially of every Latin American country.

We still must open up roads to get all of our underdeveloped countries to unite. We must at all times keep vigilance against the efforts to divide and rule and struggle to the end against those people who think of sowing seeds of discord among us. Such people only want to injure our country and to reap benefit for themselves from discord in our government.

The present indications are very clear that they are now preparing to intervene in Cuba and destroy the Cuban Revolution. The evil foreign enemies have an old method. They first begin a political offensive, propagandizing widely and saying that the Cuban people oppose communism. These false democratic leaders say that the United States cannot allow a communist country on its coastline. At the same time they intensify their economic attack and cause Cuba to fall into economic difficulties. Later they will look for a pretext to create some kind of dispute and then utilize certain international organizations they control to carry out intervention against the Cuban people. We do not have to fear an attack from some small neighboring dictatorial country, but from a certain large country, using certain international organizations, and a certain kind of pretext in order to intervene and undermine the Cuban Revolution.

But the Cuban Revolution is not a movement of a small number of people or of just a few leaders. Our Revolution is a liberation movement of the people; the people are the power behind this revolutionary movement. The present strength of the united people forces the enemy to put off his intervention. We will try to devise ways to avoid the plot of the enemy and to expose the conspiracy which aims at promoting conflicts, thus depriving the enemy of his opportunity to act.

I do not doubt that the American people are in sympathy with the Cuban Revolution. The American people can become good friends with the Cuban people. The American people will understand much better the dangerous nature of the policy of the United States government.

Interview by
Telemundo Television

⊓⊔⊓⊔⊓⊔⊓⊔⊓⊔⊓⊔⊓⊔⊓⊔⊓⊔⊓⊔⊓⊔⊓⊔⊓⊔⊓⊔

Q: Are you a communist?

A: I have been asked that question very often and I do not have to answer it because the facts speak for themselves. If you think that what we do for the people is communism, then we are communists; if you ask me if I am a member of the Partido Socialista Popular, then I would answer no.

Q: Why did you come to Cuba to fight against the Batista dictatorship if you are not a Cuban?

A: There are no differences between the countries of Latin America. I only wanted to liberate a piece of our oppressed America. I saw how democracy was destroyed in Guatemala and when I met Fidel in Mexico I thought that it was my duty to come with him to destroy a dictatorship.

Q: Do you think there is a dictatorship in Russia?

A: Yes, there is a dictatorship in the Soviet Union, even the Russians speak of the "dictatorship of the proletariat."

Q: Would you go to Russia to fight against that dictatorship?

A: Russia is not in the Americas, it is to be found in another continent and it has different customs and its racial integration is different from ours; therefore I would not engage in such an enterprise just as I would not go to the United States to defend the Negroes who are so mistreated.

Q: What would you do if a communist coup takes place in Cuba? Would you oppose it?

A: I shall probably oppose the "putsch" before anyone else but I do not think that will happen simply because they have a political party that is capable of working honestly with other parties and cooperating with the Revolution. A coup would be a surprise for me. I believe that they will not try to overthrow the revolutionary government because they are revolutionaries themselves. I seek unity. I would feel very badly if that ever occurred and I would defend the revolutionary government.

Guevara was interviewed on the television program *Telemundo Pregunta* on April 28, 1959, by a panel of reporters. *Revolución* (Havana), April 29, 1959, pp. 1, 13, and *El Mundo* (Havana), April 29, 1959, pp. 1, A8.

Q: Is the communist ideology incompatible with our national identity?

A: I do not think so.

Q: How many communists have infiltrated the government?

A: I have not made a census. For many people, everyone that thinks as I do is a communist. If that is the measurement to be used, the absolute majority of the government is communist. If we define as communist anyone that has the courage to defend his ideas, many are communist, but members of the PSP, only a few. In the Rebel Army I know of only three communists.

Q: Are you in favor of establishing diplomatic relations with the Soviet Union?

A: I am in favor of establishing diplomatic and commercial relations with all the countries of the world, and I see no reason why some countries should be excluded if they respect us and hope that we can bring about our ideals. We have relations with Trujillo and Somoza who are our declared enemies; why not with our friends?

Q: What has been Cuba's role in the invasion of Panama? [1]

A: The Revolution has to be honest above everything else, that is why it is sad to admit that Cubans participated. But they did so without our authorization. We export revolutionary ideas; we cannot export revolution. Only those who have no freedom should fight for freedom. We are only an example, everything must be done by the people themselves.

Q: What are your impressions on Dr. Fidel Castro's trip to the United States and the future relations between the United States and Cuba?

A: We shall talk with the United States on an equal basis with all the consideration that an honorable nation has toward another.

Sadly, I have very few reports on Fidel's visit to the United States. Besides what is published by Cuban papers, much of what we read comes from North American news agencies. With regard to the stand of the North American government, I would have to talk with our chief in order to give you an authorized opinion. With regard to the position taken by the North American people—as everyone knows—it has been one of warm reception.

Q: What is ahead with respect to the agrarian reform?

A: Agrarian reform had been the constant passion of the movement during the years of insurrection; during the last four months of peaceful struggle it has continued to be our passion. We shall fulfill

[1] A number of Cubans invaded Panama in June 1959; all of them were captured by the authorities of that government and it was believed that Cuba was behind the rebels. Eds.

the section of the Fundamental Law [2] that proscribes latifundia. It hurts to see large uncultivated expanses of land while some people go hungry and lack work.

Our case will be very different from that of Russia. There the state owns all the land, here we will give the land to those who work it. If the peasants want to sell the land, the state has priority over buying it.

We are also contemplating the creation of cooperatives. The government will give preference to technical and credit aid and will assure the markets for production. We will create as many cooperatives as our capital and technical resources allow. We cannot go beyond that point. It is necessary to teach the peasant the importance of cooperativism.

Technological and agricultural schools will be created. Our objective is the production of the greatest amount of goods at the lowest cost possible. We shall teach the peasant that the days of the plow and of personal work or the work of small family groups have ended.

Our orientation plan for the peasantry will be persuasive and not compulsive. We shall give him all possible technical guidance and offer him a way of selling what he has produced; but we shall not force him to accept any of these. We want to materialize the very old aspiration of having a piece of land the peasantry can call their own. We have to demonstrate that this is a serious agrarian reform, a recognition that they own the land because they work it. It is necessary to introduce technology into our agricultural production. In Santo Domingo, for instance, tobacco production per acre is twice as much as that of Cuba. The same occurs with sugar production, but if technology is introduced in this sector we shall have unemployment. The immediate and fundamental task of the Revolution is not to rescue the land used for sugar production, but rather to take the thousands of acres that are uncultivated by "poor" landowners. We cannot produce displacements if we do not offer other honest jobs; therefore, we cannot hurry on this aspect.

Q: How much did you know about Cuban agriculture when you landed in Cuba?

A: I did not know it, nor did I smoke cigars then.

Q: What is the role of the Rebel Army now?

A: It must be pointed out that although the only leader of the Revolution is Fidel Castro, the Rebel Army has great duties with the people.

[2] In 1959 the Fundamental Law was decreed by the revolutionary government; in many respects, it was a carbon copy of the 1940 Constitution. Eds.

We consider ourselves faithful interpreters of the popular will when we are right. The Rebel Army is going to be a political army because it has not been paid by anyone to defend an unjust cause. It is a people's army that created itself, moved by a revolutionary ideal. That is why it will march with the workers, the peasants, and the students on May 1. The Rebel Army has to be with the people.

The Rebel Army was born with very vague social ideas; it was a liberation army, a follower of Martí, integrated by men from the cities who had an erroneous conception of the countryside. We found vigorous support among the peasants and we became acquainted with their problems and captured the ferment that existed among them to rid themselves of old property ties. All of these made us change and shaped our social ideas. The leaders and the people have influenced each other. Indeed, this revolutionary movement is no different from any other because the people are always ready to learn everything that is taught to them. The people are always ready to defend just causes.

Q: Should the name of the Rebel Army not be changed so that it would reflect more appropriately the present situation?

A: We called the army "rebel" in the Sierra Maestra and the ideas for which it fought are the same today. We are still in a process of struggle, for we have not reached our definitive victory.

Q: Why are the people armed? Was it not Fidel Castro who said once, "Arms, what for?"

A: The arms we have are to defend the Revolution; all our enemies will know that if we are attacked, the Rebel Army and the people will fight them.

Q: Are you in favor of compulsory military service?

A: We have voluntary military service. The people have asked for arms to defend their freedom.

Q: Is it true that Ernesto de la Fé and Juan Luis Martín are in prison merely for being newspapermen?

A: When we took over the files of the repressive forces of the dictatorship, we found a plan made by Juan Luis Martín to completely liquidate freedom of the press in Cuba. He acknowledged its authorship. It is not a grave crime; it is a minor crime, but alien to his condition of newspaperman. With regard to Ernesto de la Fé, this man was in charge of BRAC.[3] There is no relationship between his condition as a newspaperman and his plan to assassinate Fidel

---

[3] Buró de Represión de Actividades Comunistas, a bureau to repress communist activities but used against anyone who opposed the dictatorship. Eds.

Castro. It is not a new plan, it was made a year ago. Besides, you know very well that he was Batista's minister of propaganda.

Our enemies are trying to divide us. But our people are united even though many efforts have been made to create division within our ranks. There is unity in the labor movement and as long as this cohesive force supports the leadership of Fidel Castro and the 26th of July Movement there will be no division. The argument of communism has been used to foster division. Raúl Castro, Alfredo Guevara,[4] and myself are accused of being communists, but our people are reacting in a positive manner. The unity of all social classes will destroy those intrigues.

Q: How did the press behave during the dictatorship?

A: You get me into quite some problems! But I shall answer you honestly—the press took very weak stands. I do not call it betrayal but weakness. As you said once, there were a number of alternatives: the mountains, sabotage in the cities, or not writing. It is sad that newspapermen can only say what the government wants; but many had very good positions. They spoke here and received a government check there.

Q: Are you referring to a list of *botelleros*[5] on which my name appears?

A: I do not personalize. I am not referring to anyone in particular, but if you want I can inform you on the matter after May 1.

Q: I hope you will do so publicly.

A: I shall do so if that is your wish.

Q: Can the Revolution improve the well-being of everyone?

A: To pretend to make a revolution that would improve every social class is impossible. The Cuban Revolution wants to distribute more evenly the wealth of the republic. If a rich man invests his money he will have no problem. There are three types of rich men: the one that lives off rents from apartment buildings and bonds; the ones that invests with foreigners and steals land in alliance with public forces; and the one who makes slaves out of peasants. Those three types of rich men will be hurt but they amount to 10,000 and on the other side we have 6 million Cubans.

We shall give guarantees to the investor. We are hungry for capital but we do not want capitalists who are too hungry. We call on the capitalists so that they will make a logical profit and then will leave behind a factory or an agricultural unit.

[4] A member of the Cuban Communist Party prior to the revolutionary seizure of power and director of the film institute of Cuba. Eds.

[5] Persons receiving sinecures from the Batista government. Eds.

Q: Many employers are using the argument that it is counter-revolutionary to demand labor improvements at this time. What do you think of that?

A: The workers have an absolute right to economic improvements. The Revolution should not be used as an argument by employers, but certain labor demands are indeed excessive. If all the demands were fulfilled, prices would increase.

Q: Who supports the Revolution?

A: The revolutionary government has two essential allies: the peasants and the workers. It is a mistake to think that a Revolution benefits all social classes, but we are not going to attack the rich; instead, we will regulate the relationship that exists between employer and employees. The rich who have inherited their wealth and have large landholdings do not have much of a chance, these will feel the weight of the Revolution. The foreign rich who invested from abroad and stole land with the consent of the state will also be hurt by the Revolution.

Q: What is the government's position on a Latin American Common Market?

A: We have a very little and difficult problem: the United States. They have always boycotted it. We cannot compete with them commercially but I believe we can make of Cuba a socially just nation and economically powerful without that common market; with a common market it would be even more so.

Q: The Inter-American Bank has begun operations with the capital deposited by twenty-one republics....[6]

A: That is a neat plan but if every dollar deposited gives a country so many votes in the Bank, then that institution becomes a corporation where naturally the United States has the last word. To believe something else is to fool oneself. Nothing will come of it. We have to break away from our economic dependence. We cannot continue to sell them 75 percent of our products; Martí said so.

Q: When will elections be held?

A: Elections will be held at the appropriate time; now the people want revolution first and elections later.

Q: Would you run for any electoral post?

A: I have no electoral appetite; if I ever run it will be because the 26th of July Movement wants me to; but I will never renounce my olive green uniform. I will only put it away temporarily.

Q: What would you consider a democracy?

[6] Original text appears edited. Eds.

A: A system where the majority enjoys as much freedom as possible; but there are a number of limitations to absolute freedom and these limitations should be carried by all of the people.

Q: How is your health?

A: I feel very good. But for twenty-nine years I have had a companion: asthma. Sometimes she gets angry but now we are on pretty good terms.

Interview with
Laura Bergquist (#1)

ᴸᴸᴸᴸᴸᴸᴸᴸᴸᴸᴸᴸᴸᴸᴸᴸᴸᴸᴸᴸᴸᴸᴸᴸ

BERGQUIST: Months back, there were predictions that Cuba would follow a "neutralist" policy of playing one power bloc off against another, without aligning with either. But more and more, you are linked economically, perhaps militarily, with the Soviet bloc. Aren't you just exchanging so-called U.S. dominance for Soviet?

GUEVARA: It is naïve to think that men who carried through a revolution of liberation such as ours, independently, did so to kneel before any master. If the Soviet Union had just once demanded political dependence as a condition for its aid, our relations would have ceased at that moment. If we maintain increasingly cordial relations with the Socialist bloc, it is because the word "submission" has never arisen.

BERGQUIST: An Australian newspaper quoted you as saying Cuba would "resist to the last drop of blood any Soviet attempt to establish a Communist satellite in Cuba." At what point does Cuba become a satellite?

GUEVARA: That reporter questioned me about a hypothetical aggression by the Soviet Union against Cuba. I wish to affirm I do not believe this possible. At the recent meeting of the Organization of American States, Peru introduced a motion against "extracontinental intervention" in this hemisphere, after receiving alms—or the promise of a small loan—from the U.S. Other countries accused a small sister nation of being a "spearhead" for Soviet penetration, without mentioning Cuba. Is this not "satellitism"? At least we have removed ourselves from the orbit of this northern "guiding star." A country becomes a satellite perhaps when its economy is dominated, its political decisions are influenced by orders from "above," and it belongs to a system aimed at maintaining the privileges of the most powerful country.

BERGQUIST: You've said Cuba suffers from a "guerrilla" complex. What is this?

GUEVARA: A tendency in many government functionaries to go on acting independently, as if they were still engaged in a guerrilla war and had complete freedom of action, taking orders only from the top chief. In short, a lack of coordination.

BERGQUIST: The Revolution, you've said, has made many "mistakes." What are they?

GUEVARA: They are errors to be expected in any revolution run by young men, lacking technicians and technique. Much money has been spent, not always wisely. There has been duplication of effort in various government agencies. Many leisure-loving officials have been permitted to continue in office. The government has been lenient in allowing its political enemies to stay on in high posts. But it is our sincere belief that our errors have been fewer and of lesser magnitude than our accomplishments.

BERGQUIST: Hitler smeared opponents of all political persuasions by calling them "Communists." Aren't you doing likewise by branding honest dissenters from the regime as "counterrevolutionaries" —equating a distinguished jurist like José Miró Cardona [one-time premier under Castro, who defected in July 1960] with Rolando Masferrer [a Batista chief, whose private army terrorized Oriente Province]?

GUEVARA: The "distinguished jurist" of whom you speak took refuge in the Argentine Embassy without anyone's having pursued him. Believe me, sooner or later, he will follow the line of Masferrer or Luis Conté Agüero [T.V. commentator and Castro biographer, who defected in April]. Conté Agüero has already stated in Miami that the "good" and "less bad" among anti-Castro elements must unite. As time goes on, the definition of "less bad" will grow steadily less rigid.

BERGQUIST: You've said the Cuban Revolution is not "exportable," because revolutions happen only in countries ripe for them. How many Latin American nations are "ripe"?

GUEVARA: More than your Department of State believes.

BERGQUIST: You protest other nations' meddling in Cuba's internal affairs. But aren't you doing just that when Castro talks of turning the Andes into the Sierra Maestra of Latin America and when you openly attack Venezuela's President Romulo Betancourt as a "prisoner of a so-called democratic regime," who should have sent members of the old regime to "the wall" [firing squad]?

GUEVARA: I was speaking before a congress of youth from many countries when I said this, and under those conditions, we can say what we choose. It was no "open" attack on Betancourt, but rather manifested our sympathy for the difficult political situation that confronts him. We haven't accused the U.S. of meddling in

Cuban affairs for *saying* our regime is of such and such a type. We do accuse it of interfering when it tells what kind of government we should have here. In Cuba, we have a government the people wish, and it's this wish we demand be respected.

BERGQUIST: Are you, as often described, the economic and social master planner of the Cuban Revolution and its "brain"?

GUEVARA: In one article that called me a "brain," my present wife was defamed as well as my first, and there were very big errors in information. Every kind of defamation has been hurled against members of the revolutionary government. Now, the corrupt U.S. press is trying to create a division in our ranks. The tactic is to advise the Leader that he is not the "brain," but someone else is, in hopes the Leader will cut his throat. Among men who have defied death shoulder to shoulder, pursuing a common ideal, this is so stupid it deserves no further comment. If anyone doubts that Fidel Castro is the Leader of this Revolution, let him come to Cuba.

BERGQUIST: I've heard you called a doctrinaire Communist and a "pragmatic revolutionary" who has learned lessons from other revolutions. What are your politics?

GUEVARA: You use the phrase "pragmatic revolutionary," and I like it. Consider that my answer. I am of a practical turn of mind. I speculate little and do not characterize myself as a theorist. I myself have been in Guatemala, Bolivia, and Mexico, and in actual study of conditions in various countries. You learn more than anything else how to avoid error. Where one really learns is in a revolutionary war; every minute teaches you more than a million volumes of books. You mature in the extraordinary university of experience. When our war began in 1956, our object was to overthrow Batista's tyranny. Cuba was an army barracks, and this caste responded to the most reactionary class of our nation, the big landlords, the parasitical capitalists, who in turn were chained to foreign colonialism. It was not enough, we found, to overthrow one man; the Revolution had to dig out the deepest roots of the evil that had taken hold of Cuba. Now our object is economic independence, as a steppingstone toward full national sovereignty.

BERGQUIST: In a *Look* interview published in the February 5, 1958, issue, Fidel Castro promised, if victorious, to establish a provisional government elected by Cuban civic bodies and hold free elections within a year. He also said, "Our 26th of July movement has never called for the nationalizing of foreign investments." Wasn't that just campaign oratory to win U.S. support?

GUEVARA: I do not remember the interview, but times are different.

It is not always possible to do what one says or wishes to do.

BERGQUIST: In jest, you once said, "Raúl Castro and I have the honor of being among the most shocking persons in Cuba." What did you mean?

GUEVARA: I took the phrase from a book by Josephus Daniels, ex-U.S. ambassador to Mexico. He told the story of an English oil magnate who, in trying to define what a Communist is, decided it is a "shocking person." Since Raúl and I greatly shock the monopolists, we've earned that name.

BERGQUIST: What changes lie ahead?

GUEVARA: What lies ahead depends greatly on the United States. With the exception of our agrarian reform, which the peoples of Cuba desired and initiated themselves, all of our radical measures have been a direct response to direct aggressions by powerful monopolists, of which your country is the chief exponent. U.S. pressure on Cuba has made necessary the "radicalization" of the Revolution. To know how much further Cuba will go, it will be easier to ask the U.S. government how far it plans to go.

Interview with
Maurice Zeitlin

ZEITLIN: Do you think that relations based on friendship and equality are still possible between the governments of Cuba and of the United States?

GUEVARA: There is no point in asking this question because Cuba has always been willing to speak with the U.S. on a basis of friendship and equality. But the U.S. apparently views our every offer to negotiate as if it were a sign of weakness rather than of a genuine desire for good relations. We do not offer to negotiate because of any weakness, but only because we desire the best possible relations with your country. Cuba asks only that the negotiations take place with no preimposed conditions.

ZEITLIN: What steps would the U.S. have to take to regain Cuba's trust?

GUEVARA: It is not a question of what the U.S. should do, but rather of what it should not do: direct aggression, blockade, sabotage, diplomatic maneuvers against us throughout Latin America, and confiscations of Cuban property—such as airplanes and ships—in North American territory.

ZEITLIN: Would Cuba be willing to discuss again the possibility of some form of long-range compensation for expropriated U.S. property?

GUEVARA: Yes, absolutely. The law has established it. The Cuban government is absolutely willing to pay as the law has established: a fund for purposes of compensation would be established from 25 percent of the value of yearly sugar sales to the U.S. over 3,000,000 tons. And we are also willing to discuss other means of compensation. But before the Cuban government can talk about this, there must be assurance that no previous conditions are imposed upon the negotiations—which must be held on the basis of absolute equality.

ZEITLIN: What is your opinion of "neutralism"?

Reprinted from Robert Scheer and Maurice Zeitlin, *Cuba: An American Tragedy* (Harmondsworth, Middlesex, England: Penguin Books), 1964, pp. 337–346, by permission of the authors and the publisher. This interview originally appeared in *Root and Branch: A Radical Quarterly*, vol. 1, no. 1 (January 1962), pp. 50–56.

GUEVARA: Neutralism is a position of more or less "equidistance." We are neutrals in the sense that we are not attached to any group, and we are not belligerents. But unfortunately, the U.S. is at war with Cuba, and for that reason whatever is bad for the U.S. is— at the moment—good for Cuba.

ZEITLIN: Do you think that Cuba can play a more constructive historical role by remaining independent in her foreign policy, criticizing or agreeing with policies irrespective of whichever bloc carries them out?

GUEVARA: Cuba has the right to live her own life and to follow the course which seems best to her. This does not mean, however, that Cuba maintains an absolute equality of opinion of the actions of both blocs. Cuba has won the right to be able to choose what she considers good. Personally, I see in the actions of the Soviet Union many things that are good for Cuba, while I see many things that are bad in the actions of the U.S. Therefore, Cuba cannot remain absolutely equidistant, although she is neutral.

ZEITLIN: One of the most distressing things I witnessed here was the unanimous and unquestioning acclaim with which the press greeted the Soviet Union's resumption of nuclear testing. Those of us who are active in the peace movement in the U.S. view the Soviet Union's resumption of tests leading possibly to increased tensions, and to a heightening of the arms race—not to speak of the fallout hazards to mankind created by the renewed testing. What is your opinion of the Soviet Union's resumption of testing?

GUEVARA: I am also very enthusiastic—because I sincerely believe that the Soviet Union wants peace, and that the reason the U.S. has not unleashed war is out of fear that it would lose it. Further, tests are necessary for perfecting new devices. The U.S. has its devices ready for explosion underground, and if the Soviet Union should fall behind, the U.S. would start a war leaving the Soviet Union in a dangerously vulnerable position. Of course, our only guarantee of peace is that there be no war. Only if there is complete disarmament can there be peace that is lasting. But since this is apparently not to be achieved immediately, precautions have to be taken—up to a certain point, so that the precautions themselves do not endanger peace. The ideal is no tests and no war.

ZEITLIN: But the arguments you give in favor of the resumption of tests by the Soviet Union are precisely the same ones used in the U.S. by militarists and right-wingers who want to maintain the Cold War, and who favor the resumption of nuclear tests by the U.S.

GUEVARA: Yes.

ZEITLIN: Yes. And it is just such arguments which the peace movement has to counter—because testing, and other such belligerent acts have a snowball effect, and can lead mankind into a holocaust from which none will return.

GUEVARA: Yes, but the arguments you have been making no longer appear brilliant, given the situation. It is frequently the case that each side in a conflict tries to place the blame for the conflict on the other. But one side is more right than the other.

An American friend was here speaking to me and lamenting the armed attack on Cuba; he based this on grounds of justice—that the revolution is just and pure and a good thing. I told him that this is not a good reason [for the U.S. not to attack Cuba]; rather, it is out of self-interest—out of fear of self-destruction, that the U.S. must not attack us.

ZEITLIN: Do you actually believe that the Soviet Union would plunge the world into a nuclear war simply to defend Cuba's revolution—little Cuba which is right next door to the U.S.?

GUEVARA: It does not make any difference what I believe; the important thing is that the Pentagon and State Department know what risk they are taking.

ZEITLIN: If the Soviet Union, which has pledged to defend you, really meant it, then why did it not attack the U.S. when the invasion of April 17 took place?

GUEVARA: Because we stopped them on the eighteenth.

ZEITLIN: Cuba's revolution has impressed people throughout the world, of widely different political and social outlooks, because of its democratic and humanist content, and its experimentation and pragmatism.

Cuba is now entering a period, apparently, in which her more or less permanent institutions will be formed. What institutions does the revolutionary government intend to establish—understanding that it still faces external and internal threats—so as to guarantee that competing points of view can be heard within the revolutionary consensus?

GUEVARA: It all depends on what you mean by a competition of ideas. When it comes to a question of interpretation of a moment of the revolution, its different tasks, and the velocity with which the revolution should be carried out—there is complete liberty to discuss that. But if you mean a parliamentary or party system in which laws may be hamstrung because they benefit the people, and the laws be discussed by the different political parties, no, that will not be allowed.

Life has created two antagonistic positions which cannot be

ignored—the revolutionary position and the counterrevolutionary position. Our task is to enlarge, as much as is possible, democracy within the revolution, and to liquidate the counterrevolution as soon as possible. As you have well said, we are pragmatic. Where our revolution will lead, what new institutions we will create, we cannot know now.

ZEITLIN: What ideas do you have as to how Cuba will assure that the people will be given meaningful alternatives between which to choose—to assure that the people will participate fully in their society, not merely as passive participants or manipulated onlookers, but as the initiators and executors of policies and programs? How, in short, will the masses be able to inject their own alternatives into the social mainstream?

GUEVARA: We cannot know now. We feel that the government's chief function is to assure channels for the expression of the popular will. What forms this will take, we cannot say yet. That will depend on the political system to be elaborated.

ZEITLIN: Have you ever considered the possibility of a representative political system based on delegates elected from the cooperatives, *granjas del pueblo*, small farmers' organizations, the unions, the university, factory committees, professional associations, regional groupings—so as to encourage the development of autonomous centers of power and initiative?

GUEVARA: Yes. We have thought about many things, done some things, but decided nothing.

ZEITLIN: When the new party is formed of the three existing revolutionary organizations now in the ORI [Integrated Revolutionary Organizations], will they retain their independent organizations, press, officers—or be expected to dissolve and join as individuals? Is the Communist Party going to have to dissolve its apparatus?

GUEVARA: No independence—nothing! One of the newspapers will be the party newspaper, maybe two of them. And these will represent not merely the views of the party but also of the government.

ZEITLIN: How will other radical tendencies—organizations other than the Revolutionary Directorate, the Communist Party, and the 26th of July, whose members will unite in the new party—be included. What about the Trotskyists, for example? Carleton Beals pointed out recently that their press here had been smashed and they were unable to complete printing copies of Trotsky's "The Permanent Revolution."

GUEVARA: That did happen. It was an error. It was an error committed by a functionary of second rank. They smashed the plates. It should not have been done.

However, we consider the Trotskyist party to be acting against the revolution. For example, they were taking the line that the revolutionary government is petty bourgeois, and were calling on the proletariat to exert pressure on the government, and even to carry out another revolution in which the proletariat would come to power. This was prejudicing the discipline necessary at this time.

ZEITLIN: You might be interested in knowing that the Trotskyists in the U.S. have been almost completely behind the Cuban Revolution, and their recent official statement on the revolution is enthusiastically approving.

GUEVARA: I do not have any opinions about Trotskyists in general. But here in Cuba—let me give an example. They have one of their principal centers in the town of Guantánamo near the U.S. base. And they agitated there for the Cuban people to march on the base —something that cannot be permitted. Something else. Some time ago when we had just created the workers' technical committees, the Trotskyists characterized them as a crumb given to the workers because the workers were calling for the direction of the factories. Several people have asked me the same question [about the Trotskyists]—but it is a problem I regard as small. They have very few members in Cuba.

ZEITLIN: The reason is not because we are specifically interested in the Trotskyists—I am hardly one—but because how they are treated is probably as good an index as any of how different political tendencies within the revolution will be treated, especially groups who differ with the Communist Party, which has always had a particular animosity for the Trotskyists, labeling anyone who disagrees with them as Trotskyists—or worse.

GUEVARA: You cannot be for the revolution and be against the Cuban Communist Party. The Revolution and the Communist Party march together. The Trotskyists say that they are against "Stalinism." But in the [1959] general strike, for instance, the Trotskyists refused to cooperate with the Communist Party.

ZEITLIN: The new party is to be based on democratic centralism, according to a little pamphlet I just read by someone named Segundino Guerra, and is to be Leninist in political outlook as well. Why? Is not Leninism irrelevant to the Cuban revolution? Perhaps if you were still trying to take power it might be relevant, but what has it got to do with Cuban traditions, with the revolution, with a government in power?

GUEVARA: What do you mean by democratic centralism? Perhaps I have a different idea of it than you have. Democratic centralism is a method of government, not only a method of conquering power.

For example, it is closely related to the Soviet system in which regional organizations have the authority to discuss measures, and their decisions are communicated through ascending organizations to the top. Democratic centralism has great importance in economic planning.

ZEITLIN: But, according to this pamphlet, factions are not going to be allowed in the new party. Will that not lead to the squashing of dissent by those in power—who monopolize the money, means of communication, in fact, the power of the state?

GUEVARA: No. Because factionalism is not the same thing as dissent. It is too bad you cannot attend the Cabinet meetings and see the wide differences expressed. What is to be condemned is that after free discussion and a majority decision, a defeated minority works outside of, and against, the party—as Trotsky did, for example. To do so is counterrevolutionary.

ZEITLIN: But it was precisely Trotsky's great tragedy that he too accepted democratic centralism, and accepted the Party as the embodiment of wisdom, and did not, therefore, struggle for his views outside the Party, nor try to organize in his defense . . . until after the expulsion from the Soviet Union.

GUEVARA: You read another version.

ZEITLIN: And it was by labeling all who disagreed with the prevailing line of the party, or who challenged the power of Stalin, "counterrevolutionaries," or by accusing them of "factionalism," that the worst aspects of Soviet politics emerged, that any genuine debate about alternative policies was completely emasculated.

GUEVARA: I prefer not to discuss the internal politics of the Soviet Union.

ZEITLIN: Everywhere one goes in Cuba, especially in Havana, there are signs with quotations from Lenin and Mao, and perhaps one from Fidel, or yourself, Raúl, or José Martí. But Cuba is in the Western hemisphere—in America. And Cuba is proud of claiming herself "the first socialist nation in America." Yet there are no signs quoting Eugene Debs, or Keir Hardie—nor even Rosa Luxembourg.

GUEVARA: Unfortunately, the people know a lot about Fidel, and a little about Raúl and Martí and me. But since they never heard of Eugene Debs or Rosa Luxembourg, they would merely ask who they are.

ZEITLIN: So? That is precisely the point. The people should know who Rosa Luxembourg was.

GUEVARA: Yes, why not. She was a great revolutionary, and she died a revolutionary, as a consequence of her political mistakes.

ZEITLIN: Many of the criticisms I have tried to make of democratic centralism, or should I say the questions I've raised about it, were made by Rosa Luxembourg, and most severely in her criticism of Leninist theory.

GUEVARA: Yes. Well, I am not accustomed to discussing theory. I try to be pragmatic. Sometimes we theorize about Cuba, sometimes about Latin America, but we never go as far as to theorize about the world:

ZEITLIN: But now I see for instance that even Fidel—in the first issue of *Cuba Socialista*, which just appeared and which is supposed to be a new theoretical journal dealing with the revolution—says that Cuba must approach its problems in the light of Marxism, something I have never known him to say publicly before, since he was hardly a Marxist.

GUEVARA: We regard Marxism as a science in development, just as, say, biology is a science. One biologist adds to what others have done, while working in his own field. Our specialty is Cuba. In Cuba we base ourselves very severely on the facts.

ZEITLIN: But of what value is Leninism in the Cuban context?

GUEVARA: The value of Lenin is enormous—in the same sense in which a major biologist's work is valuable to other biologists. He is probably the leader who has brought the most to the theory of revolution. He was able to apply Marxism in a given moment to the problems of the state, and to emerge with laws of universal validity. For example? His theory of imperialism, of the state and revolution, of the work of the party through the stages of the revolution, of his studies of the material development of production. As I remember, it is in the final Congress before his death that he had a good deal to say concerning practical methods of development—the electrification and industrialization of the country.

ZEITLIN: According to an article of yours, you view as two fundamental roles of the unions the raising of political and social consciousness, increasing workers' production, and the protection of the immediate interests of the workers. Is that correct?

GUEVARA: No. It is not a fundamental task of the unions to raise the consciousness of the workers. That is the task of ORI. Rather, their two fundamental tasks are to raise the level of production, to aid the government in its development program, and to defend the immediate interests of the workers. I have the article here. Let me read the paragraph in question to you:

The unions have ... two distinct, although complementary, functions in this revolutionary period. One of them is to grasp the idea of the organization and the goals of the Government, to discuss them at the level of the enterprise or factory, whichever it is a question of, so that the ideas will bear fruit among the workers in a spirit which makes them push forward with great impetus. The other is apparently completely opposite, but is not in reality; that is, to defend the specific and immediate interests of the working class at the level of the enterprise or factory. The establishment of a socialist system does not eliminate contradictions (between workers and management) but only modifies the form of their solution.

In another part of the essay I also said that the unions should help raise the level of the working class political and social consciousness, but I do not regard that as one of the two fundamental tasks of the unions.

ZEITLIN: In what specific ways can the workers defend themselves, and protect their interests?

GUEVARA: They have their contracts, their individual unions, their reclamation commissions, and the Cuban Federation of Labor.

ZEITLIN: What about other traditional weapons of the working class?

GUEVARA: What kind?

ZEITLIN: Can the workers strike, if they feel it is necessary?

GUEVARA: I believe yes! We maintain, however, that a strike is a defeat for the government and for the working class. For example, we had a 24-hour strike—which was solved politically as all strikes must be. The strike occurred 14 months ago. Now there are no strikes. But not because our political control has improved, but because of the rapid development of the workers' consciousness.

ZEITLIN: In the factories I visited when I spoke to the workers there, and with the many workers I spoke to on the streets also, they seemed hardly able to understand my question—which I then proceeded to explain at length, citing historical examples—as to how they could protect themselves against their factory bosses and the government, if they had to. They could not see how there could be a conflict between themselves and the government.

GUEVARA: This is the situation exactly. It is impossible for there to be a dispute between the working class, or a union, and the government, that cannot be resolved through discussion. The fact is that the factory to which I referred, in which a strike took place, has a low wage scale. Wages are frozen throughout the nation, and these workers are at a disadvantage. Now our solution has been to revise the wage scale for such work upward so as to make the wages more equitable. The factory is called Cuban Pulp.

ZEITLIN: How does Cuba hope to eliminate the workers' struggle against their work—the natural reaction against and fight against work which is often the workers' only protection. How does that problem become solved under socialism? How, to put it another way, will Cuba eliminate the workers' psychological separation and estrangement from his work which seems basic to contemporary industrial society?

GUEVARA: Automatically. When we arrive at a socialist state, the worker comes to feel the work is his own. What we are trying to do is to assure that the worker gain an understanding of his responsibility at the factory and national level.

ZEITLIN: But what of the plain drudgery that accompanies factory work—that can hardly disappear merely because a revolution has taken place. Look, I just was in a textile factory—one the workers told me you had just worked a day in—and the noise there was terrible, it almost drove me crazy, it just kept on, at a very loud roar. And the workers have to spend their every day in that. They can hardly be expected to learn to love it—whatever their level of understanding.

GUEVARA: That kind of problem is not possible to solve now. Visit the factories even in the U.S. The Czechs have developed a water-driven shuttle that is much quieter than the present ones in our factories. It is very expensive, though, and we cannot afford it. So we cannot bring many in. And most important, our first task is to make jobs for the people.

ZEITLIN: In what concrete ways can the workers control their own work? What have they to say about methods of work, changes in techniques, and such?

GUEVARA: Everything they want.

ZEITLIN: How?

GUEVARA: By way of the workers' technical councils—all the changes in the factory they want to make. Though sometimes—very often— we cannot do what they suggest. For example, the most frequent suggestion from the workers is to install air conditioning—which we cannot afford. At one meeting I attended, a worker from the mines pointed out that they work 8 hours a day in bad health and safety conditions, for low wages—and without air conditioning. He is right. But what can we do? We want to eliminate these things. But I beg a few years of you.

ZEITLIN: What role do the workers have in the actual creation of the national economic plan?

GUEVARA: They take no part in the creation of the first plan. After the first plan has been worked out by the Central Planning Commission, the specific plans are sent to the enterprises, and from there to the factories, and in the factories to the assembly of workers, where the factory plan is discussed. Here the workers discuss the possibilities of the plan for the factory and send the revised plan back up for approval, and it then becomes law. In this way the workers have a voice in the plan of the factory, but not in the national plan. The various plans require prior coordination.

ZEITLIN: What do the workers have to say over investment priorities, over how much will be alloted to the production of consumers' goods, for instance?

GUEVARA: At this moment they have nothing to say. As yet they have not finished erecting the structure—the minimal level of industrialization—to allow that. Moreover, that is a political question. To make such decisions will be the function of a political organization, and for that task, I ask you less time than for the other [that is, the elimination of the discontents and ills of work].

BERGQUIST: Many early Castro supporters certainly did not have today's Marxist-oriented revolution in mind. When you were fighting in the Sierra Maestra mountains, was this the future Cuba you envisioned?

GUEVARA: Yes, though I could not have predicted certain details of development.

BERGQUIST: Could you personally have worked with a government that was leftist but less "radical"—a government that nationalized certain industries, but left areas open for private enterprise and permitted opposition parties?

GUEVARA: Certainly not.

BERGQUIST: Historically, the extreme right and left in Latin America have combined, for different purposes, in an effort to topple "centrist" governments like Romulo Betancourt's in Venezuela. Why does Cuba level more violent attacks at Betancourt than at a dictator like Paraguay's Alfredo Stroessner?

GUEVARA: Paraguay's dictatorship is obvious. Betancourt is a traitor; he has sold out to the imperialists, and his government is as brutal as any dictatorship.

BERGQUIST: But Nasser of Egypt takes help from the "imperialist" West, as well as from the East. Has he "sold out"?

GUEVARA: No, he is a big anti-imperialist. We are friends.

BERGQUIST: You once said that Cuba would resist becoming a Soviet satellite to the "last drop of blood." But how "sovereign" were you when Khrushchev arranged with Kennedy for the missile withdrawal without consulting you?

GUEVARA: As you know from Fidel's speech, we had differences with the Soviet Union.

BERGQUIST: You've traveled widely since our last talk—from the Punta del Este Conference in Uruguay to Moscow. Since you call yourself a "pragmatic Marxist" who learns from the "university of experience," what have you learned?

GUEVARA: At Punta del Este, I learned in a shocking, first-hand way

By permission of the editors. From the April 9, 1963, issue of *Look* Magazine. Copyright 1963 by Cowles Communications, Inc.

about the *servilismo* [servility] of most Latin American govern-ments to the United States. Your Mr. Dillon was a revelation to me.

BERGQUIST: I've heard many Cubans refer to the period when Anibal Escalante was a director of ORI as "our Stalin" period. But *Anibalistas* are still in the government. What can keep them from re-gaining power?

GUEVARA: Escalante was shipped out of the country. He had to go. That period is finished. We are completely reorganizing ORI along different lines.

BERGQUIST: Bureaucracy seems a plague of most "Socialist" coun-tries. I noticed it in Moscow. Hasn't it also invaded Cuba?

GUEVARA: Bureaucracy is not unique to Socialism. General Motors has a big bureaucracy. It existed in Cuba's previous bourgeois re-gime, whose "original sins" we inherited. After the revolution, because we were taking over a complex social apparatus, a "guer-rilla" form of administration did develop. For lack of "revolutionary conscience," individuals tended to take refuge in vegetating, filling out papers, establishing written defenses, to avoid responsibility. After a year of friction, it was necessary to organize a state appara-tus, using planning techniques created by brother Socialist coun-tries.

Because of the flight of the few technicians we had, there was a dearth of knowledge necessary to make sensible decisions. We had to work hard to fill the gaps left by the traitors. To counteract this, everyone in Cuba is now in school.

During the last mobilization, we had many discussions about one phenomenon: When the country was in tension, everyone organized to resist the enemy. Production did not lessen, absenteeism disap-peared, problems were resolved with incredible velocity. We con-cluded that various forces can combat bureaucracy. One is a great patriotic impulse to resist imperialism, which makes each worker into a soldier of the economy, prepared to resolve whatever prob-lem arises.

BERGQUIST: What about Cuba's new school system, which separates many children from their parents? Isn't it completely disrupting family life?

GUEVARA: The revolutionary government has never had a definite policy, or dealt with the philosophical question of what the family should be. When the process of industrial development takes place, as in Cuba, women are increasingly at work and less at home caring for children. Nurseries must be established to leave the child somewhere. In places like the Sierra Maestra, when there can be no central schools after a certain age because pupils are too widely scattered in the countryside, we think it better for the children to receive schooling in a specialized center like Camilo Cienfuegos School City. There they can also train for their later work in life. The child spends his vacations with his family—certainly this is no worse than the "boarding schools" of the wealthy people we knew, who did not see their children for eight to ten months a year. There are the problems of families divided, where half the members are revolutionary, the other half not with the revolution—even pathetic cases of parents who left for Miami, but whose children of twelve or fourteen did not want to go. If we hurt the family, it is because we haven't thought about it, not because we are against the family.

BERGQUIST: Recently, at a trade union banquet, you noted that "youth" was conspicuously lacking among "exemplary workers" honored that night. Since this is such a "young" revolution—why?

GUEVARA: Perhaps an artificial division has arisen in the thinking of our people. In the armed defense of the revolution, young people have always been disposed to heroic adventure. Ask them to make long marches, to take to the trenches or mountains, to sacrifice their lives if need be, and they respond. But when the word "sacrifice" refers to an obscure, perhaps even boring job that has to be done daily with efficiency and enthusiasm, older people of experience still excel them. Socialism cannot be achieved by either armed fight or work alone. We must now create a new authentic national hero—a work hero whose example is contagious, as potent as any military hero's.

BERGQUIST: Finally, what of claims by Cubans that "Socialism" here is "different"?

GUEVARA: Perhaps it was more spontaneous, but we are part of the Socialist world. Our problems will be solved by our friends.

Interview with
Josie Fanon

ЛЛЛЛЛЛЛЛЛЛЛЛЛЛЛЛЛЛЛЛЛЛЛ ЛЛЛЛЛЛ

Q: Why are you in Algeria?

A: The reason is very simple. In a few days I am going to visit several African countries, and to go to Africa we have to come to Algeria first. We are also using the occasion, before we leave, to discuss general international and African problems with our brothers in the Algerian government. We are thinking of spending a few more days in Algeria.

Q: Would you give a broad outline of the position of the Cuban government in relation to Africa generally?

A: Africa represents one of the most important fields of struggle against all forms of exploitation existing in the world—against imperialism, colonialism, and neocolonialism. There exist great possibilities for success in Africa, but there are also many dangers. The positive side includes the youth of the African people's modern states, the hate which colonialism has left in the minds of the people, the very clear and profound differences between an African and a colonialist. The people are convinced that there can never be sincere friendship between the two except after the final departure of the colonialist. There are other positive aspects, too: the current potentialities for a much more rapid development than ever before due to the aid which some of the capitalist countries can also provide under certain conditions (but on this point we must be watchful).

We believe that the principal danger faced by Africa is the continually rising possibility of division among the African peoples. On one side we can find the lackeys of imperialism, on the other the people trying to free themselves along the roads best suited to them. We have valid reasons for fearing this danger. There is also the phenomenon of unequal trade between the industrialized countries and the economically dependent nations. This unequal relationship is shown in its most brutal aspects by colonialism. Even the completely independent countries risk finding themselves locked

Interview by Josie Fanon, widow of the Algerian revolutionary leader Frantz Fanon, for *Revolution Africaine. Revolución* (Havana), December 23, 1964, pp. 1, 2.

up in the prison of the international capitalist market because the large industrialized countries impose controls through their high technical development. After independence, the industrialized nations begin to exercise a kind of "economic suction" on the liberated countries and a few years later the conditions exist once again for the political domination of underdeveloped countries by industrial nations.

We believe that in Africa today the bourgeoisie still has something to say. This is quite different from Latin America where the national bourgeoisie no longer has any choice but complete submission to the orders of imperialism. In many independent African countries it is possible for the bourgeoisie, in the beginning, to develop and play a "relatively" progressive role. It can, for a time, mobilize the people and left-wing forces under the slogan of the anti-imperialist struggle, but inevitably the time comes when this bourgeoisie, and the government representing it, end up at an impasse. It is not possible for the bourgeoisie, because of its very nature, to follow the road of the masses. The only course remaining open to it is collaboration with imperialism and the oppression of the people. In short, it can be said that at present there are great possibilities in Africa due to the unrest existing in this region of the world, but there are also real dangers which we have to keep in mind. There are important economic problems to be remembered. Unequal relations in international exchanges lead to an impasse where it becomes very easy to give in to imperialism and to oppress the people whom, for awhile, they seem to serve.

Q: If you were asked to give the road of economic development best suited for the African countries, what would you answer?

A: If my advice—or rather my opinion as Cuban Minister of Industry—were asked, I would simply say that a country beginning to develop itself must, in the first stage, work—above all at organization—and that one should approach the practical problems by "using one's own head." This opinion may seem abstract and rather vague, but it is something very important.

In Africa, where many countries have already carried out very extensive nationalization, perhaps it is possible to create certain enterprises to provide products for other countries which lack them and vice versa. It is essential to work in the spirit of mutual benefit and therefore it is necessary to know each other better and to establish a relationship of confidence. At first this must be limited to very simple things. At times it may be necessary to set up small plants requiring many workers and offering jobs for many unemployed, rather than highly mechanized enterprises which employ a smaller number of workers. In certain cases, a sector must be mechanized rapidly; in other cases, this might not be the case. In fact, in a developing country most problems deal with agriculture and extractive industry, but it is quite evident that these problems are different in each nation, and that one must pay attention above all to particular realities. That's why it is impossible to give a general formula that could be applied to all countries in Africa.

Q: In your opinion, what are the perspectives of the revolutionary struggle in Latin America?

A: You know that is something close to my heart; it is my major interest. We believe that the revolutionary struggle will be a very long and very hard one. It is difficult to believe—difficult, but apparently not impossible—in the isolated triumph of the revolution in one country. Imperialism has been preparing organized repression of the people of Latin America for many years. An international of repression has been formed in many countries. Right now, in fact, in Peru, where the last battles were fought for the liberation of Latin America from the Spanish yoke, military maneuvers are being held. Different countries are participating in these maneuvers, conducted by the United States, in the Ayacucho region. What we are witnessing in this region is overt preparation for repression. And why are these maneuvers carried out precisely in this mountainous region of Peru, in this jungle zone? It is because Ayacucho is situated close to important revolutionary bases. Ayacucho was not chosen by accident.

The North Americans are paying attention to the problem of guerrilla war. They have written some very interesting things on it. They have grasped quite correctly that guerrilla war is extremely difficult to liquidate if it is not liquidated as soon as it appears. All their strategy is now oriented toward this objective, taking two main forms: first, repression; second, the isolation of the revolutionaries from their main base—the peasants. I read in a North American document the same expression used by Mao Tse-tung: "Among the people, revolutionaries are like a fish in water." The North Americans have grasped that the power of the guerrilla fighter resides in this, and they have understood that everything must be done to stop it from continuing.

Obviously, all these factors make armed struggle more difficult. But against international repression will come the inevitable and natural reply of international revolutionary struggle on the part of workers and peasants against the common enemy. That is why we foresee the establishment of a continental front of struggle against imperialism and its internal allies. This front will take some time to organize, but when it is formed it will be a very hard blow against imperialism. I don't know if it will be a definitive blow, but it will be a severe blow. It is because of this that we pose this fundamental principle: The struggle for freedom must be not only a defensive, but an offensive struggle against imperialism as well.

We will even add that the working class in the United States, because of its high standard of living, does not see well enough the contradictions existing in North American society. The living conditions of the North American workers have ameliorated these contradictions and prevent them from gaining a clear consciousness of their own exploitation. As long as they keep getting the crumbs which North American imperialism tosses them from their feast, they will not have a revolutionary consciousness.

ЛЛЛЛЛЛЛЛЛЛЛЛЛЛЛЛЛЛЛЛЛЛЛ

REPORTER: Would you like to give a summary on the Cuban experiment, or would you like us to present you with questions?

GUEVARA: If I'm to do a commentary, I would have to prepare it; please start your questions.

REPORTER: We believe there are two basic matters. One is the political organization. This is a matter we face in spite of the government, as you face it also in Cuba. It requires unification of socialist powers of various sources. This we feel has been realized by Cuba since 1961. What are the differences and obstacles which were met on the way to this unification? Is political organization that toward which you are currently working during the command of your revolutionary power?

GUEVARA: The question is of tremendous breadth because it requires speaking of the entire experiment of the Cuban Revolution. No doubt you may know that the ORI is composed of three political powers, each one of its own form.

1. The first of these is the movement called the 26th of July. This depended on a vast popular movement, presided over by the leaders of the Revolution. The leadership of this movement emerged from the bourgeoisie, from the lines of the petit bourgeoisie who were cultured and revolutionary. It was also followed and supported by active groups of strugglers. These groups represented the body of the popular masses of workers and farmers in a particular way. These supported the movement if they did participate actively in the revolutionary situation. Inside this movement, there were two parts: (1) the Sierra, and (2) the Plains. The Sierra group could almost be compared to the leftist. The Plains could be compared to the rightist, not for ideological considerations, but basically for results, in the experiment, in the struggle and the specialization of activities. Conditions of the struggle differ in the Sierra from those of the Plain. This is a matter you will not have to worry about [in Egypt]. But it was an important one on an important level for our

Al-Tali-'ah, no. 4, April 1965. Appendix to Daniel Tretiak's *Cuba and the Soviet Union: The Growing Accommodation* (Santa Monica, California: The Rand Corporation), July 1966.

own experiment. This does not mean that all elements working in the Plain are rightist and that the Sierra was free from those elements which were not competent for the situation. But the Sierra was encouraging a popular understanding in the popular social image. It was faced with strategic methods, more revolutionary than conditions were able to provide. We were talking in the Sierra about the revolutionary which depended on the peasantry, while the Plains was talking about a general revolutionary strike. This is an opinion which may seem to be more revolutionary from the point of view of tradition. What happened actually was that we (the Sierra) were able to take over the rule and get rid of Batista. Our movement enjoyed wide popularity due to its struggle—but it did not rely on suitable organization for its needs.

2. The second political power in the ORI is the Partido Socialista Popular (PSP), or in other words, the Cuban Communist Party. It did not have a left wing or a right wing, but it committed grave mistakes. Perhaps its basic error was due to its failure, in striking depth, to understand the magnitude of the spread of the revolutionary movement and the possibilities which lay within that struggle. The PSP lagged behind the big movement which rose under the leadership of Fidel Castro. After that, those comrades realized the legality and the revolutionary leadership of Castro. We (the 26th of July Movement and the PSP) began to work together and our socialist friends participated in this combined work with their identified ideology, the result of thirty or forty years of active participation in the struggle against imperialism, a struggle led by popular faces such as Mella, the founder of the party, and Soumendies, a Spaniard and a great revolutionary leader in the sugar factories, who was later assassinated. But the struggles of this party remained isolated from the popular groups due to the special attacks which were raised against them by Batista—a matter which caused some complications.

3. The third group in the ORI is the Revolutionary Directorate (RD). This is an organization which was originally formed by students. It sprang from the left bourgeois groups, combining both wings, the left and the right. It participated in the revolutionary struggle.

In truth, there were five organizations which participated in the fall of Batista: the 26th of July Movement, the PSP, the RD, the Organization of Guerrillas, and groups which originally belonged to the Revolutionary Socialist Party but had separated from it in the wake of military activities against Batista. This fifth group sprang from the original old party. It was headed by a guerrilla who was supplying us with arms through certain connections, which he maintained were in the U.S., on condition that some other people would make use of them.

REPORTER: Was Dorticós, the president of the Republic, a member of any of these groups?

GUEVARA: No, Dorticós was a member of our movement; he was a member of the "Plains" wing. He was in charge of another region; but this does not mean that he was a rightist.

Castro was at the head of the army and he was its commander in chief. We were facing some problems at that time but were unable to see them clearly at first because of the revolutionary movement which was led by the Sierra . . . ,[1] the attack on the president's palace, and getting hold of the rule and the popular enthusiasm. In 1960 there was no representation in the Congress for eighty-one communist parties, except the PSP. But in 1962 the Organizaciones Revolutionarias Integradas (ORI) attended the 22nd Congress of the Communist Party of the Soviet Union (CPSU); we unified the three political powers from the top without referring to organized elections. This was a type of orientation without a list or a defined line.

At this point, Aníbal Escalante appeared as an active leader of the PSP. He was put in charge of organizing the unified party.

Although we, the 26th of July Movement, were not organized in a proper form, our meetings before the Revolution were regular and our activities secret or semisecret. But the comrades of the PSP had enjoyed organizational experience in spite of the fact that their outlook was isolationist at the same time.

We were in need of tying the party together with the public after the Revolution; we had nationalized industries, and we replaced the bourgeois leadership in other industries. After some of those ousted had fled to the U.S., we were in need of cadres to take their place. Most of the people who participated in the 26th of July Movement were illiterate, and could not serve as cadres. But within the PSP we were able to find the cadres to take over leadership positions in industry and economy. We were in need of a large nucleus of trained personnel, because we had nationalized 98 percent of the organizations, leaving only those organizations of a professional or semiprofessional nature. The responsibility of organizing the party under these conditions was given to Escalante.

Escalante, of course, chose his old companions to occupy posi-

---

[1] Ellipses throughout in original. Eds.

tions of leadership without cleaning house, and accordingly a large number of those comrades reached high administrative positions in these organizations, and became the leaders of the party at the same time; thus, in truth, there was formed not a party represented by true leadership but an administrative party. And, at the same time, the party controlled all executive positions. Escalante gradually began to take over all important positions. He used isolationist ideas which did not allow the building up of a popular party, but which established instead a party without an active role among the public. On the other hand, the public did not know the members of the party, because their members were alienated from the people by their secret activities on the one hand and their persecution on the other. It was often necessary to transfer party members to positions which were far from their base of activities, as economic conditions required. This led to the decrease of the cadres, which in turn caused isolationism from the populace. On the other side, these isolated cadres began to commit other mistakes. Some of them faced various difficulties through their lives of struggle. Some of them reached leadership positions and enjoyed various privileges —beautiful secretaries, Cadillac cars, air conditioning. Soon they got accustomed to these things; they now preferred keeping doors shut for the sake of air conditioners, keeping the warm Cuban atmosphere outside. And outside stood the crowds of workers. And thus, a new group of people appeared, the opportunists.

REPORTER: Wasn't there a labor union organization to cope with this situation?

GUEVARA: The labor union organization had already suffered persecution from Batista. From this and also from the yellow elements of the leadership like Mujal (a type which we find in the leadership of labor unions in the United States), the true elements in labor unions were removed from the center of labor. Thus the workers could not see them. These were some of the basic reasons why we felt it necessary to organize a unified party.... The party began under the leadership of the administration. It was not founded on a true democratic basis. It was not able at this stage to win wide popularity among the people. It rather was cloaked with isolationism. The situation necessitated the 26th of March [speech of 1962] in which Fidel Castro revealed openly Aníbal Escalante's policies and from that day on, we completely changed our work methods.

The party did not enjoy effective influence among the masses nor among real [effective] organizations. Neither did it coincide with the awareness of the masses. Fidel Castro always resorted to television, not to the party, when moving the masses was necessary. And when he attempted to put his ideas into execution, the party was not at the required level of preparedness. At times he even spoiled his program because the cadre was not in agreement. In Escalante's office were seventeen television sets; this does not mean Escalante was a traitor—he is not a weak, despairing type of person but rather a man of intelligence and revolution—but only that he committed grave mistakes in these matters. . . . The fact that he had such authority in his hands was in truth a proof of the sickness of isolationism in its worst form. It is true that he benefited from this situation; he was not a traitor but also was not a saint.

We asked ourselves at that time what to do. Fidel Castro visited different organizations; on the lists of party members he requested, he found names not even known to the masses of workers. He asked about the members of the party who occupied administrative positions—who were these members? He found that they were the director, the director of employees, the director of production, the director of the economic section, and so forth. That is to say that the leadership cadre was a party of administrators only. . . . Perhaps there were one or two members of the Popular Socialist Party who for one reason or another did not occupy administrative positions. We went over these lists. Fidel Castro made clear to us the grave errors which we had committed, and we criticized ourselves deeply. We were very generous in offering our confidence, in addition to our weak revolutionary awakening and our revolutionary experiment, which lacked maturity. Our revolutionary experience was short, clear, and simple. We did not face complicated issues which would require revolutionary struggle with whatever difficulties were faced. On the other hand, we did not give the matter of building up the party enough attention. We were too involved with national problems to be concerned with party problems.

These were some of the most serious errors of this period. We decided then to face the issue of changing the situation. We drafted a plan for ourselves to correct these errors. In addition, Fidel Castro had by now acquired experience himself. We could summarize this plan as follows: We began to convene labor councils in every department at the department headquarters where workers would nominate themselves and their coworkers who were model workers. Then we discussed their qualities. These workers could be described as those of great ability and clear vision. They discussed problems openly at a time when they did not campaign or request their own election but also asked why they would be elected. We were confident that those few elected first were of the best elements, but as for the rest there was a possibility that they were not on the same high level. There was a good deal of disagreement; thus it was the right of the elected worker who was faced with attacks to defend himself. This elected worker in truth was "naked" [laid bare], from the practical point of view, in front of the labor council to defend his own work.

REPORTER: Perhaps this is a type of direct democracy to which you have resorted?

GUEVARA: Yes, definitely.

REPORTER: Remembering your speech made in Algiers, we would like to ask you this: What is your understanding of the relationship between the state and the communist party in your country? Is it true that the Cuban state rules the country in the manner of a guerrilla war?

GUEVARA: This is another big problem, and our party is still searching for the answer to two questions: First, what is the definition of a communist for us? Second, what is the role of the party? I mean, there are no organized and definite answers to these questions. Of course, there are varied and opposing thoughts on these matters. We conducted a special and a partial experiment in a practical way, but so far we have not reached a final answer in the form of a statement which could be issued by the party.

What is the role of the party? It should lead the revolutionary state; it should supervise it; the party should be the ideological power which orients the people and leads them. These are the broad lines ... but how do we put them into practice? We are agreed on the general outlines of the situation, but it is necessary that we find ways and means to put these principles into practice in the particular situations which we face. As for the definition of the communist—is it necessary that he be atheist or is it possible that he could be a believer? Should we require of him efforts in labor equivalent to the efforts of the average worker or should we expect more? Should he remain in the rear if we enter a battle in the war —should we protect him or should he be placed at the front lines to face the dangers? These are all questions still awaiting a final reply.

In connection with relations between the state and the party, what is [actually] the revolutionary state? It has various forms which are introduced through the various experiments from the October Revolution in Russia until our present day. And here we face two matters, that of form and that of content. It is necessary that we protect the revolutionary content, but it is also necessary that we should be able to change the form to fit our new situations. We realize not only our practical failure—but also our ideological failure in solving this matter. Therefore, what are the forms which we should adopt which will agree with our historical needs? What is the form which should replace the council of ministers and the parliament, for example? Our council of ministers—to this day— holds the legislative power in addition to its executive power. In addition to its right to amend the constitution it convenes as a revolutionary council—and thus we break through the spirit of bourgeois laws which we have inherited. But we did not draft a new constitution—and in spite of that fact the council of ministers granted itself the right to issue new laws and to amend the constitution. The problem is not that of drafting new laws, but of their purpose. Why do we issue them? And in what direction should they tend? We cannot say we have arrived at final decisions in these matters because we have not yet evolved the theoretical revolutionary thought which is able to give the necessary answers.

These are relations between the party and the state—between the revolutionary command and the masses, even though this has been accomplished so far in an obligatory manner. The command is aware of the revolutionary reactions on the part of the masses, yet it knows that the organizations such as labor unions, women, and youth organizations require definition of the principles upon which they operate. We shall not retain the forms of government which reflect the continuation of the struggle between the proletariat and workers. We must find ways and means by which to face the new issues brought about by removing the old situation and by building a socialist society.

REPORTER: What is your opinion of the Yugoslavian experiment in this respect?

GUEVARA: We definitely oppose the Yugoslavs, and we do not wish to use big flashy words on this subject; we are not talking about backsliding—but we also do not wish to talk about being stationary. We do not at all accuse the Yugoslavs of being agents of imperialism, and so forth—but we oppose them in a basic manner.

REPORTER: How?

GUEVARA: We believe that there are two ways in which we differ from the Yugoslav experiment: that is, in our reaction to Stalinism and in opposition to the Soviet Union to dictate to us its economic and leadership ideals.

On the other hand, we do agree with the idea that it is necessary to find new solutions in a particular way. But in their experiments the Yugoslavs mix individual economic matters with group problems, and we believe in the separation of the one from the other. The problem of workers' participation in the administration of organizations seems to us to be a separate question from the problem of workers' participation in profit.

What is happening in Yugoslavia? The power there is for the law of production—and where the law of production dominates, it surrenders the economy to capitalism. That is to say, in Yugoslavia there is imminent danger of walking toward capitalism, and it is quite possible that this economic principle will reflect on its political position. The Soviet Union produced the New Economic Policies (NEP) for a time; and if Lenin had lived, this policy would have failed in its own day. But Lenin died. Also the problems which are caused by such an economic policy change in effect when transported from point 0 degree to 1 degree in progress or from 8 degrees to 9 degrees. The matter is clearer and more critical in the second cases—East European countries were at point 4, 5, or 6 degrees—and Yugoslavia on this, followed by Poland and then Czechoslovakia. Then came Lieberman's experiments in the Soviet Union which you have discussed in your journal, *Al-Tali-'ah*.

There are problems concerning the basic concept of socialist evolution in the field of economy which are still unknown to this day. So far, crooked roads have been followed; and when it was decided to refrain from these roads, other roads were followed which did not prove to be less crooked, and thus these experiments always reached a wall impossible to climb—perhaps there is a straight road which could be sought. Everything so far has been focused on the law of production—and this means the danger of returning again to capitalism.

REPORTER: But there is not a capitalist strata ruling there now nor the political-economic and social conditions suitable for capitalism; on the contrary, the conditions are suitable for socialism.

GUEVARA: Yes, but this is only the first stage ... these communities are still in a balancing condition, and they have not finally abandoned the possibility of return to capitalism if we take the matter from the general historical point of view.

There were serious stages of evolution which took place in the Soviet Union which stand in the way of its return to capitalism, but in Yugoslavia a feudal society still existed until 1945. And we cannot say that the remains of the old society have been completely uprooted. The Soviets resorted to the "measures" of profit. But in the Soviet Union there is a growing trend toward conquering the negative elements, while in Yugoslavia the road faces toward the danger of the overwhelming outburst of these negative elements. In our trade with Yugoslavian organizations which work in the same field and at the same time compete with each other—each one is ready to cut down prices to a critical low point so as to eliminate each other from the market.... Isn't this a distinctive feature of capitalistic economy?

Then again, what does it mean when the factories which deal with "automation" distribute their increasing profits in an exceptional way among their workers alone without the workers in the plural sense receiving benefit from it?

What is the effort which the worker in such an organization exerts in comparison to that of the farmer who exhausts himself on a small piece of land, and this is the case with 85 percent of the land in Yugoslavia, where small farmers hire other farmers smaller than they. Such conditions create a privileged group and enhance elements of a capitalist nature.

We should differentiate between financial privileges and the privilege of standing in the way of the battle when the individual exerts his extreme efforts and steadfastness for readiness in the struggle ... and this is what socialism is particularly concerned with.

REPORTER: It is important to us, if possible, to get acquainted with the most important problems which were caused by the formation of a socialist organization in the industry of your country.

GUEVARA: Labor is a separate and independent element from the production of labor. The output of labor depends on the laborer, but it is also tied up with the machinery used and the advancement of the industrial society in which it operates. Accordingly, the laborer who works should not benefit at the expense of the laborer who exhausts himself while using different tools.

REPORTER: But how do you take care of the problem of barriers which stand in the way of production in your experiment? In your opinion?

GUEVARA: We do not believe that this is strictly a financial or economic matter, but that is is also an administrative and moral problem. We mean by this that a factory of good workers and bad administrators is worse than a factory of good administration and average workers. Take, for example, the cigar workers. A man produces eighty cigars a day; if we put him on a twelve-hour shift, he will be able to produce one hundred and twenty. And if we press him, he will reach one hundred and forty per day. But if we bought a machine which makes cigars, it may be possible to reach thirty-eight to forty-five times more the production of the worker, while the price of the machine may be equal to a full year of production by one worker. In other words, production does not basically depend on increased efforts and tailored means to increase production, but is a result of technical progress.

REPORTER: We wish that you would speak to us about Cuba as a base for revolution in Latin America and what difficulties or obstacles present themselves in this respect in connection with the exportation of revolution, and Peronist movement in Argentina, and so forth?

GUEVARA: Let us begin with the Peronists. Personally, I was against Peronism in the past. Perón is the result of events and factions peculiar to conditions in Latin America. There has been a struggle among North American, English, and German capitalists. England has been in a retreating stage and the Germans started a political movement during the war—of which Perón was not a leader—sympathizing with the Axis, while some elements of this movement (which was working under the emblem of nationalism) had connections with the Nazis. Argentina and Cuba and the U.S.A. were among the countries which came out from World War II as judges. We had the sugar ... they had the wheat which allowed them during this period to realize profits. And Perón gained power in Argentina during this period which was characterized by the pouring out of profits, and developed the country in the industrial direction. There were no labor laws at that time ... but it was natural that labor legislation be drafted along with the growth of the proletariat. The Yalta agreement enforced a blockade on Argentina caused by her relations with the Axis.... And Argentina at this time was able to realize a ratio of industrialization. Perón at this time reached the zenith of his popularity. During this success his wife Eva appeared ... and she adhered to general humanitarian principles and here began the struggle of the Argentinian proletariat against local capitalists. Perón attempted to hold the balance between the capitalists and the workers. The reactionary forces began to oppose Perón more and more. There was increasing opposition during his second government in step with the army, navy, and the North Americans whose capital was pouring into the country ... which necessitated friction and clashes. The Peronist movement founded a labor organization, creating a legend—but in spite of that the proletarian movement in this wealthy nation was characterized by a type of paralysis ... it lacked the spirit for struggle and the necessary organizations for struggle. Perón found himself alone, and he never climbed to the level of facing death; he escaped. He was not a hero in truth, but he was an intelligent man. He lacked a political faith—but he enjoyed excellence in maneuvering which cannot be doubted.

He succeeded in influencing the masses and in creating a legend, and he knew how to create an atmosphere that could really capture the fancy of the people. . . . There is no doubt that Perón was not the man to make big decisions and face crises such as the crisis of fighting all the Caribbean. But he left his influence on the masses. His followers were not lasting. They were on his level with the exception of one man called John Cook who spent a period of time in Cuba.

But in relation to the Cuban experiment and its beam of light on the revolutionary movement in Latin America—it has proved by practical experiment that it is possible to free the underdeveloped countries from the grip of colonialism even when all the conditions for self-revolution could not be realized.

REPORTER: Does attempting a revolutionary operation create in itself a new situation to cope with?

GUEVARA: Yes, this is a critical matter, but our Revolution was also equivalent to a sign to North American isolationism and reactionary power to recruit its forces and get ready for the battle.

More than at any other time in the past, this power is ready now to face progressive action in the future of the revolutionary movement in Latin America, although it should not be thought that the revolutionary movement in each country is united and ready for the struggle, armed ideologically in the same manner as we were. This is one of the negative aspects which was caused by the course of developments and the distribution of class power in Latin America. We developed our guerrilla warfare through practical experience, and for three years assisted in the armed battles in Guatemala, Venezuela, Colombia, and elsewhere.

LETTERS

Letter to
Fidel Castro

ЛЛЛЛЛЛЛЛЛЛЛЛЛЛЛЛЛЛЛЛЛЛЛЛЛ

Fidel:

I received the letter addressed to Piro [1] and it is already being printed. Because of its content I believe it to be a very significant document, at least as important as the Montecristi Manifesto,[2] and it is certain that it will set a historical precedent. Perhaps today it will cause quite a stir, especially in certain industrial spheres. However, Lenin has already stated that a policy based on principles is the best policy. The final result will be magnificent.

It is fantastic that we are now able to get to Manzanillo. I now actually have a small column led by Israel Oquendo at the place you indicated. I have no direct report but the news I have received secondhand indicates that they took Lourdes, captured seven men and left afterward. Some say that they have now eighty men. I am thinking of making him a captain, providing him with a teacher so he can learn to read and giving him a definite position to hold. Ramiro [3] will have informed you about my troop by now. Camilo [4] has become a true lion, in everything, and is now my right-hand man. In closing I wish to congratulate you once again on the document. I can tell you that you will always be respected for having shown the possibility of armed struggle supported by the people for all of the Americas. Now you are on the road to becoming one of the two or three in the Americas who have reached power through an armed struggle with broad popular support.

Che

This letter was written on January 6, 1958; it was a reply to a letter written by Fidel Castro to Celia Sánchez in which the United States was denounced for giving military aid to Batista. *Granma* (Havana), August 27, 1967, p. 8.

[1] The alias of Celia Sánchez, Fidel Castro's secretary. Eds.

[2] Manifesto issued in 1895 by José Martí to begin the struggle for Cuba's independence. Eds.

[3] Ramiro Valdés. Eds.

[4] Camilo Cienfuegos. Eds.

Letter to
Faure Chomon

ЛЛЛЛЛЛЛЛЛЛЛЛЛЛЛЛЛЛЛЛЛЛ

Sierra del Escambray, November 7, 1958

Mr. Secretary General of the Directorio Revolucionario,
Compañero Faure Chomón

Dear Comrade,

I am addressing you with the purpose of informing you of the last events which have occurred in the heart of Sierra Escambray.

The difficulties sprouted between us, and the organization Segundo Frente del Escambray began to turn into a crisis after the appeal of our Maximum Chief, Dr. Fidel Castro, until it culminated in open aggression against one of my captains in the zone of San Blas. This delicate situation makes it impossible to reach an agreement with the aforementioned organization.

In our last interview, I was unable to make a concrete offering due to your refusal even to talk with members of the Segundo Frente, which was a contradiction with the unity instructions which I carried from the Sierra Maestra. I consider that at the present moment the 26th of July Movement cannot talk either at a fraternal level with that institution, which opens the channels for us to carry out concrete conversations on all the points which are of interest to our respective organizations.

In official conversations held with members of the Partido Socialista Popular, they have shown a posture frankly for unity and have placed at the disposition of that unity their organization on the plains and their guerrillas in the Yaguajay front.

I can go to confer with you at the most convenient place for you; but if, due to military action, you are unable to make a direct contact with me, Major Ramiro Valdés, second military chief of this zone for the 26th of July, is authorized to effectuate the conference.

I take advantage of this opportunity to inform you that *compañero* Pompilio Viciedo [1] has reiterated his position to submit to a trial rather than to abandon our ranks; thus he will remain detained in

Bohemia (Havana), December 10, 1965, p. 56.
[1] A member of the Chomón guerrilla who killed two followers of Eloy Gutierrez Menoyo. Eds.

this camp until the total clarification of the facts. We will be grateful for any declarations which first eye-witnesses or anyone knowing the facts could make and the appearance of all of them at the trial which will be held when all the dispersed elements of proof have been gathered.

Receive a revolutionary salute.

Che
Commander in Chief, Las Villas Region, for the 26th of July Movement

Letter to
Fidel Castro

ЛЛЛЛЛЛЛЛЛЛЛЛЛЛЛЛЛЛЛЛЛЛЛЛЛЛЛ

Fidel:

At this hour I remember many things—when I met you in Maria Antonia's house, when you suggested that I come, all the tensions of the preparations.

One day we were asked who should be notified in case of death, and the real possibility of the fact affected us. Later we knew that it was certain, that in a revolution one wins or dies if it is a real revolution. Many *compañeros* died along the way to victory.

Today everything has a less dramatic tone because we are more mature. But the fact is repeated. I feel that I have fulfilled the part of my duty that tied me to the Cuban Revolution in its territory, and I bid farewell to you and the *compañeros*, your people who are already mine.

I formally renounce my positions in the party leadership, my ministry post, my rank of major, and my Cuban citizenship. Nothing ties me legally to Cuba; the only ties that bind me to Cuba are of another nature, which cannot be broken as appointments can.

Reviewing my whole life, I believe I have worked with sufficient honesty and dedication to consolidate the revolutionary triumph. My only shortcoming of some gravity was not to have trusted in you more from the first moments in the Sierra Maestra and not to have understood with sufficient celerity your qualities as a leader and a revolutionary.

I have lived magnificent days; at your side, I have felt the pride of belonging to our country during those luminous and sad days of the Caribbean crisis.

Few times has a statesman shone more than on those days; I am proud, too, of having followed you without hesitation and of identifying myself with your way of thinking, of seeing, and of assessing dangers and principles.

Other hills of the world demand the aid of my modest efforts. I can do what is denied you because of your responsibility as the head of Cuba, and the hour for us to separate has come.

Letter read by Fidel Castro on October 3, 1965. *El Mundo* (Havana), October 5, 1965. pp. 1, 8.

Let it be known that I do so with a mixture of joy and pain. Here I leave the purest of my hopes as a builder and the dearest of my dear ones, and I leave the people who took me as their son. This will give rebirth to part of my spirit. On the new battlefields, I will carry the faith which you instilled in me, the revolutionary spirit of my people, the sensation of fulfilling the most sacred of all duties— to struggle against imperialism wherever it may be. This in itself heals and cures any laceration.

I repeat once more that I free Cuba from any responsibility except what emanates from her example and that if the final hour comes to me under other skies, my last thought will be for this country and especially for you whom I thank for your teachings and example. I shall try to be loyal to you to the last consequences of my acts. I have always been identified with the foreign policy of our Revolution and continue to be. Anywhere I am, I will feel the responsibility of being a Cuban revolutionary and as such I will act. I leave my children and wife nothing material, and I am not ashamed. I am glad it is so. I ask nothing for them, as the state will give them enough with which to live and be educated.

I would have many things to tell you and our people, but I feel words are unnecessary as they cannot express what I would like to say, and it is useless to waste words.

To victory always! *Patria o muerte!*

I embrace you with revolutionary fervor.

Che

Letter to
His Parents

Dear Folks:

Once again I feel beneath my heels the ribs of Rosinante.[1] I return to the road with my lance under my arm.

About ten years ago, I wrote you another letter of farewell. As I remember, I lamented not being a better soldier and a better doctor. The latter no longer interests me; I am not such a bad soldier.

Nothing has changed in essence, except that I am more aware. My Marxism has taken deep root and become purified. I believe in armed struggle as the only solution for those peoples who fight to liberate themselves, and I am consistent with my beliefs.

Many will call me an adventurer, and I am, but of a different type, one of those who risks his skin to demonstrate his truths. It is possible that this will be the last time. I don't look forward to it, but it is within the logical realm of possibilities. If this be so, I send you a last embrace.

I have loved you very much, but I have not been able to express my feelings; I am extremely rigid in my actions and I think that sometimes you did not understand me. It was not easy to understand me, but just for today, believe me.

Now a will power I have polished with the delight of an artist will sustain these shaky legs and weary lungs. I shall do it.

Once in a while, remember this small *condottiere* of the twentieth century. A kiss to Celia, Roberto, Juan Martín, and Potón; to Beatriz, to everyone. A big embrace to you from your prodigal and recalcitrant son.

Ernesto

Last letter to his parents in Argentina, written in 1965. *Casa de las Américas* (Havana), September 1967, pp. 166–178.

[1] Rosinante: the old, worn horse of Don Quixote. Eds.

Letter to
Hildíta

⊓⊔⊓⊔⊓⊔⊓⊔⊓⊔⊓⊔⊓⊔⊓⊔⊓⊔⊓⊔⊓⊔⊓⊔⊓⊔⊓⊔⊓⊔⊓⊔

Dear Hildita:

Today I write to you even though the letter will get to you late. I want you to know that I remember you very much. I hope you are having a happy birthday. You are almost a woman and I should not write to you as one writes to little kids, that is, telling little lies.

You should know that I am far away and that I will be so for some time to come, doing all I can against our enemies. It is not much, but I do all I can and you can always be proud of your father as I am of you.

Remember that there are still many years of struggle ahead, and that when you become a full-grown woman you will have to do your part in this struggle. Meanwhile, you should prepare; be very revolutionary, which at your age means to learn more and to always be ready to support just causes. Obey your mother and do not think you are of age too early. You will get there.

You should try to be one of the best in school. Better in every sense. You know what this means: to study and to have a revolutionary attitude, in other words, good behavior, love for the Revolution, companionship, and so forth. I was not like that at your age, but I was in a different society, where every man was against the other. Now you have the privilege of living in another epoch and you should be worthy of that privilege.

Do not forget to look after your smaller brothers and sisters. Tell them to study and to behave.

Well, once again, happy birthday. Give an embrace to your mother and to Gina. Here is one, very big and strong, for you, to take care of you during the time in which we will not see each other.

Your father

Letter to his daughter, Hilda Guevara Gadea, written on February 15, 1967. *El Mundo* (Havana), October 16, 1967, p. 4C.

ЛЛЛЛЛЛЛЛЛЛЛЛЛЛЛЛЛЛЛЛЛЛЛЛ

To my children:

Dear Hildita, Aleidita, Camilo, Celia, and Ernesto, if one day you read this letter it will be because I am no longer with you. You will almost not remember me and the littlest ones will not remember me at all.

Your father has been a man who acts as he thinks and you can be sure that he has been faithful to his convictions. Grow up to be good revolutionaries. Study hard so you can master the technology that will permit you to control nature. Remember that the Revolution is what matters and that each one of us, alone, is worth nothing. Above all, always be capable of feeling deeply any injustice committed against anyone anywhere in the world. That is the most beautiful quality of a revolutionary.

Farewell, children, I still hope to see you. A big hug and kiss from

Papá

Last letter writen from Bolivia to his children. *Tricontinental Bulletin* (Havana), October 1968, p. 36.

SONG TO FIDEL

Canto a Fidel

Vámonos,
  ardiente profeta de la aurora,
  por recónditos senderos inalámbricos
  a librear el verde caimán que tanto amas.

Vámonos,
  derrotando afrentas con la frente
  plena de martianas estrellas insurrectas,
  juremos lograr el triunfo o encontrar la muerte.

Cuando suene el primer disparo y se despierte
  en virginal asombro la manigua entera,
  allí, a tu lado, serenos combatientes,
  nos tendrás.

Cuando tu voz derrame hacia los cuatro vientos
  reforma agraria, justicia, pan, libertad,
  allí, a tu lado, con idénticos acentos,
  nos tendrás.

Y cuando llegue al final de la jornada
  la sanitaria operación contra el tirano,
  allí, a tu lado, aguardando la postrer batalla,
  nos tendrás.

El día que la fiera se lama el flanco herido
  donde el dardo nacionalizador le dé,
  allí, a tu lado, con el corazón altivo,
  nos tendrás.

No pienses que puedan menguar nuestra entereza
  las decoradas pulgas armadas de regalos;
  pedimos su fusil, sus balas y una peña.
  Nada más.

Y si en nuestro camino se interpone el hierro,
  pedimos un sudario de cubanas lágrimas
  para que se cubran los guerrilleros huesos
  en el tránsito a la historia americana.
  Nada más.

This poem was written in Mexico in 1956. *Bohemia* (Havana), May 1, 1960, p. 58.

Song to Fidel

Onward,
    burning prophet of the dawn,
    down hidden and untouched paths,
    to liberate the green cayman [1] you love so well.

Onward,
    armed with the courage of Martí,
    to destroy any offense,
    swearing to triumph or die.

When the first shot sounds and awakens
    the jungle in virginal amazement,
    there, beside you, serene crusaders,
    you will find us.

When you speak on the four winds
    of land, justice, bread, and liberty,
    there, beside you, in affirmation,
    you will find us;

And when the end of the journey is reached,
    and the tyrant has been swept away,
    there, beside you, waiting for battle,
    you will find us.

And the day the beast licks its wounded side
    where the nationalizing darts have struck,
    there, beside you, with a proud heart,
    you will find us.

We will not be swayed
    when the decorated fleas come armed with gifts;
    we ask only a rifle, bullets, and a rock,
    nothing else;

And if our path be blocked by iron,
    we ask only a rosary of Cuban tears,
    so that these guerrillas' bones will be covered
    in the passing of American history,
    nothing else.

[1] *Cayman:* refers figuratively to Cuba's geographical resemblance to a *cayman* or alligator. Eds.

Bibliography

Sources [1]

Bohemia
Boletín Provincial Habana del P.P.C.
Casa de las Américas
Cuba Socialista
Diario de la Tarde
El Mundo
El Mundo del Domingo
Granma
Hoy
Humanismo
Juventud Rebelde
Lunes de Revolución
MINFAR (Ministerio Nacional de las Fuerzas Armadas)
Nuestra Industria: Revista Económica
Nuestra Industria: Revista Tecnológica
Obra Revolucionaria
Orientador Revolucionario
Revolución
Revolución, Suplemento Gráfico
Trabajo
Tricontinental, Suplemento Especial
Verde Olivo

Articles

"Un año de lucha armada," *Verde Olivo*, 5:25–39 (January 5, 1954).
"Qué es un guerrillero," *Revolución*, February 19, 1959, pp. 1–2.
"Una Revolución que comienza," *Revolución*, July 9, 1959, pp. 1–18.
"Guerra y población campesina," *Lunes de Revolución*, 19:30–31 (July 26, 1959).
"América desde el balcón afro-asiático," *Humanismo*, 8:46–48 (September–October 1959).
"La India: país de grandes contrastes," *Verde Olivo*, 1:8–9 (October 1959).
"Indonesia y la sólida unidad de su pueblo," *Verde Olivo*, 1:8–9 (October 1959).
"Recupérase Japón de la tragedia atómica," *Verde Olivo*, 1:8–9 (October 1959).
"Intercambio comercial y de amistad con Ceylán y Pakistán," *Verde Olivo*, 1:8–9 (November 16, 1959).

[1] With the exception of *Humanismo*, published in Mexico, all sources are published in Havana. References within each group are listed chronologically.

"Yugoslavia, un pueblo que lucha por sus ideales," *Verde Olivo*, 1:8–9 (November 23, 1959).
"El cachorro asesinado," *Humanismo*, 8:79–81 (November 1959–February 1960).
"Canto a Fidel Castro," *Bohemia*, 52:58 (May 1, 1960).
"Notas para el estudio de la ideología de la Revolución Cubana," *Verde Olivo*, 1:10–14 (October 8, 1960).
"Un pecado de la Revolución," *Verde Olivo*, 2:26–29 (February 1961).
"Cuba, excepción histórica o vanguardia en la lucha anticolonialista?" *Verde Olivo*, 2:22–29 (April 9, 1961).
"Discusión colectiva; decisión y responsabilidad únicas," *Trabajo*, 2:40–47 (July 1961).
"Parte oficial de guerra del Che, trasmitido por Radio Rebelde," *Revolución, Suplemento Gráfico*, December 16, 1961, p. 1.
"Tareas industriales de la Revolución en los años venideros," *Cuba Socialista*, 2:28–46 (March 1962).
"Editorial," *Nuestra Industria: Revista Tecnológica*, 1:2–3 (May 1962).
"El ataque a Bueycito," *Revolución*, August 24, 1962, p. 10; August 25, 1962, p. 10; August 27, 1962, p. 10.
"Industria de guerra," *Revolución*, August 29, 1962, p. 10.
"El cuadro, columna vertebral de la Revolución," *Cuba Socialista*, 2:17–22 (September 1962).
"Contra el burocratismo," *Cuba Socialista*, 3:1–7 (February 1963).
"Consideraciones sobre los costos de producción como base del análisis económico de las empresas sujetas a sistema presupuestario," *Nuestra Industria: Revista Económica*, 1:4–12 (June 1963).
"Guerra de guerrillas: un método," *Cuba Socialista*, 3:1–17 (September 1963).
"Sobre el sistema presupuestario de financiamiento," *Nuestra Industria: Revista Económica*, 2:3–23 (February 1964).
"La banca, el crédito, y el socialismo," *Cuba Socialista*, 4:23–41 (March 1964).
"La Conferencia para el Comercio y Desarrollo en Ginebra," *Nuestra Industria: Revista Económica*, 2:3–8 (June 1964).
"La planificación socialista, su significado," *Cuba Socialista*, 4:13–24 (June 1964).
"Cuba, su economía, su comercio exterior, su significado en el mundo actual," *Nuestra Industria: Revista Económica*, 2:3–12 (December 1964).
"El socialismo y el hombre en Cuba," *Verde Olivo*, 5:14–18, 66 (April 1965).
"Palabras del Che a la juventud," *Verde Olivo*, 6:15–20 (October 1965).
"Las tácticas y la estrategia de la revolución latinoamericana," *Verde Olivo*, 8:2–5 (October 2, 1968).

Articles published under pseudonyms
1. *Francotirador* (all published in *Verde Olivo*)
"El Payaso macabro y otras alevosías," 1:17, April 10, 1960.
"El más peligroso enemigo y otras boberías," 1:7, April 17, 1960.
"El Desarme continental y otras claudicaciones," 1:9, April 24, 1960.
"No seas bobo, compadre, y otras advertencias," 1:15, May 2, 1960.

"La democracia representativa sur-coreana y otras mentiras," 1:21, May 8, 1960.

"Cacareo, los votos argentinos y otros rinocerontes," 1:21, May 15, 1960.

"Los dos grandes peligros, los aviones piratas, y otras violaciones," 1:11, May 22, 1960.

"El salto de rana, los organismos internacionales, y otras genuflexiones," 1:15, May 29, 1960.

"Estambul, Puerto Rico, Caimanera, y otras 'bases de discusión,'" 1:17, June 5, 1960.

"Idígoras, Somoza, y otras pruebas de amistad," 1:61, June 12, 1960.

"El plan Marshall, el plan Eisenhower, y otros planes," 1:29, June 19, 1960.

"Nixon, Eisenhower, Hagerty, y otros toques de atención," 1:15, June 26, 1960.

"La acusación ante la OEA, las Naciones Unidas, y otras fintas," 1:17, July 10, 1960.

"Las bases de submarinos, las de cohetes, y otros engendros," 1:12, July 17, 1960.

"Beltrán, Frondizi, y otras razones de peso$," 1:15, July 24, 1960.

"La 'Corte de los Milagros' y otros motes de la OEA," 1:15, July 31, 1960.

"Para muestra basta un botón y otras historias breves," 1:9, August 7, 1960.

"Había una vez un central azucarero y otras leyendas populares," 1:18, August 14, 1960.

2. *Advice to the Combatants* (published in *Verde Olivo*, Havana, with the exception of the last entry)

"Moral y disciplina de los combatientes revolucionarios," 1:50–51, March 17, 1960.

"La disciplina de fuego en el combate," 1:29, May 8, 1960.

"Solidaridad en el combate," 1:52–53, May 15, 1960.

"El aprovechamiento del terreno, I, II, III," 1:32–33, May 22, 1960; 1:27–29, May 29, 1960; 1:28–29, June 5, 1960.

"El Contra-ataque, I y II," 1:18–20, June 26, 1960; 1:40–42, July 17, 1960.

"Las ametralladoras en el combate defensivo, I, II, III, y IV," 1:30–31, July 24, 1960; 1:32–33, July 31, 1960; 1:93–94, August 7, 1960.

"La artillería de bolsillo, I, II, y III," 1:10–11, September 24, 1960; 1:62–63, October 8, 1960; 1:24–26, October 22, 1960.

"Consejos al combatiente" (MINFAR, Dpto. de Instrucción, 1961?), 47 pp.

Letters, messages, decrees

"Cartas a Camilo Cienfuegos," *Juventud Rebelde*, October 20, 1967, p. 5.

"Carta a Fidel Castro," *Granma*, October 16, 1967, p. 14.

"Carta a Fidel Castro," *Granma*, October 16, 1967, p. 13.

"Carta a Fidel Castro," *Verde Olivo*, 5:9 (January 1964).

"Al pueblo de Las Villas," *El Mundo del Domingo*, December 30, 1962, p. 2.

"Carta a José E. Martí Leyva, de Oriente," *Juventud Rebelde*, October 19, 1967, p. 6.

"Carta a Carlos Franqui," *Revolución*, March 11, 1959, pp. 1, 6.

"Carta a Mial, Departamento Militar de La Cabaña," *Granma*, October 16, 1967, p. 17.

"Carta a Miguel Angel Quevedo," *Hoy*, June 6, 1959, pp. 1, 5.

"Telegrama a Conrado Rodríguez," *Revolución*, January 8, 1960, pp. 1–2.

"Carta a José Tiquet, de México," *Juventud Rebelde*, October 19, 1967, p. 6.
"Opiniones autografiadas en el álbum de la exposición china," *Hoy*, March 16, 1961, p. 6.
"Circular a jefes de empresas consolidadas," *Diario de la Tarde*, January 11, 1962, p. 6.
"Acuerdo Número 6, del Consejo de Dirección del Ministerio de Industrias," *Orientador Revolucionario*, 7:10–11 (April 1962).
"Carta a la Dra. Aleida Coto Martínez," *Juventud Rebelde*, October 19, 1967, p. 5.
"Carta a los compañeros de la Planta Ensambladora de Motocicletas," *Boletín Provincial Habana del P.P.C.*, no. 10, February 15, 1967.
"Circular a los jefes del Ministerio de Industrias," *Nuestra Industria: Revista Económica*, 3:73 (August 1963).
"Carta a María Rosario Guevara, de Marruecos," *Juventud Rebelde*, October 17, 1967, p. 3.
"Carta a Pepe," *Granma*, October 16, 1967, p. 17.
"Carta a Fidel Castro," *El Mundo*, October 5, 1965, pp. 1, 8.
"Carta de despedida a sus padres," *Casa de las Américas*, 7:166–178 (September 1967).
"Mensaje a los pueblos del mundo a través de la Tricontinental," *Tricontinental, Suplemento Especial*, April 16, 1967, pp. 5–24.

Speeches, interviews, conferences

"Entrevista de prensa," *El Mundo*, January 5, 1959, pp. A1, 47.
"Entrevista telefónica con el diario *Correo de la Tarde*, de Buenos Aires," *El Mundo*, January 5, 1959, p. A7.
"Declaraciones a la prensa," *Hoy*, January 6, 1959, p. 2.
"Declaraciones afirmando que no acepta cargos," *El Mundo*, January 8, 1959, p. A14.
"Discurso en el acto organizado en su honor por el Colegio Médico Nacional en el cual se le declaró médico cubano honorario," *Revolución*, January 16, 1959, p. 2.
"Discurso en el homenaje que le rindieron en el Palacio de los Trabajadores, los obreros cubanos," *El Mundo*, January 20, 1959, p. A8.
"Charla pronunciada en la Sociedad 'Nuestro Tiempo,' el 27 de enero de 1959," *Revolución*, January 29, 1959, pp. 1, 6.
"Comparecencia en el programa de TV 'Comentarios Económicos,' el 11 de febrero de 1959," *Revolución*, February 12, 1959, pp. 1, 4.
"Palabras iniciales en el recital de Nicolás Guillén, en la Cabaña," *Hoy*, February 21, 1959, p. 1.
"Palabras en el acto de apoyo al Movimiento de Integración Nacional en el Sindicato de Plantas Eléctricas, el 4 de abril de 1959," *Hoy*, April 7, 1959, pp. 1, 3.
"Palabras en el Fórum Tabacalero," *Hoy*, April 11, 1959, pp. 1, 4.
"Discurso en la Conferencia organizada por Unidad Femenina Revolucionaria, el 11 de abril de 1959," *Hoy*, April 12, 1959, pp. 1, 3.
"Palabras en el acto de clausura de la Exposición de Industrias Cubanas, en la Escuela de Medicina de la Universidad de la Habana," *Hoy*, April 19, 1959, pp. 1, 3.
"Discurso en el acto de entrega de $30,000 para la Reforma Agraria por los

trabajadores tabacaleros en la CTC," *Revolución*, April 27, 1959, p. 3.
"Discurso en el acto de graduación del primer grupo de soldados que terminaron su entrenamiento militar en la Escuela de Reclutas de la Fortaleza de la Cabaña, el 28 de abril de 1959," *Hoy*, April 29, 1959, pp. 1, 3.
"Comparecencia en el programa 'Telemundo Pregunta,'" *El Mundo*, April 29, 1959, pp. A1, A8.
"Discurso en el acto del 1 de mayo en Santiago de Cuba," *Revolución*, May 2, 1959, p. 11.
"Discurso en el acto de las Milicias Obreras y Populares de Bejucal, el 3 de mayo de 1959," *Hoy*, May 7, 1959, pp. 1, 6.
"Palabras en el acto de apertura de la Universidad de la Habana, el 11 de mayo de 1959," *Hoy*, May 12, 1959, pp. 1, 5.
"Conferencia en la Universidad de la Habana, el 25 de mayo de 1959," *Revolución*, May 26, 1959, pp. 1, 14.
"Palabras a los periodistas en relación con su viaje a Egipto," *Revolución*, June 6, 1959, pp. 1, 2.
"Conferencia de prensa en la República Árabe Unida," *Hoy*, June 20, 1959, pp. 1, 7.
"Conferencia de prensa en la République Árabe Unida," *Hoy*, July 1, 1959, pp. 1, 4.
"Entrevista con J. Nehru, efectuada en Nueva Delhi, India, el 1 de julio de 1959," *Revolución*, July 2, 1959, pp. 1, 5.
"Conferencia de prensa en Jakarta, Indonesia," *El Mundo*, July 31, 1959, p. 1.
"Conferencia de prensa en Ceilán," *El Mundo*, August 9, 1959, p. 2.
"Conferencia de prensa en Belgrado, Yugoslavia," *El Mundo*, August 16, 1959, pp. 1, 10.
"Conferencia de prensa a su regreso a Cuba, el 8 de septiembre de 1959," *Hoy*, September 9, 1959, pp. 1, 7.
"Comparecencia en el programa 'Comentarios Económicos,' el 14 de septiembre de 1959," *Revolución*, September 15, 1959, pp. 1, 16.
"Entrevista con estudiantes extranjeros," *Revolución*, September 18, 1959, pp. 1, 9.
"Palabras en el duelo del comandante Juan Abrantes y el teniente Jorge Villa," *Revolución*, September 26, 1959, p. 19.
"Conferencia en la Academia José Antonio Echeverría de la Policia Nacional Revolucionaria," *Revolución*, October 1, 1959, pp. 1, 16.
"Discurso en el Parque Central sobre educación y cultura popular, el 8 de octubre de 1959," *Hoy*, October 9, 1959, pp. 1, 7.
"Discurso en el acto de honradez y honestidad de la CTC el 14 de octubre de 1959," *El Mundo*, October 15, 1959, pp. 1, 7.
"Discurso en el acto del Tercer Distrito Militar Leoncio Vidal en Santa Clara para conmemorar el 10 de octubre," *Hoy*, October 18, 1959, p. 10.
"Discurso frente al Palacio Presidencial el 26 de octubre de 1959, con motivo del restablecimiento de los tribunales revolucionarios," *Revolución*, October 27, 1959, p. 4.
"Entrevista con un periodista de *Revolución* en las oficinas del Departamento de Industrialización del INRA," *Revolución*, October 29, 1959, pp. 1, 17.

"Entrevista grabada en La Habana y transmitida por Radio Rivadavia de Buenos Aires," *Revolución*, November 3, 1959, pp. 1, 6.

"Entrevista con Carlos Franqui al tomar posesión como presidente del Banco Nacional de Cuba," *Revolución*, November 27, 1959, p. 1.

"Discurso en conmemoración del fusilamiento de los estudiantes de medicina el 27 de noviembre de 1871," *Hoy*, November 28, 1959, pp. 1, 7.

"Entrevista concedida a un periodista del diario *Prensa Libre* de Guatemala," *Revolución*, December 1, 1959, p. 10.

"Discurso en el encuentro con la Juventud Cívica Unida en El Caney, Oriente," *Hoy*, December 2, 1959, pp. 1, 7.

"Discurso en la Universidad de Las Villas, en ocasión de su investidura como Doctor Honoris Causa de la Facultad de Pedagogía, el 28 de diciembre de 1959," *Revolución*, December 31, 1959, pp. 1, 2.

"Discurso en la ciudad de Santa Clara, en el acto de clausura del Día del Ejército Rebelde," *Revolución*, December 29, 1959, p. 6.

"Discurso resumen del acto, homenaje a José Martí, el 28 de enero de 1960," *Revolución*, February 1, 1960, p. 18.

"Conferencia en la Asociación de Colonos de Cuba, el 29 de enero de 1960," *Revolución*, January 30, 1960, p. 16.

"Comparecencia en el programa 'Ante la Prensa,' el 4 de febrero de 1960," *Revolución*, February 5, 1960, pp. 1, 14.

"Discurso en el teatro de la CTC-R, en ocasión de la entrega de un nuevo donativo para armas y aviones, el 7 de febrero de 1960," *Hoy*, February 9, 1960, pp. 1, 7.

"Palabras en el acto de entrega de diplomas y premios a los 100 obreros que más se han distinguido en el mes de enero de 1960; celebrado el 22 de febrero de 1960," *Revolución*, February 23, 1960, pp. 1, 2.

"Discurso en el acto de entrega de la fortaleza militar de Holguín al Ministerio de Educación, como Centro Escolar, el 24 de febrero de 1960," *Hoy*, February 26, 1960, p. 7.

"Palabras en la Asamblea Nacional de Colonos, el 26 de febrero de 1960," *El Mundo*, February 27, 1960, p. 8.

"Palabras en la Universidad de la Habana, el 2 de marzo de 1960," *El Mundo*, March 3, 1960, pp. 1, 12.

"Conferencia inaugural en el programa de television 'Universidad Popular,' sobre Soberanía política e independencia económica, trasmitida el 20 de marzo de 1960," *Revolución*, March 21, 1960, pp. 1, 8.

"Discurso en el acto conmemorativo del 1 de mayo, en Santiago de Cuba," *El Mundo*, May 3, 1960, p. C13.

"Discurso en la inauguración de la Exposición Industrial en Ferrocarril, el 20 de mayo de 1960," *El Mundo*, May 22, 1960, pp. A1, D3.

"Conferencia televisada del ciclo Cuba Avanza, el 18 de junio de 1960," *Obra Revolucionaria*, 11:3–15 (June 16, 1960).

"Conferencia en el acto de clausura del ciclo de cultura y adoctrinamiento en la Escuela Técnica Industrial José B. Alemán, el 1 de julio de 1960," *El Mundo*, July 3, 1960, pp. 3, 10.

"Discurso en el acto en apoyo al Gobierno Revolucionario, el 10 de julio de 1960," *Obra Revolucionaria*, 3:43–44 (July 16, 1960).

"Discurso en el acto de apertura del Primer Congreso Latinoamericano de

Juventudes, el 28 de julio de 1960," *Obra Revolucionaria*, 20:13–20 (August 25, 1960).

"Discurso en el acto de inauguración del curso de adoctrinamiento organizado por el Ministerio de Salud Pública, el 20 de agosto de 1960," *El Mundo*, August 21, 1960, p. 6.

"Discurso en el acto conmemorativo del segundo aniversario de la partida de la columna invasora Ciro Redondo, celebrada en el campamento de las Mercedes, Sierra Maestra, el 28 de agosto de 1960," *El Mundo*, August 30, 1960, pp. 1, 12.

"Discurso en el acto de clausura de la Plenaria Nacional Tabacalera, celebrada el 17 de septiembre de 1960," *El Mundo*, September 18, 1960, pp. 2, 4.

"Discurso en la Asamblea, General Popular en Camagüey en respaldo a la Declaración de La Habana, el 18 de septiembre de 1960," *El Mundo*, September 20, 1960, p. A12.

"Declaraciones formuladas con motivo de la nacionalización de tres bancos norteamericanos," *El Mundo*, September 20, 1960, p. A10.

"Discurso en la despedida de las Brigadas Internacionales de Trabajo Voluntario, el 30 de septiembre de 1960," *El Mundo*, October 1, 1960, pp. 1, 8.

"Palabras en la graduación de alumnos de la Escuela de Capacitación Cívica 'Frank País,'" *Verde Olivo* 1:11–13 (October 15, 1960).

"Conferencia de clausura del ciclo de charlas del Banco Nacional de Cuba," *El Mundo*, October 21, 1960, p. 1.

"Declaraciones a su llegada a Checoslovaquia," *Revolución*, October 24, 1960, pp. 1, 12.

"Comparecencia televisada en Praga," *Revolución*, October 27, 1960, pp. 1, 8.

"Entrevista concedida a periodistas en Moscú," *Revolución*, November 2, 1960, pp. 1, 11.

"Entrevista en Moscú con el periodista Dennis Ogden del *Daily Worker*," *Revolución*, November 4, 1960, pp. 1, 2.

"Palabras a su llegada a Pekín," *Revolución*, November 18, 1960, pp. 1, 4.

"Palabras durante su visita a Ediciones en Lenguas Extranjeras en Moscú," *El Mundo*, November 23, 1960, p. B3.

"Palabras en el acto de bienvenida que le ofrecieron en la ciudad de Shangai," *El Mundo*, November 29, 1960, pp. A1, B4.

"Palabras pronunciadas en Pyongyang, en respuesta a las de solidaridad del Primer Ministro Kim Il Sung," *Hoy*, December 4, 1960, pp. 1, 14.

"Discurso al pueblo chino," *Revolución*, December 9, 1960, p. 20.

"Declaraciones en una reunión de 'Amistad Cubano-Soviética,' en Moscú, efectuada en el Palacio de los Trabajadores," *El Mundo*, December 11, 1960, pp. A1, A2.

"Comparecencia televisada para informar al pueblo de las gestiones realizadas por los países socialistas de Europa y Asia, el 6 de enero de 1961," *El Mundo*, January 7, 1961, pp. 1, B2, B4.

"Palabras para despedir el duelo en el sepelio de los combatientes de las FAR," *Revolución*, January 11, 1961, pp. 1, 11.

"Discurso durante su visita a la planta de Nícaro," *Revolución*, January 21, 1961, p. 16.

"Discurso en Cabañas, P. del Río, para recibir a los milicianos pinareños al regreso de sus puestos de combate el 22 de enero de 1961," *Revolución*, January 23, 1961, p. 1.

"Discurso en la clausura de la Convención Nacional de Consejos Técnicos Asesores, el 11 de febrero de 1961," *El Mundo*, February 12, 1961, p. A6.

"Discurso en la entrega de diplomas a los obreros destacados en la producción, el 22 de febrero de 1961," *Revolución*, February 23, 1961, p. 1.

"Entrevista con un periodista de *Revolución* por haber sido designado Ministro de Industrias," *Revolución*, February 27, 1961, pp. 1, 11.

"Palabras de respuesta a una invitación del diario argentino *Novedades Gráficas* para que concurriera a una mesa redonda sobre 'Las relaciones cubano-norteamericano' en Buenos Aires," *El Mundo*, March 18, 1961, pp. 1, B2.

"Charla sobre 'El Papel de la Ayuda Exterior en el Desarrollo de Cuba,' en el ciclo sobre Problemas Económicos, el 9 de marzo de 1961," *Verde Olivo* 2:24–25 (March 19, 1961).

"Discurso en el Primer Encuentro Nacional Azucarero, celebrado el 28 de marzo de 1961," *El Mundo*, March 29, 1961, pp. 1, A5.

"Discurso en el acto de inauguración de la fábrica de lápices José A. Fernández," *El Mundo*, March 31, 1961, pp. 1, A6.

"Declaraciones en la reunión efectuada en industrias con dirigentes del organismo," *Revolución*, April 10, 1961, pp. 1, 13.

"Palabras en la clausura de la exposición china," *El Mundo*, April 12, 1961, pp. 1, B2.

"La conferencia sobre 'La industrialización en Cuba,' el 30 de abril de 1961," *El Mundo*, May 3, 1961, pp. A5, A8.

"Discurso en el 26° aniversario de la muerte de Antonio Guiteras, efectuado en la Industria Eléctrica 'Antonio Guiteras' el 8 de mayo de 1961," *Revolución*, May 9, 1961, pp. 1, 3.

"Discurso en el Centro Gallego organizado por la Casa de la Cultura con motivo de la visita del general Lister, el 2 de junio de 1961," *Revolución*, June 3, 1961, pp. 1, 7.

"Discurso en el acto de clausura del Campo Internacional de Trabajo de la UIE el 4 de junio de 1961," *Revolución*, June 5, 1961, pp. 1, 10.

"Palabras en el acto de entrega de premios a los obreros mas destacados en la producción el mes de mayo de 1961," *Revolución*, June 23, 1961, pp. 1, 5.

"Palabras en la apertura del curso de adiestramiento para funcionarios y empleados del MININD y sus empresas consolidadas," *Revolución*, June 24, 1961, pp. 1, 4.

"Discurso como delegado de Cuba ante el Consejo Interamericano Económico y Social (CIES) el 8 de agosto de 1961," *Revolución*, August 10, 1961, pp. 5–7.

"Conferencia de prensa en Punta del Este, el 9 de agosto de 1961," *Revolución*, August 11, 1961, p. 5.

"Discurso en la Universidad de Montevideo en agosto de 1961," *Revolución*, August 19, 1961, pp. 5, 7.

"Discurso en la Conferencia del CIES, fundamentando la oposición de Cuba a firmar la 'Carta de Punta del Este,'" *Revolución*, August 18, 1961, p. 6.

"Declaraciones al periódico *El Popular* de Montevideo," *Hoy*, August 19, 1961, p. 3.

"Comparecencia televisada para informar al pueblo sobre el resultado de la Conferencia Economica de Punta del Este, el 23 de agosto de 1961," *Obra Revolucionaria*, 29:3–16 (August 24, 1961).

"Discurso en la Primera Reunión Nacional de Producción, celebrada en el Teatro Chaplin el 26–27 de agosto de 1961," *Obra Revolucionaria*, 30:107–128 (August 26, 1961).

"Discurso en la clausura de la Primera Asamblea de Producción de la Gran Habana, celebrada en el Centro Gallego," *Obra Revolucionaria*, 38:7–15 (October 12, 1961).

"Charla con funcionarios y Empleados del MININD," *El Mundo*, October 7, 1961, pp. 1, 2.

"Palabras en reunión efectuada en el salón de actos del MININD," *Revolución*, October 26, 1961, pp. 1, 11.

"Discurso en la inauguración de la planta de sulfometales 'Patricio Lumumba,'" *El Mundo*, October 31, 1961, pp. 1, 7.

"Palabras en la reunión con directores de Empresas Consolidadas y dirigentes sindicales," *El Mundo*, November 5, 1961, p. A2.

"Palabras en el acto de despedida a los becarios que salieron a estudiar en los países socialistas," *Revolución*, November 7, 1961, p. 9.

"Discurso en el acto celebrado en la fábrica de pinturas Clipper," *El Mundo*, November 16, 1961, pp. 1, A2.

"Discurso en el banquete ofrecido por el MININD a los trabajadores de ese organismo que participaron como delegados en los Congresos Obreros," *El Mundo*, November 26, 1961, p. B2.

"Discurso en la escalinata de la Universidad de la Habana el 27 de noviembre," *El Mundo*, November 28, 1961, pp. 1, 5.

"Discurso en el XL Congreso Nacional de Trabajadores," *Revolución*, November 29, 1961, pp. 3–4.

"Discurso en el acto inaugural de la fábrica de galletas 'Albert Kuntz' en Guanabacoa," *Revolución*, January 4, 1962, p. 10.

"Discurso en la Asamblea General de Trabajadores Portuarios, Sección Sindical de la Habana, en el espigón No. 1 'Margarito Iglesias,'" *El Mundo*, January 7, 1962, pp. 1, A5.

"Declaraciones con respecto al estudio del Mínimo Técnico," *Hoy*, January 11, 1962, p. 3.

"Comparecencia televisada en un programa especial de 'Ante la prensa,'" *Revolución*, January 29, 1962, p. 2.

"Palabras con motivo de la entrega de premios a los vencedores en la emulación de los Círculos de Estudio en el Ministerio de Industrias," *Revolución*, February 1, 1962, pp. 1, 7, 8.

"Palabras en el acto de inauguración de la Escuela de Capacitación Técnica para obreros," *Revolución*, February 2, 1962, pp. 1, 6.

"Discurso en el acto de apertura del curso académico 1962–63 en la Universidad Central de Las Villas," *Hoy*, February 3, 1962, p. 5.

"Declaraciones al semanario *Principios* de Buenos Aires," *El Mundo*, March 4, 1962, pp. 1, 9.

"Discurso en una reunión con los Directores y Responsables de Capacitación de las Empresas Consolidadas y Secretarios de Educación y de

Trabajo de los 25 sindicatos nacionales," *Trabajo*, 3:12–15 (March 1962).

"Discurso en la clausura de la Plenaria Nacional Azucarera," *Obra Revolucionaria*, 13:5–8, April 17, 1962.

"Discurso en el acto clausura del Primer Consejo Nacional de la CTC-R," *Obra Revolucionaria*, 13:10–16 (April 17, 1962).

"Palabras en la cooperativa 'Ramón González Coro' en Quivicán," *Diario de la Tarde*, April 17, 1962, p. 4.

"Discurso en el acto de entrega de premios a los 45 obreros más distinguidos en la producción del Ministerio de Industrias," *Revolución*, May 2, 1962, pp. 4, 5, 7.

"Charla en el MININD con los delegados obreros extranjeros asistentes a los actos del 1 de mayo de 1962," *Revolución*, May 5, 1962, pp. 1, 6.

"Conferencia en el Aula Magna de la Universidad de la Habana," *Revolución*, May 12, 1962, pp. 1, 6.

"Palabras en el acto conmemorativo del 152 aniversario de la independencia argentina," *Revolución*, May 26, 1962, pp. 1, 8.

"Discurso en el acto de entrega de premios a los técnicos y obreros más destacados durante los meses de marzo y abril," *Revolución*, June 9, 1962, pp. 1, 5.

"Palabras en la Asamblea de trabajadores de la Refinería 'Ñico Lopez' de Regla," *Revolución*, June 12, 1962, p. 10.

"Discurso en el acto de entrega de premios a los obreros más destacados en la producción," *Revolución*, June 29, 1962, pp. 2, 5.

"Entrevista con Vadim Listov de la revista soviética *Tiempos Nuevos*," *Revolución*, July 10, 1962, p. 1.

"Palabras en el acto efectuado en los molinos de harina 'José A. Echeverría' en Regla," *El Mundo*, August 1, 1962, pp. 1, 8.

"Palabras en el acto inaugural del astillero 'Chullima' en las márgenes del río Almendares," *Revolución*, August 16, 1962, pp. 1, 2.

"Discurso en el acto organizado por la CTC-R en homenaje a los trabajadores que superaron las metas de producción y para recibir las herramientas y equipos donados por los trabajadores," *Revolución*, August 22, 1962, p. 5.

"Palabras en la textilera 'Camilo Cienfuegos' de Guines," *Hoy*, September 11, 1962, p. 6.

"Discurso en el acto de entrega de premios a los obreros y técnicos del MININD más destacados durante el mes de julio," *El Mundo*, September 15, 1962, p. 1.

"Discurso en el acto de conmemoración del II aniversario de la integración de las Organizaciones Juveniles," *Obra Revolucionaria*, 30:15–23 (October 23, 1962).

"Entrevista concedida a Sam Russell, corresponsal de *Daily Worker* de Londres," *Revolución*, December 6, 1962, pp. 1, 5.

"Discurso pronunciado en el acto conmemorativo de la muerte del general Antonio Maceo," *Obra Revolucionaria*, 33:4–6 (December 10, 1962).

"Discurso en el acto de graduación de alumnos de la Escuela de Superación Obrero 'Lenin' efectuada en el teatro del plantel 'Valdés Rodríguez,'" *Revolución*, December 15, 1962, pp. 1, 2.

"Palabras en el acto de entrega de premios a los trabajadores ejemplares y técnicos mas sobresalientes durante los meses de agosto a octubre de 1962," *El Mundo,* December 16, 1962, pp. 1, A5.

"Discurso en la clausura de la Plenaria Nacional Azucarera," *El Mundo,* December 20, 1962, pp. 7, 8.

"Discurso en el acto de graduación de alumnos de la Escuela para Administradores 'Patricio Lumumba,' el 21 de diciembre de 1962," *El Mundo,* December 22, 1962, p. 7.

"Discurso en el acto de clausura de la primera escuela popular," *El Mundo,* January 27, 1963, pp. 1, B3.

"Discurso en el hotel, 'Habana Libre' en el homenaje a los técnicos y obreros más destacados durante 1962," *El Mundo,* January 29, 1963, p. 2.

"Discurso en la entrega de los premios especiales a técnicos y obreros del Ministerio de Industrias," *El Mundo,* February 2, 1963, pp. 1, 2.

"Discurso en la Plenaria Azucarera Nacional en Camagüey," *El Mundo,* February 10, 1963, pp. B2, B6.

"Discurso en el acto de inauguración de la primera etapa de la fábrica de alambre en Nuevitas," *Revolución,* February 11, 1963, p. 5.

"Entrevista para la televisión canadiense en los campos de Camagüey," *Revolución,* February 12, 1963, pp. 1, 10.

"Discurso en la asamblea general celebrada por los obreros de la Textilera Ariguanabo para hacer la presentación de los trabajadores de ese centro con condiciones necesarias para ser miembros del PURS, el 24 marzo de 1963," *El Mundo,* March 26, 1963, pp. 4, 12.

"Palabras en el acto de inauguración de la planta procesadora de cacao en Baracoa," *Revolución,* April 2, 1963, pp. 2, 5.

"Discurso en el tercer chequeo nacional de la III Zafra del Pueblo en Santa Clara, el 6 de abril de 1963," *El Mundo,* April 7, 1963, pp. 1, 5.

"Discurso en el homenaje a técnicos y obreros de fábricas consolidadas más destacados durante 1962, el 30 de abril de 1963," *Trabajo* 4:53–56 (May 1963).

"Discurso en el almuerzo ofrecido al personal del periódico *Hoy,* con motivo de su 25 aniversario el 16 de mayo de 1963," *El Mundo,* May 21, 1963, p. 17.

"Palabras de despedida a la delegación del Ejército Nacional Popular de Argelia en la recepción del 20 de mayo de 1963," *Hoy,* May 21, 1963, p. 5.

"Entrevista con el periodista mexicano Víctor Rico Galán," *Verde Olivo* 4:58–59 (June 30, 1963).

"Declaraciones durante su estancia en Argelia en julio de 1963," *Revolución,* July 11, 1963, pp. 1, 2; July 24, 1963, pp. 1, 5.

"Declaraciones en *Revolution Africaine,*" *El Mundo,* July 13, 1963, pp. 1, 2.

"Palabras en el Seminario sobre Planificación de Argelia," *El Mundo,* July 16, 1963, p. 7.

"Entrevista con periodistas en Argelia," *Revolución,* July 24, 1963, pp. 1, 5.

"Entrevista con estudiantes norteamericanos que visitan a Cuba," *Revolución,* August 2, 1963, pp. 1, 5.

"Entrevista con visitantes latinoamericanos," *El Mundo,* August 21, 1963, pp. 1, 5.

"Palabras en la entrega de premios del torneo de ajedrez entre trabajadores del Ministerio de Industrias," *El Mundo*, August 25, 1963, pp. 1, 8.

"Palabras al terminar la jornada de trabajo voluntario en la fábrica de madera Antonio Cornejo," *Revolución*, August 26, 1963, pp. 1, 3.

"Discurso resumen en el Primer Encuentro Internacional de Profesores y Estudiantes de Arquitectura el 29 de septiembre de 1963," *El Mundo*, October 1, 1963, pp. 5–6.

"Palabras en la entrega de diplomas a los obreros de vanguardia durante los meses de enero a marzo de 1963," *El Mundo*, October 27, 1963, pp. 1, 2.

"Entrevista en la sección 'Siquitrilla,'" *Diario de la Tarde*, November 11, 1963, p. 8.

"Discurso en la clausura del seminario sobre Documentación de obras para las inversiones," *El Mundo*, November 19, 1963, pp. 1, 7.

"Discurso en el acto de clausura del Forum de la Energía Eléctrica celebrado el 24 de noviembre de 1963," *El Mundo*, November 26, 1963, pp. 1, 8.

"Discurso en la graduación de 400 alumnos de las Escuelas Populares de Estadística y de Dibujantes Mecánicos," *El Mundo*, December 17, 1963, pp. 1, 8; December 18, 1963, pp. 5, 6.

"Discurso en el acto de clausura de la Semana de Solidaridad con el pueblo de Vietnam del Sur, el 20 de diciembre de 1963," *El Mundo*, December 21, 1963, p. 5.

"Información al pueblo sobre la implantación de las normas de trabajo y la escala salarial, el 26 de diciembre de 1963," *El Mundo*, December 27, 1963, pp. 1, 5, 7, 11.

"Discurso en la inauguración de la planta 'Plásticos Habana,'" *El Mundo*, December 30, 1963, p. 2.

"Palabras en la Central Termoeléctrica de Mariel," *El Mundo*, January 4, 1964, p. 5.

"Discurso en la entrega de Certificados de Trabajo Comunista el 11 de enero de 1964," *El Mundo*, January 12, 1964, pp. 1, 10.

"Entrevista para la sección 'Siquitrilla' del periódico *Revolución* durante un viaje al centro de rehabilitación de Uvero Quemado [Guanacahabibes]," *Revolución*, February 4, 1964, p. 6.

"Necesidad para el desarrollo de nuestra industria," *El Mundo*, February 26, 1964, pp. 1, 8.

"Palabras en el acto de entrega de premios a los obreros vanguardia del Ministerio de Industrias," *Revolución*, March 5, 1964, p. 3.

"Charla con los obreros de la fábrica de cemento 'Mártires de Artemisa,'" *Revolución*, March 12, 1964, pp. 1, 2.

"Discurso en la entrega de premios a los trabajadores que resultaron vencedores en la Emulación Nacional de 1963, el 14 de marzo de 1964," *El Mundo*, March 15, 1964, pp. 11–12.

"Discurso en la Conferencia Mundial de Comercio y Desarrollo, celebrada en Ginebra el 25 de marzo 1964," *El Mundo*, March 26, 1964, pp. 1, 11.

"Conferencia de prensa en Ginebra, el 31 de marzo de 1964," *El Mundo*, April 1, 1964, pp. 1, 2.

"Entrevista por televisión en Suiza el 11 de abril de 1964," *Verde Olivo* 5:62–64 (April 26, 1964).

"Declaraciones en Argelia," *Revolución*, April 16, 1964, pp. 1, 5.

"Discurso en la planta mecánica 'Fábrica Aguilar Noriega,' el 3 de mayo de 1964," *El Mundo*, May 5, 1964, pp. 1, 5.

"Discurso en la clausura del Seminario 'La Juventud y la Revolución,' " *El Mundo*, May 10, 1964, p. 10.

"Discurso en Isla de Pinos, el 10 de mayo 1964," *El Mundo*, May 12, 1964, p. 2.

"Discurso en la inauguración de la fábrica de bujías 'Neftalí Martínez,' el 17 de mayo de 1964," *El Mundo*, May 19, 1964, p. 7.

"Palabras a los integrantes de varias Unidades Militares que participan en la IV Zafra del Pueblo en Camagüey," *El Mundo*, May 27, 1964, pp. 1, 8.

"Discurso en la apertura de la Plenaria Provincial de la CTC de Camagüey, el 12 de junio de 1964," *El Mundo*, June 12, 1964, pp. 1, 5.

"Discurso en honor a los macheteros y jóvenes comunistas que ganaron la emulación en el Ministerio de Industrias," *El Mundo*, July 27, 1964, pp. 1, 8.

"Discurso en la inauguración de la segunda etapa de la fábrica de alambre 'Gonzalo Esteban Lugo,' el 12 julio de 1964 en Nuevitas, Camagüey," *Hoy*, July 14, 1964, p. 8.

"Discurso en el combinado del lápiz 'Mitico Fernández,' el 18 de julio de 1964," *Hoy*, July 19, 1964, p. 9.

"Discurso en la fábrica de bicicletas 'Heriberto Mederos,' en Caibarién, el 19 de julio de 1964," *El Mundo*, July 21, 1964, pp. 1, 2.

"Discurso en el acto de inauguración de la Industria Nacional Productora de Utensilios Domésticos en Santa Clara, el 24 de julio de 1964," *Revolución*, July 25, 1964, p. 11.

"Discurso en la entrega de Certificados de Trabajo Comunista a los obreros del Ministerio de Industrias, el 15 de agosto de 1964," *El Mundo*, August 16, 1964, p. 6.

"Palabras en el acto de conmemoración del sexto aniversario de la Invasión por las columnas Antonio Maceo y Ciro Redondo," *Verde Olivo* 5:4–5 (September 13, 1964).

"Discurso en el acto de entrega de premios a los ganadores de la Emulación Socialista en el Ministerio de Industrias, el 22 de octubre de 1964," *Revolución*, October 23, 1964, pp. 1, 2, 5, 6.

"Discurso en la presentación de los militantes del PURS en la refineria 'Ñico López,' el 23 de octubre de 1964," *Hoy*, October 24, 1964, p. 1.

"Discurso en la inauguración de la fábrica de brocas 'Alfredo Gamonal,' el 28 de octubre de 1964," *Revolución*, October 29, 1964, pp. 1, 2.

"Discurso en el homenaje a Camilo Cienfuegos, el 28 de octubre de 1964," *El Mundo*, October 29, 1964, p. 8.

"Palabras en el acto celebrado en la Casa de la Amistad con motivo de la creación de la Sociedad Amistad Soviético-Cubana en Moscú, el 11 de noviembre de 1964," *El Mundo*, November 12, 1964, pp. 1, 7.

"Entrevista con un periodista uruguayo del periódico *El Popular* celebrada en Moscú el 12 de noviembre de 1964," *Revolución*, November 13, 1964, pp. 1, 2.

"Entrevista en Moscú con periodistas soviéticos," *Hoy*, November 18, 1964, p. 3.

"Discurso al resumir la Gran Plenaria Provincial de Administradores de Empresas y Fábricas del Ministerio de Industrias en Oriente," *Hoy*, November 29, 1964, p. 5.

"Discurso en la conmemoración del octavo aniversario de los hechos del 30 de noviembre de 1956 en Santiago de Cuba," *El Mundo*, December 1, 1964, p. 7.

"Palabras en la Universidad de Oriente, donde sostuvo un encuentro con estudiantes y profesores de la Facultad de Technología y Economía," *Revolución*, December 3, 1964, pp. 1, 2.

"Discurso en la XIX Asamblea General de las Naciones Unidas el 11 de diciembre de 1964," *El Mundo*, December 12, 1964, pp. 7, 9.

"Discurso en la XIX Asamblea General de las Naciones Unidas usando el derecho de réplica para responder a los representantes de Costa Rica, Nicaragua, Venezuela, Colombia, Panamá, y Estados Unidos, el 11 de diciembre de 1964," *El Mundo*, December 12, 1964, pp. 1, 9.

"Comparecencia en el programa 'Face the Nation,' el 14 de diciembre de 1964," *El Mundo*, December 15, 1964, p. 9.

"Entrevista durante su visita a Argelia, concedida a Josie Fanon, redactora de asuntos internacionales y latinoamericanos del semanario *Revolution Africaine*," *Revolución*, December 23, 1964, pp. 1, 2.

"Palabras a jovenes argelinos y al semanario *Jeunesse*, órgano oficial de la Juventud del Frente de Liberación Nacional de Argelia, en los salones del Palacio del Pueblo en Argelia, el 23 de diciembre de 1964," *Revolución*, December 26, 1964, pp. 1, 2.

"Entrevista con Serge Michel, jefe de redacción del diario *Alger Ce Soir*," *Revolución*, December 28, 1964, p. 6.

"Declaraciones en su visita a la República de Mali," *El Mundo*, January 2, 1965, pp. 1, 2.

"Entrevista en el diario *L'Etincel* de Accra, el 18 de enero de 1965," *El Mundo*, January 19, 1965, pp. 1, 2.

"La acción neocolonialista en la América Latina y algunas consideraciones sobre la unidad de acción necesaria entre Africa, Asia, y Latinoamerica," *El Mundo*, January 20, 1965, pp. 1, 2.

"Declaraciones en una reunión con dirigentes sindicales de Ghana," *El Mundo*, January 20, 1965, p. 2.

"Conferencia en el Instituto ideológico Kwame Nkrumah," *El Mundo*, January 22, 1965, pp. 1, 2.

"Declaraciones para el Departamento de Programas Internacionales de la radio y la televisión argelinas," *El Mundo*, January 28, 1965, pp. 1, 7.

"Entrevista en *Alger Ce Soir* de Argelia el 30 de enero de 1965," *El Mundo*, January 31, 1965, pp. 1, 8.

"Declaraciones a *Prensa Latina* en Dar es Salam (Tanzania) el 18 de febrero de 1965," *Revolución*, January 19, 1965, pp. 1, 2.

"Discurso en el Segundo Seminario Económico de Solidaridad Afro-asiatica, pronunciado en Argelia el 24 de febrero de 1965," *El Mundo*, February 25, 1965, pp. 1, 5.

"Declaraciones en la República Árabe Unida," *El Mundo*, March 11, 1965, p. 5.

"Entrevista exclusiva al semanario *Liberation*," *El Mundo*, March 25, 1965, pp. 1, 2.

Books

El Diario de campaña del Che Guevara en Bolivia. Havana: Instituto del Libro, 1968.

La guerra de guerrillas. Havana: MINFAR, 1960.

Pasajes de la guerra revolucionaria. Havana: Edición Nacional, 1963.

Prologue to *Biografía del tabaco habano,* by Gaspar García Gallo. Havana: Comisión Nacional del Tabaco, 1961.

Prologue to *Geología de Cuba.* Havana: Departmento Científico de Geología, 1964.

Prologue to *La Guerra del pueblo, ejército del pueblo,* by Vo Nguyen Giap. Havana: Editora Política, 1964.

Prologue to *Mi aporte a la revolución cubana,* by Alberto Bayo. Havana: Imprenta Ejército Rebelde, 1960.

Prologue to *El partido marxista-leninista.* Havana: Dirección Nacional del PURSC, 1963.

Che Guevara on Guerrilla Warfare, (ed.) H. C. Peterson. New York: Praeger, 1961.

The Complete Bolivian Diaries of Che Guevara and Other Captured Documents, (ed.) Daniel James. New York: Stein and Day, 1968.

Che Guevara Speaks: Selected Speeches and Writings, (ed.) George Lavan. New York: Merit Publishers, 1968.

Episodes of the Revolutionary War. Havana: Book Institute, 1967.

Ernesto Che Guevara: Obra Revolucionaria, (ed.) R. F. Retamar. Mexico: Ediciones Era, 1967.

Venceremos! The Speeches and Writings of Che Guevara, (ed.) John Gerassi. New York: Macmillan, 1968.

Index

F
1788
G773
1969

Guevara, Ernesto,
1928-1967.

Che: selected works
of Ernesto Guevara

DATE			